Nicholas Wells
R. Dean Taylor

SAMS
Teach Yourself

StarOffice®
for Linux™
in 24 Hours

SAMS

A Division of Macmillan Computer Publishing
201 West 103rd St., Indianapolis, Indiana, 46290 USA

Sams Teach Yourself StarOffice® for Linux™ in 24 Hours

Copyright © 1999 by Sams Publishing

International Standard Book Number: 0-672-31412-6

Library of Congress Catalog Card Number: 98-87844

Printed in the United States of America

First Printing: March 1999

01   00   99   4   3   2   1

Trademarks

Warning and Disclaimer

EXECUTIVE EDITOR
Jeff Koch

MANAGING EDITOR
Brice Gosnell

PROJECT EDITOR
Kevin Laseau

COPY EDITOR
JoAnna Kremer

INDEXER
Bruce Clingaman

PROOFREADER
Billy Fields

TECHNICAL EDITOR
Aron Hsiao

SOFTWARE DEVELOPMENT SPECIALIST
Jack Belbot

INTERIOR DESIGN
Gary Adair

COVER DESIGN
Aren Howell

LAYOUT TECHNICIANS
Ayanna Lacey
Heather Miller
Amy Parker

Contents at a Glance

Introduction 1

PART I PREPARING TO USE STAROFFICE **3**

1 Installing StarOffice 5

2 Getting Started with StarOffice 25

3 Using the Explorer and the Desktop 45

4 Configuring StarOffice 65

5 Importing and Exporting StarOffice Documents 89

6 Creating Graphics with StarDraw 109

PART II CREATING DOCUMENTS WITH STARWRITER **125**

7 Creating a New StarWriter Document 127

8 Formatting Your Document 143

9 Using Advance Formatting Tools 159

10 Using Tables, Indexes, and Other Special Features 181

11 Adding Graphics to Documents 201

12 Using Spellcheck and the Thesaurus 219

PART III CREATING SPREADSHEETS WITH STARCALC **233**

13 Creating Spreadsheets with StarCalc 235

14 Entering Spreadsheet Data 257

15 Using Formulas, Functions, and Names 275

16 Formatting Your Spreadsheet 291

17 Adding Charts and Graphics to Spreadsheets 311

18 Using Database Functions 331

PART IV WORKING WITH PRESENTATIONS **349**

19 Creating Presentations with StarImpress 351

20 Adding Graphics and Charts to Your Presentation 373

21 Formatting and Giving Your Presentation 389

PART V USING INTERNET AND SCHEDULING FEATURES IN STAROFFICE   **417**

22   Creating Internet Documents with StarOffice   419

23   Using StarOffice Email and Newsgroup Features   443

24   Using StarSchedule   465

     Index   485

Table of Contents

INTRODUCTION   **1**

PART I PREPARING TO USE STAROFFICE   **3**

HOUR 1 INSTALLING STAROFFICE   **5**

Reviewing Linux System Requirements 5
   Checking Your Environment Variables 6
   Single-User and Network (Multiuser) Installations 6
   Checking File Permissions and Library Versions 7
   Using Different Linux Systems...8
Obtaining a License Key for StarOffice..8
Installing a Single-User Version of
   StarOffice 5 9
   Choosing an Installation Option 13
   Using the Custom Installation Option..15
   Finishing the Installation 16
Preparing for a Networked Installation 17
   Installing the Server Side of a Networked Install 18
   Installing a Client User for a Network Installation.........................20
Updating or Removing the StarOffice Installation.......................................22
   Modifying the StarOffice Installation 23
   Deinstalling StarOffice 23
   Repairing StarOffice 24
In the Next Hour..24

HOUR 2 GETTING STARTED WITH STAROFFICE   **25**

Starting StarOffice 25
   Setting Your PATH Variable 26
   Starting StarOffice from a Command Line.......................................27
   Using StarOffice in KDE 28
   Making an Icon for Looking Glass 29
Defining Parts of the StarOffice Window 32
   Understanding the Overall Layout of StarOffice 33
   Using the Function Toolbar..34
   Reading the Status Bar 36
   Using the Start Bar 38
   Using the Toolbars...39

Using the Explorer Window 40
    Viewing the Beamer 41
    Using the Explorer Icons...41
In the Next Hour..43

HOUR 3 USING THE EXPLORER AND THE DESKTOP   45

Using the Explorer Window 45
    Viewing the Beamer 47
    Using Right-Click Menus 47
    The Address Book 48
    The Bookmarks Folder 49
    The Gallery 49
    The Recycle Bin 51
    The Samples Folder..51
    Your Work Folder 52
    Your Workplace 53
Defining Parts of the Desktop 53
    The Desktop Versus the Work Folder 54
    The Desktop Icons...55
    Adding Your Documents to the Desktop 55
    Removing a Document from the Desktop..57
    Viewing Properties of an Item on the Desktop 58
    Switching Between Documents and the Desktop 59
    Viewing Multiple Document Windows...60
    Using the Start Menu..60
Reviewing the Menus 60
    Using Keyboard Shortcuts..61
In the Next Hour..63

HOUR 4 CONFIGURING STAROFFICE   65

Changing What's on the Menus and Toolbars 65
    Selecting Menu Items to Display 66
    Configuring the Toolbar Contents..68
    Setting Which Toolbars Are Displayed..71
Setting the General Options 72
    Reviewing Your User Data 72
    Setting Your Save Options 73
    Reviewing Your StarOffice Paths 75
    Setting Language Options 77

Setting Other Global Options 79
    Setting Up Keyboard Shortcuts...79
    Setting What to Display in the Status Bar 80
    Configuring AutoCorrection 81
Setting Up StarOffice Printers 84
    Using the Printer Setup Utility 84
    Adding Another Printer Type 86
    Setting the Default Printer...86
    Changing the Print Queue Used by a Printer 86
    Configuring a Printer...87
In the Next Hour...88

HOUR 5 IMPORTING AND EXPORTING STAROFFICE DOCUMENTS   89

Importing Word Documents 89
    Using Microsoft Word 6.0/95 and Word 97 Files.....................................90
    Reviewing Styles in Imported Files 91
Importing Other Word Processor Documents..93
    Using WordPerfect Files 93
    Using Other Word Processor Files 94
    Using Text Files..95
    Using HTML as an Interchange Format 96
Exporting StarWriter Documents 96
Reviewing Imported and Exported Documents 98
Importing Excel Spreadsheets 100
    Reading Excel 5.0, Excel 6.0/95 and Excel 97 Files 100
Importing Other Spreadsheet Formats 101
    Using Lotus 1-2-3 Spreadsheet Files 101
    Using Other Interchange Formats 102
Exporting Spreadsheets for Use in Other Programs..103
Reviewing Imported and Exported Spreadsheets...104
Importing and Exporting Presentations 106
    Exporting StarImpress Presentations...106
Importing and Exporting Graphics...107
In the Next Hour...108

HOUR 6 CREATING GRAPHICS WITH STARDRAW   109

Vector and Raster Graphics 109
    Raster images..110
    Vector Images 110
Creating a New StarDraw Image 111
    Reviewing the StarDraw Screen 112
    Changing the View of the Page..113
    Inserting a New Object 114
Modifying StarDraw Objects 116
    Changing Colors 119
    Arranging Objects 120
    Grouping Objects..121
Adding Text to the Drawing 121
In the Next Hour..124

PART II CREATING DOCUMENTS WITH STARWRITER   125

HOUR 7 CREATING A NEW STARWRITER DOCUMENT   127

Starting from Scratch with StarWriter 127
    Using the Start Menu...128
    Using the New Menu..128
    Using the Desktop 130
    Using a Template..130
    Using the AutoPilot 131
Opening an Existing StarWriter Document 133
Entering and Modifying Text 134
Saving Your Document...134
    Selecting a Location for Your Files..135
    Learning to Save Early, Save Often 135
    Resaving with a New Document Name 136
Printing Your Document...136
Setting Options for All Text Documents 138
    Choosing Which Parts of a Document Are Displayed 138
    Choosing How the Document Layout Is Displayed 139
    Changing the Default Fonts for Text Documents 139
    Setting Text Document Printing Options 140
    Setting Table Options 141
In the Next Hour..142

HOUR 8 FORMATTING YOUR DOCUMENT   **143**

Setting Character Styles 143

    Choosing a Font..144

    Using Bold, Italic, and Underline 145

    Adding a Hyperlink 148

Choosing Paragraph Settings 150

    Setting Line Spacing and Paragraph Indents 151

    Setting Paragraph Alignment...151

    Setting Tabs 152

    Using Other Paragraph Formatting Features..............................154

Arranging the Page 154

    Setting the Page Margins and Paper Size 154

    Defining Basic Page Numbering and Layout 155

    Adding a Header or Footer to Each Page 156

The Default Format Setting 158

In the Next Hour...158

HOUR 9 USING ADVANCED FORMATTING TOOLS   **159**

Using Footnotes 159

    Creating a Footnote 161

    Editing a Footnote 163

    Deleting a Footnote 163

Customizing Footnote Options...164

    Setting Footnote Position 165

    Setting Up Automatic Numbering...165

Using Columns 166

    Defining Columns 167

    Adding Columns to an Existing Document 169

    Working with Columns 170

Using Text Styles 170

    Explaining the Concept of Styles 170

    Reviewing the Style Command...171

    Opening the Stylist Window 173

    Applying a Style 174

    Reviewing the Stylist..174

    Reviewing the Attributes of a Style 176

Creating Your Own Styles 177

    Creating a Style by Example..178

In the Next Hour...180

HOUR 10 USING TABLES, INDEXES, AND OTHER SPECIAL FEATURES   181

Working with Tables 182
    Inserting a New Table 182
    Converting Between Text and Tables 184
    Formatting a Table..185
    Adding New Columns and Rows 186
    Splitting and Merging Cells 187
    Formatting Tables 189
Creating an Index 192
    Inserting Index Markers 193
    Inserting the Index..195
    Updating an Index 197
Numbering and Outlining 197
    Using Auto Numbering Outlines...197
    Using Bullets and Line Numbering...199
In the Next Hour 200

HOUR 11 ADDING GRAPHICS TO DOCUMENTS   201

Importing Graphics...201
    Placing Graphics in Your Document..202
    Using Other Linux Programs to Convert Graphic Formats 204
    Creating New Images in the Image Editor 205
Formatting Images in Your Document 208
Selecting a Graphic to Edit...208
Moving and Resizing Images 210
    Setting Alignment and Text Wrapping 211
    Using Layers 214
    Adding a Border 214
    Using the Object Dialog Box 216
Adding Horizontal Lines 217
In the Next Hour..218

HOUR 12 USING SPELLCHECK AND THE THESAURUS   219

Using AutoCorrect 219
    Setting AutoCorrect Options 220
Using Auto Spellcheck 223
    Turning Auto Spellcheck On or Off 223
Spellchecking Your Document 225
    Using the Pop-Up Spelling Menu 225
    Activating the Spellcheck Dialog Box 228

Searching the Thesaurus 230

    Searching for More Meaning 231

    Using the Thesaurus from the Spelling Dialog Box 231

In the Next Hour 231

PART III CREATING SPREADSHEETS WITH STARCALC   233

HOUR 13 CREATING SPREADSHEETS WITH STARCALC   235

Opening a New StarCalc Spreadsheet 235

    Using the Start or New Menus 236

    Using the Desktop 236

    Using a Template..237

Opening an Existing StarCalc Spreadsheet 240

Saving Your Spreadsheet 241

Printing Your Spreadsheet 242

    Setting the Print Area 242

    Using the Fit-to-Page Feature 244

    Turning Grid Lines On or Off..246

    Choosing the Page Format 247

Setting Spreadsheet Options 249

    Choosing What to Display Onscreen 249

    Setting Input Options..251

    Adding a Grid to a Spreadsheet 252

    Setting Calculation Preferences..254

In the Next Hour 255

HOUR 14 ENTERING SPREADSHEET DATA   257

Navigating in StarCalc 257

    Moving with the Mouse or Keyboard 257

    Understanding Cell References 258

    Naming a Cell or Range 259

    Selecting a Range of Cells 261

    Selecting Rows or Columns 262

Working with Sheets..263

    Naming a Sheet 263

    Adding Another Sheet 265

    Protecting a Sheet 266

    Hiding Cells..269

Entering Data in Your Spreadsheet..270

    Entering Numbers, Dates and Text 270

    Cutting, Pasting, and Moving 272

In the Next Hour 273

HOUR 15 USING FORMULAS, FUNCTIONS, AND NAMES   **275**

Labels and Formulas...275
    Entering Cell References...276
    Entering Numbers and Labels...276
    Editing a Cell...278
Entering Formulas..278
Using Functions 279
    Using Functions to Simplify Formulas 279
    Finding Functions 280
    Editing a Function 283
    Using the Mouse to Enter Cell References...284
    Recalculating Your Spreadsheet...286
Using More Advanced Functions...286
    Using a Financial Function 287
In the Next Hour..290

HOUR 16 FORMATTING YOUR SPREADSHEET   **291**

Changing Fonts and Sizes..291
    Formatting Cell by Cell..293
    Setting a Font and Size 293
Setting Number Formats in Cells..298
    Using the Object Bar to Set Number Formats 298
    Adjusting Decimal Places 299
    Using the Number Formatting Dialog Box...301
Adjusting and Inserting Rows and Columns 302
    Adjusting Row Height and Column Width 302
    Inserting and Deleting Rows..305
    Inserting and Deleting Columns 308
In the Next Hour..309

HOUR 17 ADDING CHARTS AND GRAPHICS TO SPREADSHEETS   **311**

Adding a Graphic to a Spreadsheet 311
    Importing a Graphic File..312
    Editing an Imported Graphic..314
Creating a Chart 314
    Selecting a Data Set..315
    Starting a Chart 316
    Selecting a Chart Type 317
    Selecting a Chart Variant..319
    Labeling Your Chart 321

Modifying and Formatting a Chart..324
   Selecting a Chart to Modify 325
   Reviewing the Edit Options on a Chart 325
   Changing a Color in the Chart 326
   Changing the Numbers on an Axis 328
In the Next Hour 329

HOUR 18 USING DATABASE FUNCTIONS   **331**

Defining Database Terms 332
Using Data Validation..333
   Setting up Data Validation Criteria 334
Sorting Database Records...339
   Selecting Data to Sort 339
   Setting the Sort Criteria...341
   Reviewing Sorting Options 341
Filtering Data Records 343
   Using Automatic Filtering...343
   Using the Standard Filter...345
In the Next Hour 348

PART IV WORKING WITH PRESENTATIONS   **349**

HOUR 19 CREATING PRESENTATIONS WITH STARIMPRESS   **351**

Creating a New StarImpress Presentation 351
   Slides and Pages 352
   Making Use of Presentation Templates..353
   Using a Slide Layout 355
   Using the AutoPilot 356
Creating Individual Slides 360
   Adding a Layout to a Slide 361
   Inserting a New Slide 362
   Entering Text on a Slide 363
   Adjusting Paragraphs...364
   Setting Font Options 366
Saving Your Presentation 367
   Exporting Slides in Graphics Formats 368
   Exporting as a Web Presentation...370
In the Next Hour 372

HOUR 20 ADDING GRAPHICS AND CHARTS TO YOUR PRESENTATION   373

Importing and Editing Graphic Files 373
    Importing an Existing Graphic File...374
    Moving and Resizing an Imported Graphic 375
    Editing an Imported Graphic File 375
    Adding Actions to Graphics 377
Drawing Your Own Graphics 379
    Adding Lines and Rectangles 380
Using Charts from Spreadsheets...385
    Importing a Chart 385
    Inserting a spreadsheet 386
In the Next Hour..387

HOUR 21 FORMATTING AND GIVING YOUR PRESENTATION   389

Arranging Your Slides 389
    Choosing a Master View 390
    Moving Between Slides..391
    Using the Background Mode..392
    Selecting Other Views 393
Rearranging Slides Using the Slide Sorter...396
    Moving Slides 396
    Copying and Pasting Slides...397
    Deleting Slides..398
Defining Transitions Between Slides 398
SpellChecking Your Presentation 402
Adding Speaker Notes 403
Setting Presentation and Slide Show Options 405
    Setting Presentation Options 405
    Setting the Slide Show Options..407
Running a Slide Show 410
Preparing Hardcopy Slides 412
    Setting the Page Size...412
    Defining Printing Options 413
In the Next Hour..415

PART V   USING INTERNET AND SCHEDULING FEATURES IN STAROFFICE   417

HOUR 22   CREATING INTERNET DOCUMENTS WITH STAROFFICE   419

Setting Internet Options 419
Choosing Internet Server Options...420
Setting up Internet Searching 424
Setting up Internet Protocols...425
Using the StarOffice Browser...427
Opening a Web Document 427
Inserting Automatic Links in StarWriter Documents 428
Inserting Manual Links in StarWriter Documents 430
Inserting Links in Spreadsheets and Presentations 431
Saving URLs in the Explorer 432
Working with Web Documents..433
Saving Existing Documents for the Web 434
Creating New HTML Documents 435
Adding Other HTML Elements..438
In the Next Hour 441

HOUR 23   USING STAROFFICE EMAIL AND NEWSGROUP FEATURES   443

Configuring Email Accounts 443
Setting up a POP3 Account..444
Setting up a Separate Email Outbox 447
Activating Your Email Settings..448
Sending Emails 450
Starting an Email Message 450
Including Attachments in an Email...452
Sending the Email Message 454
Sending a Document as Email 455
Using Other StarOffice Internet Functions..456
Browsing an FTP Site 456
Configuring the Newsgroup Reader..459
Creating a News Icon 459
Choosing Newsgroups to View 461
Reading Newsgroup Postings 461
Posting a New Message to a Newsgroup 462
Updating Explorer Icons 463
In the Next Hour 463

HOUR 24 USING STARSCHEDULE   **465**

How StarSchedule is Organized 465
Using the Task List 467
    Creating New Tasks..467
    Reviewing Task Details..468
    Setting up Task Categories 472
    Setting up Other Users 473
    Changing the Task List Layout 475
    Filtering the Task List 477
Using the Event Calendar...478
    Changing the Events View 478
    Adding items to the Calendar 481
    Filtering the Calendar Events 481
    Setting up Reminders and Recurring Events 482
Congratulations...484

About the Author

Nicholas D. Wells (nwells@xmission.com) is the author of several books on Linux-related subjects, including the forthcoming *Sams Teach Yourself KDE in 24 Hours*. After leaving Novell to join Linux-based start-up Caldera, Inc., he worked as the Director of Marketing for several years before realizing that writing about technology was more fun than selling it. He left Caldera to write and consult full-time. When he's between projects, he likes to read history books, learn foreign languages, and travel to new places with his wife, hoping to find the new best place to go diving.

R. Dean Taylor has over 14 years of channel-marketing experience in the computer industry working for companies such as Sanyo/Icon, IBM, WordPerfect, and Novell. He is currently responsible for channel marketing for Caldera Systems, Inc. Although he has extensive experience in the computer industry, this is his first experience with professional writing and has found it to be extremely rewarding. When he is not working or spending time with his wife and four daughters, you will find him on a river fly fishing. Finally, he gratefully recognizes Nicolas' generosities for space sharing on the outside of the book, for doing most of the work, and especially for his patience and guidance.

Dedication

This book is dedicated to my wife, Anne, who encouraged me follow my dreams, quit my day job on a song and prayer, and start writing full-time.

—Nicholas Wells

Acknowledgments

This project took a lot longer than originally planned because of the new version of StarOffice that showed up just as I was finishing it. Despite the additional work and delays this caused, my editor at Sams, Jeff Koch, continues to be a pleasure to work with under tight deadlines, striving to make the book as accurate and up-to-date as possible.

My coauthor, Dean Taylor, provided much-needed help, writing or reviewing several of the chapters along the way.

And of course, none of this would have happened without Anne's support and encouragement.

—Nicholas Wells

Tell Us What You Think!

As the reader of this book, *you* are our most important critic and commentator. We value your opinion and want to know what we're doing right, what we could do better, what areas you'd like to see us publish in, and any other words of wisdom you're willing to pass our way.

As an Executive Editor for the Operating Systems team at Macmillan Computer Publishing, I welcome your comments. You can fax, email, or write me directly to let me know what you did or didn't like about this book—as well as what we can do to make our books stronger.

Please note that I cannot help you with technical problems related to the topic of this book, and that due to the high volume of mail I receive, I might not be able to reply to every message.

When you write, please be sure to include this book's title and author as well as your name and phone or fax number. I will carefully review your comments and share them with the author and editors who worked on the book.

Fax: 317.581.4663

Email: lowop@mcp.com

Mail: Executive Editor
          Operating Systems
          Macmillan Computer Publishing
          201 West 103rd Street
          Indianapolis, IN 46290 USA

Introduction

Writing a book about a Linux application is something new. The publication of this book marks a new step for Linux books—until now, all the books about Linux have focused on the operating system. With the incredible growth of Linux, now approaching 8 million users, books about how to use Linux applications are becoming available—starting with this one.

StarOffice is a complete office suite modeled on Microsoft Office 97. It was developed by StarDivision, a German company that has enjoyed tremendous success in Europe. StarOffice for Linux is their first venture into other parts of the world, and promises to be a boon to Linux users.

If you're familiar with Office 95 or Office 97, many of the features of StarOffice will be familiar to you. StarOffice includes advanced features such as automatic indexes, integrated drawing tools, spreadsheet database functions, chart designers, and a macro programming language called StarBASIC (although that topic isn't discussed in this book).

If you're not familiar with Microsoft Office, but you have been using Linux, you'll love working with StarOffice. It provides everything you need to create documents, spreadsheets, databases, and presentations. No more giving a presentation about Linux using PowerPoint. You can also use StarOffice as an integrated Internet tool—read email and newsgroups, browse the Web, and download from FTP sites, all within the same comfortable interface.

If you're new to Linux, this book is a great place to start. After you have Linux installed, the step-by-step approach walks you through the StarOffice installation, creating basic documents, and using the features of windows and dialog boxes. Before long, you'll be using StarOffice as your primary application in Linux.

In addition to documents, spreadsheets, and presentations, StarOffice 5 includes several major improvements over previous versions. These improvements include the following:

- A complete scheduling program (similar to Microsoft Outlook) with tasks, event calendars, and pop-up reminders for recurring or one-time events.
- A powerful vector-based drawing tool, StarDraw, to create drawings that can be integrated into other StarOffice documents.
- Redesigned Internet access tools, including new emailing and newsgroup reading interfaces.
- Improved stability, based on the latest Linux libraries (glibc), plus a new, easy-to-use installation program.

One of the highlights of StarOffice 5 is the capability to import and export Microsoft Office 97 files, so you can share work with others who aren't using StarOffice. (You can also check out the StarDivision Web site at `http://www.stardivision.com` for information about the Windows version of StarOffice.)

This book introduces you to the leading edge of Linux personal productivity applications. We hope you'll enjoy reading it, and maybe even make StarOffice the most-used application on your Linux system.

PART I

Preparing to Use StarOffice

Hour

1 Installing StarOffice

2 Getting Started with StarOffice

3 Using the Explorer and the Desktop

4 Configuring StarOffice

5 Importing and Exporting StarOffice Documents

6 Creating Graphics with StarDraw

HOUR 1

Installing StarOffice

This hour guides you through the process of installing StarOffice on your Linux system. Although installing StarOffice is quite simple, review the information presented here to ensure a smooth installation. The key to a smooth installation, no matter which Linux system you're running, is to be certain that the correct system libraries are installed and available to StarOffice.

Reviewing Linux System Requirements

If you follow the information in this section, you can get StarOffice running on basically any Linux system that meets the listed requirements. The system requirements for installing StarOffice 5 are listed in Table 1.1.

TABLE 1.1 SYSTEM REQUIREMENTS TO INSTALL STAROFFICE 5 FOR LINUX

Description	Requirement
Linux kernel version	2.0.*x* (or later stable version)
Linux library version	libc6, also called glibc2, version 2.0.7 (other library versions can be installed on your Linux system, but the correct version must be available to StarOffice, as described in the sections that follow)
System Memory	32MB RAM
Hard Disk Space	11–140MB, depending on installation type
X Window System graphics	256 or more colors or grayscales

Although these requirements are straightforward, note that compared to many Linux programs, StarOffice requires a fair amount of memory and hard disk space. The more you have, the more smoothly StarOffice runs.

Checking Your Environment Variables

StarOffice uses the LANG environment variable to determine which international number, currency, and dictionary settings to use. The default setting is en_US for U.S. English. If you need to change to British English, use the following command from any command line before running StarOffice:

```
export LANG=en_GB
```

> Because the default language for StarOffice is U.S. English, you don't have to worry about setting the LANG variable unless you want to try other languages.

Single-User and Network (Multiuser) Installations

One of the benefits of using Linux is the true multiuser capability of the operating system. Several people can be logged in across a network and use the files and services from a single Linux system.

StarOffice allows a network installation, which enables you to install StarOffice from a main location (such as /opt or /usr/local) and then install a relatively small (2–9 MB) client portion that enables a user to have access to the StarOffice installation without installing the entire (huge) product in every home directory.

Even if you're using Linux just as your desktop, using a network installation is an easy way to allow multiple user accounts to access StarOffice without using 140MB for each user's copy.

Checking File Permissions and Library Versions

Most problems with StarOffice installation occur for one of the following reasons:

- You don't have sufficient file permissions to create the directories and files needed during installation.
- You don't have the correct libraries installed to run the setup program or to run StarOffice.

If you use a single-user installation, you'll be installing StarOffice in your home directory, so permission to create files is no problem.

If you intend to use a network installation, you probably want to be logged in as root (or as a user with some system administration rights) to create the StarOffice installation and install the new system libraries if necessary. The directory in which you install StarOffice must be accessible for read access by all the users who will be running StarOffice from that location. The commands to set the permissions for the StarOffice directory are provided later in this hour as the setup procedure is described.

StarOffice 5 requires that you have the following two items installed on your system:

- ld-linux.so.2
- libc-2.*.so (any version number can replace the *)

The installation procedure described in this hour includes installation of the glibc libraries that are included with the StarOffice 5 product because many Linux systems don't include these libraries.

Red Hat Linux 5 or later and Debian 2 or later both use the new glibc libraries required by StarOffice. Caldera's OpenLinux 1.3 and Slackware 3.6, however, are still based on the older libc5 libraries. If you have trouble getting StarOffice to run, follow the complete installation procedure outlined in this hour——it installs the necessary libraries on systems that don't already have them.

The libraries that are installed take up a few extra megabytes on your system, but are used only by StarOffice and don't interfere with anything else you're doing on your Linux system.

Using Different Linux Systems

StarOffice for Linux was originally "sponsored" by Caldera, Inc., a leading Linux vendor. Caldera worked with Star Division to have the StarOffice suite ported to Linux. As the popularity of Linux and StarOffice for Linux have grown, StarDivision has ensured that StarOffice works with all Linux systems that meet the requirements described previously. The README files included with the StarOffice program describe some hints for working with StarOffice on specific Linux distributions, including OpenLinux, Red Hat, Suse, Slackware and Debian.

Although many Linux programs are stored and distributed as RPM-formatted files, StarOffice for Linux uses a separate installation program described later in this hour. You don't need to have the rpm tool installed on your Linux system to install StarOffice.

> Replacing libraries on a stable Linux system is not a good idea. Instead, follow the installation procedure in this hour to make the needed library version available only to StarOffice.

Obtaining a License Key and Customer Number

Before you can install StarOffice 5, you must have a license key and a Customer Number from StarDivision. The license key is a long alphanumeric code; the Customer Number is a seven digit number. Both are entered during the installation of StarOffice.

To obtain your own license key and Customer Number, visit the StarDivision Web site at http://www.stardivision.com or http://www.stardivision.de (German version) and go to the StarOffice for Linux download page.

Follow the steps onscreen to download a copy of StarOffice for Linux. You'll need to register some personal information (including your name, address, and email address). After confirming this information, a Registration Data screen provides you with a license key and a Customer Number. Print out this screen and keep it for your records. You can't install StarOffice without this information.

At this point you can either exit your browser (if you already have a copy of StarOffice 5) or continue and download StarOffice. The download file is about 64 MB.

Once you have downloaded the StarOffice archive to a temporary directory, you must unpack it so that you can install the product. The downloaded file is a tar archive. You can unpack it with a command like this:

```
$ tar xvf /tmp/so501.tar
```

The archive is not compressed (it is not in .tgz format) because it contains files that are already compressed. Don't use the z option in your tar command.

Installing a Single-User Version of StarOffice 5

StarOffice is installed by a setup program, just like most Windows programs with which you might be familiar. After running a small script to install the correct system libraries in a StarOffice directory, you can run setup to install StarOffice.

The network installation procedure is described in the later part of this hour. A network installation of StarOffice differs from a single-user installation only in the location of the StarOffice files and the capability of multiple users to run StarOffice at the same time.

To install StarOffice, follow these steps:

1. Log in as the user for which you are installing StarOffice, and start the X Window System if it isn't already running.

2. Open an xterm command-line window.

3. Change to the directory that contains the StarOffice archive that you downloaded:

   ```
   $ cd /tmp/so50/1
   ```

4. Change to the glibc2_inst directory:

   ```
   $ cd glibc2_inst
   ```

5. If you're running a tcsh or (pd)ksh shell, start an sh shell (the StarOffice installation scripts were written for bourne-compatible shells):

   ```
   $ sh
   ```

6. Start the StarOffice preparation script (note the dot-space-dot-space):

   ```
   $ . ./soprep
   ```

7. Respond to the first prompt by entering the name of the directory in which the new StarOffice libraries will be installed. This will be the lib/ subdirectory below where you intend to install the StarOffice program:

   ```
   glibc2 directory [/opt/Office50/lib] ? /home/nwells/Office50/lib
   ```

The soprep script installs the libraries in that directory and returns to a command prompt. Within the text that appears onscreen, you see a notice that the libraries were installed successfully.

> If the libraries are not installed successfully (often because of limited permissions in the library directories), the installation of StarOffice fails. You might need to attempt a network installation first, followed by a single user installation (see the next section of this hour), or contact your system administration to prepare the system as root.

8. Change to the main StarOffice installation directory. (Don't leave the bash shell! Some environment variables needed by the setup program were set by the soprep script.)

   ```
   $ cd ../so501_inst
   ```

9. Start the setup installation program:

   ```
   $ ./setup
   ```

   A message might inform you that the window manager has not defined icons, so defaults are being used. This is harmless.

After a few seconds, the StarOffice graphic appears and the installation process begins.

The first screen to appear is a welcome screen, shown in Figure 1.1. Press Next to continue the installation.

FIGURE 1.1

The first screen welcomes you to StarOffice.

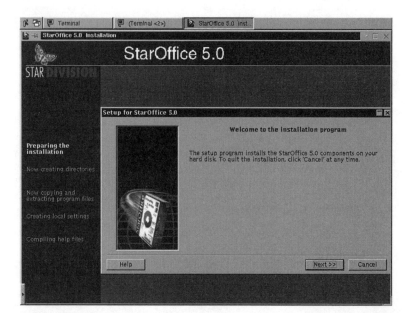

The next screen that appears shows the StarOffice license agreement (see Figure 1.2). The license agreement defines how you can use your copy of StarOffice for Linux. Read the license agreement carefully, and then press Accept to continue.

FIGURE 1.2

The license agreement defines how you can use your copy of StarOffice for Linux.

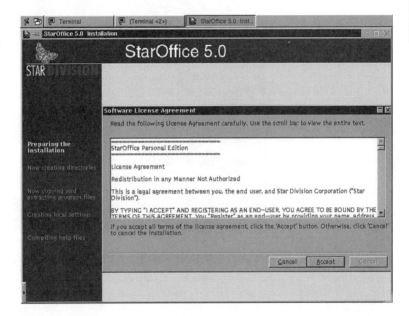

Perhaps because of the complications involved with running multiple versions of Linux, the next screen displays installation and use hints for StarOffice. You can read through these, and then choose Next to continue the installation.

In the next screen, you enter your personal information. (See Figure 1.3.) This information is used to customize document templates, create email messages, and so on.

You must enter all of the information that you entered on the StarDivision Web site to obtain your Customer Number and license key. This information is coded to the license key itself; if you don't enter precisely the same information, the license key does not work and you cannot install StarOffice.

FIGURE 1.3

The User Data screen enables you to personalize your copy of StarOffice.

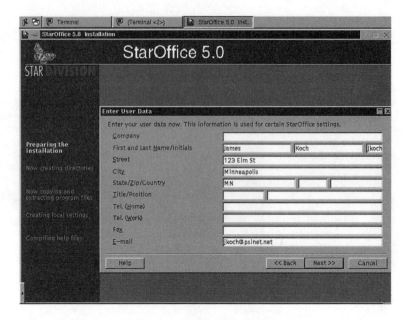

If you need to update, modify, or add to the personal information that you enter in this screen, you can do so at anytime by using the Tools menu. Choose Options, General, and select the User Data tab. This might necessitate getting a new license key, however.

Choose the Next button to continue. An information screen warns you that the User Data information must match what you entered on the StarDivision Web site. Use the Back button to return and edit the information if necessary. (You can also use the Back button twice to change the User Data screen if the license key that you enter fails.) Choose Continue to go on.

In the next screen (see Figure 1.4) you enter the Customer Number and license key that you obtained from the StarDivision Web site. When you press Next, the key is checked against your personal information. If you entered the correct key, the next screen

Entering the license key is difficult. If you use so much as an extra space after your first name, entering the license key that you received does not work. Use the Back button twice to check the User Data screen if necessary. Also watch for swapped characters in the license key, such as zero and the letter *O*.

FIGURE 1.4

The license key and Customer Number must be entered correctly before you can continue with the installation.

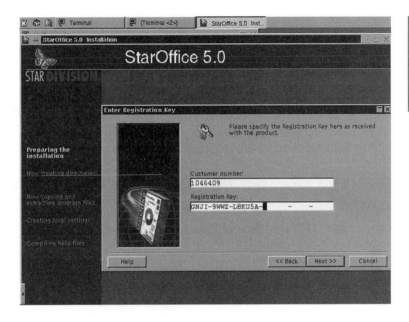

appears.

Choosing an Installation Option

The next decision that you have to make is which components of StarOffice you want to install. As mentioned earlier, StarOffice is not a small program, so you can choose to leave some parts out of the installation.

Remember, however, that the integrated nature of StarOffice means that most of the program is shared among all the components. That means that you can't leave out a large component such as the StarImpress presentation software.

If you do need to save hard disk space, you can leave out things such as the following:

- Clipart or Graphics collections
- Templates
- Help files
- Sample documents

You can choose one of several installation options, as shown in Figure 1.5.

The easiest choice is the Standard Installation. This takes a lot of space (139MB, plus 20MB extra during installation), but provides you with graphics, templates, help files, dictionaries, and so forth. If you choose the Standard Installation button, you have about 160MB of free hard disk space.

FIGURE 1.5

You can select which
components of
StarOffice to install by
selecting an installa-
tion option.

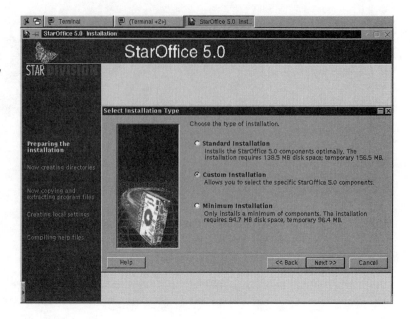

If you have KDE on your system, choose the Custom installation option to automatically add StarOffice to your KDE menus. Details are provided in the next section.

If you don't have that much space, you can choose the Minimum Installation button. This requires a mere 97MB of hard disk space, but doesn't install things such as the help files and sample documents (which will be referred to in later hours for some of the examples). Choose Next to continue. (If you chose the Custom installation option, refer to the following section after completing the next screen.)

Next you'll see the screen where you can select the Installation directory. Because you're doing a single user installation, the default directory that is shown is probably a good choice. It is probably something such as /home/nwells/Office50. If you want to change it, choose the Browser button and select another directory.

If you don't install StarOffice in the same place that you designated for the libraries when running the soprep script, the program might not run after installation is complete.

If you selected the Standard or Minimum installation options and choose Next, the screen in which you select components of StarOffice, described in the following section, does not appear.

Using the Custom Installation Option

If you enjoy setting things up yourself, you can choose the Custom Installation option. When Custom Installation is selected, the screen that appears after the installation directory is chosen enables you to select which components of StarOffice to install. (See Figure 1.6.)

FIGURE 1.6

The Custom Installation option enables you to select which components of StarOffice you want to install.

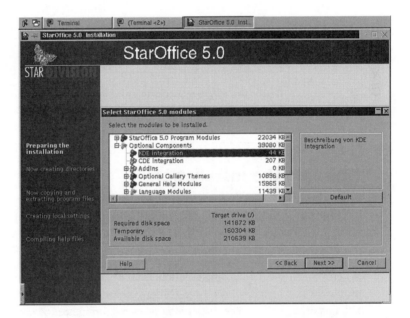

From this screen, you can select which components you want to install. Clicking on a plus sign opens a sub-list of components. The icons are used to indicate which components are selected:

- A solid color indicates that all of that component is selected for installation.
- A fuzzy color indicates that part of that list of components will be installed.
- An empty (black outlined) icon indicates that the component will not be installed.

StarOffice uses the same set of underlying functionality for the word processor, the spreadsheet, the presentations software, and so on. If you leave out a key section, none of these will function. Instead, you can save space by selecting which sample documents, templates, help files, and so on you want to install.

To deselect options from the list, follow these steps:

1. Click on the plus sign (+) to the left of the type of item that you want to deselect. That item expands to display its contents.

2. Click on the plus sign for sublevel components, if necessary.

3. Click on the icon or name of an item that you don't want to install. The icon goes blank and the Required disk space line in the bottom of the screen is updated to reflect the new space requirements.

4. Click again on any icon that you want to reselect so that it is included in the installation.

5. When you have selected and deselected all the components that you want to use, continue the installation by choosing the Next button.

> If your Linux system is running KDE as its desktop, open the Optional Components list and choose the KDE Integration icon to automatically add StarOffice to your KDE menu during installation.

Finishing the Installation

When you have finished selecting the installation directory and setting any custom installation options, the next screen shows that the installation is ready to begin. At this point you can use the Back button to return to any previous screen to alter your entries, or you can choose the Complete button to begin installing StarOffice.

When you choose the Complete button, StarOffice is installed. (See Figure 1.7.) A progress bar, which displays the percentage completed for the installation, appears on the left side of the screen. The installation takes 5–25 minutes to complete, depending on the speed of your system components.

After most of the files are installed (at 99% complete), a dialog box tells you that the Installation is complete. Choose the Complete button to close the dialog box and end the installation program.

FIGURE 1.7

The progress bar in this screen shows how the file installation is proceeding.

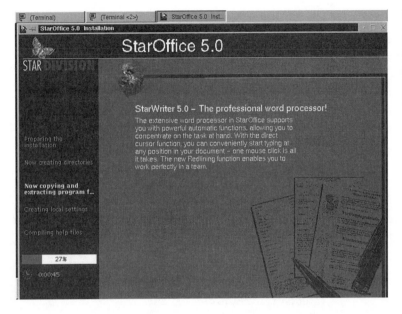

The installation program also places a filed named .sversionrc in your home directory.

If you aren't interested in learning about a network installation, you can jump right to Hour 2, "Getting Started with StarOffice."

Preparing for a Networked Installation

A networked installation of StarOffice is very useful if you have several users on your Linux system and have purchased several licenses of StarOffice. It enables you to install StarOffice in a single location where more than one user can use it. This saves a lot of disk space because each user doesn't need a copy of StarOffice in his or her home directory.

Of course, if you're using an evaluation or free download version of StarOffice, you can use the networked installation with multiuser accounts to evaluate how it all works (a separate license key is required for each user)——just don't run your business on it.

A network installation of StarOffice is easier than a single-user installation. The differences are the location where the bulk of StarOffice files are installed and the need to install a small set of files (with a license key) for each user who accesses the networked installation of StarOffice. The following steps summarize a networked StarOffice installation (details are provided in the next section):

1. Install StarOffice using the /net option. That is, install the libraries if necessary (as described previously), and then use a command such as the following:

   ```
   $ ./setup /net
   ```

   When prompted for the location at which StarOffice files will be installed, choose a common application area such as /opt or /usr/local. (No license key is required for this step because no one can use a networked installation without first installing a user to access it).

2. Obtain a license key for a user. Log in as that user.

3. Run the setup program from the bin/ directory of the networked StarOffice installation. For example, use the following command:

   ```
   $ /opt/Office50/bin/setup &
   ```

   The network installation is almost identical to the Single User installation described in the first half of this hour, except that no libraries need to be installed first.

The sections that follow walk you through a network installation for StarOffice.

Installing the Server Side of a Networked Install

The system requirements for the networked installation are the same as for a single-user installation.

To start a networked installation, follow these steps:

1. Log in as a user with enough administration privileges to install StarOffice to the desired location (usually this is the root user).

2. Start the X Window System if it isn't already running.

3. Open a terminal window and change to the StarOffice directory:

   ```
   # cd /tmp/so501/
   ```

4. Change to the glibc2_inst directory:

   ```
   $ cd glibc2_inst
   ```

5. If you're running a tcsh or (pd)ksh shell, start an sh shell (the StarOffice installation scripts were written for bourne-compatible shells):

   ```
   $ sh
   ```

6. Start the StarOffice preparation script (note the dot-space-dot-slash):

   ```
   $ . ./soprep
   ```

7. Respond to the first prompt by entering the name of the directory name in which the new StarOffice libraries are to be installed. This is the lib/ subdirectory below where you intend to install the StarOffice program:

   ```
   glibc2 directory [/opt/Office50/lib] ?
   ```

   (Just press Enter if the /opt directory shown is correct.)

   The soprep script installs the libraries in the selected directory and returns to a command prompt. Within the text that appears onscreen, you see a notice that the libraries were installed successfully.

> If the libraries are not installed successfully (often because of limited permissions in the library directories) the installation of StarOffice fails. Review the library descriptions in the first part of this hour and the README files in the StarOffice directories.

8. Change to the main StarOffice installation directory. (Don't leave the sh shell! Some environment variables needed by the setup program were set by the soprep script.)

   ```
   $ cd ../so501_inst
   ```

9. Start the setup installation program with the network option:

   ```
   $ ./setup /net
   ```

   A message might inform you that the window manager has not defined icons, so defaults are being used. This is harmless.

   After a few seconds, the StarOffice graphic appears and the installation process begins. The first screen to appear is a welcome screen, just as in a single user installation. Press Next to continue the installation.

10. Review the license agreement screen and choose Accept to continue.

11. Review the Important Information screen and choose Next to continue.

12. Choose the type of installation you want (Standard, Custom, or Minimum) and choose Next to continue.

    If you choose a Custom installation, review the steps in the Single User installation section for help on selecting components to install. In particular, choose the KDE option if your Linux system uses the KDE desktop.

If you include KDE Integration in the networked installation, each user also has KDE integration installed automatically.

13. Enter the directory in which the networked StarOffice program is to be installed.

    The setup program uses the home directory of the user that you are logged in as by default (for example, /root/Office50). You'll need to use the Browse button or enter another directory, such as /opt/Office50, for networked use.

14. Choose the Complete button from the next screen to begin the installation. (Use the Back button if you need to change a selection in a previous screen.)

    The installation begins copying files. When this is completed, a dialog box informs you that the installation has finished.

Installing a Client User for a Network Installation

The networked installation of StarOffice that you just completed cannot be run directly. Instead, follow up the network installation by installing StarOffice for a user.

To start the installation process for a network user, follow these steps:

1. Log in to your Linux system using the username that will use StarOffice as a networked user.

2. Start the X Window System, if it isn't already running, and open a terminal window.

3. Start the setup program in the bin/ directory of the networked StarOffice installation:

   ```
   $ /opt/Office50/bin/setup
   ```

   A welcome screen appears. Choose Next to continue.

4. Review the license agreement and choose Accept to continue with the installation.

5. Review the Important Information screen and choose Next to continue.

6. Enter as much information as you choose in the User Data screen (shown in Figure 1.8).

   You must enter at least the information that you provided to StarDivision to obtain your license key. Review the information in the single user installation procedure if you have questions about using this screen.

7. The next screen to appear enables you to select either a standard workstation installation or a Standard Installation (local). (See Figure 1.9.)

FIGURE 1.8

The User Data screen requires at least the information you entered to obtain your license key from StarDivision.

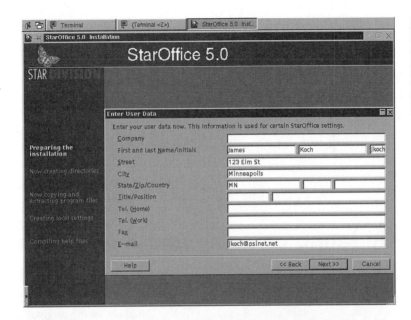

FIGURE 1.9

The workstation installation or a full local installation can be selected.

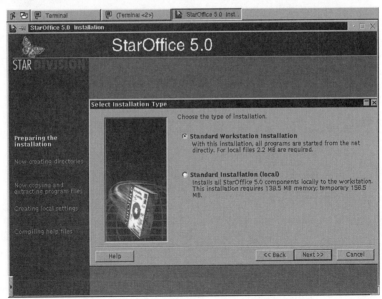

The Standard Installation (local) installs all the StarOffice files in the current user's home directory, requiring about 140MB. The Workstation installation requires only 2.2MB (about 9.5MB with libraries).

8. Choose the desired installation directory within your home directory for the StarOffice files. You'll need between 3 and 10MB of space within your home directory.

9. Choose the Complete button to install the StarOffice files.

> If you selected the KDE components during the network installation, a dialog box tells you that StarOffice was added to your KDE Panel.

10. Choose Complete in the final screen to close the installation program.

Updating or Removing the StarOffice Installation

After you have StarOffice installed, you might want to change the installation. For example, if you didn't install the help files or templates in the original installation, you might want to add them to your system later.

You might even need to remove StarOffice from your Linux system. Although StarOffice is pretty much self-contained in the Office50 directory, it always helps to have a `deinstall` utility.

All these tasks can be completed by starting the `setup` utility after StarOffice is installed. The `setup` utility detects that StarOffice is already installed on your system (for the current user) and presents you with options that are different than those in the original installation.

Start the `setup` utility within the program directory of StarOffice:

```
$ /opt/Office50/bin/setup &
$
```

The `setup` program starts up, but it doesn't look like it did the first time. The options presented now (see Figure 1.10) are

- Modify installation
- Deinstallation
- Repair

The next sections take you through these options.

FIGURE 1.10

The setup utility pre-sents different options after StarOffice is installed.

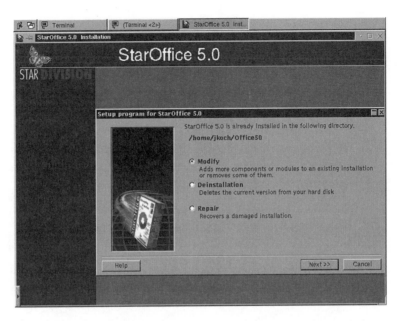

Some of these options require that you have access to the StarOffice archive that you downloaded and used to install StarOffice. These original files may be needed to alter or update your installation.

Modifying the StarOffice Installation

When you installed StarOffice, you had a choice of installation options. If you chose the Custom Installation option, you selected which components you wanted to install.

If you start the setup utility again——after you've completed the original installation——and choose the Modify option, you can add to or remove from the list of components that you originally installed.

The screen where you select the components to install is basically the same as the Custom Installation screen described in the Single User installation procedure. You can choose the items that you want to have included in your StarOffice installation.

Deinstalling StarOffice

If you decide you need to take StarOffice off your system, the best way to do it is with the De-Install option in the setup program.

> You can use the rm command to erase the StarOffice directory, Office50—
> but use caution with the rm command. Don't forget to remove the .sver-
> sionrc file in your home directory, as well.

Repairing StarOffice

The final option in the post-installation setup program is to Repair your StarOffice installation. Use this option if something has happened to your Linux filesystem that makes StarOffice unable to run.

You can compare this to having a really bad crash in Microsoft Windows. Instead of reinstalling the system or application, you can run the setup utility and use the Repair button.

The Repair feature can determine which parts of StarOffice are missing or misplaced, and whether file versions are incompatible. As with modifying the installation, this provides a convenient alternative to backing up your data and configurations and reinstalling StarOffice.

Again, you might need access to the original StarOffice archive files that you downloaded so that the Repair utility can retrieve any missing files from the StarOffice original source. This is only the case, however, if the networked installation of StarOffice is damaged.

In the Next Hour

Hour 2 describes how to start the StarOffice program that you installed in this hour. You learn how to use a command line (within the X Window System) or a desktop icon to start the program.

In addition, the next hour walks you through the basic interface elements of the StarOffice window, so you start to become familiar with the screen that you'll be seeing throughout this book.

HOUR 2

Getting Started StarOffice

In this hour, you will learn how to start StarOffice, as well as some hints for using StarOffice within several popular Linux graphical systems.

After you learn how to start StarOffice, you will learn some basics about the layout of the StarOffice window and how to start navigating around it as you create your documents.

Starting StarOffice

Starting the StarOffice program is like starting any other program in Linux. You just enter the name of the program on a command line. There are two rules:

1. You must be running the X Window System—the graphical interface to Linux. If you're in character mode, StarOffice can't run. It's strictly a graphical program.

2. You need to be logged in with the same username that you used to install StarOffice. StarOffice is normally installed in your home directory.

> If you created a network installation for StarOffice while logged in as root, you must still create a per-user installation from the /bin directory of the network StarOffice installation. See Hour 1, "Installing StarOffice," for details.

> If you are using KDE and chose the KDE Integration option while installing StarOffice, proceed to the section "Using StarOffice in KDE."

Setting Your PATH Variable

First, try an experiment. Open a terminal emulator window in X (an xterm window) and enter the following command:

```
$ soffice
bash: soffice: command not found
```

Your system probably can't start StarOffice. The program for StarOffice can't be located automatically unless you include the subdirectory that contains the StarOffice binary in the PATH environment variable.

To add the StarOffice path to your PATH environment variable, enter the following command:

```
$ export PATH=$PATH;~/Office50/bin
```

By adding the StarOffice binary directory to the PATH environment variable, your Linux environment can locate your StarOffice program binaries.

If you want to add this information to your shell startup so that you don't have to enter it each time you start Linux, add the command just given to your .profile script in your home directory. (The .profile script is executed each time you log in to Linux.)

> Hidden files in your Linux filesystem begin with a period—for example, .profile or .bashrc. You can see them by using the ls command with the -a option:
>
> ```
> $ ls -a
> ```

If you use bash, you can add the updated PATH command to your start-up script by executing the following command:

```
$ echo 'export PATH=$PATH:~/Office40/bin` >>.bashrc
```

> The commands used in this hour assume you're running the bash shell, which is the default shell for almost all Linux systems. Some users prefer using other shells, such as sh, csh, or tcsh. Some commands that have been demonstrated (such as export) don't work the same way in other shells.

2

Starting StarOffice from a Command Line

With the PATH variable set correctly, you can start StarOffice from any graphical xterm window with the following command:

```
$ soffice
```

However, it's better to add a space and an ampersand afterward:

```
$ soffice &
$
```

This starts StarOffice as a background application to the xterm in which you are typing. Put simply, that means that the xterm command line is still usable. In the first example, without the &, the xterm is busy running StarOffice and isn't of any further use to you.

If you don't want to worry about setting the PATH variable described in the previous section, you can always start the StarOffice program directly from the StarOffice binary directory. From any directory, the command is as follows:

```
$ ~/Office50/bin/soffice &
```

Now here's how to make it more convenient to start StarOffice from your Linux Desktop.

> It's normal for StarOffice to take a full minute or more to start, even on a 400MHz Pentium system.

The first time you start StarOffice, you'll see a message indicating that some initial organization is being done. This only happens the first time you start StarOffice.

You'll also see a dialog box asking if you want to register your copy of StarOffice immediately. (See Figure 2.1.) If you have an Internet connection established on your computer (via modem or other connection) and want register immediately, choose Yes. Otherwise, choose No. You can see in the dialog box the date on which your evaluation copy of StarOffice will stop working.

FIGURE 2.1

When you start StarOffice, a dialog box asks if you want to immediately register your copy of StarOffice with StarDivision.

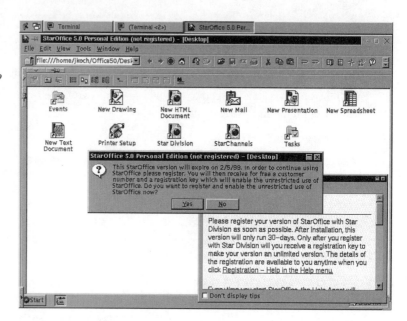

Using StarOffice in KDE

If you're running one of the latest versions of Linux, the chances are fair that you're using the KDE desktop environment. You can recognize KDE in most cases by the large *K* on the panel at the bottom of the screen.

If you are using KDE, you need to have included the KDE integration component as you installed StarOffice. That option (part of the Custom Installation choice) adds the StarOffice program, the setup program (for maintenance of StarOffice), and the Printer Setup program psetup to your main KDE menu under the applink (local applications) menu entry. (See Figure 2.2.)

FIGURE 2.2

StarOffice can be automatically added to your KDE menus during installation.

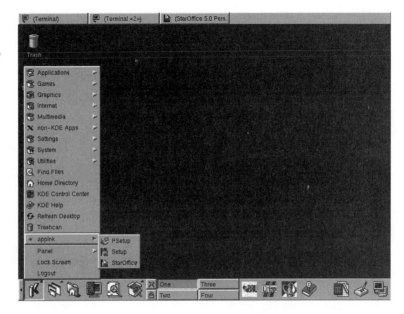

If you used this installation option, you can start StarOffice by selecting it from the applink submenu on your KDE menu.

You can also make StarOffice start automatically when you start KDE. To make StarOffice start automatically, go to the Autostart folder *on your* KDE desktop and add a link to the StarOffice binary, which is normally located at

`/home/`*username*`/Office50/bin/soffice`

Every program with a link in the Autostart folder is started each time KDE starts running.

You can make a link from the Autostart folder to the StarOffice program with the following command:

`$ ln -s ~/Office50/bin/soffice ~/Desktop/Autostart`

Making an Icon for Looking Glass

If you're using Caldera OpenLinux 1.3 or a previous version, you have the Looking Glass Desktop installed by default, or available as an option. (See Figure 2.3.) You can add a StarOffice icon to the Desktop so that you can always start StarOffice by just double-clicking on the StarOffice icon. To add the icon, follow these steps:

FIGURE 2.3

The Looking Glass desktop is common among OpenLinux users.

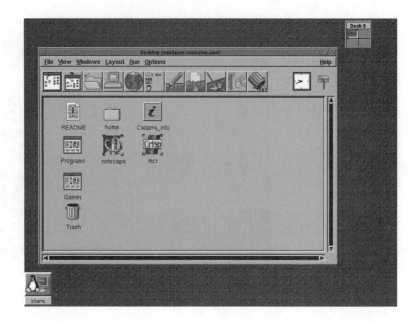

1. Choose File, Open from the Desktop main menu. The dialog box in Figure 2.4 appears.

FIGURE 2.4

The Open Directory Window dialog box in the Looking Glass Desktop.

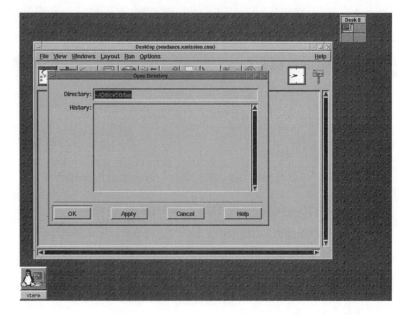

2. In the Open Directory Window dialog box, enter the directory in which the StarOffice program files are located, which is normally

   `~/Office50/bin`

3. After a Directory Window opens for the StarOffice program directory, look for the file within the Window. (See Figure 2.5.)

FIGURE 2.5

The Directory Window containing the StarOffice program files.

The StarOffice program

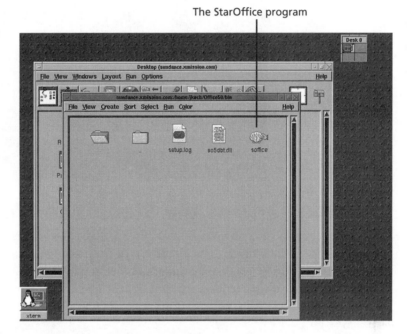

4. Click on the icon for the file soffice and drag it to the main Desktop area; release the mouse button. The icon remains on your Desktop.

5. Any time you want to start StarOffice, just double-click on the StarOffice icon on the Looking Glass Desktop. (See Figure 2.6.)

FIGURE 2.6

*The Looking Glass
Desktop with a
StarOffice icon added.*

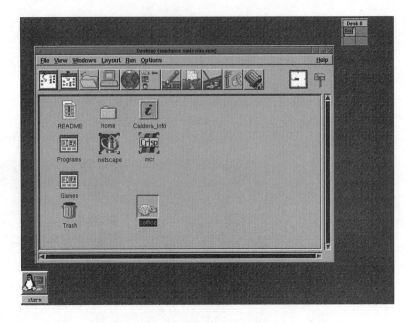

Defining Parts of the StarOffice Window

When you first start StarOffice, after closing the dialog box that requests that you register StarOffice, it looks similar to Figure 2.7. Because StarOffice has some integration that you're probably not used to with other office packages, here's a review of the parts of the screen that you see immediately:

FIGURE 2.7

*StarOffice appearance
at startup.*

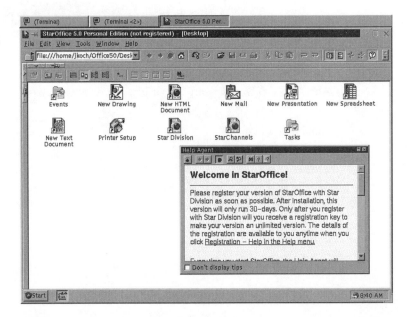

- **The menus and toolbars are probably familiar to you from many office software packages**—The menu items are used to select actions; the toolbars are shortcuts to various menu items. You'll learn more about them later. StarOffice includes several different toolbars.

- **The middle or main section of the window is the StarOffice Desktop**—Like other Desktops that you've seen in Linux or other operating systems, the Desktop provides icons that you can choose to initiate various actions. The icons on the StarOffice Desktop either open a Help file or open a new file of a certain type.

- **The Help window opens each time you start StarOffice**—You can close it by clicking the Close icon in the upper right corner of the window. Help is always available from the Help menu or by pressing F1. (Unless F1 is already used for something by your window manager.)

- **The bottom line of a StarOffice document window is the Status bar**—The Status bar contains information about the file that you're working on, such as the page you're on, the size of the current file, and the date and time. When no document is open, no status bar is displayed.

- **Beneath the Status bar is the Start bar, which contains the Start button (similar to the main menu button in KDE or Windows 98)**—Icons and the filenames of currently open documents are also provided on the Start bar to quickly switch between the documents that you have open (equivalent to switching between them using the Window menu).

> StarOffice tries to expand to full screen when it opens. If you're using KDE, StarOffice might cover up the panel or taskbar. In this case, you'll need to resize the StarOffice window (or press the Maximize button) in order to see the Status bar and Start bar.

Now you can look more carefully at the parts of the StarOffice window that you haven't seen in other graphical programs.

Understanding the Overall Layout of StarOffice

To understand the things you'll be doing with StarOffice, it's probably best to start thinking of the StarOffice window as a Web browser rather than as an office software package.

To begin with, notice the box in the middle of the top toolbar (The Function toolbar) that resembles an URL from your Web browser. Actually, it is an URL, but it probably starts with the word *file* because you're viewing your Desktop, which is actually just a file stored in your Linux filesystem.

You can use the file:// descriptor to view other local files. In fact, when you load a document or spreadsheet, the filename is displayed with a file:// URL. This is similar to opening a local HTML or text file in a Netscape browser.

> The StarOffice Desktop and other features described in this hour are located in your StarOffice directory. For example, the Desktop is located at ~/Office50/Desktop, and the Explorer contents are at ~/Office50/explorer.

You can also use StarOffice to browse the Web. To see this in action, if you have an active Internet connection, try entering another URL in the text entry box—for example, type the following:

```
http://www.cnn.com
```

You will learn about using StarOffice with the Internet in Hours 22, "Creating Internet Documents with StarOffice," and 23, "Using StarOffice Email and Newsgroup Features."

Most of the other features of StarOffice that you'll learn about are implemented within this browser-like design. StarOffice just happens to be a browser that can edit documents and spreadsheets, run slide shows, maintain databases, and so on.

To return the StarOffice window to the main Desktop display, choose the icon with the picture of a drafting table (a desktop), just to the right of the Start button on the Start bar.

Here's a closer look at the features on the Function toolbar that contains the URL box.

Using the Function Toolbar

The Function toolbar (shown in Figure 2.8) is composed of icons that are used within all parts of StarOffice. Taken together they look like a combination of the icons you know from your Web browser and your favorite office software.

You can see a brief description of each of these icons by leaving your mouse cursor sitting on the icon for a couple of seconds. The following is a description of each of the icons, looking from left to right on Figure 2.8:

- **The Link icon** —Represents a link to the document that you're currently viewing. Move the mouse pointer over this icon and click to drag a link to this icon to any location within StarOffice. A typical use is to add a document to your list of bookmarks in the Explorer's Bookmark folder.

- **The URL window** —Displays the URL of the document that you are currently viewing. You can enter any URL on the Web here if you have an Internet connection. This field often displays URLs that you are unfamiliar with (often starting with private or component) when you are viewing StarOffice tools such as the Address Book.

- **The URL history arrow** —Enables you to view previously visited URLs. Click on this drop-down list arrow. You can select any document in the drop-down list to change to that document.

FIGURE 2.8

The Function toolbar in StarOffice.

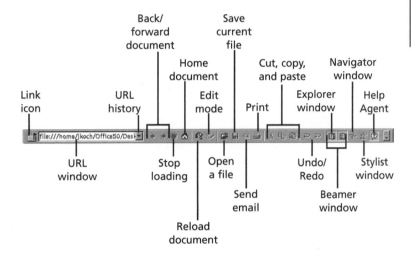

Documents in the history list might not be available if your network or Internet connections have changed since you viewed a document.

- **The Back arrow** —Changes to the previously viewed document. After using the Back arrow to visit a previously viewed document, use the Forward arrow to return to later documents.

- **The Stop sign** —Turns red like a stop sign if a document is being loaded, locally or from the Internet. You can click the icon to stop the document from loading.

- **The Home button** —Takes you to your Home document. You'll learn how to set your Home document in Hour 4, "Configuring StarOffice," in the Browser Options dialog box.

- **The Reload icon** —Reloads the current document. Use this icon to refresh an Internet document or a local document that has changed since it was last loaded.

- **The Edit icon** —Indicates that the current document is being edited. Some documents cannot be edited. Often you can start to edit an Internet Web page by saving a local copy and using the Edit icon to start editing.

- **The Open and Save icons** —Are used to open a new local document or to save the current document, as in most graphical programs.

- **The Send icon** —Used when you are writing an email or newsgroup message (see Hour 24, "Using StarSchedule").

- **The Print icon** —Immediately prints the current document to the current default printer.

- **The Cut, Copy, and Paste icons** —Function as in most other graphics programs. Use them to move around text and other parts of any file you're working with in StarOffice.

- **The Undo and Redo icons**—Revert to repeat your last editing action. You can set the number of saved editing steps when you configure StarOffice.

- **The Explorer icon**—Makes the Explorer window visible or hidden.

- **The Beamer icon**—Makes the Beamer window visible or hidden.

- **The Navigator icon**—Makes the Navigator window visible or hidden.

- **The Stylist icon**—Makes the Stylist window visible or hidden.

- **The Help Agent icon**—Makes the Help Agent window visible or hidden.

Some of the Function bar icons change depending on the type of document you're working with. You'll look at those as they're needed in later hours.

With that basic description of the Function bar, you can explore some of the other parts of StarOffice, starting with the status bar.

Reading the Status Bar

The status bar in StarOffice is similar to the status bar in most other popular graphical applications, but it contains some unique features as well.

You can hide the status bar if you want more room onscreen for your documents. Choose Status Bar from the View menu; choose it a second time to display it again. The status bar is shown in Figure 2.9 as it appears when you begin editing a document . The Status bar includes, from right to left, the following components:

FIGURE 2.9

*The StarOffice status
bar.*

- **The date and time**—These are taken from your Linux system information.
- **The Modified indicator**—An asterisk (*) appears in this field to show when information has been entered but not saved to disk. Each time you save your document, the indicator disappears until you enter something new that needs to be saved.
- **The Hyperlink status**—This toggles between HYP and SEL to indicate how to work with hyperlink references. Click on this part of the status bar to change it. If HYP is displayed, clicking on a hyperlink jumps you to the document referred to in the link; if SEL is displayed, the text of the link is selected (highlighted).
- **The Insert indicator**—When INSRT is displayed, your typing inserts new characters; when OVER is displayed, your typing overwrites the existing text in your document. You can change this by pressing the Insert key on your keyboard or by clicking on that part of the status bar.
- **The size indicator**—This displays the relative size of the document being viewed. You can change the size by choosing Zoom from the View menu or by clicking the right mouse button on that part of the status bar. The right-click selection menu is displayed in Figure 2.10.

FIGURE 2.10

*The Zoom selection
menu is displayed
when you right-click
on the current size in
the status bar.*

- **The style**—This displays the paragraph style for the paragraph in which the cursor is currently located. Also displays the character style if it's not the default setting for that paragraph style. (Paragraph styles are described in Hour 9, "Using Advanced Formatting Tools.") You can see a list of the styles that are defined for the current document by choosing Stylist from the Format menu.
- **The page count**—The page count is displayed as two numbers: the page that the cursor is on and the number of pages in the document. If you double-click on the page count section of the status bar, the Navigator window appears. With the Navigator window, you can move to any part of the current document by selecting a page number, a table, an index marker, or any other part of the document. The Navigator window is shown in Figure 2.11.

> The page count is not displayed if you select Online Layout from the View
> menu.

FIGURE **2.11**

*The Navigator
window.*

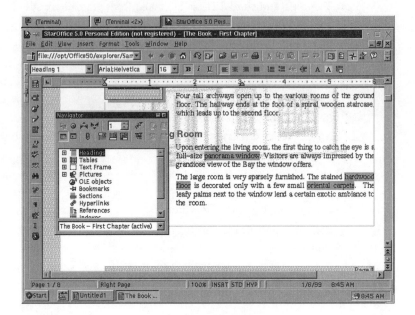

Using the Start Bar

The Start Bar is separated from the Status Bar when your document windows in
StarOffice are not maximized to fill the StarOffice window. A Status Bar appears at the
bottom of each document window, whereas the Start Bar always appears at the bottom of
the StarOffice window.

The Start Bar includes the following items:

- **The Desktop icon**—No matter how many documents you have open, this icon
  always appears on the Start bar to the right of the Start menu. Click the Desktop
  icon to bring the StarOffice Desktop into view; you can choose from the icons
  there to open a new file or other items you've placed there.

- **Buttons for each open document window**—Enable you to switch to any open
  document by clicking one of the buttons on the Start Bar.

- **The Start menu**—Similar to the K menu in KDE or the Start menu in MS Windows, the Start menu shows a list of options for new document types you can open, utilities you can start, and previously edited documents. The first level of the Start menu is shown in Figure 2.12. The Start menu is always visible on the left edge of the Start bar at the bottom of the main StarOffice window.

FIGURE 2.12

The first level of options on the StarOffice Start menu.

Most sections of the status bar can be sized however you want them. You can even size some of them into oblivion. When you move the mouse pointer near the border between two parts of the status bar, the mouse pointer changes to a double arrow. Just click and drag to resize that part of the status bar.

Using the Toolbars

The toolbars in StarOffice are similar to toolbars you've used in other office suite programs; StarOffice just uses more of them. The default display has both a Function toolbar and an Object toolbar. The icons on the Object toolbar change depending on what type of work you're doing. The icons on the Function toolbar stay relatively constant.

You can choose to hide or redisplay any of these Toolbars by selecting them from the View menu, under the Toolbars submenu.

When you start working on a document, the Main toolbar is also visible, as shown in Figure 2.13. It is located on the left side of the StarOffice window and is used to insert objects of different kinds into your documents. Because this is often the easiest way to quickly add a feature, you learn how to use the icons on the Main toolbar as you explore formatting and inserting objects into your documents in Part 2, "Creating Documents with StarWriter."

FIGURE 2.13

The Main toolbar enables you to insert many types of objects into your document.

Using the Explorer Window

The Explorer window is shown in Figure 2.14. It can be viewed any time by choosing Explorer from the View menu. The Explorer gives you a treelike structure on which you can locate and store documents of different types, including templates, Web pages, and documents that you've created.

FIGURE 2.14

The Explorer window in StarOffice.

Click here to view or hide the Explorer.

Click here to pin or overlay the current document

The Explorer is also where resources such as email accounts, StarSchedule event calendars, and newsgroup accounts are accessed.

Using the Explorer might remind you of using things such as the file manager in Windows 3.1 or the file system Explorer in Windows 95. The difference is in the extras that StarOffice provides as preconfigured types of information that are listed in the Explorer window for easy access.

You'll see the Explorer used for examples throughout the rest of this book.

Viewing the Beamer

As you explore the icons in the Explorer window, you'll view many different types of information and system resources. One way to view these items is in the Beamer window. If the Beamer isn't onscreen, some items from the Explorer window appear in the main viewing window, but this makes it harder to use them in your documents.

The Beamer window is similar to a little catalog or listing where information is displayed. The Beamer window appears just below the toolbars.

To view the Beamer window, select Beamer from the View menu.

With the Beamer window onscreen, it is easier to see how useful the different parts of the Explorer can be. In general, the items displayed in the Beamer window can be dragged and dropped into the document that you're working on.

Using the Explorer Icons

The sections that follow define some of the default items included in the Explorer and show you how to try them yourself :

- **The Address Book**—The address book is a collection of mini-databases (each one called a *Table*) where you can store names, addresses, and other information for people you know. You can create custom queries and forms for these Tables, and add new information as needed.

- **Bookmarks**—Bookmarks are pointers to documents that you might want to view or edit again in the future. The bookmarks folder is similar to using bookmarks in any Web browser, except that in StarOffice you can also use bookmarks for local documents that you're editing instead of just for documents on the Web.

  If you want to add a file that you're viewing to the bookmark folder, just drag and drop the Link icon onto the Bookmark folder in the Explorer. (The Link icon is a folder with a triangle-flag on it, located just to the left of the URL window in the Function toolbar.)

If you click on the Bookmarks folder, a few predefined bookmarks appear in the Beamer window.

- **Gallery**—StarOffice comes with a collection of hundreds of graphics that you can use for your own documents. These graphics are located in the Gallery folder of the Explorer. You can browse through the graphics in the Gallery and insert any of them into a document, spreadsheet, or presentation you're preparing.

- **The Help folder**—Contains StarOffice help topics that you can browse and view.

- **The Recycle Bin**—Most graphical operating systems have a recycle bin where you can place documents that you no longer need. The Recycle Bin in StarOffice provides this feature for your Linux system. By default, documents are not actually erased until you empty the Recycle Bin.

You can place any unwanted file on your StarOffice desktop in the Recycle Bin by dragging its icon to the Recycle Bin folder.

Dragging a Desktop icon to the Recycle bin places the actual file in the Recycle bin, not just a Desktop pointer to it.

When you click on the Recycle Bin icon, the list of files stored in the Recycle Bin appears in the Beamer window.

To empty the Recycle Bin, use the right-click pop-up menu.

The Recycle bin is actually a directory located at ~/Office50/explorer/Trash.

The delete function in Linux is permanent. When you delete files by emptying the Recycle Bin, you cannot recover the files that were deleted. If you select the Empty Immediately option for the Recycle Bin, everything placed in the Recycle Bin is permanently deleted from your system.

- **Samples**—The Samples folder contains templates and sample documents that you can use to prepare your own documents in StarOffice. Later, some of these sample documents are used to show you some of the features of StarOffice.

If you did a custom StarOffice installation and de-selected the Sample documents, the Samples folder is empty.

- **StarSchedule**—Contains the icons used to access the task list and events calendar for StarSchedule features (see Hour 24.)
- **Work Folder**—The Work Folder is like your personal storage area. When you save a file in StarOffice, the default location to save it in is the Work Folder. When you choose the Work Folder icon, all the files that you've stored in the Work Folder area appear on the Desktop area, where you can double-click on any document to open it.

When you view the Work Folder, you're actually viewing the contents of the directory ~/Office50/explorer/WorkFolder.

- **Workplace**—The Workplace is a way to graphically access the filesystem on your Linux computer. When you click on the plus sign next to the Workplace icon, the contents of the root directory of your Linux system appear. Subdirectories appear as folders in the Explorer window; files appear in the Beamer window where you can work with them directly.

In the Next Hour

The usefulness of the Explorer window will become obvious as you begin to use StarOffice. The next hour, "Using the Explorer and the Desktop," describes more about using the Explorer. You'll see examples of how it can help you work more efficiently as you walk through creating and managing documents in later hours.

In Hour 3 you'll learn how to use the Explorer and Beamer windows with your Desktop. You'll also see examples of using the Explorer to access and save files, and of using the Desktop to store commonly used files for easy access.

HOUR 3

Using the Explorer and the Desktop

In this hour, you learn the details of using the Explorer window to access StarOffice resources in your documents.

You also learn how to get around the Desktop and associated Start menu to quickly start editing new or existing documents.

This hour builds on the overview of the StarOffice window presented in Hour 2, "Getting Started with StarOffice." You'll have some opportunities to try the things that you are shown, so you might want to have StarOffice running in front of you as you read.

Using the Explorer Window

In Hour 2, you learned about the Explorer window. In this hour, you dig deeper into how to use the Explorer window as you work in StarOffice.

The Explorer window as it appears after you install StarOffice is shown in Figure 3.1. The Explorer gives you a treelike structure in which you can locate and store documents of different types, including templates, Web pages, and documents that you've created. In addition, you use the Explorer to create and access most Internet resources in StarOffice.

FIGURE 3.1

The Explorer window in StarOffice.

The StarOffice Explorer window isn't just for documents, however. It provides a quick interface to many specialized resources that StarOffice provides. With the Explorer, you can access these resources with a couple of mouse clicks instead of searching through subdirectories.

To use items listed in the Explorer window, follow these two rules:

- If an item has a plus sign (+) to the left of it, click on the plus sign to display the contents of that item. (The Gallery item is an example.) The plus sign then changes to a minus sign (-), which you can click on to close the view of the item.

- If an item doesn't have a plus sign to the left of it, as is the case with the Recycle Bin item, click on the icon or the word itself (Recycle Bin) to show the contents of that item in the Beamer window.

You also can double-click on an item in the Explorer window to display its contents in the main viewing area. This is convenient if you don't have the Beamer open, but it can get in the way if you're working with open documents.

> If the Explorer window takes up too much room on your screen, click the
> stick pin icon on the right edge of the Explorer to make the window appear
> on top of your document. Then use the arrow icon to view or hide the
> Explorer as needed.

You'll see the Explorer used for examples throughout the rest of the book.

Viewing the Beamer

As you're learning the parts of the Explorer window, you'll view many different types of
information and system resources. The best way to view these items is usually in the
Beamer window.

To view the Beamer window, choose Beamer from the View menu. The Beamer window
is like a little catalog or listing where special information is displayed; it appears just
below the toolbars.

With the Beamer onscreen, it is easier to see how useful the different parts of the
Explorer can be. Why is the Beamer so useful? In general, the items displayed in the
Beamer can be dragged and dropped into the document that you're working on. You'll
walk through some examples as you explore the items in the Explorer.

The following sections define each of the items shown in the Explorer window and
describe how you can try them yourself.

In order to try the examples that follow, you need to have a document open. To open a
blank StarWriter document, double-click on the New Text Document icon. (Use the Start
bar Desktop icon to switch to it first, if necessary.)

With the Explorer and Beamer windows visible, you're ready to look at the default items
in the Explorer.

Using Right-Click Menus

Many options in the Explorer are accessed using a right-click menu. To see the main
right-click menu, click your right mouse button on the word Explorer in the top line of
the Explorer window. The pop-up menu, with the New and Document submenus opened,
is shown in Figure 3.2.

FIGURE 3.2

Pop-up menus are used to access many features in the Explorer window.

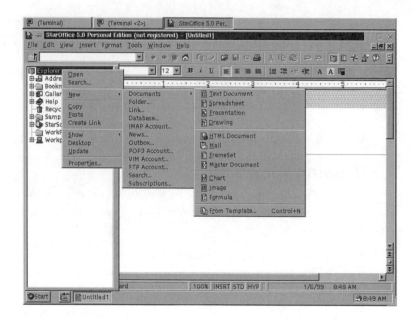

The Address Book

The address book is a collection of mini-databases (each one called a Table) in which you can store names, addresses, and other information about people you know. You can create custom queries and forms for these Tables, and you can add new information as needed.

Follow these steps to view the sample table in the Address book and to see how you might use it:

1. Expand the tree, if necessary, by clicking on the plus sign (+) to the left of the Address Book icon; this opens the Address Book.

2. Click on the plus sign to the left of the Tables icon to open the list of Tables.

3. Click on the address item. The sample addresses appear in the Beamer window.

4. Click on one of the gray buttons at the far left, near one of the addresses in the Beamer window, to select that record. (The display that appears is shown in Figure 3.3.)

5. Click on and drag the arrow to the left of the name, releasing the mouse button within your document window.

6. Use the Database columns dialog box to select which parts of the address book entry are to be inserted into your document, and what form they will take (table, text, and so on). When you choose OK, the data from the address book appears in your document.

FIGURE 3.3

The Beamer window with a sample Address Book entry selected.

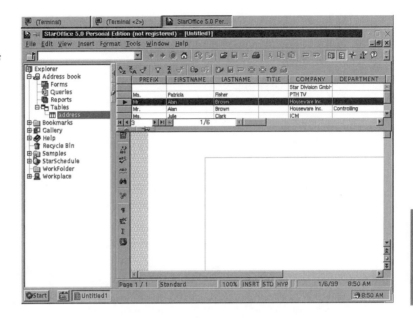

 You can create new tables by right-clicking on the Tables item in the Address Book and choosing New, Table, and then AutoPilot or Table Design.

The Bookmarks Folder

Bookmarks are pointers to documents that you might want to view or edit again in the future. The bookmarks folder is like using bookmarks in any Web browser, except that in StarOffice you can use bookmarks for local documents as well as for documents on the Web. If you want to add a file that you're viewing to the bookmark folder, just drag and drop the Link icon onto the Bookmark folder in the Explorer. (The Link icon is a folder with a triangular flag on it, located just to the left of the URL window in the Function toolbar.)

If you click on the Bookmarks folder, a few predefined bookmarks appear in the Beamer window.

The Gallery

StarOffice comes with a collection of hundreds of graphics that you can use for your own documents. The Gallery collection includes many types of images, including the following:

- **Bullets**—Small graphics that you can use to highlight items in a list
- **Rulers**—Horizontal lines that you can use to graphically separate sections of a document
- **Textures**—Colors and patterns that you can use to form a distinctive background for your documents (but don't make your text unreadable!)

You might recognize that these graphics are most useful in creating Web pages, as described in Hour 22, "Creating Internet Documents with StarOffice." However, they can also be useful for other documents.

All these graphics are located in the Gallery folder of the Explorer. You can browse through the graphics in the Gallery and insert any of them into a document, spreadsheet, or presentation you're preparing.

Use a graphic from the Gallery by following these steps:

1. If necessary, click on the plus sign (+) to the left of the Gallery icon to expand the Gallery tree.
2. Click on the Bullets icon. A collection of bullet icons appears in the Beamer window. (This is shown in Figure 3.4.)

FIGURE 3.4

The Beamer window with bullet graphics from the Gallery displayed.

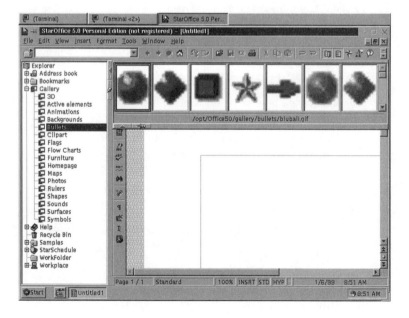

3. Scroll around the Beamer window until you find the graphic that you want.

4. Click and drag that icon, releasing the mouse button over your document. A copy of the graphic is inserted into your document.

The Recycle Bin

Most graphical operating systems have a recycle bin where you can place documents that you no longer need. The recycle bin in StarOffice provides this feature for your StarOffice documents. By default, documents are not actually erased until you empty the Recycle Bin.

You can place any unwanted file from the StarOffice Desktop or Explorer folders in the Recycle Bin by dragging its icon to the Recycle Bin folder.

When you click on the Recycle Bin icon, the list of files stored in the Recycle Bin appears in the Beamer window.

The Explorer Recycle Bin lists in parentheses the number of files that are currently in the Recycle bin (no number is shown if no files are present).

To work with the Recycle Bin, click on the Recycle Bin icon with your right mouse button. You can then choose to empty the Recycle bin to permanently delete the files it contains (thus freeing up that disk space).

The Recycle Bin pop-up menu does not include the option to Empty Recycle Bin unless the Recycle Bin contains at least one file.

No undelete command exists in Linux—the delete function is permanent. When you delete files by emptying the Recycle Bin, you cannot recover the files that were deleted.

The Samples Folder

The Samples folder contains templates and sample documents that you can use to prepare your own documents in StarOffice. You'll look at some of these sample documents later to see some of the features of StarOffice.

If you didn't use the Standard installation for StarOffice, the Samples folder might be empty.

Your Work Folder

The Work Folder is your personal storage area. When you save a file in StarOffice, the default location in which to save it is the Work Folder, described in Hour 7, "Creating a New StarWriter Document." When you open the Work Folder item, all the files that you've stored in the Work Folder appear in the Beamer or on the Desktop area; you can then double-click on any document to open it. Figure 3.5 shows how the Work Folder might look after you've saved a few StarOffice files in it.

FIGURE 3.5

The StarOffice Work Folder with some user-created documents stored in it.

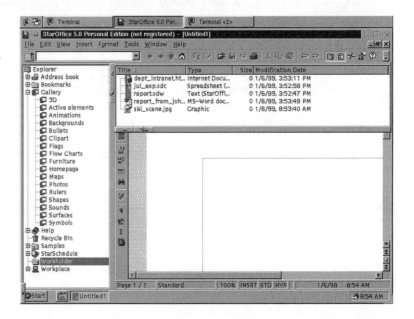

Of course, the Work Folder is actually just a directory on your hard disk (~/Office50/explorer/WorkFolder). In fact, the graphics in the Gallery and the other Explorer items are also stored in distinct subdirectories on your hard disk. The Explorer window is useful because it makes opening files that you work on regularly more convenient—you don't have to browse through the entire Linux filesystem.

Your Workplace

The Workplace is a way to graphically access the filesystem on your Linux computer. When you click on the plus sign next to the Workplace item, the contents of the root directory of your Linux system appear. Subdirectories appear as folders in the Explorer window; files appear in the Beamer window so that you can work with them directly.

Figure 3.6 shows how the Explorer and Beamer windows might look while you are exploring your local filesystem.

FIGURE 3.6

You can explore your local filesystem from the Explorer window's Workplace icon.

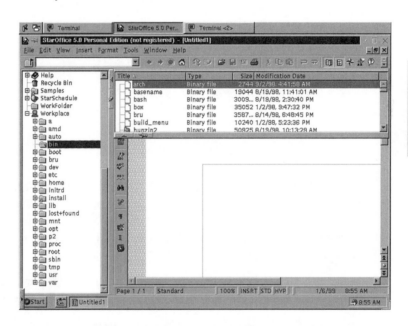

If you store your documents in the Work Folder (the default when you save a file), you probably won't often use the Workplace item. On the other hand, you might want to import graphics stored on other parts of your hard disk, open text documents that weren't originally created in StarOffice, or drag and drop files to new locations on your Linux system. The Workplace in the Explorer window works well for any of these tasks.

Defining Parts of the Desktop

The Desktop is the main viewing area of the StarOffice window. When you first start StarOffice, it appears as shown in Figure 3.7. This section describes the icons on the Desktop and shows how you can use them to get started with StarOffice.

FIGURE 3.7

The StarOffice
Desktop at startup.

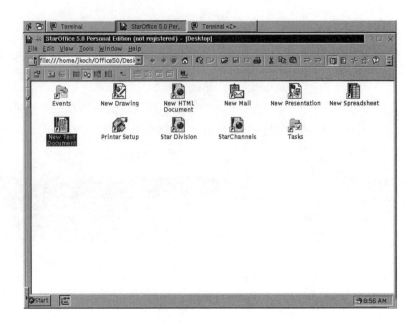

The idea behind the Desktop (and behind the Explorer window and icon bars, for that matter) is that you can have immediate access to most tasks in StarOffice without having to remember which menu they're located on. Often, you never have to view a standard menu. You can just choose an icon or an item on the ever-present Start menu to initiate an action.

In the sections that follow, the icons and tools on the Desktop are described in more detail so that you can use them to start creating documents in Hour 7.

The Desktop Versus the Work Folder

Both the Desktop and the Work Folder in the Explorer window are places to store your work.

Normally, you store all your documents in the Work Folder. You can create subdirectories to organize your work and divide files into different types (such as spreadsheets and presentations).

However, some documents are always more active than others. Documents that you are working on from day-to-day are normally placed on the StarOffice Desktop so that they are only a click away when you start StarOffice. When a document is finished or less important than others, it can be moved back to the Work Folder for permanent storage, leaving the Desktop uncluttered for current projects.

In the sections that follow, you learn how to move files between these two areas of StarOffice.

The Desktop Icons

Several types of icons are included on the default StarOffice Desktop:

- **New documents**—Double-clicking on any of these icons opens a new document of the named type. One example is the icon labeled New Spreadsheet.
- **HTML documents (Web pages)**—These documents are related to the StarOffice home pages at StarDivision, the creator of StarOffice. One example of these is the icon labeled StarDivision.
- **Programs**—Programs can also be stored on the Desktop. One example is the icon labeled Printer Setup, which runs the program `psetup`.
- **Explorer links**—Because some features, such as StarSchedule, can only be accessed via the Explorer, the Desktop includes links to those items. One example is the icon labeled tasks, which opens the Task List screen (see Hour 24, "Using StarSchedule").

The StarOffice Desktop isn't just for these default files. On the Desktop you're actually seeing the contents of a special subdirectory on your Linux system. You can see this in the URL window of the function bar when you're viewing the Desktop. The following URL is displayed (with your username, of course):

`file:///home/dtaylor/Office50/Desktop/`

Because the Desktop is always quickly available by clicking on the Desktop icon in the lower-left of the status bar, storing your daily work files on the Desktop makes them easy to access.

Adding Your Documents to the Desktop

You can add any of your documents to the Desktop so that you can immediately find them. Just follow these steps:

1. Make sure on the View menu that both the Beamer and the Explorer windows are open.
2. In the Explorer window, open the Workplace folder.
3. Within the Explorer window, browse in the Beamer until you locate the work file that you want to move to the Desktop.
4. Click and drag the file's icon from the Beamer, dropping it on the Desktop (see Figure 3.8).

FIGURE **3.8**

The StarOffice
Desktop with a user
file added.

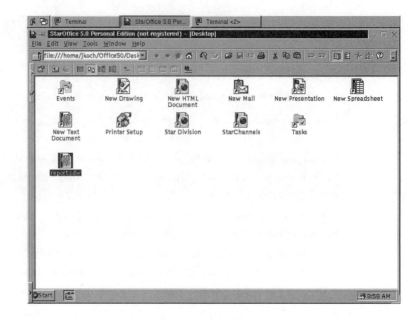

When you move a file to the Desktop, you're moving the actual file to a different subdirectory. Use the same drag-and-drop procedure when you want
to move the file off the Desktop. Deleting the file from the Desktop erases
the file from your system.

When you drop an icon onto the Desktop, sometimes it doesn't appear on
the Desktop even though the file has been moved. To refresh the Desktop
display, choose the Display Details icon from the Object toolbar. When you
choose the Display Icons icon on the toolbar, the new file appears on the
Desktop.

You can add many files to your Desktop, arranging them to suit your work needs. You
can even delete some of the help files on the Default Desktop and use the Help menu
instead when you need to open an Online Help file. Figure 3.9 shows a sample Desktop
with a collection of personal files.

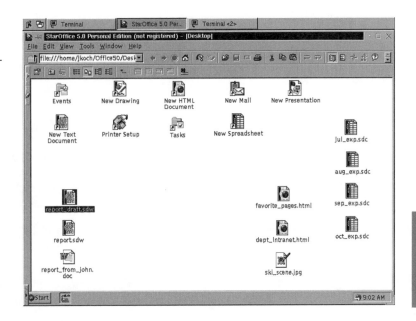

FIGURE 3.9

The StarOffice Desktop with a collection of personal work files.

Removing a Document from the Desktop

The easiest way to move a document from the Desktop to a folder in your Workplace is to drag the icon from the Desktop to a folder in your Workplace (within the Explorer).

If you want to delete a file that's stored on your Desktop, another choice is to drag and drop the icon from the Desktop to the Recycle Bin icon in the Explorer window.

If you want to delete a file directly from the Desktop, however, you can follow these steps:

1. With the mouse pointer over the icon of the file that you want to delete, click the right mouse button. The pop-up menu shown in Figure 3.10 appears.

2. Choose Delete from the pop-up menu.

3. Use the Confirm Delete dialog box to confirm that you want to erase this item from the Desktop and from your filesystem. The icon and the file it represents are deleted.

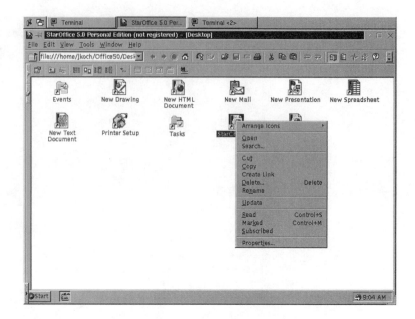

FIGURE 3.10

A pop-up menu
appears when you
right-click on a
Desktop icon.

Viewing Properties of an Item on the Desktop

The right-click menu that you just used to delete a Desktop icon has many other uses. The menu changes depending on the type of icon that you right-click. In general, however, the menu shown in the previous figure applies.

One of the things that you'll use the right-click menu for is to view the properties of a document on your Desktop—to see its size, its date of creation, and so on.

When you right-click on any Desktop icon, you can choose the Properties item from the pop-up menu. The dialog box in Figure 3.11 appears. Different types of files have slightly different dialog boxes.

From the Properties dialog box, you can view properties such as

- The type of document (StarWriter, subdirectory Folder, HTML, StarCalc, MS Word, and so on)
- The size of the document
- The date and time that the file was created and when it was last modified
- Information about accessing the document on the Internet (if appropriate to the file type)

FIGURE 3.11

The Properties dialog box tells you all about any file on your StarOffice Desktop.

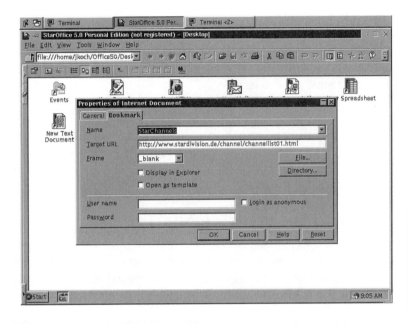

In addition to the Properties item, you can see many other options on the right-click menu that you can explore to arrange the icons on your Desktop and work with your Desktop files.

Switching Between Documents and the Desktop

With all your key working documents stored on your StarOffice Desktop for easy access, you might be asking what makes the Desktop so convenient.

You can always switch to the Desktop by selecting it from the Window menu. The easier way, usually, is to click on the Desktop button on the left end of the Start bar (see Figure 3.12). Because this button is always visible, you're always just one click away from viewing all the files on your Desktop.

FIGURE 3.12

The Desktop button on the status bar means you're always just one click away from viewing the StarOffice Desktop.

Click here at any time
to reach the Desktop.

Viewing Multiple Document Windows

When you have multiple documents open in StarOffice, you can display each one in a window smaller than the main StarOffice window so that parts of multiple documents are visible at the same time.

These *floating windows* each include a Status bar for the document in that window.

Use the small buttons on the upper-right corner of the document window to create a floating window while viewing a document. As with non-floating, full-sized windows, you can use the Windows menu or the buttons on the Start Bar to make any document visible.

Using the Start Menu

The Start menu is a great way to access many StarOffice features. Not only are menu items provided to start new documents of many types, but you can also use the Start menu to open recently edited documents (their names are saved and shown on the Documents submenu), just as you do in Microsoft Windows 98.

Bookmarks and Help files are also listed in separate submenus on the Start menu for quick access.

If you're using KDE on your Linux system, and you selected KDE Integration when you installed StarOffice, you have two other features available in the Start menu:

- The Program Files submenu includes everything from the KDE Main Menu, so you can start any program on the KDE menu directly from within StarOffice.

- The KDE Control Center is included in the Settings submenu, so you can configure KDE from the Start menu selections.

Reviewing the Menus

The menus in StarOffice will be very familiar to you if you've used other office suite software. The items are arranged in a similar pattern that is easy to learn.

The catch is that StarOffice, unlike MS Office, isn't composed of several components such as MS Word and MS Excel. Instead, everything is part of one program: StarOffice.

Therefore, the menus don't have to change much between different document types. In fact, most of the menu items remain the same for any document that you're working on. This makes it easy to find the command that you need on the menus.

When you work with different types of documents, you'll see that the following menus remain constant most of the time:

- **File menu**—Items for working with entire files or documents, such as opening and saving
- **View menu**—Items for choosing what you view on your StarOffice window
- **Window menu**—Items for arranging and selecting among all the open documents in your StarOffice session
- **Help menu**—Items for different online help tools

On the other hand, some of the menus change quite a bit. For example, the formatting options for a spreadsheet and a word processing document require different commands, so the items listed on the Format menu change according to what you're working on.

Using Keyboard Shortcuts

Computer users seem to fall into two camps. The first prefers to use a mouse, feeling that typing is for content and not for controlling a computer program. The second type prefers the keyboard, and only touches the mouse as a last resort.

Graphical programs make it easy to learn a new application, but they require you to use the mouse. Most graphical programs in Windows and Macintosh also have keyboard shortcuts to accommodate users who prefer using the keyboard. These shortcuts are a great way to quickly perform tasks without using the mouse. Most Linux programs don't have these shortcuts, but StarOffice for Linux does!

Two kinds of keyboard shortcuts are provided in StarOffice. The first uses the Alt key to open a menu and regular keystrokes (letters, arrows, and the Tab key) to select an option.

The second type of shortcut is called an Accelerator key. By pressing the Ctrl key in combination with other keys, you can immediately execute an action such as saving or printing a file, or bolding a block of selected text.

Following is an example of using the Alt key to perform a task—opening a new StarCalc spreadsheet:

1. While holding down the Alt key, press the *f* key (this is usually written as Press Alt+F). The File menu appears.
2. Press the *n* key. The New item is selected, and the New submenu appears.
3. Press the *s* key. The Spreadsheet item is selected, and a new spreadsheet document appears on your screen.

4. Looking back at the menus that you selected using the keyboard, notice how can you tell which keys to use for these shortcuts: each one is underlined (see Figure 3.13).

FIGURE 3.13

Menu shortcut keys are underlined.

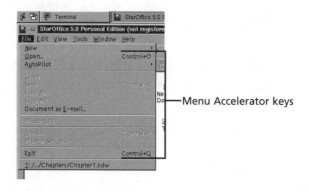

Menu shortcut keys

To open a menu, hold down the Alt key and press the underlined key; to select an item within the menu, just press the underlined key.

Accelerator keys are even quicker. Look again at the File menu (see Figure 3.14). Anytime you press Ctrl+O, the Open File dialog appears as if you had selected Open from the File menu (using Alt+F and O, or by using the mouse).

FIGURE 3.14

The Accelerator keys are always listed on the right side of a menu item.

Menu Accelerator keys

How can you tell what the Accelerator keys are for a task? Just look at the right side of a menu item to see whether a key combination is shown there.

In the Next Hour

In the next hour, "Configuring StarOffice," you'll learn how to set options for how StarOffice behaves and how to modify StarOffice menus and toolbars to suit your preferences. You'll also explore how to check settings for things such as how often documents are autosaved, how many levels of undo are allowed, and where StarOffice looks for your document files.

3

Hour 4

Configuring StarOffice

In this hour, you learn how to set options that affect your working environment in StarOffice. That environment includes defining what items are included on your menus and toolbars, as well as special features such as auto-spellchecking.

Options that affect specific document types such as spreadsheets or HTML documents are discussed in the hours that describe working with those document types.

All the global options described in this hour are set from the Tools menu, and most are part of the Configure or Options items.

Changing What's on the Menus and Toolbars

StarOffice provides more flexibility than you will probably ever want. Almost everything you see on the screen can be changed to fit your work environment and preferences.

Two things that you work with regularly can be easily modified: menus and toolbars. Menus and toolbars can be configured to contain exactly the commands and icons that you want to have immediately accessible.

Start by exploring how you can change the StarOffice menus to suit your tastes.

Selecting Menu Items to Display

If you're new to StarOffice, you probably can't imagine why you'd want to change the menu structure—especially because everything you'll see in this book is based on the default menus!

After you've used StarOffice for a while, however, you might find that you want the menus to more closely match another application that you use. Perhaps, for example, you regularly use a command that's hard to access via the default menu structure (maybe it requires you to go through three submenus and a dialog box). In either case, setting up the menus to match your preferences makes StarOffice easier to use.

All the commands used in StarOffice are available as menu items. You can select any of them from a list and position them anywhere in the menu structure.

In fact, you can also write your own programs in StarOffice BASIC (a macro language for StarOffice) and assign custom commands to a new menu item. That, however, is beyond the scope of this book.

To take a look at the menu items, choose Configure from the Tools menu. The menu configuration dialog box opens. Select the Menu tab to see the menu configuration options, as shown in Figure 4.1.

You'll notice a few things in this figure:

- The menu structure (main menus and submenus or menu items) is indicated in the top list box by the indentation of the items.
- The keyboard shortcut for each menu item in the Menu item list has a tilde (~) in front of it. For example, the AutoPilot menu item has a tilde in front of the u, indicating that pressing *u* selects this menu item (after pressing Alt+F to open the File menu).
- A command name is shown to the right, in square brackets, for each menu item.
- Categories of functions or commands are listed in the Category field.
- All the available commands for the selected functions category are listed in the Command list in the dialog box.

FIGURE 4.1

The Menu tab of the Configuration dialog box shows the commands associated with each menu item.

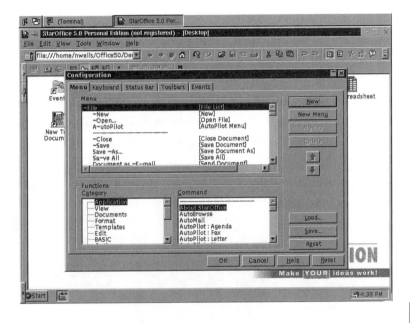

The Configuration dialog box configures the menus for the document type that you're viewing. If you want to change the default menus for spreadsheets, open a spreadsheet (even a blank one) before selecting Configure from the Tools menu.

There are hundreds of functions listed in the different categories. When you select an item in the Category list, the Commands list shows commands in that category. You can learn a lot about the functions available in StarOffice by browsing through a few of the command lists.

For example, suppose that each week you create a small newsletter with an index. You update the index several times as you write. Right now, you have to choose this command from the default menus under Tools, Update, All Indexes. If you want to make this command appear at the top of the Edit menu, follow these steps:

1. Open a StarWriter word processor document so that the changes that you make to the menus affect the word processor menus.

2. Choose Configure from the Tools menu and select the Menu tab.

3. In the Category list, scroll down and select Edit. The list of commands changes to show editing commands.

4. In the list of commands, scroll down and select Update Indexes.

5. In the Menu list, scroll down and select ~Edit.

6. Press the New button to insert the command that you selected into the Edit menu.

7. Press the OK button to finish your changes.

8. Click on the Edit menu. The Update Indexes item is listed first (as in Figure 4.2). It's probably gray because you're using a blank document that doesn't yet have indexes to update.

FIGURE 4.2

The Update Indexes item has been inserted as part of the Edit menu.

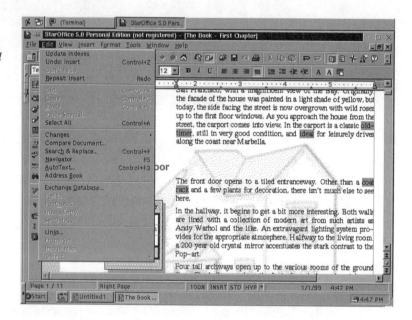

To see a short description of any command in the Command list, click on it and leave your mouse pointer in place for a second. A yellow pop-up description of that command appears. (You must first select Extended Tips from the Help menu for the pop-ups to appear.)

Configuring the Toolbar Contents

Configuring which icons are on the StarOffice toolbars is probably even more useful than customizing your menu items because toolbar icons are always just a mouse-click away.

As you saw in Hour 2, "Getting Started with StarOffice," StarOffice has a lot of toolbars: the Function Toolbar, the Main Toolbar, and the Object Bar, which in turn contains many sub-toolbars. Different versions of these toolbars appear depending on what type of document you're editing and what object is selected in that document.

When you configure these toolbars, you have access to the same complete list of StarOffice functions that is available for defining your own menu items. Each one has an icon of some type assigned to it (you can change those, too).

Defining all the toolbars can get complicated, but the following simple example shows you what you can do; you can explore on your own after that.

As you practice changing the toolbars or menu items, you might find that you don't like some of the changes that you've made. You can always press the Reset button in the Configuration dialog box to restore the settings to what they were when you first opened the dialog box. Pressing the Default button restores the default StarOffice settings, as if no changes had been made since StarOffice was first installed.

Suppose you create a lot of documents that have tables in them, but you don't like having the Main Toolbar (which includes the Insert Table icon) visible on your screen.

You can easily add the Insert Table icon to the Function toolbar by following these steps:

1. Choose Configure from the Tools menu.

2. Choose the Toolbars tab. The list of toolbars appears, as shown in Figure 4.3.

FIGURE 4.3

The Toolbars tab of the Configuration dialog box is the starting point for configuring the icons on your StarOffice toolbars.

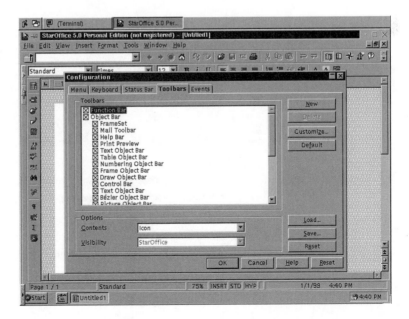

4

3. Scroll down in the Toolbars window and click on Function Toolbar. (Notice all the different Object toolbars that are listed—this list changes depending on what you're doing in StarOffice.)

4. Choose the Customize button. The Customize Toolbars dialog box appears (see Figure 4.4).

FIGURE 4.4

The Customize Toolbars dialog box enables you to add any command icon to a toolbar by dragging it.

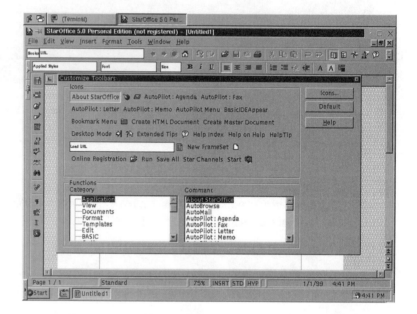

5. Scroll down the Category list and click on Insert.

6. Scroll down the Command list and click on Insert Table. Notice which icon is highlighted in the top part of the dialog box (see Figure 4.5).

7. Click and drag the Insert Table icon from the Customize Toolbars dialog box and drop it on the Function Toolbar (outside the dialog box) in the position where you want it.

8. If you need to move the icon, click and drag it to another location on the Function Toolbar.

9. If you want to remove any icons that are currently on the Function Toolbar, click and drag them off the toolbar, dropping them anywhere on the screen except in the Customize Toolbars dialog box.

10. When you are done modifying the Function Toolbar, close the Customize Toolbars dialog box by clicking on the tiny x in the upper right corner of the title bar.

FIGURE 4.5

*The Insert Table icon
is highlighted when
you choose it from the
Command list.*

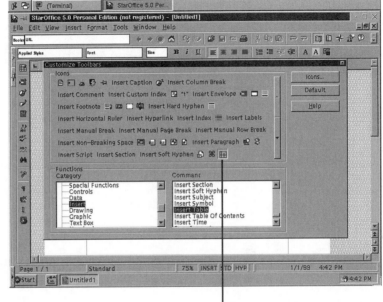

The Insert Table icon

If you make a mess of your toolbars during this exercise, choose Default in
the Toolbars tab of the Configuration dialog box—the default StarOffice
toolbar is restored.

Starting with the Configuration dialog box, each of the toolbars can be configured as this
example illustrates.

From the Toolbars tab in the Configuration dialog box, you can also set whether the toolbars display icons (when icons are available), text, or both. Just select an option from the
Contents field after you select a toolbar to edit.

The StarOffice toolbars are very flexible. Experiment with the different toolbar options,
try changing icons, and move icons around on the toolbars to see how you can set up
your environment to fit your work habits.

Setting Which Toolbars Are Displayed

The easy part of setting up your toolbars is deciding which ones you want to display.
From the View menu, you can select Toolbars and check or uncheck any of the four toolbars. (See Figure 4.6.)

FIGURE 4.6

You can select which toolbars to display from the Toolbars item of the View menu.

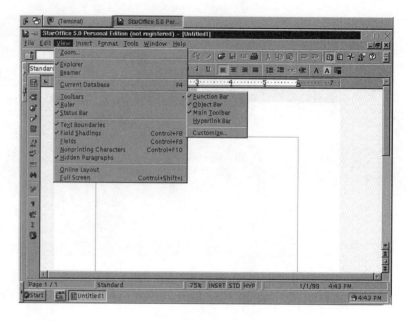

Menus and toolbars aren't the only things you can set up within StarOffice. The next section describes some of the other global options that you can configure.

Setting the General Options

Although you can set options independently for spreadsheets, HTML files, presentations, and so on, some settings apply to all documents that you create.

These general settings are controlled by the General Options dialog box, which you can view by selecting Options from the Tools menu, and then selecting General.

The sections that follow review the most important settings in the General Options dialog box.

Reviewing Your User Data

When you installed StarOffice in Hour 1, "Installing StarOffice," you had the option of entering some personal data during the installation. This User Data is stored in StarOffice for use in template documents, in email and newsgroup postings, and so on.

If you need to review or change any of your personal information, go to the General Options dialog box (choose Options, Tools, General) and choose the User Data tab. (See Figure 4.7.)

FIGURE 4.7

The personal information stored in the User Data tab can be reviewed or altered as necessary.

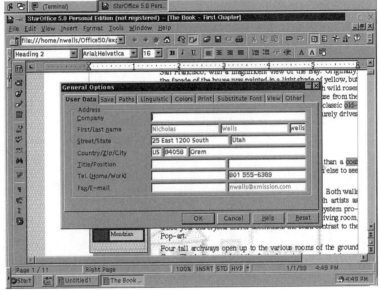

You can click on any of the fields to enter new data. Just click the OK button when you're done to store your changes.

If you change the name or email address fields, your registration code needs to be updated, which requires a new license key from StarDivision.

Pressing Cancel in the General Options dialog box closes the dialog box without saving any updates you've entered. Pressing Reset leaves the dialog box open but resets all the information to what it was before you entered any changes.

Setting Your Save Options

The Save settings in the General Options dialog box enable you to determine how your work is protected. In general, the more protection you have against power failures, bad edits, and other oops! situations, the better off you are as you work.

Using features such as automatic save is so fast on today's PCs that you won't notice any interruption in your work; but this feature can sure save you when you think you've lost a day's worth of work.

To see your Save options, open the General Options dialog box and choose the Save tab (see Figure 4.8).

FIGURE 4.8

The options in the Save tab determine how your documents are protected against losing data.

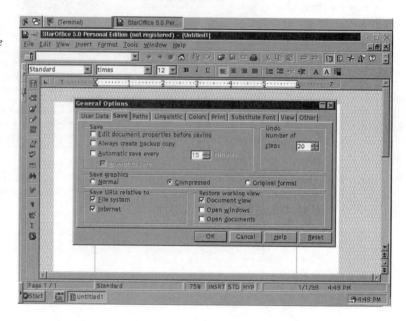

Remember, the Save options described here apply to all types of documents that you create in StarOffice, from word processing documents to email messages and presentations.

The key items in the Save tab are

- **Edit document properties before saving**—If this item is checked, you'll see a Properties dialog box for your document as you save it. This option enables you to review information about the document each time you save it. This is useful in cases in which you need to update a revision number or check other document information.

- **Always create backup copy**—If this item is checked, StarOffice creates a backup copy of every document. This obviously doubles the space required for your documents and can add a few seconds as you save your files, but the added safety might be worth it to you.

Backup copies are stored in the /~Office50/backup directory with the extension .bak. You can use the Open item on the File menu to browse this directory and select a backed-up document to load.

- **Automatic save every *xx* Minutes**—Autosave is one of the nicest features of any modern office software. When you check this option, StarOffice automatically creates a new backup file every few minutes (you determine how often in the Minutes field). If your work is unexpectedly interrupted, you lose only a few minutes' work, even if you never officially saved the document you're working on. The time required for the Autosave on most computers isn't even noticeable.

- **Undo Number of steps**—This option enables you to set how far you can back up in your work using the Undo item on the Edit menu. More undo levels adds to the memory requirements of your system, but can be a great help if you do a lot of editing on large or important files.

The two Save options—Always create backup copy and Automatic save every *xx* minutes—are turned on by default in many word processors, such as Microsoft Word. However, they are off by default in StarOffice. Turn these options on and leave them on as you work in StarOffice.

4

If you're working on a laptop, automatic save and backup features can use extra battery power by running the hard drive more often. Use your judgment as to whether the backup or the battery life is more important to you.

Reviewing Your StarOffice Paths

If you've worked with Linux for very long, you know that one of the greatest sources of trouble with Linux software can be determining where things are stored in the filesystem.

StarOffice is a large program, and you might want to store parts of it in nonstandard locations to fit what you're doing with the rest of your Linux system.

The Paths tab in the General Options dialog box enables you to set up the subdirectory where each part of StarOffice is stored. Most of these subdirectories are probably fine as they're set up by default. Following is a look at a couple that you might want to change.

The Path tab of the General Options dialog box is shown in Figure 4.9.

FIGURE 4.9

Paths (subdirectories) can be altered for most of the files used by StarOffice.

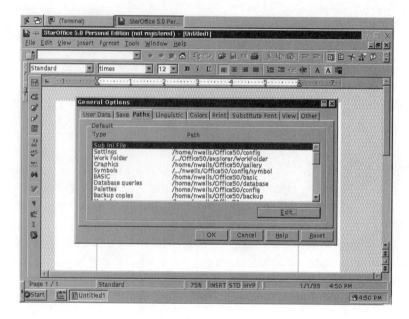

The list of paths includes most of the special directories that StarOffice uses for things such as the Explorer window's Work Folder, the Bookmarks, and the Desktop itself.

Other paths relate to things that have not been described yet, such as the subdirectory in which backup documents are saved. You might want to change a path for one of the following reasons:

- You want all your working files stored in a separate part of your home directory.
- You want your working files and backup files stored in another directory that's backed up each evening by your system administrator.

The location used by default when you save any new document is determined by the Work Folder path.

To make any changes to a path, select the path that you want to edit from the list and choose the Edit button.

A file browser such as the one in Figure 4.10 appears; you can select the subdirectory that you want to apply to the path that you selected.

FIGURE 4.10

When you edit a path, you use a standard file browser window to choose a new subdirectory.

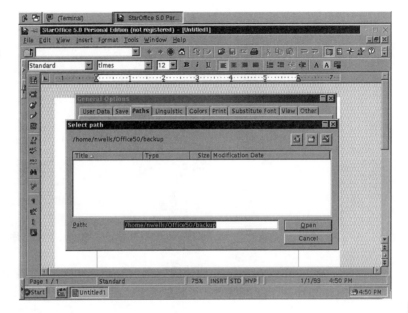

Setting Language Options

The language options available in StarOffice are a great help in making your writing correct and professional. Although not as advanced as some of the latest tools in Word or WordPerfect, StarOffice still provides many great language features.

To set the basic language features, open the General Options dialog box (choose Tools, Options, General) and select the Linguistic tab. The dialog box in Figure 4.11 appears.

The Check spelling box shows a few rules that are applied when you use the Spell Checker. The default options are set to

- **All caps**—Always spell-check words that are all capital letters.
- **Words with numbers**—Always spell-check words that include numbers.
- **Case insensitive**—Don't look for words with wrong capitalization.
- **Don't check special regions**—Don't spell-check in special areas of the document, such as headers and footnotes.
- **Don't spell check using all available languages**—Use only the current default language.

FIGURE 4.11

FIGURE 4.11

The Linguistic tab determines your spelling, hyphenation, and language options.

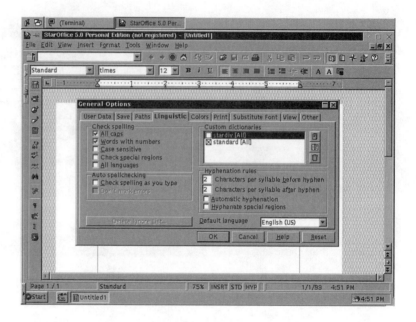

The Auto spellchecking feature (turned off by default) checks your spelling as you type, underlining in red any word not found in the dictionary. Figure 4.12 shows a document with a few underlined (misspelled) words caught by the auto-spellchecker. Auto spellchecking is described in more detail in Hour 12, "Using Spell-Check and the Thesaurus."

FIGURE 4.12

Auto spellchecking uses a wavy underline to show words that can't be identified.

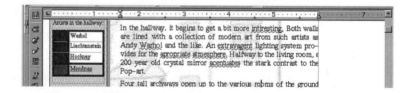

The hyphenation rules define how words at the end of lines are hyphenated into two parts. Unless you're working on a report with special formatting requirements, you can probably leave these settings at their default values.

Remember, though, that the Default language shown in the lower-right of the Linguistic tab of this dialog box determines how words are hyphenated. Each language has hyphenation rules coded into a dictionary that StarOffice uses to hyphenate your documents.

The General Options dialog box includes other options beyond what you've seen here, including the capability to set view options (see the View tab), standard colors (see the Colors tab), and the program language if you have more languages than just English installed (see the Other tab).

Setting Other Global Options

A few other option settings might come in useful as you customize your StarOffice environment. All these options are configured by items on the Tools menu.

Setting Up Keyboard Shortcuts

At the end of Hour 3, "Using the Explorer and the Desktop," you learned how to use the keyboard to complete StarOffice tasks. From the Configuration dialog box, you can set up many of these keyboard shortcuts.

To set up your own keyboard shortcuts, or to change the defaults that StarOffice uses, choose Configure in the Tools menu and select the Keyboard tab. This dialog box is shown in Figure 4.13.

FIGURE 4.13

The Keyboard tab of the Configuration dialog box enables you to define actions for special key combinations.

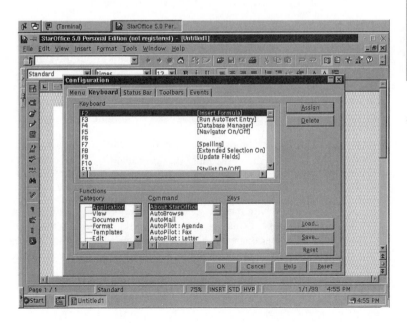

As you scroll down the list in the Keyboard field, you'll see the function keys listed, as well as key combinations such as Ctrl+*letters*, Shift+Ctrl combinations, and so on.

In the bottom half of the dialog box, you'll recognize the lists of categories and commands that you saw earlier in this hour when you learned about setting up menus and toolbars.

The process for creating key assignments is similar to the one for setting up menus and toolbars:

1. Select a category that contains the action to which you want to assign a keyboard shortcut. The command list updates to include commands from the category that you select.

2. Select the specific command that you want from the command list.

3. Select a keyboard combination from the Keyboard list.

4. Choose the Assign button. The command that you selected appears next to the keyboard shortcut you selected.

5. Press OK to close the dialog box. Now you can try pressing the keyboard combination you selected to execute your command.

Setting What to Display in the Status Bar

You learned about the default status bar in Hour 2, but the status bar in StarOffice (like everything else) can be modified to suit your preferences.

From the Configuration dialog box, choose the Status Bar tab (see Figure 4.14). Note that most of the items listed are checked by default, but some are not.

By checking any of the items in the list, you can add them to the status bar. If it becomes crowded, uncheck the items that you don't want.

As with many of the other configuration options shown in this hour, the status bar changes depending on the type of file that you're viewing. If you alter the status bar while viewing a spreadsheet, and then you open a word processor document, the default status bar for word processor files remains unchanged.

FIGURE 4.14

The status bar can be configured to display the information that is most useful to you.

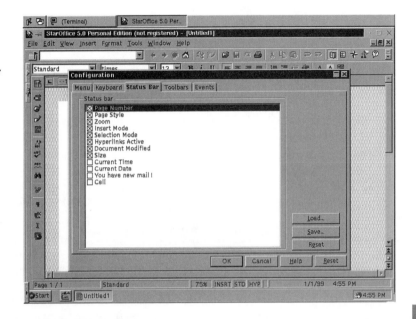

Configuring AutoCorrection

4

One of the most powerful features of StarOffice can also be one of the most challenging to configure; hopefully you won't have to change much!

The AutoCorrect feature watches what you type and changes it when an error is detected. Some users, both good typists and bad, find this very annoying. But because nearly all of us make errors, such as typing *hte* instead of *the*, the AutoCorrect feature can be a great help.

If you need to override the AutoCorrect feature, first enter the text as you type and allow the AutoCorrect to fix it. Then use the mouse or arrow keys to return to the spot at which you want to override the correction. Use the Delete or backspace key to erase and then reenter the letters as you want them (taking care not to press the spacebar afterward). The AutoCorrect does not change them.

By configuring the AutoCorrect feature, you can enjoy the benefits of it without the annoyances.

AutoCorrect can be configured by selecting AutoCorrect/AutoFormat from the Tools menu (when viewing an open document). The four tabs show you the many options that the AutoCorrect feature can watch for and correct.

The first two tabs—Replace and Exceptions—contain lists of words to be replaced or corrected, and exceptions to the autocorrection rules. You can add to or delete items from these lists to match your needs. (The Replace tab is shown in Figure 4.15.)

FIGURE 4.15

The Replace tab of the AutoCorrect dialog box enables you to configure which misspellings are to be corrected.

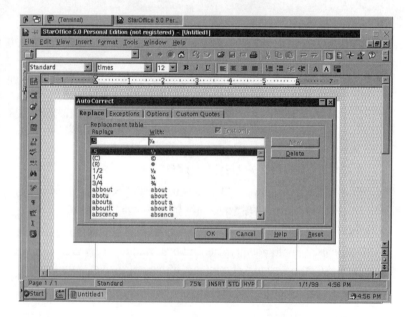

For example, if your work regularly includes an abbreviation that isn't listed in the Exceptions, the AutoCorrect feature always capitalizes the word that follows the abbreviation. You can add the abbreviation to the Exceptions list to prevent that autocorrection from occurring.

Most of the items in the Replace list are misspellings such as replacing *thier* with *their*. If you use other words that you often misspell, you can add them to the Replace list.

What if you don't want to use autocorrection at all? You can change to the Options tab (see Figure 4.16) and uncheck the first two boxes: Use replacement table.

FIGURE 4.16

*The AutoCorrect
options define special
actions that the
AutoCorrect feature
can include.*

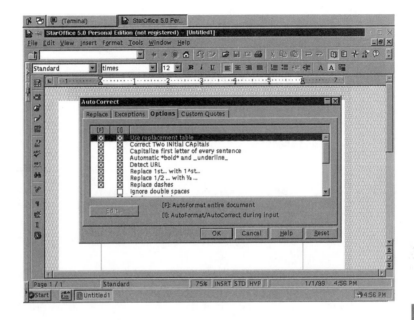

Other options determine how sentences are started as well as corrections to common
mistakes that occur during rapid typing.

If you don't want to see misspelled words underlined, review the Auto spellchecking
options in the General Options dialog box, in the Linguistic tab. Choose Options from
the Tools menu, and then choose General Options.

The Main toolbar provides an icon to toggle Auto spellchecking on and off.
See Figure 4.17.

FIGURE 4.17

*An icon on the Main
toolbar can be used
to toggle Auto
spellchecking on
and off.*

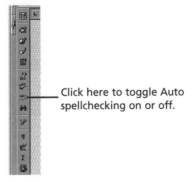

Click here to toggle Auto
spellchecking on or off.

4

You'll find more things that you can set up in StarOffice to suit your work style, but you know the main configuration options and where to find them.

Setting Up StarOffice Printers

StarOffice uses the standard Linux printing system to print your documents. However, StarOffice also enables you to set up different printer drivers to take advantage of additional printer features.

> All the printers that StarOffice supports natively are PostScript printers. If you need to use a non-PostScript printer, configure your Linux system to use a filter program such as GhostScript.

If you have printing already set up on your Linux system, you can begin using StarOffice and print documents without using the steps in this section. Using more advanced features of your printer, such as changing paper trays or duplex printing mode, can all be done using the Printer Setup utility described here.

Using the Printer Setup Utility

Use the Printer Setup utility to select a default printer, configure it, and work with the printer fonts. You can start this utility by double-clicking on the Printer Setup icon on your StarOffice desktop. (See Figure 4.18.)

You can also run this program by starting the psetup program from a graphical command line. The psetup utility is located in the same directory as the main StarOffice program.

> If you installed StarOffice using the Network/Workstation installation method, you might not be able to alter the printer setup; however, you can review it using the Printer Setup icon.

FIGURE 4.18

Double-click on the Printer Setup icon on the desktop to begin configuring StarOffice printers.

When you start the `Printer Setup` program, the Printer Installation dialog box appears, as shown in Figure 4.19.

4

FIGURE 4.19

You can select and configure printers using the `Printer Setup` utility.

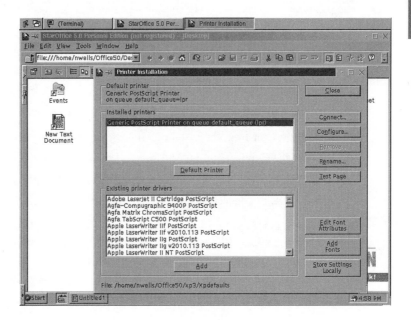

By default, a single Generic PostScript printer is selected for use on the default Linux printer queue. Learning all about Linux printing is a huge task, so just take a look at how to use the key features of this dialog box to set up printers for StarOffice.

Adding Another Printer Type

To add a printer from the list of existing printers (for which StarOffice has some driver support), double-click on the printer name in the Existing printer drivers list. That printer is moved to the Installed printers list, where it can be configured for use.

Setting the Default Printer

The default printer is the one to which StarOffice automatically prints when you print any document.

To make one of the installed printers the Default printer, select that printer in the Installed printers list by clicking on it. Then choose the Default Printer button under the Installed printers list.

Changing the Print Queue Used by a Printer

A print queue is a named location where files that are to be printed are placed. You might find it useful to set up multiple print queues if you have a printer with regular and letter-head paper, or if several users are sharing a printer and you want to keep their print jobs separate.

Any printer can be connected to any print queue. If printer A is connected to print queue B, when a user prints a file to print queue B, the physical device printer A (and its associated printer driver) are used to print the file.

To set the print queue for any installed printer, follow these steps:

1. Select a printer from the Installed printers list by clicking on it.
2. Choose the Connect button. The dialog box in Figure 4.20 appears.
3. Select an existing print queue from the list shown by clicking on it.
4. Choose OK to connect this installed printer to the selected print queue.

The default name for the Linux print queue (which is used by default on the generic printer that is automatically installed) is lpr. You'll see a definition for a print queue called lpr when you view the Connect dialog box. All the print queue definitions are taken from your Linux printing configuration file (usually /etc/printcap).

FIGURE 4.20

From the Connect dialog box, select the print queue that an installed printer services.

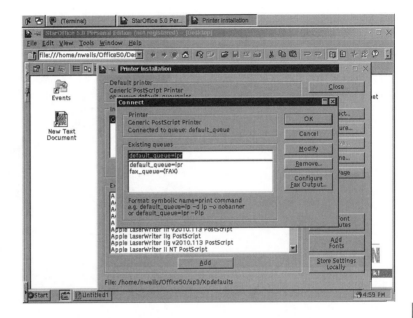

Configuring a Printer

You can set configuration information for any installed printer. Just follow these steps:

1. Select the printer that you want to configure by clicking on its name in the Installed printer list.

2. Choose the Configure button. The dialog box in Figure 4.21 appears.

3. Select the settings that you want as the default for all documents printed to this printer and print queue.

These settings can be overridden for any document using features on the StarOffice menus. If you set the defaults that you prefer here, however, you don't have to make the changes on every document you create.

Unfortunately, StarOffice doesn't use standard PostScript printer definition files. The options available with the listed PostScript printers are very limited.

In addition to these basic printer settings, many configuration options are available relative to the fonts that are used by the printer. To view and edit the font information, select a printer from the Installed printer list and choose the Edit Font Attributes button or the Add Fonts button.

FIGURE 4.21

The Configure dialog box enables you to define default settings for every document printed to the selected printer.

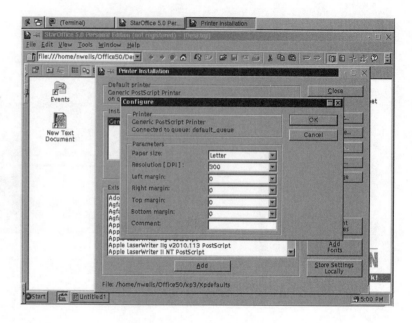

In the Next Hour

In the next hour, "Importing and Exporting StarOffice Documents," you'll learn about exchanging StarOffice files with other software packages. You'll see how to import files that were created using other Office software or the Internet, and how to export your StarOffice documents so that other users who don't have StarOffice can use them with their own programs.

HOUR 5

Importing and Exporting StarOffice Documents

In this hour, you learn about how to import and export documents between StarOffice and other office software that you or your colleagues need to use.

It isn't likely that you'll be using exclusively StarOffice from now on, at least not for your boss and all your co-workers.

Fortunately, StarDivision thought the same thing and provided StarOffice with a strong list of file conversion filters. With these automatic filters, you can exchange files with many different word processors, spreadsheets, and presentation programs. They're not perfect, but in this hour, you learn how to make the best of what StarOffice provides.

Importing Word Documents

Some people think that the most-used import filter for any word processor is Microsoft Word. StarDivision came to the same conclusion and provided the strongest support for Word documents.

StarOffice supports Word 6.0/95 and Word 97 file formats very well, and it supports RTF format.

Using Microsoft Word 6.0/95 and Word 97 Files

The best input filter in StarOffice is for Word 6.0/95 and Word 97 files. When you use the Open file dialog box (see Figure 5.1), the familiar Microsoft Word icon is even used for any Word files stored on your Linux filesystem. Ironic, isn't it?

FIGURE 5.1

The familiar Word icon is used for any Word documents displayed in the Open file dialog box.

StarOffice files

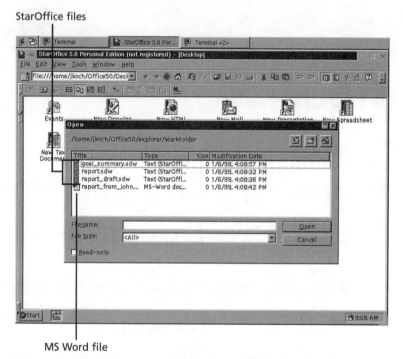

MS Word file

You can open a Word 6.0/95 or Word 97 document with the same steps that you use to open StarOffice documents, using the Open file dialog box. You can store Word documents on your StarOffice Desktop and double-click to start editing them.

Of course, when you save any Word document that you've been editing, you need to watch the file format to see that it's set correctly. If you open a Word document, edit the document, and use Save or Save As, by default StarOffice uses the Word 6.0/95 or Word 97 filter to save the document. You'll learn more about saving different file formats later in this hour.

A message often appears when you save in Word format to remind you that some features might not transfer to Word format, and therefore you might lose some information. If this is a concern, save a copy in native StarOffice format as well.

Although the StarOffice filters for Word documents are good, be careful about assuming that everything converts from a StarOffice file saved as Word 97 to a native Windows copy of Word 97.

In particular, things such as macros, footnotes, headers, tables, and so on might not convert or might be formatted incorrectly in native Word 6.0/95 or Word 97.

It's a good idea to save a StarOffice-formatted document—or at least a backup of the Word-formatted document that you intend to pass on to a colleague—until you've heard from that person that the file can be opened and is correctly formatted.

Reviewing Styles in Imported Files

A favorite feature of Word is the paragraph styles that are used to assign font and spacing characteristics (among others) to one paragraph at a time. Hour 9, "Using Advanced Formatting Tools," covers StarOffice styles.

When you import a Word document, the styles from the Word document are added to the current StarOffice style list. You can see these in the Paragraph Styles window. (Press F11 or choose Stylist from the Format menu; see Figure 5.2.)

If you know your Word document well, you might be troubled that your paragraph styles aren't listed in the Paragraph Styles window. Take heart. Change the drop box at the bottom of the Paragraph Styles window from Automatic to All Styles—or better, to Applied Styles.

With Applied Styles selected, only the paragraph styles that were imported from your Word document are listed in the Paragraph Styles window. The characteristics of the paragraph style are imported intact.

5

FIGURE 5.2

*When you import a
Word document, you
can review any styles
added to the document
by viewing the
Paragraph Styles
window.*

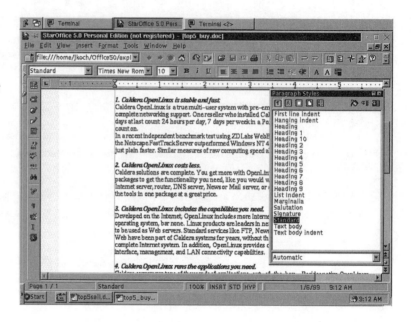

You can review your imported styles from the Style Catalog dialog box using the following steps:

1. Choose Catalog from the Styles & Templates submenu under the Format menu.
   The Style Catalog dialog box appears. (See Figure 5.3.)

FIGURE 5.3

*From the Style Catalog
dialog box, you can
edit the setting for any
style.*

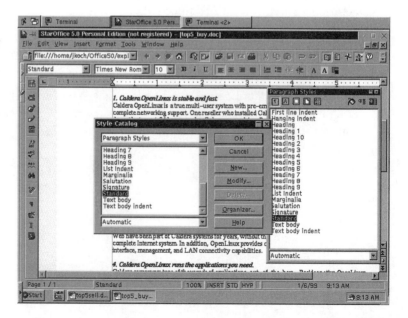

2. Choose Applied Styles from the drop-down list.

3. Select the style that you want to review.

4. Choose Modify. The Paragraph Style dialog box appears. (See Figure 5.4.)

FIGURE 5.4

The Paragraph Style dialog box describes everything about a selected paragraph style.

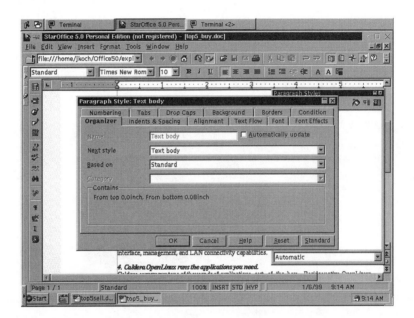

5. Select any of the tabs to see the settings for the imported style. The Font and Indents & Spacing tabs are usually a good place to start.

Importing Other Word Processor Documents

Other than Microsoft Word documents, you can have documents in dozens of other formats. The sections that follow describe how to open other documents in StarOffice.

Using WordPerfect Files

WordPerfect is arguably the second most used word processor in the world. StarOffice, however, has never heard of it. You won't find WordPerfect listed in any of the format selection dialog boxes of StarOffice.

If you have a WordPerfect file that you want to edit in StarOffice, you need to open the file in WordPerfect. Then use the Save As command in WordPerfect to save the file in one of the following formats:

- Word 6.0 or Word 95
- Word 97
- Rich Text Format (RTF)

Depending on the version of WordPerfect that you're using, all these options might not be available in the WordPerfect Save As dialog box.

When you open the newly saved document in StarOffice, the format is determined for you as the file is opened. If the format can't be recognized, an error message tells you so. (See Figure 5.5.)

FIGURE 5.5

When you open a file in an unrecognized format, StarOffice displays an error message to indicate that the file can't be read.

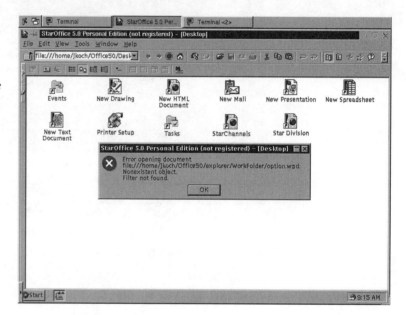

Using Other Word Processor Files

StarOffice doesn't support any other word processing formats. The best option for using documents created by other word processors is to use the Save As dialog box to save the document in one of the formats listed in the WordPerfect section: Word 6.0/95, Word 97, or RTF.

This is the preferred order for using the filters for any other word processor. However, you might need to try several of the filters to see which one retains the most information during the conversion.

Obviously, this situation is less than ideal, especially if you have to regularly exchange documents between StarOffice and another word processor such as Ami Pro. For each document, you have two conversions: from Ami Pro to an intermediate format such as RTF, and from RTF to StarOffice.

Rich Text Format (RTF) is a widely supported format that is intended to be cross-platform. Because it includes many formatting features, such as character formats, footnotes, and tables, it is often a good choice for conversions between word processing formats. In addition, RTF is included as a conversion option, both reading and writing, with every major word processor.

Using Text Files

When you're using Linux, text files seem to crop up fairly often. Text files can be read directly into StarOffice without specifying a format.

Text files use a .TXT extension and have a specific icon in StarOffice to help you recognize them. (See Figure 5.6.)

FIGURE 5.6

A text file, shown here on the StarOffice Desktop, has its own icon style.

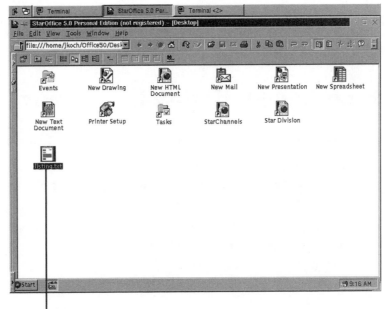

Icon for a text document

StarOffice reads in text files created in both UNIX/Linux and in DOS/Windows. StarOffice manages the different methods of marking the end of each line as the files are imported.

Using HTML as an Interchange Format

You'll hear more about this in Hour 22, "Creating Internet Documents with StarOffice," but StarOffice is designed to work well with the Internet. In fact, HTML is one of the prime formats that StarOffice can read and write.

HTML is not listed in the previous sections as a word processor interchange format because HTML is severely limited compared to word processor formats. At the least, it's designed for different goals, so using HTML to convert between Word 97 and StarOffice, for example, does not preserve all the formatting and document data from the original file.

Nevertheless, if you're working with colleagues who are Web-savvy, or who are more interested in reading your document that in editing or altering your document, HTML can be an effective format for your documents.

You can choose HTML as the format in the Save As dialog box (described previously). StarOffice can read in (*import*) any HTML Web page, including one that you've saved from StarOffice.

Exporting StarWriter Documents

If you need to share documents created in StarWriter with a colleague that uses another word processor, the other word processor is not likely to read StarOffice files.

Instead, you need to export your StarOffice files in a format that can be read by another word processor. StarOffice provides several export filters from the Save As dialog box (see Figure 5.7):

As with preparing a file for import into StarOffice, the main formats to use for exporting to other word processors are as follows:

- Word 95
- Word 97
- Word 6.0
- Rich Text Format
- Plaintext (several varieties)

FIGURE 5.7

From the Save As dialog box, you can select one of several export file formats.

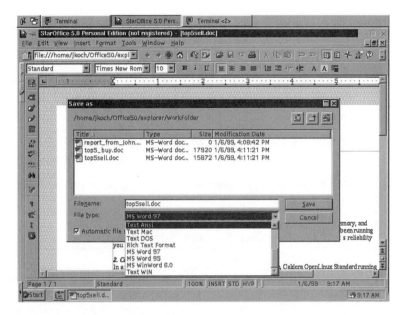

To save a StarOffice document in another format, follow these steps:

1. Choose Save As from the File menu. The Save As dialog box opens.

2. Select a format from the File type drop-down list.

3. Enter a different name for the document.

4. Select the directory in which the new file is to be saved (remember that you can't save the file directly to a floppy disk unless you have it mounted in your Linux system).

5. Choose OK to save the document.

After you've saved a StarOffice document in a format such as Word, RTF, or plaintext, you can use that document in any word processor that can import that format. The reason StarDivision selected these formats is that every major word processor can import these formats.

Most word processors, in fact, can determine the file format automatically and apply the correct conversion to the native format. For example, if you open a Word 6.0 document in WordPerfect 8 for Windows, the file imports automatically and appears on your screen.

In some cases, a word processor can't determine the format of a file. In such a case, you normally choose the format from a dialog box that lists the available filters.

Reviewing Imported and Exported Documents

Any time you move a document between word processors that use different formats—for example, reading a Word file into StarOffice—check the document to see how well the conversion worked.

Although we've had good luck with the Word filter in StarOffice (which is recommended for most uses in this hour), you might have problems with some features.

Table 5.1 shows the key import and export filters available in StarOffice, and how you can use them.

TABLE 5.1   KEY IMPORT AND EXPORT FILTERS IN STAROFFICE

Format	Comments
HTML	Strong filter in StarOffice, but useful mostly for Internet/Web posting and sharing between systems without other word processors (difficult to edit exported documents).
RTF	A good choice for word processors and text processing systems that don't support Word format.
Word 6.0/95	The preferred choice for exchanging files with anyone who can read Word format.
Word 97	A strong filter in StarOffice, but best to use only for export when you know the recipient has Word 97 because Word 95 can't read Word 97 files.
Plaintext	Useful for exporting to email systems without HTML capability, or for other text file needs (such as configuration files).
StarOffice	StarOffice formats can only be read by StarOffice; use other formats when you need to exchange files with users who don't have StarOffice.

In all word processors, some conversion filters work better than others. Importing one type of file might work well, but importing another type might leave a document full of errors.

Table 5.2 lists some things that you can check to see how converted documents have fared, as well as some problems you might encounter after importing and exporting files.

TABLE 5.2 SOME ITEMS TO CHECK AFTER IMPORTING A DOCUMENT

Item to check	Potential problems
Total number of pages	Small changes in fonts or line spacing can make a document longer or shorter.
Page numbers, footnotes, headers, and footers	These items outside the text margins might overlap or be in different positions. Also check the font used.
Font	A different default font might be substituted.
Graphics	Different graphics formats can be supported in the new word processor, making some graphics gray boxes. Positioning of graphics might also be off.
Columns	Alignment, gutter, and text flow of columns might not be correct.
Tables	Spacing of cells (width/height), shading, or special fonts might not have been applied.
Document properties	Document meta-information, such as author and date created, might not be imported even though the new word processor has those features.
Special markers	Markers for things such as index and table of contents might be inserted as normal text instead of as hidden markers. If they are hidden, they might not generate the correct index or other list.
Macros and templates	Documents that rely on a template or macro to display properly won't work in the new word processor. You'll have to research how to imitate or develop the necessary substitute formatting.

5

Importing Excel Spreadsheets

It is the same with spreadsheets as it is with word processing: file conversion and sharing with Microsoft Office products is stronger than with any other office software.

Reading Excel 5.0, Excel 6.0/95 and Excel 97 Files

The best input filter for spreadsheets in StarOffice is the Excel filter. In fact, it's the only StarOffice filter made especially for spreadsheets. When you use the Open file dialog box (see Figure 5.8), the familiar Microsoft Excel icon is used for any Excel files found in that directory.

FIGURE 5.8

The familiar Excel icon is used for any Excel spreadsheets that are displayed in the Open file dialog box.

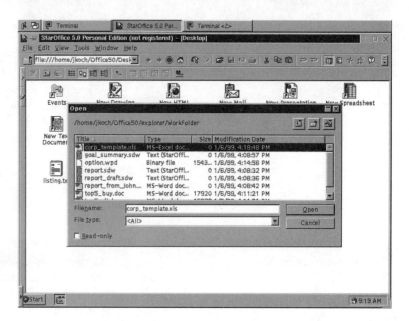

You can open Excel files from versions 5.0, 6.0, 95, or 97 within StarCalc. Just use the same steps that you use to open other StarOffice documents (using the Open File dialog box). You can store Excel documents on your StarOffice Desktop and double-click to start editing them.

Of course, when you save any Excel document that you've been editing, you need to watch the file format to see that it's set correctly. If you open an Excel spreadsheet, edit that spreadsheet, and use Save or Save As, StarOffice uses the same Excel *filter* (version) that was used to read in the file.

When using the StarOffice filter to save documents in Excel format, be careful to check large or complex spreadsheets the first time you import them or when moving them back and forth between Microsoft Office and StarOffice. There haven't been problems exchanging files with native Excel users, but we might not be stretching the capabilities of the filter with a lot of complex charts, formulas, and so on.

> It's a good idea to save a StarOffice-formatted spreadsheet—or at least a backup of the Excel-formatted document—that you intend to pass on to a colleague until you've heard from that person that the file can be opened.

Importing Other Spreadsheet Formats

Besides Microsoft Excel spreadsheets, you can have spreadsheets in several other formats. The sections that follow describe how to open other documents in StarOffice.

Using Lotus 1-2-3 Spreadsheet Files

Lotus 1-2-3 is arguably the second most-used spreadsheet in the world. StarOffice, however, does not give it much attention.

Lotus 1-2-3 1.0 is listed in the Select Filter dialog box as an option when you open a file with an unrecognized format. (See Figure 5.9.) But this Lotus filter opens the spreadsheet in StarWriter as a word processing document, which isn't of much use to you.

FIGURE 5.9

The Select Filter dialog box enables you to select the correct format for the file that you want to import into StarOffice.

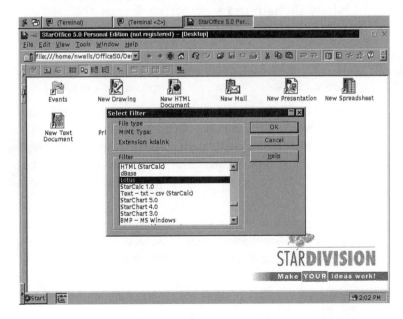

If you have a Lotus 1-2-3 spreadsheet that you want to edit in StarOffice, you'll need to open the file within Lotus 1-2-3 and then use the Save As command to save the file in one of the following formats:

- Excel 4.0, 5.0, 95, or 97
- HTML
- DIF

Using DIF and HTML is described a little later in this hour. Depending on the version of Lotus 1-2-3 that you're using, all these options might not be available in the Lotus Save As dialog box.

If you can use the Excel option to save your Lotus 1-2-3 spreadsheet, the file type is detected automatically and the file opens in StarOffice without a problem. If the format cannot be recognized, the Select Filter dialog box (shown previously) appears, and you can select the correct format.

 Although this is really the only way to use Lotus 1-2-3 spreadsheet files, the combination of a non-Microsoft export filter in Lotus and a non-Microsoft input filter in StarOffice can lead to uncertain results. Check your imported spreadsheet carefully for errors, and keep backup copies until you're certain that the transfer worked.

Using Other Interchange Formats

StarOffice doesn't really support any other native spreadsheet formats. It does, however, provide the *Data Interchange Format* (*DIF*), which can be used successfully in some cases. DIF is intended for use with databases more than with spreadsheets, but it is a widely used standard format that any spreadsheet can most likely save in.

The best option for using spreadsheets created by other programs is to use the Save As dialog box to save the document in an Excel format. Using both an input filter and an output filter on your spreadsheet increases the chance that a problem might occurring; however, the StarOffice input filter for Excel really provides the best option because it is so much further along than any other interchange format for spreadsheets with StarOffice.

Although StarOffice handles HTML text very well, using comma-delimited text—or even HTML—won't preserve the formulas that are part of your spreadsheet. It only preserves the values that are calculated from those formulas.

Therefore, if you want to use your spreadsheet to show someone your results, HTML is fine. If you need to continue working on the spreadsheet, however, HTML is useless.

Exporting Spreadsheets for Use in Other Programs

If you need to share StarOffice spreadsheets with a colleague that uses another spreadsheet program, the other program is not likely to read StarOffice files. None of the other popular spreadsheets—Lotus 1-2-3, Quattro Pro, Microsoft Works—support importing StarOffice spreadsheet files.

Instead, you'll need to export your StarOffice spreadsheet files in a format that can be read by the other spreadsheet program.

StarOffice provides the following useful spreadsheet export filters from the Save As dialog box:

- Excel 4.0, 5.0, 95, and 97
- HTML
- dBase (a database format)
- Text

To save a StarOffice spreadsheet in another format, follow these steps:

1. Choose Save As from the File menu. The Save As dialog box opens.
2. Select a format from the File type drop-down list.

 As described in the previous sections, the best option for exporting a file for use in another word processor is Excel. (Use the latest version of Excel that the target computer has installed.) If you use any of the other formats listed previously, some formatting or formula information will be lost during the conversion.

3. Enter a different name for the document.
4. Select the directory in which the new file is to be saved (remember that you can't save the file directly to a floppy diskette unless you have it mounted in your Linux system).
5. Choose OK to save the document.

5

After you've saved a StarCalc spreadsheet in a format such as Excel, you can use that spreadsheet in any program that can import that format. Because of the popularity of Excel, any program released after the release of Excel 5 probably has this capability.

In fact, most spreadsheet programs determine the file format automatically, based on the file extension or content, and apply the correct conversion to the Excel format. For example, if you open an Excel 5 spreadsheet in Lotus 1-2-3 version 3.1 for Windows, the file imports automatically and appears on your screen.

In some cases, a spreadsheet program can't determine the format of a file. In such a case, you normally choose the format from a dialog box that lists the available filters.

Reviewing Imported and Exported Spreadsheets

Any time you move a spreadsheet between programs using a non-native format—for example, reading an Excel file into StarOffice—check the spreadsheet to see how well the conversion worked.

Although we've had good luck with the Excel filter in StarOffice (which is recommended for almost all spreadsheet exchanges), you might have problems with some fea-

In all spreadsheet programs, some conversion filters work better than others. Importing one type of file might work well, whereas importing another type might leave a spreadsheet full of errors. Check any important areas after importing a spreadsheet.

tures.

Table 5.3 lists some things that you can check to see how converted spreadsheets have fared, in addition to listing some problems that you might encounter after importing and exporting files.

TABLE 5.3 ITEMS TO CHECK AFTER IMPORTING A SPREADSHEET

Item to check	Potential problems
Total number of sheets in the spreadsheet	The current sheet of an imported spreadsheet might be intact, but the entire "Workbook" might not have been imported correctly. Check the names and arrangement of multiple sheets in a multi-sheet spreadsheet.
Page numbers, footnotes, headers, and footers	These items outside the page margins might overlap or be in different positions. Also check the font used.
Font	A different default font might be substituted.
Graphics and charts	Different graphics formats might be supported in the new word processor, making some graphics gray boxes. Positioning of the graphics might also be off.
	Chart styles or formatting options available might be different. Check charts for data consistency (do they still make sense when you read the numbers?), as well as making sure that they still look good.
Formulas	Most formulas are simple enough and common enough to transfer fine, but long or complex formulas that rely on absolute cell references or a special order in which operations are performed might not calculate in the same way. Add parentheses where needed to force calculation in the correct order.
Functions	If a function that was available in the original spreadsheet program is not available in the new program, an obvious error appears in the cell. More dangerous are complex or rarely-used functions that might have different meanings or parameter order and therefore appear to work, but actually function slightly differently.
Document properties	Document meta-information, such as author and date created, might not be imported even though the new spreadsheet program has those features.
Special Features	Features such as data validation and input help notes, sheet protection, and user-defined functions might not import correctly, leaving the data in the cells correct, but making use of the spreadsheet by others less intuitive.

continues

5

TABLE 5.3 CONTINUED

Item to check	Potential problems
Macros and Templates	Spreadsheets that rely on a template or macro to display properly probably won't work in the new spreadsheet program. You'll have to research how to imitate or develop the necessary substitute tools.

Importing and Exporting Presentations

Presentations in StarImpress include most of the features you'll find the in the popular PowerPoint program. The details of creating presentations can be found in Hour 19, "Creating Presentations with StarImpress."

Unfortunately, the import and export capabilities of StarImpress are not impressive.

Although StarOffice lists PowerPoint 97 in the Select Filter dialog box as a supported file type for importing documents, it is difficult to get it to read in native PowerPoint files.

> If you keep your presentations simple, you might have better luck trying to import your PowerPoint 97 presentations into StarOffice.

The best solution for importing a presentation created in another program such as PowerPoint or Corel Presentations is to save the presentation as a series of HTML documents, and then to use StarOffice as a Web browser to view the presentation on your Linux system.

Exporting StarImpress Presentations

When you create a StarImpress presentation that you want to use on a computer system that does not have StarOffice, your best choice is to use the Export item on the File menu to export the presentation as a set of HTML documents.

You can also select a graphic format to export the current slide as a bitmapped image.

Importing and Exporting Graphics

StarOffice supports a long list of graphics formats. Hour 11, "Adding Graphics to Documents," describes how to import graphic images into a document. This same process can be used to import saved image files into spreadsheets, presentations, or StarDraw files.

When you create a bitmapped image in the Image Editor (described in Hour 11), or a vector image in StarDraw (described in Hour 6, "Creating Graphics with StarDraw"), you can export that image in any of several bitmapped or vector graphics formats. To do so, choose Export from the File menu (see Figure 5.10).

FIGURE 5.10

The Export dialog box enables you to create many graphic formats from a StarDraw or Image Editor file.

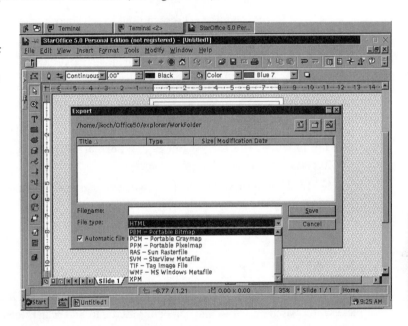

The following formats are supported for import and export:

The file extension designations used in the Export dialog box are all three letters, based on the Microsoft Windows standard for which StarOffice was originally written. You might need to rename your exported files with different file extensions so that your Linux programs recognize them. This is true with JPG (JPEG), HTM (html), and others.

- **HTML**—Not really a graphics format, but you can export a drawing as a graphic within an HTML page
- **BMP**—Used in MS Windows
- **PNG (Portable Network Graphic)**—Used on UNIX systems
- **EPS (Encapsulated PostScript)**—Widely used vector format
- **GIF**—The most used format on Web documents
- **JPG**—JPEG is a loss-y format used for photos and some Web graphics; JPEG produces very small files
- **MET**—An OS/2 graphics format
- **PCT**—PICT is a bitmapped format used by Macintosh computers
- **PBM (Portable Bitmap)**—Used on UNIX systems and others
- **PGM (Portable Gray Bitmap)**—Used on UNIX systems and others
- **PPM (Portable Pixelmap)**—Used on UNIX systems and others
- **RAS**—A bitmapped format used by Sun computers
- **SVM**—A StarView metafile, used in previous versions of StarOffice
- **TIF (TIFF, or the Tagged Image File Format)**—The most widely used bitmap format for professional graphics work
- **WMF (Windows Meta Files)**—Vector-based graphics files used by MS Windows programs
- **XPM**—A bitmapped format used in the X Window System

In the Next Hour

The next hour describes how to use the StarDraw features of StarOffice to create complete vector-based drawings that can be inserted into StarWriter documents or used by themselves. You can create flyers, brochures, or Web graphics (when exported correctly). You'll see the basic tools provided by StarDraw to create these graphics.

Hour **6**

Creating Graphics with StarDraw

In this hour, you learn how to create vector-based graphics using the StarDraw tools in StarOffice. The drawing and editing tools of StarDraw are explained, as are adding text and modifying colors in the graphic images that you create.

Vector and Raster Graphics

The first thing that needs to be explained before using StarDraw to create a graphic is the difference between a vector-based graphic image and a raster-based (also called bitmapped) graphic image.

Raster images

Most of the images you've seen, such as computerized photos and graphics on the Web in GIF for JPEG format, are *raster* graphics. These can be created in raster, or bitmap, drawing programs such as Adobe PhotoShop, PaintShop PRO, CorelPAINT, or the Image Editor in StarOffice (see Hour 11, "Adding Graphics to Documents").

If you have created graphics using programs such as CorelDRAW, the GIMP, or Adobe Illustrator, you've used *vector* drawing programs.

What's the difference? A file containing a bitmapped graphic image contains a piece of information for each *pixel* (bit) in the image. Every line, or raster, in the image must be described in this way, with color, brightness, and other information stored for each pixel.

Of course, the information stored for all those bits can be compressed. Using fewer colors requires less space to describe each bit, and areas that are the same color can be compressed using file formats such as GIF and PCX. But the information for each pixel is still extracted when the image is displayed.

Raster graphics are best for photos, scanning the Web, and very small images such as icons. Raster graphics are easier to work with and display in a computer than vector-based images are.

Vector Images

Vector-based images describe how to draw an image on a blank page. So instead of a set of color information for every dot on the screen, a vector image might have the following instructions:

1. Draw a circle with a center at point 100,150 and with a radius of 50 pixels, and fill it with color number 12.

2. Draw a line from point 25,25 to point 100,25. Make it black, and 5 pixels wide.

These examples of drawing commands can be stored in a vector drawing program using very little space. Using vector drawing commands also means that the image can be scaled to any size without seeing the *stairstep* or *pixelation* that comes from resizing bitmapped images.

Of course, it isn't easy to describe a photograph of a castle using drawing commands like these—but the commands get a lot more complicated than you might think. Bitmapped images are the best choice for some things, but for many business graphics applications, vector graphics are the right choice.

StarDraw is a vector-based drawing program. You can use the Image Editor in StarOffice if you need to create bitmapped images. The advantages of using StarDraw for a graphics project include

- Graphics files are smaller than equivalent bitmapped images, unless you're creating a very complicated image.
- Graphics can be resized for display on different screens or printed formats.
- Objects within StarDraw images (objects are described later in this hour) can be individually modified.

Vector images are useful for flyers, business graphics such as boxes and brochures that have a lot of text, and page layout tasks such as newsletters.

The following section shows you how to create a new StarDraw image and start working with the drawing tools that StarDraw provides.

Creating a New StarDraw Image

To start a new StarDraw image, double-click on the New Drawing icon on the StarOffice desktop, or choose Drawing from the Start menu or New submenu on the File menu.

A newly opened drawing screen is shown in Figure 6.1.

FIGURE 6.1

A new StarDraw drawing includes rulers and color tools to create your graphic.

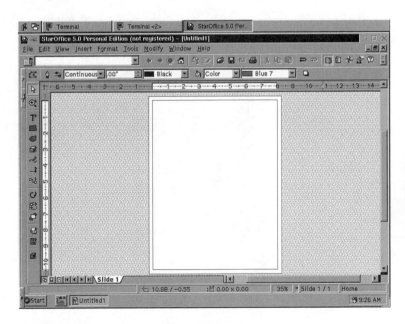

6

Reviewing the StarDraw Screen

Following are some points to notice on this screen:

- A Slide 1 tab is shown below the page. This is similar to a page number, although most of your drawings will only have one page. The StarDraw and StarImpress presentation programs share many features.

- The Object toolbar above the page shows several drop-down lists that you can use to modify objects' colors and other properties. This procedure is described later in this hour.

- The Main toolbar to the left of the page shows drawing tools that you can select. You'll use these in a moment to start drawing.

- Rulers are shown to the left of and above the page. The rulers are probably displaying inches, but you can alter that with the Drawing Options Layout tab.

- The status bar (if you have it visible via the View menu) displays your pointer position as you move the mouse, the size of the page view (as a percentage), and a few other pieces of information.

As you work with icons on the Main toolbar (on the left side of the screen), you'll notice that most of them have a tiny arrow in the upper right corner. This indicates that you can click and hold on that icon to change its function.

For example, if you click and hold on the square icon, a pop-up window appears in which you can select which type of object you want to create (see Figure 6.2).

FIGURE 6.2

The square icon on the Main toolbar displays a pop-up selection box in which you choose what you want to create.

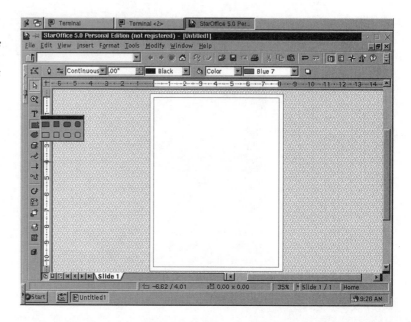

In the pop-up selection box for a square, your choices include the following:

- Create a filled-in rectangle using the current color.
- Create a filled-in square using the current color. (This is the default selection.)
- Create a filled-in rectangle with rounded corners using the current color.
- Create a filled-in square with rounded corners using the current color.
- Create a rectangle (unfilled).
- Create a square (unfilled)
- Create a rectangle with rounded corners (unfilled).
- Create a square with rounded corners (unfilled)

These choices make it easier to create just what you need in your drawing. Each of the icons includes a similar set of choices. If you leave the mouse pointer over one of the choices, a pop-up message tells you what that selection is used for.

Changing the View of the Page

The simple drawing you'll create here won't fill the entire page, so start by zooming in so that you can see better the objects you create. Follow these steps:

1. Click and hold on the Zoom icon (showing a page by default), and then choose the magnifying glass with a plus sign (see Figure 6.3).

FIGURE 6.3

The Zoom options enable you to alter the page view by selecting an area to view.

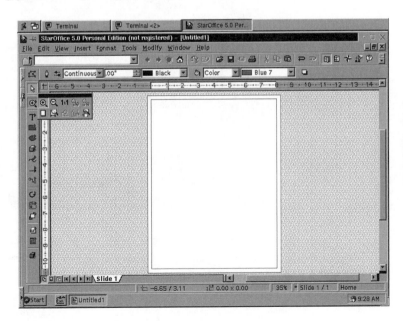

6

2. Move the mouse pointer to the page. The pointer changes to a magnifying glass with a plus sign in it. Click and drag to outline about one-fourth of the page.

3. When you release the mouse button, the page changes to show only the area that you selected. Zooming doesn't alter any objects on the page—it only changes how closely you're viewing them.

> You can change the view back to the page view by choosing either the Entire Slide option or the Entire Page option from the Zoom pop-up selection box.

Inserting a New Object

To insert an object into your drawing, click on one of the drawing icons on the Main toolbar. For this example, choose the 3D object icon, hold down the mouse button, and then choose the *torus* (ring) from the selection window. (See Figure 6.4).

FIGURE 6.4

To draw an object, choose a drawing icon from the Main toolbar.

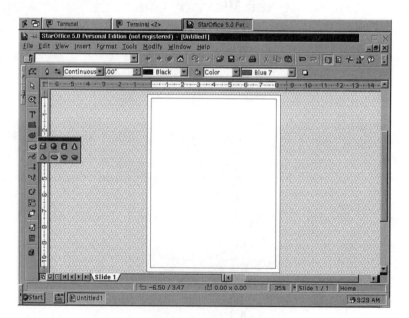

Now move the mouse pointer to the center of the visible area of the document, click and drag to outline a rectangle, and release the mouse button. A 3D torus object appears on the screen. (See Figure 6.5). Notice the following:

FIGURE 6.5

Objects can be drawn by clicking and dragging the mouse with the selected object tool.

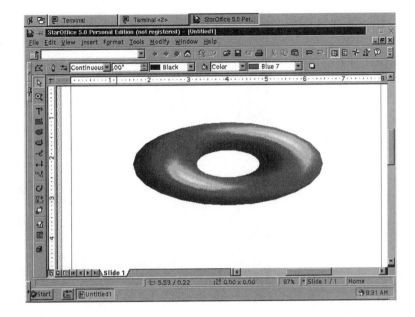

- The new object is selected, indicated by the green handles surrounding it. This means that you can immediately modify this object if necessary.
- The 3D object is filled in with the current fill color. (3D Objects always use a fill to show shading.)
- The 3D object icon is no longer selected on the Main toolbar. The focus has reverted to the arrow selection tool, with which you can select objects or areas in the drawing.

If you make a mistake as you draw the object, you can press the Delete key after creating it (while it still has the green selection handles) to immediately delete the object. Then you can draw it again.

6

Now, use the following steps to add another object:

1. Click on the Lines & Arrows icon and choose the line with an arrow on each end.
2. Click and drag the mouse pointer horizontally across the middle of the first object you created.
3. As you finish the line, hold down the Shift key to make the line perfectly horizontal, and then release the mouse button. Figure 6.6 shows the results.

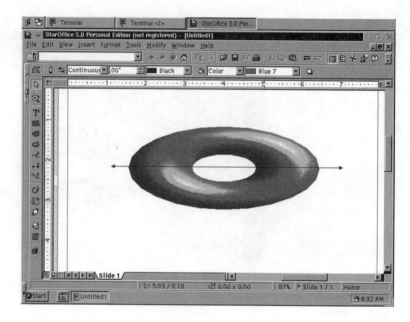

FIGURE 6.6

*A line with or without
arrows can be added
using the Lines &
Arrows tool.*

In the next section, you'll modify these basic objects to suit your needs for this drawing.

Modifying StarDraw Objects

The basic objects you've drawn can be modified in many ways. The first step in modifying any object is to first select it. To select an object, choose the Arrow icon (the Select tool on the Main toolbar) and click on the object that you want to select.

> If you can't select the right object because many objects are too close together, click on any object; then use the Tab or Shift+Tab keys to select each object in the drawing in turn. Watch the green selection handles and the status line messages to see when you have selected the desired object.

To begin, work on the line you just created. Select it so that green handles appear on each end.

Only a few of the options you can use to modify these sample objects are explained here; however, here you will see how to access the modification process, where additional options are available.

Now move the mouse pointer so that it sits on top of the line (the mouse pointer points in a different direction) and press the right mouse button. Choose Line from the pop-up menu. The Line dialog box appears (see Figure 6.7).

FIGURE 6.7

The Line dialog box enables you to modify the features of a line.

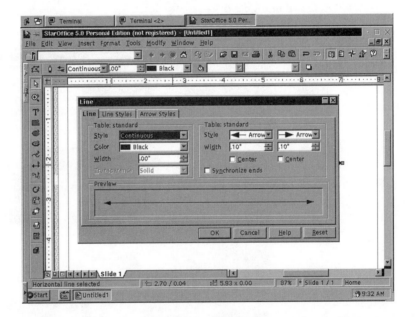

With a line selected, you can also choose Line from the Format menu, but using the right-click pop-up menu only shows those options that apply to the selected object (for example, no 3D effects option appears for the Line object).

6

To make this line heavier, in the Line tab, enter 0.2 in the width field (assuming that you're using inches—choose another number, if necessary). Now choose Ultrafine dashes from the Style field on the left side of the dialog box.

Finally, in the Style field on the right side of the dialog box (where the arrow heads are visible), choose none from both drop-down lists. (Assume that you decided that you don't want arrowheads on this line.) From the Arrow Styles tab, you can choose any graphic image as the arrowhead.

Choose OK to close the Line dialog box and apply your changes to the line object. The result is shown in Figure 6.8.

FIGURE 6.8

The modified Line object has no arrows, and a different width and style.

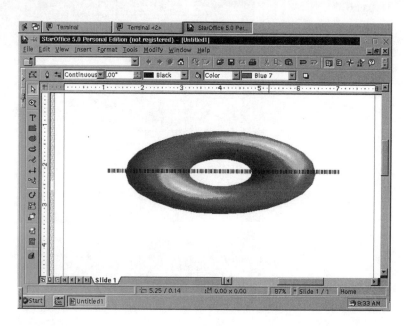

 Any selected object can be moved by clicking and dragging it, or by choosing position and size from the format menu.

Next modify your torus object. Click on the object to select it. Now click and drag on the bottom, middle, green handle to resize the torus. An outline shows you the new size. Release the mouse button when you're finished. The object is redrawn at the new size.

Now double-click on the torus object (just click again if it's still selected with green handles). Red handles now appear, and the mouse pointer changes to the rotate tool. Click and hold the left mouse button. An outline of the box enclosing the torus rotates in three dimensions as you move the mouse. When you release the mouse button, the torus is redrawn. The red handles remain, however.

> With the torus selected, you can also select the Draw Effects icon on the Main toolbar to rotate the object.

Click in the white space outside of the selected object to deselect it.

Changing Colors

Most objects in StarDraw can have a color associated with them. Objects are generally composed of an outline and a fill color. You can choose to make both the outline and the fill invisible, or you can use a color (including black) to display them.

With any object selected, you can use the drop-down lists on the Object toolbar to set the outline and fill options.

For example, with the torus selected, choose Continuous from the drop-down line style box that currently shows the word *invisible*.

Then choose invisible from the drop-down fill style box that currently shows the word *Color*. The result is shown in Figure 6.9.

Choose Undo from the edit menu twice to revert to the filled torus.

> The line style and color and the fill style and color can also be modified by choosing Line and Area on the Format menu. The Colors tab of the Area dialog box gives you greater control over color than do the drop-down lists on the Object toolbar.

6

FIGURE 6.9

*You can select colors
for the fill and outline
of each object. This
Figure shows an invis-
ible dill color and a
continuous black
outline.*

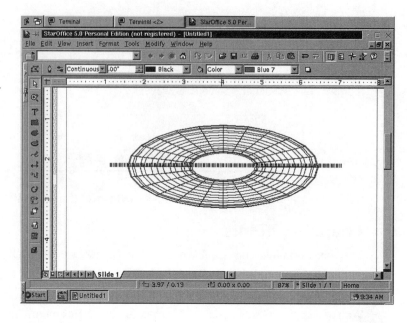

Arranging Objects

As you create objects, they are layered on top on one another. Thus, the last item created is the top item visible; it covers any items that are created before it.

But you don't always want things to stay that way. To alter the arrangement of the layered objects, select an object, right click on it, and choose Arrange from the pop-up menu. The Arrange submenu enables you to move an object forward or backward by one object, or to the front or back of the entire drawing (as if it was the first or last object created). By selecting different objects and using these options, you can arrange the overlapping of all the objects in your drawing.

StarDraw also has a feature called layering, in which multiple objects are placed on different layers and modified, viewed, or printed as a set. This advanced feature is beyond the scope of this introduction to StarDraw, but you can choose Layer from the Insert or Format menus to begin experimenting with layers.

Grouping Objects

When you have a drawing containing many objects, it can be helpful to work with many objects in the drawing as a group (for example to resize, move, or change their color simultaneously).

For example, suppose your line and torus form the core of a fancy new logo. After you've established the look that you want, you'll need to resize them both at the same time.

You can select both objects at the same time and use the Position and Size dialog box on the Format menu.

But you can also group the objects together so that they are tied to one another; selecting one selects both and editing either edits both. This enables you to use graphical tools to resize the objects, and makes using other features more convenient.

This is especially true when the objects that you want to use together comprise a group of 10, 50, or many more objects. It doesn't make sense to select them all each time.

In addition, when you have a complex drawing, it can be very difficult to precisely select the object that you want among the many others onscreen. By creating a group of objects, you can tie together associated objects to work on them simultaneously.

To create a group, follow these steps:

1. Click on the line to select it.
2. Hold down the Shift key and click on the torus. Now both objects are selected.
3. Choose Group from the Modify menu. The two objects are grouped together, and now show only one set of green handles.

Adding Text to the Drawing

6

Most drawings include text of some sort that labels or explains the drawing. StarDraw images are not intended to be used for newsletters or other text-heavy projects (although it's certainly possible to use StarDraw for such purposes). Nevertheless, StarDraw includes many text manipulation options.

To add text to a drawing, choose the text tool from the Main toolbar (with a large T on the icon) and click the location in the drawing at which you want the text placed. Then start typing:

- To finish entering text, click the mouse somewhere outside of the text field in which you're typing.
- To edit the text that you've entered, choose the Text tool again and click on a text field that you've previously typed in. Or just double-click on the text that you've entered using the select tool.

Text in a StarDraw image is not paragraph-oriented. Each line comprises a separate object, each of which can be modified individually (however, you can also modify several objects at the same time by selecting them all before choosing an option).

Enter two lines of text in your sample drawing, as shown in Figure 6.10.

FIGURE 6.10

Text objects can be added to any drawing with the Text tool. Text can then be modified as needed.

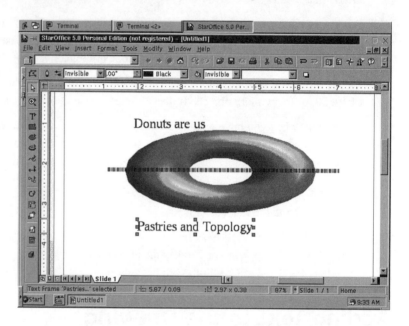

After entering the text, select and drag the text objects to the exact position in which you want them.

Now you can modify the text in several ways. To begin, you need to select the text object to be edited, and then select all the text in the object (so that it's all blocked out in black).

With a block of text selected, the Object toolbar changes to display options similar to those you use when you work with text documents: font, type size, alignment, bold or italic, and so on.

You can choose a new font and size to make the type look right. This can be done from the drop-down lists in the Object toolbar, or by choosing Character from the Format menu.

Your revised drawing, with text, is shown in Figure 6.11.

FIGURE 6.11

You can format text objects for font, type style, and size, and then position them by dragging them to the precise location that you choose.

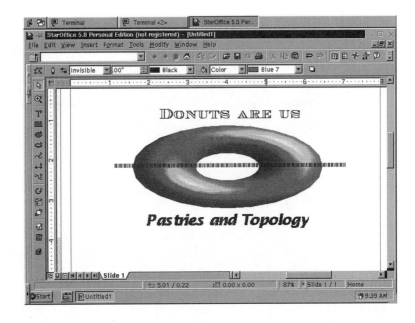

You can also try the Fontworks item under the Format menu to flow text around curves and objects; or try the Text Animation tab (choose Text from the Format menu).

You'll find some items in StarDraw that refer to OLE objects—ignore them. They are left over from the conversion of StarOffice from Windows to Linux (the two versions are identical).

6

StarDraw is an impressive, full featured drawing program comparable to CorelDRAW. There is not time here to even mention many of the useful or fun features that StarDraw provides. To continue exploring StarDraw, draw some basic objects and see what features are available on the Edit, Insert, Format, Tools, and Modify menus.

In the Next Hour

In the next hour, you will begin creating text documents with StarOffice using the StarWriter word processing features. You will learn to open new or existing documents, and then enter and edit text using StarOffice menus and toolbars. You will also learn how to set configuration options that apply only to your text documents, and how to print those documents.

PART II

Creating Documents with StarWriter

Hour

7 Creating a New StarWriter Document

8 Formatting Your Document

9 Using Advanced Formatting Tools

10 Using Tables, Indexes, and Other Special Features

11 Adding Graphics to Documents

12 Using SpellCheck and the Thesaurus

Hour 7

Creating a New StarWriter Document

In this hour, you learn how to create a new StarOffice word processor document, and then save and print that document. Documents in StarOffice can be started in several ways; you'll learn the most useful ones.

In addition, this hour describes how to start entering text in your document and how to set default options for your text documents.

Starting from Scratch with StarWriter

StarOffice provides so many ways to open a new document that you'll hardly know which one to choose. The sections that follow walk you through the methods that you're most likely to use.

When you start a new StarWriter word processing document, you're really just opening another window in the StarOffice main window. Any other documents you have open, as well as the StarOffice Desktop, all stay active, though they might be hidden from view.

The sections that follow describe how to open a new StarWriter document. This can be done in several ways:

- **Using the Start button in the bottom left corner of the StarOffice window—** Click Start and then choose Text Document from the pop-up menu.
- **Using the New menu—**Choose New from the File menu and then Text Document from the New submenu.
- **Using the Desktop—**Double-click on the New Text Document icon. Switch to the Desktop using the Desktop icon on the Status bar if necessary.
- **Using a Template—**Choose New from the File menu; then choose From Template.
- **Using the AutoPilot—**Choose AutoPilot from the File menu; then choose a Document type (agenda, fax, and so on) from the AutoPilot submenu.

Using the Start Menu

The easiest way to start a new StarWriter document is to select Text Document from the Start menu. The Start menu is always visible in the lower left corner of the StarOffice window.

When you click on Start, a pop-up menu appears. The top part of the menu lists new file types that you can start. Choose Text Document to start a new StarWriter word processing document.

Using the New Menu

After you start StarOffice, the Desktop is displayed. You can open a new document by choosing New from the File menu, and then selecting Text Document from the New submenu. (See Figure 7.1.) You can see that StarOffice enables you to create many types of files. When this book refers to a document, it means a StarWriter word processing file.

Notice in the New submenu that an icon is shown next to each item. You'll soon learn to recognize these icons for the file types that they represent in StarOffice.

When you choose Text Document from the New submenu, a new word processing document appears in the main StarOffice window; the Desktop is no longer visible (see Figure 7.2).

Using the Start menu or the Desktop (see the next section) are both faster than using the File menu to open a new document.

FIGURE 7.1

The New submenu enables you to select which document type you want to start working with.

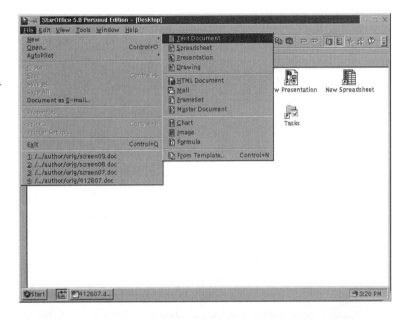

FIGURE 7.2

A new document, ready for editing.

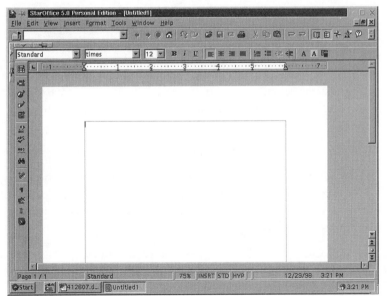

7

Using the Desktop

After you start StarOffice and you're looking at the Desktop, you can immediately start a new document by double-clicking on the New Text Document icon in the upper-left corner of the default Desktop. (See Figure 7.3.)

FIGURE 7.3

The New Text Document icon on the Desktop opens a new document.

The New Text
Document icon

 When you rearrange the StarOffice Desktop with your own files, be careful not to delete the New Text Document icon or you won't have the option to quickly start new documents.

Using a Template

If you know what type of document you're creating, you can save time by starting with a document template. A template has all the formatting and standard information for a particular type of document—all you have to do is enter your text.

To open a template, choose New from the File menu; then choose From Template from the New submenu. The Templates dialog box appears, as shown in Figure 7.4.

From the Text Document Templates dialog box, select the category of document that you need from the Categories list. When you select a category, a list of templates appears in the Templates list. Click on a template and click the OK button to open a new document based on that template.

The categories include templates for presentations, spreadsheets, and different documents. When you select a template, a file of the corresponding type is opened.

 If you used a minimum or custom install that didn't include the StarOffice templates, the Text Document Templates dialog box is empty.

FIGURE 7.4

Documents can be started from many different StarOffice templates.

Beyond templates, StarOffice provides a more customized way to create a new document: the AutoPilot.

Using the AutoPilot

A StarOffice AutoPilot is a series of dialog boxes that ask you questions about what you want to do. They then use the information that you entered to complete the task for you.

AutoPilots are provided in StarOffice for many tasks, including creating several types of new documents. Using the AutoPilot takes more time than opening a template but the results are customized to fit exactly what you want.

An AutoPilot is similar to a Wizard in some Microsoft Windows applications.

As an example, you can use the AutoPilot to create a new memo. Choose AutoPilot from the File menu, and then select Memo. The first screen of the Memo AutoPilot dialog box appears (see Figure 7.5).

7

FIGURE 7.5

*The AutoPilot can be
used to create a cus-
tomized memo.*

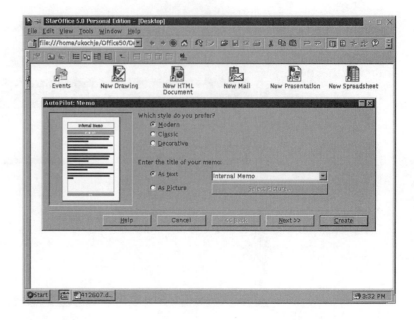

After you select the options in this dialog box that fit the memo that you want to create,
click the Next>> button. The next part of the dialog box appears, and you can enter more
details about the memo.

> The information you provided in the User Data tab of the General Options
> (choose Options from the Tools menu, and then General Options) provides
> some of the information used by the AutoPilot.

The memo AutoPilot dialog box contains a total of four screens in which you enter information, followed by one which displays a checkered flag and tells you that the AutoPilot
is ready to create your memo. When you're done, press the Create button and the memo
document is opened with everything in place except the words you enter. All the formatting, graphics, and so forth are taken care of.

AutoPilots are provided for the most commonly used document types. Many more templates are provided than AutoPilots, but the AutoPilots enable you to customize your
document without learning all the commands you might need to use.

Also, AutoPilots can be used even if you didn't install the document templates.

Opening an Existing StarWriter Document

The Open File
icon

After all this information about starting a new StarOffice document, you still might need to open an existing document.

As in most graphical programs, you can open the Open dialog box with the folder icon on the Main toolbar (see Figure 7.6).

If you prefer, you can choose Open from the File menu. In either case, the Open dialog box appears, as shown in Figure 7.7.

FIGURE 7.7

You select which existing file to open from the Open dialog box.

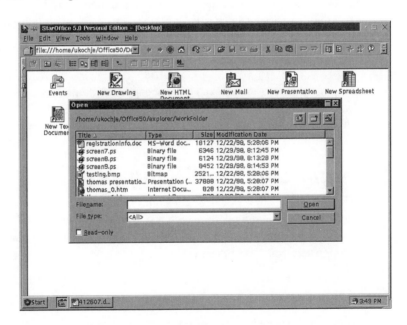

The default location displayed by the Open dialog box is the Work Folder. You can change which subdirectory is in the Path tab of the General Options (described in Hour 4, "Configuring StarOffice").

7

You can also click and hold on the icon to the far right at the top of the dialog box to see a drop-down list from which you can choose the directory that you want to view. Options include the Explorer window, the Workspace, and the root directory of your Linux filesystem (/).

If you need to move to another location in your Linux filesystem, click the Parent Directory icon to move up one level in the directory structure.

Notice that even in Linux, StarOffice tries to match the icon for each file to the file type. For example, if you have a Microsoft Word file, it appears with the standard Word document icon.

To select a subdirectory and view its contents, double-click on it.

When you know which file you want to open, select it and choose the Open button. If the file isn't in StarOffice format, you might be prompted to help StarOffice determine the file format so it can be opened for editing in StarOffice. Hour 5, "Importing and Exporting StarOffice Documents" describes the details of working with other file formats in StarOffice.

You can also open a document directly from the Work Folder in the Explorer. Just double-click on the Work Folder, and then double-click on the file that you want to open.

Entering and Modifying Text

When you have a new or existing document onscreen, you can enter text and use standard keys to move around the screen just as you do in any text editor or other Linux program. Just be certain that your StarOffice window has focus so that your keystrokes appear where you expect them to.

Saving Your Document

After you've entered the text of your document, you'll want to save it to your hard disk.

To open the Save As dialog box, press the disk icon on the Main toolbar (see Figure 7.8) or choose Save from the File menu.

FIGURE 7.8

The disk icon on the Main toolbar saves your document. If the document doesn't have a name yet, it opens the Save As dialog box.

The disk icon

The disk icon is gray (so you can't click on it) unless you have a document open, with changes. Each time you save your document, the icon goes gray until you make other edits.

Selecting a Location for Your Files

When you open the Save As dialog box to save a document to disk, the subdirectory that appears in the dialog box is the StarOffice Work Folder. If you enter a filename and choose OK, your document is saved in the Work Folder, which is actually a subdirectory of the StarOffice directory.

The advantage to saving your files in the default Work Folder is that your files are always available from the Explorer window (as you learned in Hour 3, "Using the Explorer and the Desktop").

On the other hand, you might prefer that your StarOffice files are located with other word processing or personal files; or, you might have separate directories where you want to store your word processing files, spreadsheets, presentations, and so forth.

You can change the default so that the StarOffice Save As dialog box always starts at a different location in the Linux filesystem: Change the Work Folder path in the General Options dialog box. (See Hour 4 for details.)

Learning to Save Early, Save Often

It doesn't take too many disasters before people start planning for them. If you've ever lost several days' work, or even a productive hour's work because of a power glitch, a system crash, or some other problem, you probably save documents regularly.

Of course, Linux never seems to crash. Still, why not get in the habit of using that handy little key combination any time you pause to think during your typing: Press Ctrl+S.

After you've saved a document the first time, and have given it a document name, you can update it on your hard disk by using the Ctrl+S Accelerator key combination. You

7

can see this listed next to the Save item in the File menu, but choosing that menu item all the time isn't nearly as convenient as pressing the Accelerator keys.

If you're more a mouse person than a keyboard person, you can click on the floppy disk icon to update your document on the hard disk. If you've already saved the file once, you don't have to enter the document's name again.

Resaving with a New Document Name

Sometimes, you might also need to save your document with a new name.

For example, suppose you open a file that you previously sent to someone. You need to alter the name and resend it to another friend. If you just choose Save or press Ctrl+S, you'll erase the original version of the file.

Instead, after you've opened the original file, immediately choose Save As from the File menu. Enter a new name for the file and choose OK. Now you can make changes to the file and save it without losing the information in the original file.

Printing Your Document

Printing your document can be very easy—or very difficult. For the easy version, just press the printer icon on the Main toolbar (see Figure 7.9).

FIGURE 7.9

The printer icon on the Main toolbar immediately prints the current document.

The printer icon

The current document is printed immediately, without even opening a dialog box.

That is, the document is printed if you have printing correctly configured on your Linux system and a valid printer driver selected and configured in StarOffice.

Unfortunately, if you haven't yet set up printing in Linux, it's beyond the scope of this book to describe how to do it. Some information is provided in Hour 4. For complete information, check out a copy of *Sams Teach Yourself Linux in 24 Hours.*

Your Linux system probably has a printer setup utility of some sort. You can also edit the /etc/printcap file in a text editor—this is the "difficult" version of printing your document.

If your Linux printing is working, you can set a few other options for printing your document beyond pressing the printer icon on the toolbar.

Before you print a document, you might want to see how it will look on the printed page. You can do this by choosing Page View/Print preview from the File menu while you're viewing a document. Figure 7.10 shows a Page View.

FIGURE 7.10

A Page View of your document shows how it will look on a printed page.

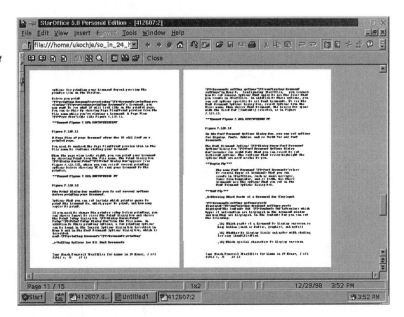

You need to uncheck the Page View/Print preview item in the File menu if you want to continue editing your document.

When the page view looks right, you can print your document by choosing Print from the File menu. The Print dialog box appears (see Figure 7.11); you can select several printing options before choosing OK to send your document to the printer.

Options that you can set include the printer queue to print the document to, which pages to print, and how many copies to print.

If you need to change the printer setup before printing, you can choose Cancel to close the Print dialog box and choose the Print Setup dialog box from the File menu. In addition to these printing options, a few other options can be found in the General Options dialog box (described in Hour 4), and in the Text Document Options dialog box, which is described in the following section.

7

FIGURE 7.11

*The Print dialog box
enables you to set sev-
eral options before
printing your docu-
ment.*

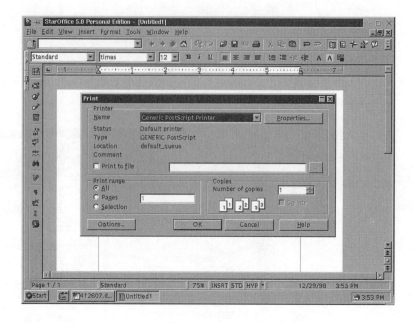

Setting Options for All Text Documents

In Hour 4, you learned how to set General Options that apply to all the files that you create in StarOffice. In addition to these options, you can set options specific to all text documents. To see the Text Document Options dialog box, select Options from the Tools menu, and then choose Text Document. The dialog box opens with the first tab (Contents) selected, as in Figure 7.12.

The Text Document Options dialog box includes eight tabs that you can select to set different options. The sections that follow highlight the options that will be the most useful to you.

> The name *Text Document* refers to several types of documents that you can
> create in StarOffice, such as email messages, faxes from templates, and so
> forth. All these documents use the options that you set in the Text
> Document Options dialog box.

Choosing Which Parts of a Document Are Displayed

The Contents tab determines which types of information are displayed in the document window, and how they are displayed. In the Contents tab you can set the following options:

- Which parts of a document to display onscreen or to keep hidden (such as tables, graphics, and notes)
- Whether to display fields and notes with shading for easy identification
- Which special characters to display onscreen (things such as paragraph marks and tabs can be indicated with a visible character)

FIGURE 7.12

In the Text Document Options dialog box, you can set options for display, fonts, tables, and so forth for all text documents.

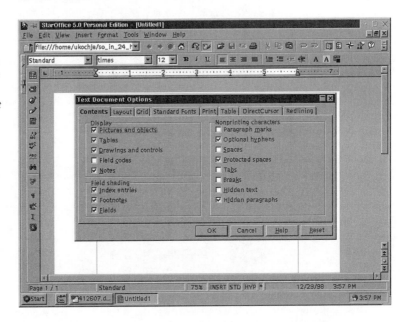

Choosing How the Document Layout Is Displayed

The Layout tab defines options for measurements and other features that determine how formatting options are applied or viewed. In the Layout tab you can set the following options:

- How far apart the default tab stops are set
- Which measurement system to use in the document for rulers, indents, and so forth (for example, picas, inches, or millimeters)
- Which windowing options are available for the document (rulers and scrolling)

In the Grid tab you can turn on a visible grid, or just "snap to" an invisible grid and set the resolution of the points on that grid.

Changing the Default Fonts for Text Documents

When you create a new StarOffice document and start entering text, StarOffice uses a certain font or typeface for your document.

7

In the Standard Fonts tab, shown in Figure 7.13, you can set the default fonts that are used for documents. Different fonts can be specified for different paragraph styles, including setting fonts for headings, indexes, and captions, in addition to the standard font for body text.

FIGURE 7.13

Default fonts for the main styles in a text document are set in the Standard Fonts tab of the Text Document Options dialog box.

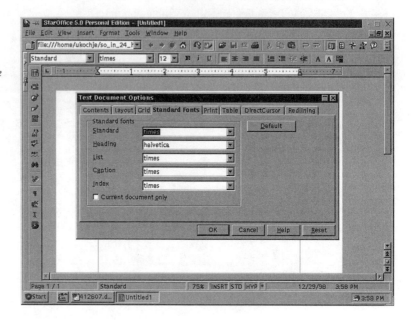

If you prefer, you can check a box to set these fonts just for the current document, rather than for all text documents.

When you want to change the default font for one of the paragraph types, use the drop-down list to select from the installed StarOffice fonts.

Setting Text Document Printing Options

In the Print tab, shown in Figure 7.14, you can select which parts of a text document are printed. For example, you can turn on printing of special fields, tables, and so forth, or you can select to print only left or right pages.

As another example, suppose you're working on a document that contains many graphics. You can choose to print the document without printing any of the graphics or drawings while you're revising the early drafts of the document; or, you might choose to print the document without any of the notes that you've added.

FIGURE 7.14

Printing for a text document can be configured in the Print tab of the Text Document Options dialog box.

The Options button in the Print dialog box (opened from the File menu) enables you to go directly to the Text Document Options Print tab.

Setting Table Options

The final tab that is described for setting Text Document Options applies to Tables. In the Table tab you can set how the table size is affected by your editing.

Specifically, you can set the default width and height for columns and rows when you insert a new table, as well as whether changes to a cell's contents affect the entire table size or just the adjacent parts of the table.

The Text Document Options dialog box includes a few additional options that you can see in the figures or experiment with as you work, but the options that you're most likely to use as you create documents have been covered here.

7

In the Next Hour

In the next hour, "Formatting your Document," you begin learning how to format your documents. You'll use basic character and paragraph formatting commands to set up the look of your document, and you'll explore page formatting tasks that affect how a document is arranged on paper.

HOUR **8**

Formatting Your Document

In this hour, you learn how to format your document. You'll want to have a document open to use for the examples that are given (or just type in some text). The figures show sample text that has been typed in to demonstrate what is being described.

Formatting determines what fonts are used and how they're displayed, how lines and paragraphs are aligned, and how the page is arranged.

More advanced formatting tools are described in Hour 9, "Using Advanced Formatting Tools," but you'll quickly see that StarOffice provides a full set of formatting options. They're even easy to use! Most of the StarOffice basic formatting options are the same as those in Microsoft Word or Corel WordPerfect.

Setting Character Styles

The font in which a document is written gives it a certain feel when you read it; the font can make the document casual or business-like, or it can make the document easier or harder to read.

Fonts can be loosely grouped into fixed-spacing fonts, which are often used to indicate computer output, and proportional fonts, which are much easier to read. Also, fonts can be *serif*—with little ledges like the text you're reading now—or *sans-serif* (French for "without serif"). Sans-serif fonts are good for headlines, but are considered more tiring for large amounts of text.

The term *font* usually refers to the typeface, such as Times, Helvetica, or Courier. Other characteristics of the typeface—character attributes—are normally defined separately because they are used much more frequently.

Choosing a Font

A font can be applied to an entire document, to just a paragraph, or even to a character. For example, the entire document might be in the Times font, but words that describe computer commands can be in Courier font.

Before you enter text, you can select a font for the text that you enter. After you've entered text in a document, you can select text that you want to appear in a different font and apply that font.

To apply a new font to selected text, follow these steps:

1. Select the text to which you want to apply a font by either clicking and dragging the mouse pointer, or by holding down the Shift key and using the arrow keys.

2. Choose Character from the Format menu. The Character dialog box appears (see Figure 8.1).

> You can also select a font from the drop-down list in the Object toolbar, if that toolbar is displayed. However, you're about to explore the other character formatting options, so use the dialog box for now.

3. Select a font from the Font list. The Preview window in the dialog box shows you how your selected text looks in the font that you selected from the list.

4. If you want the font to be sized differently than the surrounding text, choose a size from the Size list.

5. Choose OK to apply the font and close the dialog box.

Text sizes are displayed in *points,* a printers' term you'll become familiar with as you use StarOffice. Standard text is sized at either 10 or 12 points; headlines usually start at 14 points and go up from there.

FIGURE 8.1

The Character dialog box enables you to set characteristics for a selected block of text.

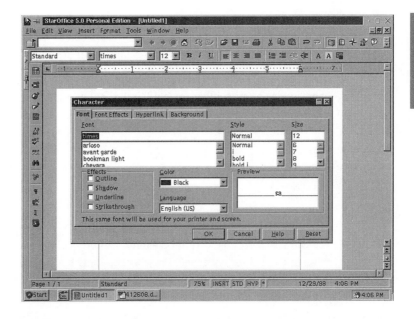

 An inch is 72 points; so, if you want a headline that is 1/2-inch high on a printed page, for example, use a 36-point font. The size of fonts onscreen rarely corresponds to their correct point size.

You'll probably only set a new font for headlines, captions, or certain words in your documents, but other font characteristics are much more commonly used.

Using Bold, Italic, and Underline

The font settings that you'll work with continually are those such as bold, italic, and underline.

While you're in the Character dialog box, you can see which options are available in the font that you select by looking in the Style list. If you choose a specialized font, for example, italic might not be available.

You can select any of these styles, and then press OK to apply them to selected text. If no text is selected, they apply to any new text that you enter at the current cursor position.

When you're typing in text, however, it's tedious to open this dialog box and select a style just to set a word in italic type. Instead, you'll want to use one of the following methods for the three most common font settings (bold, italic, and underline):

- Select the text to which you want to apply the setting. Then choose one of the icons on the Object toolbar for bold, italic, or underline (see Figure 8.2).

FIGURE 8.2

The bold, italic, and underline icons on the Object toolbar are a fast way to change font settings.

The bold, italic, and underline icons

- You can also select the text to be altered and press Ctrl+B for bold, Ctrl+I for italic, or Ctrl+U for underline. Pressing the same keys a second time reverses the setting. (If bold or italic is not available in the current font, nothing happens when you press these keys.)

The Effects section of the Font tab in the Character dialog box includes the following options:

- Outline
- Shadow
- Underline
- Strikethrough

StarOffice can apply these effects to any font that you select.

If you want to see the more advanced settings, open the Character dialog box and choose the Font Effects tab. (See Figure 8.3.) Here, you can set things such as superscript and subscripts, double underlining, small caps, and blinking text (which everyone prefers you don't use).

Following are some examples to show you what these effects can do:

1. Select a block of text in your document.
2. Open the Character dialog box from the Format menu.
3. Choose the Font Effects tab (this example works with whatever font you're using).
4. Click on the Small caps option in the More effects area.
5. Choose OK to apply your changes. The result is shown in Figure 8.4.

FIGURE 8.3

The Font Effects tab contains many advanced options for controlling the appearance of your documents.

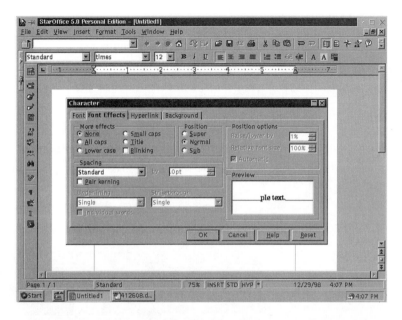

FIGURE 8.4

You can apply small caps to any font.

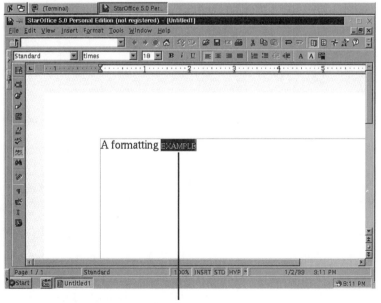

Small caps

Now select the last few characters of the text that you marked as small caps:

1. Open the Character dialog box from the Format menu and select the Font Effects tab.

2. Select the Super radio button in the Position area of the dialog box. The Position options area becomes active.

3. Uncheck the Automatic check box.

4. Change the Raise/Lower field to 75% (raise the superscript).

5. Change the Relative font size to 100% (make the superscript the same size as regular text).

6. Choose OK to apply your changes to the selected text. The result is shown in Figure 8.5.

FIGURE 8.5

The Font Effects tab enables you to define exactly how superscript text is sized.

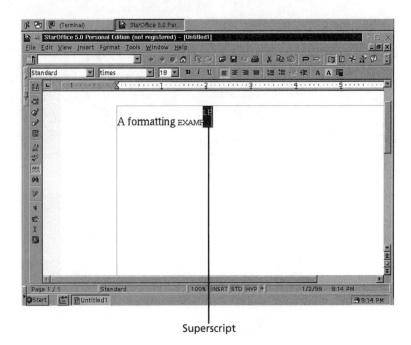

Superscript

Adding a Hyperlink

Another setting you can apply to a selected block of text, such as a word or sentence, is a *hyperlink*. You can create a link as if your document were being viewed on the Web. Any StarOffice document can contain hyperlinks.

If you export a document with hyperlinks (see Hour 5, "Importing and Exporting StarOffice Documents"), the hyperlinks won't appear in the other word processor.

8

To add a hyperlink to a block of text, follow these steps:

1. Select the word or sentence that you want to be linked to an URL.
2. Choose Character from the Format menu.
3. Choose the Hyperlink tab (see Figure 8.6).

FIGURE 8.6

The Hyperlink tab of the Character dialog box enables you to assign an URL link to any block of text.

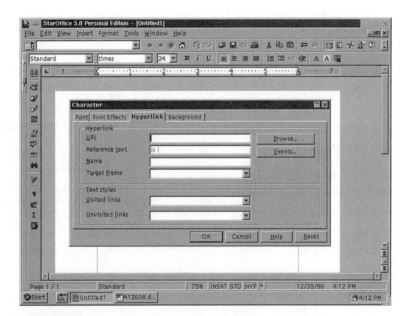

4. Enter an URL in the URL field. You can enter a local file (use the Browse button if you need to) or an URL for any document on the Web.
5. Choose OK to apply the hyperlink and any changes you've made in the other tabs in the Character dialog box.

The Hyperlink tab also contains several other features related to using StarOffice with the Internet, which you can explore on your own.

The following sections describe how to expand your formatting skills to complete paragraphs.

Choosing Paragraph Settings

As with character formatting, paragraph formatting can apply either to the block of text that you've selected or to all the text that you enter after indicating a change.

In this case, *paragraph* means all the text that you enter between the times that you press Enter. This is often several lines because of the auto–line-wrapping in word processors.

Formatting for paragraphs refers to the way in which the indents and spacing for lines in that paragraph are handled, how tabs are spaced, whether text is left- or right-justified, and so forth.

All the paragraph formatting for your StarOffice documents is done in the Paragraph dialog box, which you can open by choosing Paragraph from the Format menu. (See Figure 8.7.)

FIGURE 8.7

All paragraph formatting is done from the Paragraph dialog box.

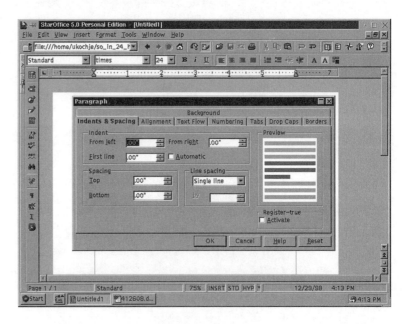

The exceptions to this are a few icons on the object toolbar; you will learn about these icons in a moment.

8

To see how to use the paragraph formatting options, place the cursor in a paragraph that you want to edit. You don't have to select the paragraph text—StarOffice applies your changes to the entire paragraph. Choose Paragraph from the Format menu.

Setting Line Spacing and Paragraph Indents

Start with the Indents and Spacing tab (select it if it's not showing). The following are the options:

- **Indents**—Indicate that text in the selected paragraph is moved further in (or out, using negative numbers) from the margins (which you'll review in the Page formatting section). Left and right indents indicate how much extra space to leave on each side of the page for this paragraph.

- **First line indent**—Enables you to create either an indented paragraph with a further indented first line or a hanging indent by setting the Left indent to a higher number than the First line indent.

- **The Spacing**—(Top and Bottom fields are shown) Indicates how much empty space will appear preceding and following the current paragraph. Unless you need to align a paragraph with a printed form or complete other special tasks, you can probably leave these settings unchanged.

- **Line spacing drop box**—Determines how the lines in the paragraph are spaced based on how high each line of text is. Put simply, you can select single-spaced, double-spaced, or 1.5-spaced lines. Other options are listed for the typesetters among us.

As you change the numbers in any of these fields, glance at the Preview window on the right side of the dialog box. The picture displayed there shows you how your changes affect the lines of text in the current paragraph.

Setting Paragraph Alignment

In the Paragraph dialog box, you can also select the alignment for the lines of the current paragraph. Most documents that you create will use the default left-aligned or left-justified setting.

Some reports that you write might require full justification, meaning text on both the left and right margins is aligned. Right alignment and centered text lines are normally used only for headlines or occasional special effects.

The Alignment tab of the Paragraph dialog box (see Figure 8.8) includes options for each of these alignment types. Again, the Preview area at the right of the dialog box shows you roughly how the alignment option will look.

FIGURE 8.8

The Alignment tab enables you to define the justification setting for a paragraph.

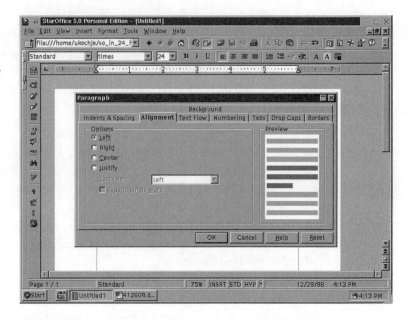

Setting the paragraph alignment is a task that you might need to do regularly for headlines or other paragraphs. StarOffice provides a few icons on the Object toolbar to instantly apply an alignment setting to the current paragraph.

The icons on the toolbar indicate left, centered, right, or full justification, respectively, as shown in Figure 8.9.

FIGURE 8.9

The Object toolbar icons for paragraph alignment immediately apply a setting to the current paragraph.

Paragraph
alignment
icons

Setting Tabs

Select the tab labeled Tabs in the Paragraph dialog box to set tab stops and types for the current paragraph.

In the Position field of the Tabs tab (see Figure 8.10), you can enter a tab stop and then press the New button. That tab stop is added to the list. The measurement method for the number you entered is determined by the General Options (as described in Hour 4, "Configuring StarOffice").

FIGURE 8.10

*The Tabs tab of the
Paragraph dialog box
enables you to enter
and configure tab
stops.*

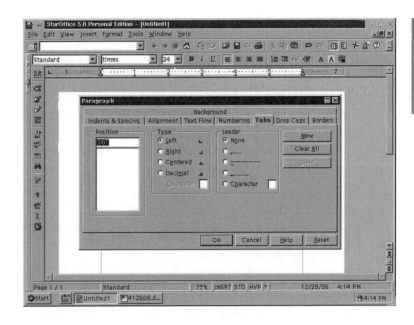

8

If you select a tab stop from the list, you can choose Clear to remove it.

> Remember that these tab stops apply only to the current paragraph or the
> currently selected block of paragraphs.

After you've added the tab stops in the positions that you need for the current paragraph,
you can configure each of those tab stops.

To configure a tab stop, follow these steps:

1. Select a tab stop in the list following the Position field.

2. Choose which type of justification will be used for text entered at that tab stop.

3. If the type you choose is Decimal, you can change the character to anything you
   want, instead of a decimal (.).

4. Choose a Leader, if you want one (the leader characters fill in empty spaces when
   you press the Tab key).

5. Choose another tab position to configure, if necessary. All the tab settings (and
   other paragraph settings) take effect when you press OK in the dialog box.

Several other paragraph formatting settings are included in the Paragraph dialog box, including defining text flow options and colors for a paragraph. Leave those for later exploration; now look at how to format and arrange the pages of your document.

Using Other Paragraph Formatting Features

StarOffice provides other formatting features that are less commonly used, but which can add some variety to the appearance of your documents. The Drop Caps tab enables you to define a large initial letter on the current paragraph, such as you'd see at the beginning of a newsletter or magazine article.

The Borders and Background tabs enable you to define an outlined box around the current paragraph and to specify the background color of the current paragraph, respectively. These features are great for highlighting blocks of text in unusual ways. You'll see similar borders and background features as you format graphics and characters.

Arranging the Page

Beyond the character and paragraph settings, you need to set up the pages through which the paragraphs flow. You can open the dialog box to organize the page layout of your document by choosing Page from the Format menu.

Unfortunately, StarDivision chose to place an advanced formatting tool as the default first tab on this dialog box (the Organizer tab). You'll learn about organizing styles in this tab in Hour 9.

Setting the Page Margins and Paper Size

After you have the Page dialog box open, choose the Page tab, as shown in Figure 8.11. From this tab of the dialog box you can set the margins, page layout, and paper size.

All four sides of the printed page are represented by the four Margins fields: Left, Right, Top, and Bottom. You can use the tiny arrows next to the fields or you can type in a number. The measurement used is the one you defined in the General Options (see Hour 4).

The Paper format area defines what type of paper your document will be printed on. You can select a paper size and either Portrait or Landscape printing.

Depending on your printer setup, the default paper size might be A4, a European paper size that makes all your documents look strange if you live in the U.S. Check the paper size for the first few documents you create to be sure that it's set to Letter.

FIGURE 8.11

You set the margins, paper size, and page orientation in the Page tab of the Page dialog box.

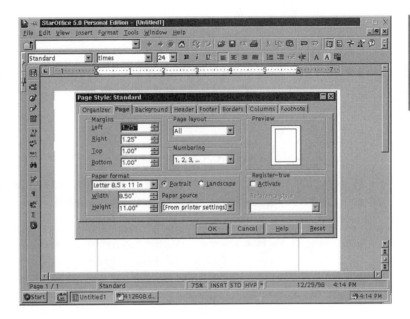

The Preview area shows you what effect your changes will have, both by the size and shape of the white box (representing the page) and by the black margin lines within the white box.

Defining Basic Page Numbering and Layout

The Numbering field enables you to set the numbering style for the document: letters, Arabic numerals, or Roman numerals.

The page numbering is set from the Page Numbering item on the Tools menu. Unfortunately, the power of the page numbering feature is not what it could be, compared to other word processing systems.

> If you need to set up different page numbering styles (using the Page dialog box) or starting numbers (using Page Numbering from the Tools menu), use separate document files.

Finally, you can set which pages in your document these settings apply to. This setting is not nearly as flexible as it could be; if you've used FrameMaker or WordPerfect, you might be disappointed to see that you can apply different formats to only a limited set of pages, rather than setting new information for each and every page as needed.

The Page layout drop-down list enables you to define that the current layout applies to

- All left-side pages (even numbered).
- All right-side pages (odd numbered).
- Left and right (Mirrored) in coordination. In this case, the Left/Right margin fields change to Inner/Outer.
- All the pages in the document.

Adding a Header or Footer to Each Page

Working with headers and footers in StarOffice is convenient. Instead of using hidden codes and reference pages, StarOffice places a separate box on each page in which you can click and start entering text for the header or footer.

In the Page dialog box, you can configure headers from the Header tab (see Figure 8.12). By definition, a header or footer is included on every page of your document, so if you don't want to include them on some parts of a larger document, use separate document files.

FIGURE 8.12

The Header tab in the Page dialog box is used to configure headers.

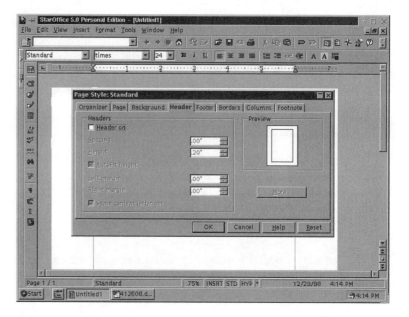

The following definitions will help you set up your headers:

- The header is off by default; you can check this box when you want to use a header.

- The Spacing field defines how much space is left between the header text and the top of the regular body text in your document.
- The Height field defines how tall the header is, but
  - The Autofit height check box can be selected to make the height fit whatever text you enter in the header.
  - The header always uses the top margin of the page that you set in the Page tab of this dialog box.
  - If you check the Autofit height box, you can set left and right margins for the header because these also affect the height of a multiline header.
- You can also check the Same content box to mirror each header onto both left and right pages of your document.

Now you can switch to the Footer tab to configure a footer for each page. (See Figure 8.13.) Of course, if you didn't have a header, you can still have a footer.

FIGURE 8.13

The Footer tab is part of the Page dialog box.

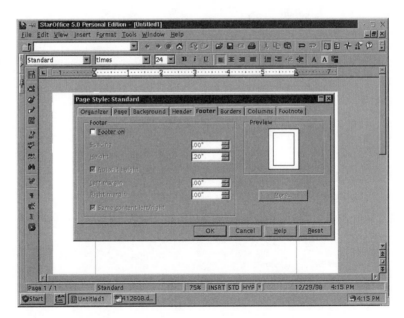

The footer is turned off by default. Check the Footer on box before trying any of the other options.

With the footer on, the same options are available as with the header. But now look at the Preview window on the right side of the dialog box. Whenever you enable both headers and footers, the Preview window shows you both. Any changes that you make in the spacing or height of either is reflected in the Preview window of both tabs.

The Default Format Setting

As you experiment with formatting, and then begin to format your documents, you'll occasionally do something complex that was better left undone.

If you change your mind immediately, you can choose Undo from the Edit menu. If you realize it only later, you can always revert to the default setting for the selected area or current paragraph.

Any time you want to have text revert to the default style, you can choose Default from the top of the Format menu. Any formatting that you set is discarded, and the default format is used for that area of your document.

In the Next Hour

In Hour 9, you will learn about styles and other advanced formatting options. A *style* is a collection of formatting information that can be applied all at once to a block of characters or to a paragraph. You can set up your own styles, but there is also a default style.

HOUR 9

Using Advanced Formatting Tools

In this hour, you learn how to use advanced formatting tools such as footnotes, columns, and text styles. StarOffice provides many formatting tools beyond what you learn here, but these are the formatting options that will be most useful to you.

You'll learn how to insert, edit, and delete footnotes, as well as to set up custom footnote options. You'll also learn how to define and use columns. Finally, you'll learn about using styles to quickly format your document.

Using Footnotes

Those small notes you sometimes see at the bottom of a page are called *footnotes*. These notes provide additional information (usually parenthetical in nature) about the text within the document.

> If these extra notes are located at the end of a document instead of at the bottom of each page, they're known as *endnotes*. Endnotes are created in the same manner as footnotes in StarOffice.

A footnote consists of two parts: the marker in the body of your document and the footnote text, located either at the bottom of the page or at the end of your document. These two parts are shown in Figure 9.1.

Footnote marker

FIGURE 9.1

A footnote marker and the footnote text to which the marker refers.

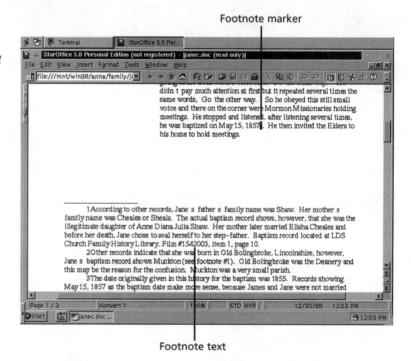

Footnote text

In the next section, you learn how to create, edit, and delete footnotes. Before you begin, however, here's a look at the two footnote menu items in StarOffice:

- The Footnote option under Insert Menu is the command that you use to place a footnote marker and text into the body of the document.

- The Footnote option under the Tools menu is used for customizing your Footnote Options.

Creating a Footnote

Creating a footnote in a StarWriter document is quite easy: Just place the cursor in the body of the text where you want the footnote marker to appear. Then choose Footnote from the Insert Menu (see Figure 9.2).

FIGURE 9.2

Choose Footnote from the Insert menu to create a new footnote.

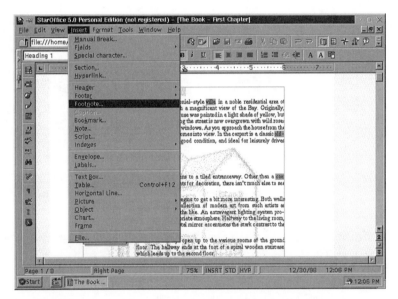

After you select the Footnote option under the Insert Footnote Menu, an Insert Footnote dialog box appears (see Figure 9.3). In this dialog box, you can select between two options:

- **Automatic**—This is the default setting (it's always selected when the dialog box opens, even if you've chosen Character for a previous footnote). The Automatic setting uses the StarOffice defaults. Until you change the footnote settings (you'll learn how later in this hour), the Automatic option uses the next number in your footnote sequence for this document as the marker for this new footnote.

- **Character**—If you don't want sequential numbers or letters, you can define what character or characters you want to insert in the body of the text as a footnote marker. The Character option allows up to ten characters to be entered.

FIGURE 9.3

*The Insert Footnote
dialog box showing
the two options:
Automatic and
Character.*

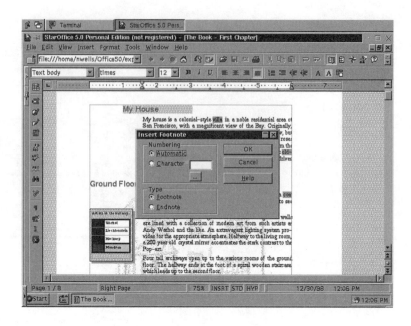

Choose OK in the Insert Footnote dialog box to continue. Two things happen immediately (see Figure 9.4):

- The marker is inserted into the body of your text.
- The cursor jumps to the end of the page, where you can start entering the text for the footnote.

FIGURE 9.4

*When you insert a
footnote, the marker
appears and you can
immediately enter the
footnote text.*

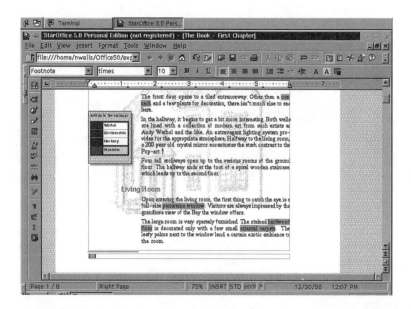

StarOffice automatically renumbers all footnotes as you work. You don't have to insert footnotes in order throughout your document.

When you've entered the text for the footnote, press the Page Up key or click on the body of your document.

9

Editing a Footnote

Editing a footnote is also easy. If you place your mouse pointer next to a footnote marker in your document, the pointer changes to a hand. If you click on any footnote marker, the cursor jumps to the footnote text, and you can edit it as needed.

If you prefer, you can also scroll down the page. When you see the footnote text, click anywhere in the footnote to begin editing it.

If you place the mouse pointer on the footnote number in the footnote text area and click, the cursor moves to the marker in the body of your text. This is a great way to find where footnote or endnote references are located in a document.

Deleting a Footnote

You can delete any footnote by highlighting the footnote marker and pressing delete. This deletes the footnote marker and the footnote text; other footnotes are renumbered as necessary.

You can use the keyboard or the mouse to delete a footnote. To use the keyboard, place the cursor after the footnote marker and press the backspace key. To use the mouse, position the mouse pointer near the footnote marker until the pointer changes to a hand. Click and drag across the footnote marker so that it's selected. Press Delete to delete the footnote.

You can use Undo on the Edit menu if you delete a footnote and then change your mind.

Customizing Footnote Options

StarOffice enables you to customize footnote options for each document you create. This section discusses how to customize the most useful footnote options. Options that you can set include designating that footnotes appear at the end of each page, the end of each paragraph, or the end of your entire document (endnotes). In addition, you can define how the automatic numbering of footnotes functions.

All the footnote options are set from the Footnote Options dialog box, which you can access by selecting Footnote from the Tools menu. (See Figure 9.5.)

FIGURE 9.5

In the Footnote Options dialog box, you can set the location, numbering, and style of your footnotes.

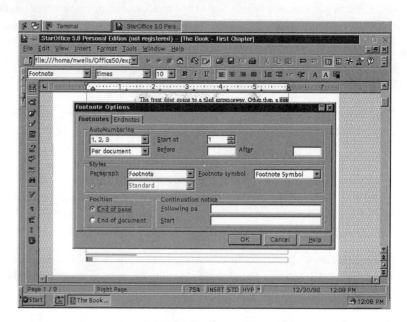

The Footnote Options dialog box is divided into four areas:

- **Position**—Determines where footnotes are placed in your document
- **Auto numbering**—Determines how the automatic numbering functions (used when you select Automatic instead of Character in the Insert Footnote dialog box)
- **Styles**—Determines the formatting of the footnote text (this will make sense after you've read the section on styles at the end of this hour)
- **Continuation notice**—Determines what message is placed between pieces of a footnote that must be split between two pages (try entering a long footnote and you'll quickly see how this is used)

Setting Footnote Position

The Position area of the Footnote Options dialog box describes where the text for foot-notes that you insert is placed in your document. The default selection for the position is End of page, which means that for any footnote that you insert on a page, the text for that note is placed at the bottom of the same page. The only exception is footnotes that wrap to the next page if tables or numerous footnotes interfere with the formatting.

If you want to change your footnotes to endnotes, select End of document; StarOffice places all the footnotes at the end of your document, after all the text that you type.

Setting Up Automatic Numbering

The Auto numbering area enables you to determine three things about the automatic numbering of footnotes in your document:

- What is used to number the footnotes (Arabic numerals, roman numerals, small letters, or capital letters). If you have a lot of footnotes, don't use roman numerals.
- How often the numbering is restarted.
- What the markers start with each time they are restarted.

Just as with the other automatic formatting features of StarOffice, such as outlining and bulleted or numbered lists (see Hour 10, "Using Tables, Indexes, and Other Special Features"), you can select which system to use for numbering your footnotes.

This flexibility enables you to use various numbering systems without having to use the Character option to type in a letter or special number for each footnote. It also keeps the footnote numbering accurate.

The automatic numbering that is provided for footnotes can be restarted at regular inter-vals. For example, you can have footnote markers 1 and 2 on the first page, and when you add a new footnote marker to page 2, the footnote marker can begin at 1 again. The options include the following:

- Each page can have a separate set of numbered footnotes.
- Each chapter can have a separate set of footnotes.
- The entire document can use a single footnote numbering system, from beginning to end.

9

Per chapter numbering of footnotes is used with multifile documents that use a Master document. This isn't discussed in this book.

If you choose the End of Document position for your footnotes (making them endnotes), the numbering option for each page doesn't make sense, so it doesn't appear in the list.

Finally, you can select the starting footnote number for the document. This starting number is used as the first footnote number for this file. This is used for Master Documents that include several files.

The starting footnote number is not used for per page or per chapter numbering options, which restart at 1 automatically.

The starting number is always shown as an Arabic numeral, even if you've selected letters or roman numerals as footnote markers. Think of the starting number as the sequential number to start with rather than the actual character. If you choose 5 as the Start at number and capital letters as the markers, for example, the first footnote is E.

The defaults for Auto numbering are 1,2,3, Per document, and 1 (for Start at). After you've tried these options, you can experiment with the Styles and Continuation notice options to see how they can improve the usefulness of your footnotes in StarOffice.

Using Columns

When you want to format text that flows in multiple vertical columns, such as in a newspaper or magazine, you can use the Columns feature.

The Columns feature aligns your text into standard newspaper-style columns. In other words, each page can have multiple columns. The text that you type flows from the bottom of one column to the top of the next column.

Although you can't do everything in StarOffice that you can in a page layout program such as Quark Express or PageMaker, StarOffice enables you to define the number of columns you want, the spacing between the columns, and the width of the line that separates the columns.

Defining Columns

You can define your columns before you begin entering your text, or you can format your document into columns at any time during the creation of the document.

The tab where you define columns is part of the Page dialog box. To view this area, select Page from the Format menu; then select the Column tab within the Page dialog box. (See Figure 9.6.)

FIGURE 9.6

You can define columns within the Page dialog box.

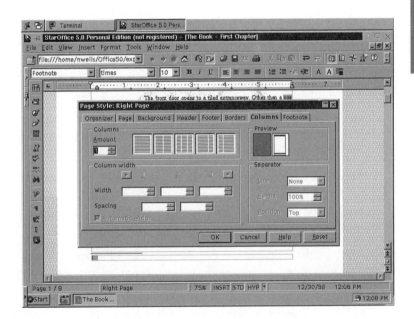

For these examples, assume that you can use standard column widths, which means that you don't have to worry about all the measurements in the Column width area of the dialog box.

If you select more than one column, you can uncheck the Automatic width feature and manually adjust the width of each column.

Always change the Spacing field to a nonzero value; the default value of zero means that text in adjacent columns is touching, and therefore can't be read easily.

Instead, look at the Preview and the Columns areas. You can adjust the number in the Amount field (a strange field name) to change the number of columns in the document. An easier method, however, is to click on one of the little pictures that shows how you want your columns set up.

The automatically set choices include:

- One column (regular noncolumn text)
- Two and three columns (for newspaper style text)
- Two columns, with the left or right column narrower (for newsletters or special formatting tricks)

Click on any of these figures and the Preview figure changes to show you how the text in your document will look.

The Separator area of the Columns tab enables you to define a line between each column. The default line size is None. If you want to add a line between the columns in your document, you can select a line width from the drop-down list.

After the Line field has a size selected, you can set a value in the Height field. This number is the percentage of the height of the text column. For example, if your top and bottom margins are both one inch and your paper is 11 inches tall, using a 100% Height creates a 9-inch line.

If you set the Height to less than 100%, you can also set the position of the line, placing it even with the top or bottom of the column, or centered vertically between columns. The same line specifications apply between all columns.

Figure 9.7 shows a document divided into two columns, with standard column widths. A line between columns is .01 point wide, and 100 percent high (the full distance between top and bottom margins).

Recall that you can create a columns definition any time you want. To create columns in a new document, follow these steps:

1. Open a new text document (notice that there are currently no columns).
2. Select the Columns tab of the Page dialog box accessed through the Format|Page menu.
3. Select the number of columns you want.
4. Change the Spacing field in the Column width section to .1 or .2 inches.
5. Define a line to separate the columns (if you want one).
6. Choose OK.

FIGURE **9.7**

A sample document with columns and a line defined between them.

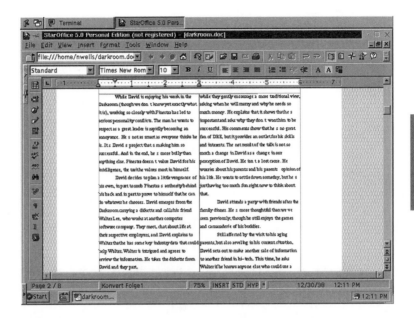

The document shows outlines for columns as you've defined them. As you type, the text wraps from the bottom of one column to the top of the next column.

Adding Columns to an Existing Document

If you already have a document and want to change its layout to include columns, place the cursor anywhere in the body of the document and follow these steps:

1. Select Page from the Format menu and choose the Columns tab.

2. Define the number of Columns you want by selecting one of the pictures in the Columns area.

3. Change the Spacing field in the Column width section to something such as .1 or .2 inches (as you prefer).

4. Define a line to separate the columns (if you want one).

5. Choose OK.

StarOffice immediately formats your document according to the columns that you defined. Unfortunately, you can't set columns for just a part of your document. It's all columns—in the same style—or no columns.

Working with Columns

When you set up columns, each page of your document is like multiple pages of text with narrow margins, formatted onto one page. Beyond that distinction, other functions of StarOffice work the same within columns as they do in regular documents:

- **Tables can be inserted into columns**—The table cannot, however, extend beyond the boundary of a column.
- **Graphics can be added to a page with columns**—As with regular pages, the graphic box can be resized and moved as you choose. The column boundaries don't restrict movement.
- **A frame can be inserted on a page with columns**—The frame can be moved and sized without being restricted by the column borders.

> If you need to add a table that spans several columns, insert a Frame and add text and a table within the Frame. We haven't discussed Frames, but you can experiment with them.

- **Index markers and footnote markers can be added to text in columns**—The correct placement and page numbers apply.

Using Text Styles

Styles are an advanced formatting feature that enables you to quickly format a block of text with several formatting options.

Styles are included in most major word processors, including Word, WordPerfect, and FrameMaker. This section describes how to set up and use styles in StarOffice.

Explaining the Concept of Styles

When you use the standard formatting options described so far (mostly in Hour 8, "Formatting Your Document"), you can set up text that is bold or double-spaced, or that has many other options set. StarOffice refers to this as *soft-formatting*; this is ironic because it can be pretty hard to set up these formatting options for your entire document.

The alternative is to use styles. A style is a named set of formatting attributes that you can apply all at once. If you need to make a single word bold, it's easy to select it and press the Bold icon on the object toolbar.

Suppose, however, that you have a long document with quotations scattered throughout. Each quotation paragraph needs to be spaced differently, with different margins, and in italics (those professors are sticklers for format).

Instead of choosing each formatting attribute for each paragraph, you can define a style—call it `Quote`—and then quickly apply that style to each quotation paragraph. When you apply the Quote style, all the formatting that you defined is applied at once to that paragraph.

9

Similarly, blocks of characters can have a style. For example, suppose you need to set all computer commands in a document to bold, italic, courier font. A style enables you to apply all these attributes at the same time.

Styles can be especially useful when you want to experiment with different formats. For example, assume you've formatted each of the headings in a large document with 24-point Bold Helvetica font. If you need to change all the headings to 20-point Italic Times font, it will take a long time to modify the document by hand.

With a style defined for the heading, however, you can change the attributes of the style—and all the paragraphs marked with that style change immediately.

The Style command allows you more power in quickly formatting a document.

Reviewing the Style Command

Before you start using the Style command, here's a look at a potentially confusing issue in StarOffice.

If you click the right mouse button on any block of text, a formatting menu appears. Part of that menu includes a Style submenu (see Figure 9.8).

This same type of information is shown in a different arrangement in the Character dialog box, which you can open from the Format menu by selecting Character, and then the Font tab (see Figure 9.9).

Please note that both of these style settings (as shown in the preceding figures) define font characteristics for a selected block of text, from a character to an entire document. This is a great way to change small amounts of text at a time; it can be a problem, however, if you want to change all the headings in a document, for example. Don't confuse these style settings with the paragraph styles described in this section.

A better way to manage the look and feel of your document is to assign a predefined set of characteristics to a style name. You can then assign these style names to any text you choose. Then, instead of changing the text one paragraph at a time, you can change them all at once by redefining the named style.

FIGURE 9.8

The Style submenu appears when you right-click on any text.

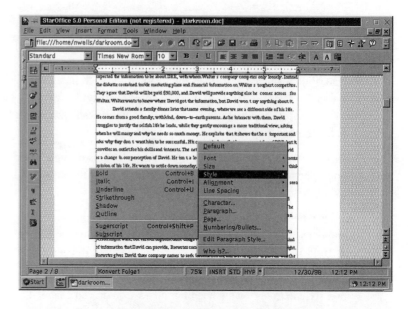

FIGURE 9.9

Formatting information labeled Style is also shown in the Font tab of the Character dialog box.

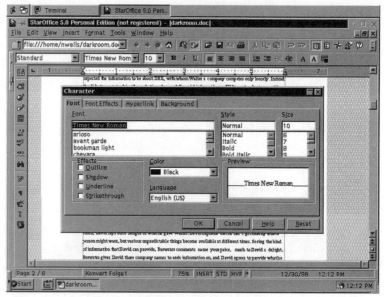

The styles discussed here are accessed in two places:

- **The Styles and Templates submenu on the Format menu**—From this menu item, you create or import named styles.

- **The Stylist item on the Format menu**—A miniature version of the Stylist is part of the Object toolbar. From the window that this item opens, you apply a named style to a block of text.

Opening the Stylist Window

The Stylist window contains a list of named styles that are defined for the document that you're viewing. Each document can have a different set of named styles.

You can import styles from another document into the current document by using Load from the Styles & Templates submenu on the Format menu.

From the Stylist window, you can apply any named style to a block of text in your document. You can open the Stylist window in one of three ways:

- Click on the Stylist icon near the right end of the Function toolbar (see Figure 9.10).

FIGURE 9.10

The Stylist icon on the Format toolbar opens the Paragraph Styles window.

The Stylist icon

- Press the F11 key.

Depending on your keyboard mapping for X and your window manager or desktop configuration, pressing F11 might not open the Paragraph Styles window.

- Select Stylist from the Format menu.

In any case, the Paragraph Styles window opens (see Figure 9.11).

FIGURE 9.11

The Paragraph Styles
window lists available
styles.

Applying a Style

When you have the Paragraph Styles window open, you can apply a named style to any text in your document. You'll learn more about creating styles in the next section, but first here's a look at how to apply a style.

The styles and text in this example won't match your document, but you can still see how styles are used. Follow these steps:

1. Place your cursor in a paragraph of text to which you want to apply a new style.
2. Double-click on a style name in the Paragraph Styles window. Notice that several things might change in your text paragraph, depending on which style you double-clicked on. The indents or margins, the font, the size, or other features might all have changed.
3. Try double-clicking on another style and watch the text change.
4. With the Paragraph Styles window still open, click on another paragraph in your document to move the cursor to that document.
5. Double-click on any style and watch the text paragraph change.

That's how easy it is to use a style to format your document. In the next section, you learn more about how to use the Paragraph Styles window with styles that are predefined, or with styles that you define.

Reviewing the Stylist

The Stylist window is a quick-access method of applying a named style to a block of text. You can also choose a style from the drop-down list in the Object toolbar (see Figure 9.12), but other things can be done only in the Stylist window.

FIGURE 9.12

The drop-down list of styles in the Object toolbar enables you to apply a style to text.

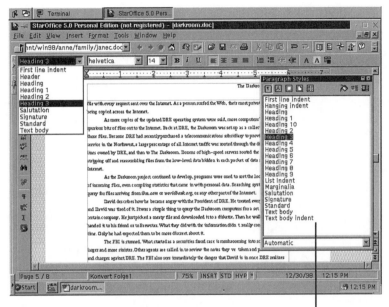

Drop-down styles list

The drop-down list of styles on the Object toolbar includes only styles that are already applied to at least one paragraph in your document. You'll want to use the Stylist window for initial document formatting.

Notice the eight icons across the top of the Stylist window. The five icons on the top-left determine which type of styles are displayed in the Stylist. (See Figure 9.13.)

FIGURE 9.13

These five icons in the Stylist window determine which type of styles are listed in the window.

These five icons indicate the type of style listed.

Because formatting can apply to different areas, Styles can also be applied at different levels. The five icons represent the following:

- **Paragraph styles**—Apply to a complete paragraph. These include formatting items such as indents, fonts, sizes, and so forth.

> The examples in this hour revolve around paragraph styles, but the same principles apply to the other types listed in the Stylist window.

- **Text styles**—Apply to blocks of characters and generally include formatting options such as italic, bold, and font type.
- **Frame Styles**—Apply to Frames in your document. (Frames are not covered in this book. A *frame* is similar to inserting a graphic in your document, but you can type in it.)
- **Page styles**—Define formatting for an entire page, such as margins and paper size.
- **Numbering styles**—Define how numbered and outlined lists are formatted.

You will use some other parts of the Stylist window in the examples that follow.

Reviewing the Attributes of a Style

Using a style is only half the fun. If you want to understand how your document is formatted and be ready to create your own styles (discussed in the next section), you need to see what formatting attributes are part of a named style.

To see the parts of a named style, view that style in the Paragraph Style dialog box. Use one of the following options:

- Click on a style in the Stylist window to select it, and then right-click anywhere in the window. Choose the Modify item from the pop-up menu.
- Choose Styles and Templates from the Format menu, and then choose Catalog from the submenu that appears. Select a paragraph style from the list and choose the Modify button.

Using either method, the Paragraph Style dialog box appears (shown in Figure 9.14).

FIGURE 9.14

The Paragraph Style dialog box shows the many attributes that are set for a named paragraph style.

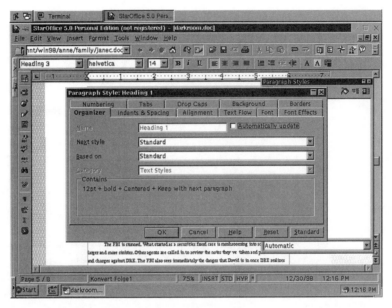

The attributes that you can review in this dialog box are as follows:

- Indents and line spacing
- Font and font effects (StarOffice calls them Styles in the Character dialog box)
- Tab settings
- Alignment (for example, centering)
- Background colors and paragraph borders

Explore these tabs to see what settings are in effect for the paragraph style you selected. In the next section, you learn two ways to quickly create your own named style in addition to the ones listed by default in the Stylist window.

Creating Your Own Styles

Now that you've seen styles in action from the Stylist window, you're ready to create your own styles. The pedantic way to create a new style is to follow these steps (We won't go into detail on this one):

1. Choose Styles and Templates from the Format menu, and then choose Catalog from the submenu that appears. The Style Catalog appears (see Figure 9.15).

FIGURE 9.15

The Style Catalog is a good access point for everything having to do with named styles in your document.

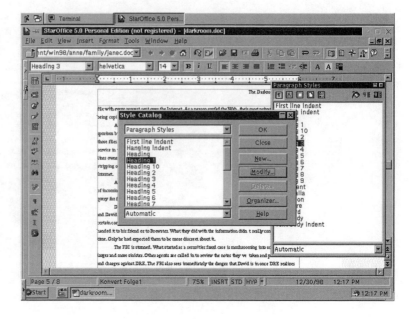

2. Choose the New button.

3. Enter a name for the new style on the first tab, Organizer.

4. Review each tab in the dialog box, entering the correct formatting detail for the style that you want to create.

5. Choose OK to finish creating the new style.

You're probably in a bigger hurry than that, however, so here's an easier way to create a new style: It's called Style by Example.

Creating a Style by Example

A Style by Example enables you to format a paragraph just as you want it to look, and then to say to StarOffice, "Record how that paragraph looks and duplicate it at my command."

The advantage to Style by Example is that you don't have to wade through all the dialog boxes to see whether you're missing something in the formatting. You can use the standard formatting options that you've been learning about to set up a paragraph, and then name it as a style.

To create a named style by using a sample paragraph that you have already formatted in the style that you want to use, follow these steps:

1. Open the Stylist window.

2. Click on the paragraph in your document that you have formatted, so that the cursor is in that paragraph.

3. Click on the New Style by Example icon (the middle icon of the three on the right side). (See Figure 9.16.)

9

FIGURE 9.16

The New Style by Example icon creates a new style based on the text at the current cursor location.

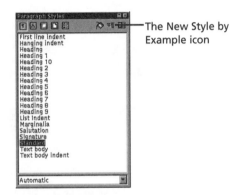

The New Style by Example icon

4. When the Create Style dialog box appears (see Figure 9.17), enter a name for the style that you are creating.

FIGURE 9.17

Enter a name for the style that you want to create by example.

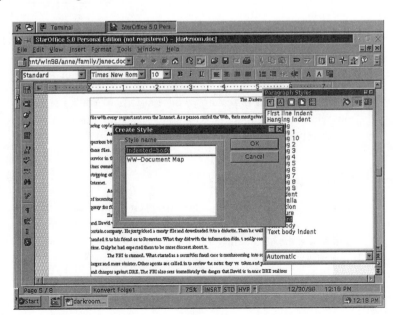

5. Choose OK. The style name you entered is added to the Stylist window. Its attributes are those of the paragraph in which the cursor was positioned.

In addition to creating a New Style by Example, you can create a new style based on an existing style. This can be a lot quicker than setting all the needed formatting options—if the style you want is similar to another existing style, but with a few modifications.

To create a style based on another style, follow these steps:

1. Place the cursor in a paragraph of the style that you want to use as a basis for your new style.

2. Open the Paragraph Styles window.

3. Right-click anywhere in the Paragraph Styles window.

4. Choose New from the pop-up menu that appears. The Paragraph Style dialog box appears.

5. The settings in this dialog box are those of the current paragraph. Notice that the Based on field contains the name of the style for the paragraph in which the cursor is located.

> The Based on style is not the style highlighted in the Stylist window when you select New from the pop-up menu. It is always the style of the current text paragraph.

6. Enter a name for your new style in the Name field.

7. Change any formatting areas that you want in this new style.

8. Choose OK to add the new style to the list of styles for this document.

Styles are a powerful feature within StarOffice. You've seen only the most basic features of styles, but it will still be enough to make the formatting of your documents go a lot more smoothly.

In the Next Hour

In the next hour, you'll learn how to insert and format tables in your StarOffice documents. In addition, you'll learn how to generate automatic indexes for your documents, and to use the automatic outlining and numbering features.

HOUR 10

Using Tables, Indexes, and Other Special Features

In this hour, you learn you how to use some of the more common features of StarOffice beyond the standard formatting discussed in Hours 8, "Formatting Your Document," and 9, "Using Advanced Formatting Tools."

Specifically, many of your documents will include tables. In this hour you learn how to insert and modify StarOffice tables. Also, if you work on any large documents (more than, say, 20 pages), you might want to use the automatic index generation in StarOffice. Finally, this hour explores some other useful features such as using outline mode and automatic bulleted lists.

Some of these features are much easier to show you if you have an existing document. At times, a reference is made to one of the sample documents that comes with StarOffice. In any case, you're probably starting to work with your own documents, so you can try out the tasks on your own.

Working with Tables

Tables are a great way to organize data. When you need to present a list that has components that correspond to each other, a table can be the perfect presentation. It makes it easier for a person who is reading your document to scan the information quickly and to find relationships between parts of the data that you present.

Tables are easy to start and edit in StarOffice, either from the menus or from the Object toolbar. In this hour, you learn how to work with both. When it seems appropriate, you also get a tip about how using StarOffice compares with the operation of other word processors with which you might already be familiar.

Inserting a New Table

Suppose you're creating a document that discusses the languages used around the world. You want to insert a table that lists a few countries that you're interested in and the languages spoken in those countries.

To insert this simple table (which you'll also use for further examples), follow these steps:

1. Position your cursor where you want the table inserted.

2. Choose Table from the Insert menu. The Insert Table dialog box appears (see Figure 10.1).

FIGURE 10.1

In the Insert Table dialog box, you can specify the size of a new table.

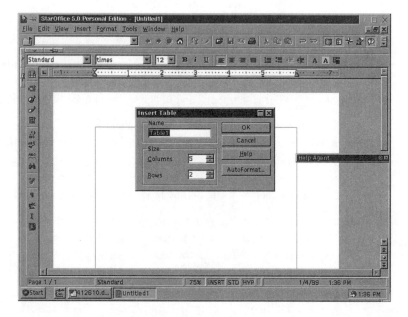

3. Enter a table name in the Name field (you can leave the default name if you prefer).

4. Enter the number of columns and rows that the table will contain in the corresponding fields.

This example creates a small table with two columns and five rows. You'll expand it as you learn other table features.

5. Choose OK to create the new table (see Figure 10.2).

FIGURE 10.2

The new table created for this "languages" example.

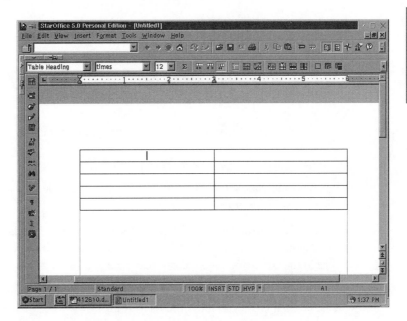

Following is a much quicker method for inserting a table:

1. Make sure that the Main toolbar is visible onscreen (select it in the View|Toolbars menu if it isn't already selected).

2. Click and hold the Insert icon (the top icon on the Main toolbar).

3. Drag over to the Table Insert icon (don't release the mouse button yet).

4. Drag down in the grid that appears until the number of highlighted columns and rows matches the size of the table that you want to insert (see Figure 10.3).

FIGURE 10.3

A table can quickly be inserted via the Main toolbar.

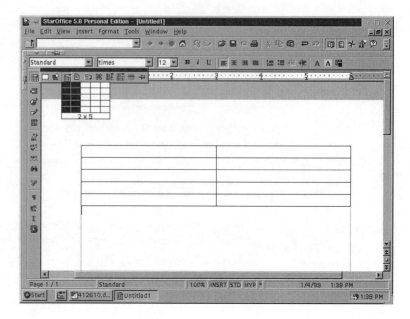

5. Finally, release the mouse button. The table is inserted into your document.

Converting Between Text and Tables

Another method that you might need to use to create a table involves converting an existing list or block of text into a table.

The StarOffice conversion to tables isn't as smart as it could be, however. Arrange your text so that all the cells on a single row of the table that you want to create are on a single line in the text before you convert to a table.

If you don't arrange the text in this manner, you can't tell how many columns StarOffice will use when it creates a table from the text lines.

Each item that is in its own cell in the table needs to be separated from the next item by a tab, a comma, or a semicolon.

Use the following steps to convert text to a table:

1. With your text arranged, select all the text that you want included in the table.

2. Choose Convert Text to Table in the Tools menu (this item is not available on the menu until you select a block of text).

3. The Convert Text to Table dialog box appears. Select which separator you want to use to divide items on each line: comma, tab, or semicolon (if you use paragraphs, your table will only have one column).

4. Choose OK to create the new table from your block of text.

Formatting a Table

When you have a table inserted into your document, you can enter text into the table cells. Move between cells using the following hints:

- Click in any table cell to place the cursor in that cell.
- Use the Tab key to advance the cursor to the next cell.
- Use Shift+Tab to back up to the previous cell.

After you have entered text in your table, you're likely to need to update the formatting or size of the table.

Notice that the Object toolbar changes when you move the cursor to any table cell. Instead of standard text formatting tools such as bold, italics, and centering text, the Object toolbar includes icons for Insert Row, Split Cells, and Border formatting.

To see a short description of any button on the Object toolbar, move the mouse pointer over that icon and leave it there for a moment. A yellow pop-up description appears for that icon.

When you insert a new table in your document, the top row of the table is automatically formatted using the Table Heading style. The rest of the cells use the Table Contents style. You learned about styles in Hour 9.

Taking the table of languages in Figure 10.4 as a starting point, suppose that now you need to add some information to the table. The following section steps through how to perform some common table functions.

10

FIGURE 10.4

This table of languages is the basis for several table formatting examples.

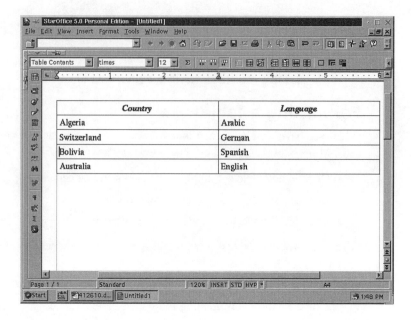

Adding New Columns and Rows

With your cursor positioned within an existing table, the Format menu expands with an entire new section that includes the Table options used in the following steps:

1. You can insert a new column or a new row by selecting Insert from the Row or Column submenu of the Format menu.

2. The Insert Columns or Insert Rows dialog box appears. Enter the number of columns or rows that you want to insert.

3. Select whether they are to be inserted before the current cursor position (to the left or above) or after (to the right or below).

4. Choose OK to insert the new rows or columns.

You can also insert new rows by moving to the last cell of the table and pressing the Tab key. This method can be used only to add another row to the end of the table, however.

Another quick method is to use the icons on the Object toolbar. The Insert Row button inserts an empty row below your current cursor position. The Insert Column button splits the current column in two. The Insert Row and Insert Column buttons are shown in Figure 10.5.

FIGURE 10.5

*The Insert Row and
Insert Column buttons
on the Object toolbar
provide a quick way to
expand a table.*

The Insert Row and Insert Column buttons

The Insert Row and Insert Column buttons might not be visible on your
toolbar unless you scroll down to them.

Splitting and Merging Cells

10

Building on the sample table of languages shown in the previous figures, you can add
additional columns and rows to hold more information. For example, another column
might hold the population of each country, or each country might include multiple languages.

The logical way to extend the sample table to make space for these items is to either split
a language cell into two rows instead of one, or to merge a country cell with the one
below it to make one larger cell.

To create this type of table, enter all the data that you want to include, with new rows
and columns for each item, (see Figure 10.6).

FIGURE 10.6

*This table includes
multiple entries for
each country, but it
isn't formatted well.*

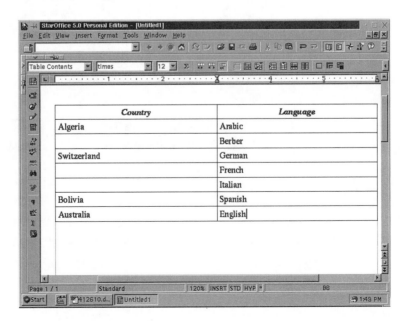

When the data is in place, you can split and merge cells to make the formatting look better.

> The Merge operation in StarOffice is called *joining* cells in most other word processors.

For example, you can use these steps to correct the formatting:

1. Select Switzerland and the two empty cells below it.
2. Choose Cell from the Format menu.
3. Choose Merge from the Cell submenu. The cells are merged to form one large cell (see Figure 10.7).

FIGURE 10.7

You can use Merge to join cells.

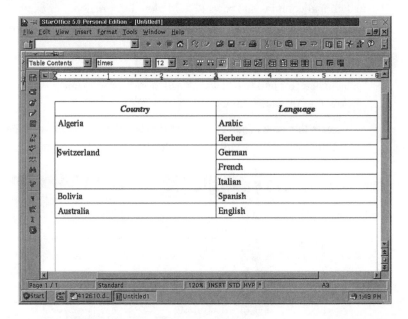

To split a cell, select that cell and choose Split from the Cell submenu of the Format menu.

The Split Cells dialog box appears; you can select whether to split the cell horizontally or vertically, and how many cells to create from the one cell (see Figure 10.8).

FIGURE 10.8

The Split Cells dialog box enables you to determine how to split one cell into several cells.

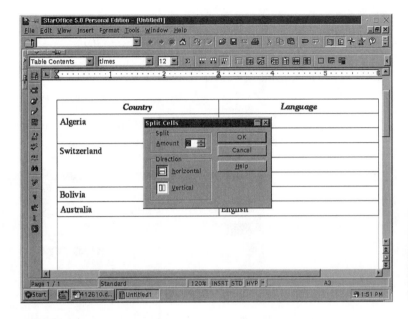

Using split and merge, you can create complex tables that effectively organize your data in a way that makes sense.

You can also use the Merge button on the Object toolbar to merge cells.

You can fix the appearance of a table by making certain borders invisible, instead of using merge and join operations; but then the Tab key doesn't move between cells as you expect it to, and the text alignment looks bad.

Formatting Tables

Most of the formatting that you'll need for a simple table is automatic in StarOffice. However, you can also choose to set dozens of options for a table.

Although the Object toolbar changes when your cursor is inside a table, you can still use most of the same functions, either from the keyboard or from the format menu. For example, you can do the following:

- Press Ctrl+B to set the selected table text to Bold.

- Press Ctrl+I to set the selected table text to Italic.

- Open the Paragraph dialog box in the Format menu and choose the Alignment tab to center a block of text.

Still, most of the formatting for your tables is best done in the Table Format dialog box, which you can open by selecting Table from the Format menu (see Figure 10.9). This option won't appear unless your cursor is within a table.

FIGURE 10.9

You can set most table format options in the Table Format dialog box.

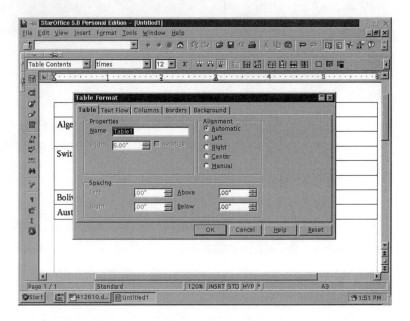

Although you won't walk through every option in this dialog box now, you'll find that the options are similar to the regular text formatting options described in Hour 6, "Creating Graphics with StarDraw." In summary, some things that you can set in the tabs of this dialog box include the following:

- Left/right/center alignment for cells in the entire table (you can set alignment for individual cells that overrides this tablewide setting)

- Top/bottom alignment within a cell (again, you can override this for an individual cell from the Cell submenu of the Format menu)

- The width of each column in the table (see Figure 10.10)

FIGURE 10.10

The Columns tab of the Table Format dialog box enables you to set the width of each column.

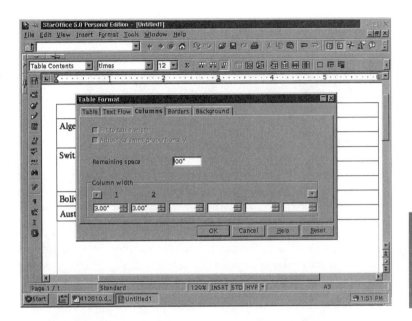

• The borders for the entire table or for individual cells (see Figure 10.11)

FIGURE 10.11

The Borders tab of the Table Format dialog box enables you to set border properties for all cells or for a single cell in a table.

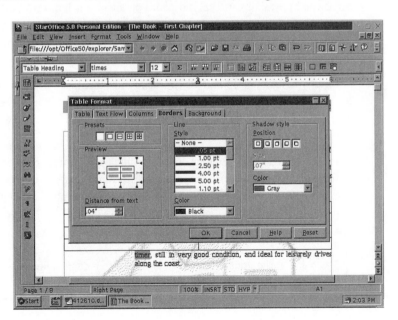

10

- The background color for the entire table or for any cells in the table

 Many of the table formatting options can be set from the Object toolbar, including the borders and background color for any selected cells.

Creating an Index

Indexing a document is tedious business. Unless you're a professional indexer (there are such things) or you like using boxes of 3×5 index cards (as did the late science writer Isaac Asimov), you'll appreciate the indexing features of StarOffice.

Indexes aren't used just for books like this one, although you can certainly write and index your book in StarOffice. Indexes add a professional touch to any document that's longer than a dozen pages. They help a reader skim a large amount of text or find just the right piece of information.

Creating an index in StarOffice consists of two steps, which are outlined in detail in the following sections.

First, you insert index markers in your document. Each index marker is associated with the term or concept next to the marker. That is, you insert a marker that says `Apache tribe, history of`, at the beginning of the sentence or paragraph that describes the history of the Apaches.

Second, you insert or update the index. In this step, StarOffice processes all the index markers found in your document (or in the multiple files in a Master document) and assembles the text from the index markers, in alphabetical order, with the page numbers where each marker was found.

Each time you add text to your document, the page number on which an index marker is found can change. But with the index markers in place, you can just update the index again to have the index include all the correct page numbers. Updating an index takes only a few seconds and requires no input from you.

 The update process for a StarOffice index is called *generating* the index in many other word processors.

Now try creating a simple index using these steps. Use one of the StarOffice sample documents because you need a document to index. You can use your own document, or follow along in the sample document.

To begin, open the following StarOffice sample document:

`Office50/explorer/samples/text_documents/chapters/chapter1.sdw`

You can open this document by using the Explorer window. Follow these steps:

1. Expand the Samples tree in the Explorer.

2. In the Samples tree, expand the Text Documents tree.

3. Double-click on the Chapters folder. The contents of the Chapters folder appear on the Desktop.

4. On the desktop, double-click on the Chapter1 file.

This document is shown in Figure 10.12.

10

FIGURE 10.12

The Chapter1 sample document.

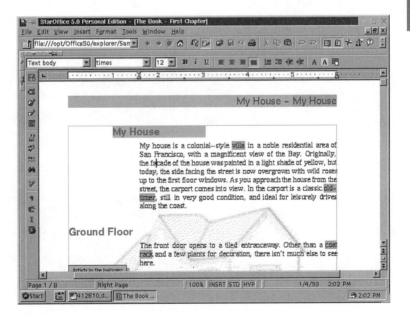

Inserting Index Markers

Insert an index marker next to any term in your document that you think a reader might want to find in the index. Because the sample document Chapter1 is about houses, assume that the reader is interested in housing terms.

This sample document already includes many index markers. Add your own to them and then review the index that these markers create.

Before adding new index markers to the sample chapter, save the file under a different name so that you can modify it without altering the original sample file. Follow these steps after loading the Chapter1 file:

1. Choose Save As from the File menu.

2. Enter a new name for the file (for example, enter ~/chap1new to save it in your home directory with the name chap1new).

3. Choose OK to save the document and close the dialog box.

To add a new index marker, follow these steps:

1. In the first line, select the text colonial-style.

2. From the Indexes submenu of the Insert menu, choose Entry. The Insert Index Entry dialog box appears, as in Figure 10.13.

FIGURE 10.13

Use the Insert Index Entry dialog box to place an index marker in your document.

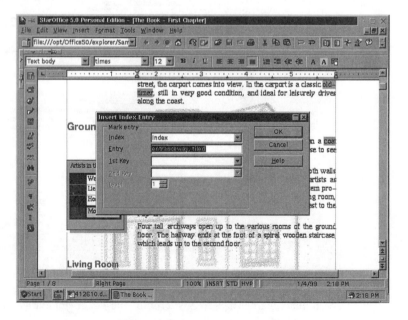

3. Choose Index from the drop-down list of the Index field. (Table of Contents is another option in this field, but you're creating an index entry.)

4. The option that you selected—`colonial-style`—is shown in the Entry field. This is the alphabetized index entry that you're creating.

5. Choose OK to insert the index entry into your document. The selected option (`colonial-style`) is shown in gray to indicate the entry.

Other words in this sample document are already index entries and appear in gray. You can turn the gray words on or off by selecting Field Shadings from the View menu.

Add one more index entry. In this example, the index entry doesn't have to match the words that you select, although they are the basis for the entry:

1. In the first line of the second paragraph, place the cursor near the option `tiled entranceway`.

2. Choose Entry from the Indexes submenu of the Insert menu. The Insert Index Entry dialog box appears.

3. Select Index from the drop-down list of the Index field.

4. In the Entry field, enter this text:

   `Entranceway, tiled`

5. Choose OK to insert the Index Entry marker.

This index entry is alphabetized under `Entranceway` instead of under `Tiled`. A good index will include both entries, to help readers locate the information by looking for either term.

You can add as many index entries as you think your document needs. If the index entry matches the selected text, the text is highlighted after the entry is added. If no text was selected or if the entry doesn't match the selected text, a mark is placed between words. These marks appear in gray when you select Field Shadings from the View menu.

StarOffice provides additional options that you can use when you create index entries, including multiple entries and keys that are used to combine multiple entries under a single alphabetic entry (see the `sheets` entry in the sample index in the next section.)

Inserting the Index

When you have added all the index entries that you need, you're ready to insert the actual index into your document.

For this example, move your cursor to the end of the Chapter1 document. Choose Index from the Indexes submenu of the Insert menu. The Insert Index dialog box appears (see Figure 10.14).

10

FIGURE 10.14

*Use the Insert Index
dialog box to place the
actual index in your
document.*

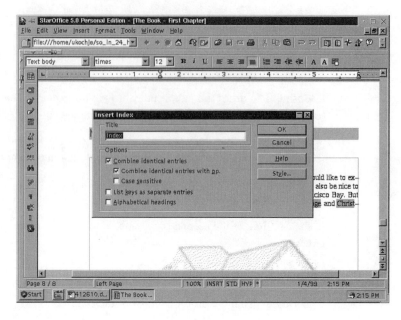

You can review the options presented in the dialog box, but for a basic index, just choose
OK. The completed index, based on all the index entries in this file, is inserted at the end
of your document because you moved your cursor there. (See Figure 10.15.)

FIGURE 10.15

*The index is created
automatically, based
on the index entries
that you place in your
document.*

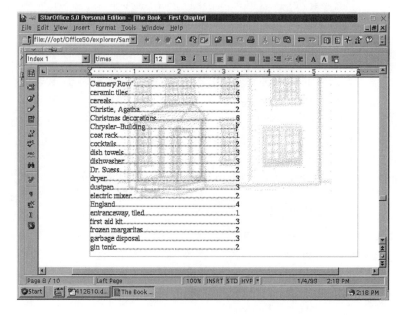

Updating an Index

When you have the index in place, you might still need to add or remove information from your document. This can involve adding and deleting words that are marked as index entries. It can also mean moving text around so that the page numbers in the index aren't correct.

StarOffice enables you to update the index without worrying about the location of the index entries in the document.

Any time you need to update the index with the latest index entries and correct page numbers, select Update from the Tools menu and choose Current Index or All Indexes from the submenu. The specified index entries are instantly reexamined and corrected in your document.

Numbering and Outlining

10

For many documents, both in business and in creative work, you need to create a structured outline or numbered list that you then expand or work from to create a larger document.

StarOffice provides line numbering, automatic bullets, and automatic outlines to help you structure a document without keeping track of all the numbers of letters as you go.

The sections that follow describe the easiest ways to use StarOffice to automate a structured document such as an outline, or to add line numbering or automatic bullets to your text.

Using Auto Numbering Outlines

Whenever you need to create an outline in StarOffice, you can turn on the outline feature to have StarOffice do the work for you.

Suppose you're writing an outline for a book. Before you start writing the outline, follow these steps:

1. Place your cursor where you want the outline to begin.
2. Choose Numbering/Bullets from the Format menu. The Numbering/Bullets dialog box opens.
3. Choose the Outline tab (see Figure 10.16).
4. Select which style of outline level markers you prefer by clicking on one of the boxes.

FIGURE 10.16

The Outline tab enables you to define how an automatic outline is to be structured.

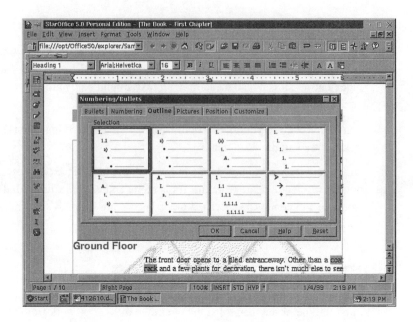

5. Optionally, choose the Customize tab (see Figure 10.17). From this tab you can set up the format of each outline level exactly as you prefer. Spacing, numbering, bullet graphics, indent amount, and other settings can all be controlled separately for each outline level.

FIGURE 10.17

In the Customize tab of the Numbering/Bullets dialog box, you can set numbering and spacing options for each outline level.

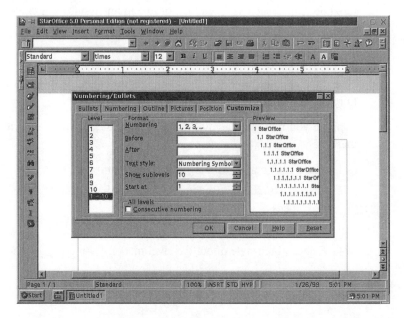

6. Choose OK to close the Numbering/Bullets dialog box. The first outline number appears.

With the outline started, you can type the text of the first outline item and press Enter. Each time you press Enter, the next number in the outline appears.

Continue to enter outline items, following these two rules:

- If the outline needs to be indented further (lower level in the outline), press the Tab key before you type the item.

- If the item needs to be raised to a higher level in the outline, press Shift+Tab before typing the entry.

When you have entered all the outline items, press Enter on a blank line to indicate the end of the outline. The last outline number disappears.

10

The gray shading on the outline level numbers doesn't appear when you print the document. You can turn it off by deselecting Field Shadings from the View menu.

Using Bullets and Line Numbering

You can use bullets and numbering the same way that you use outlining in StarOffice:

1. From the Format menu, choose Numbering/Bullets.

2. Choose the Bullets or Numbering tab.

3. Select a style from the boxes shown.

4. Choose OK.

A bullet or number is shown at the beginning of the current line. When you type text and press Enter, the next number or another bullet appears (see Figure 10.18).

As with outlining, press Enter on a blank line to end the automatic addition of a bullet or line number.

When you need to use a bulleted list or numbered list, you can also add those features after you've entered the text.

Just select any block of text and then open the Numbering/Bullets dialog box. When you select the bullet or numbering option and choose OK, your selection is applied to all the selected lines.

FIGURE 10.18

Automatic bullets or numbering are available in many formats.

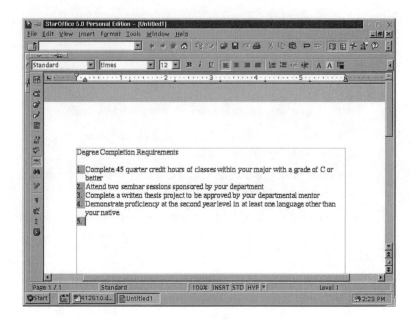

The Pictures tab in the dialog box is just like the Bullets tab, except that it uses small graphics as bullets. This is probably best used in Web pages that are to be viewed in color.

In the Next Hour

In Hour 11, "Adding Graphics to Documents," you'll learn how to add graphics to your StarWriter documents. You can either import existing graphic files of many different formats or create your own drawings using the built-in Image Editor or StarDraw tools. You'll also learn to edit how images are positioned and displayed in your document.

HOUR 11

Adding Graphics to Documents

In this hour, you learn how to add the graphic images and figures that you create to your documents. You also learn how to position and edit a graphic.

StarOffice includes StarDraw for creating vector-based graphics (see Hour 6, "Creating Graphics with StarDraw"), and the Image Editor for creating bitmapped graphics. Both types of graphics can be inserted into documents as described in this hour.

StarWriter documents can also use standard line drawing and borders. In this hour, you learn how to insert and position such elements in a document.

Importing Graphics

Pictures or diagrams add a lot to any document. Because StarOffice can create Web pages so readily, you'll probably use a lot of graphics as you create documents in StarOffice.

Instead of using StarDraw or the StarOffice image editor (which you'll learn about later in this hour), you can create the images you need in a standard Linux package such as GIMP or Xpaint. Both of these excellent tools are included in nearly every Linux distribution.

After you've created a graphic or downloaded one that you want to add to your document, you're ready to import the graphic into your StarOffice document.

Placing Graphics in Your Document

StarOffice includes a clip art library of dozens of images that you can insert into your documents. You can also use most graphics in standard formats. (A list of major supported formats is included in the next section.) In this hour, you learn how to use both clip art and other imported graphics.

To prepare for this example, open a document that you've been working on and check both the Explorer and the Beamer in the View menu so that they're visible on your screen. Then follow these steps:

1. Click on the plus sign (+) next to the Gallery in the Explorer window.

2. Choose a category of clip art by clicking on it. Choose Maps. The graphics in that group appear in the Beamer. (See Figure 11.1.)

FIGURE 11.1

Clip art can be viewed in the Beamer window.

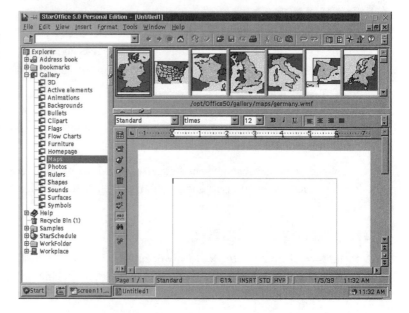

3. Scroll through the Beamer until you find an interesting graphic.

4. Click on the graphic in the Beamer and drag it to the main document window.

5. Release the mouse button in the location within the document in which you want the graphic placed. The graphic isn't placed at the current cursor location.

You've just inserted a graphic into your document. The image is selected, as shown by the green handles around it. (See Figure 11.2.) A little anchor is also shown. The anchor is provided mainly for reference purposes; it indicates where the graphic is anchored in the document. Because you can use your mouse to drag the document wherever you want it, the anchor doesn't matter much in text documents.

FIGURE 11.2

A graphic is selected after being dragged into a document.

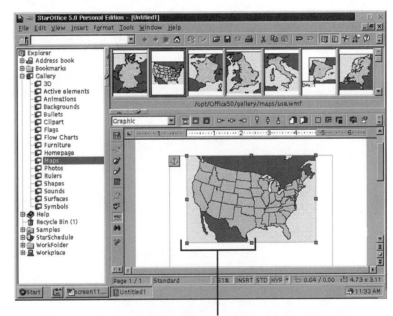

11

Handles show that the graphic is selected.

A little later, you'll look at how to work with the graphic that you've inserted. First, however, you will try two other methods of inserting a graphic.

Remember that the Workplace item in the Explorer window is a method of browsing your entire Linux filesystem. With the Beamer open, you can open the Workplace icon in the Explorer and locate a graphic in your Linux filesystem.

As you browse the directories in the Explorer, you can click on any directory (rather than the plus sign next to the directory) to see a listing of the files that the directory contains in the Beamer window.

When you see a graphic file in the Beamer window that you want to insert in your document, click on the icon or filename in the Beamer window and drag it to a spot in your document.

If the file is in a graphics format that StarOffice can read (more on that soon), the graphic appears in your document.

Finally, you can use the old-fashioned method of inserting graphics into your document. Choose Picture from the Insert menu and then choose From File on the submenu. The Insert Picture dialog box appears, as shown in Figure 11.3.

FIGURE 11.3

From the Insert Picture dialog box, you can select a graphics file to insert.

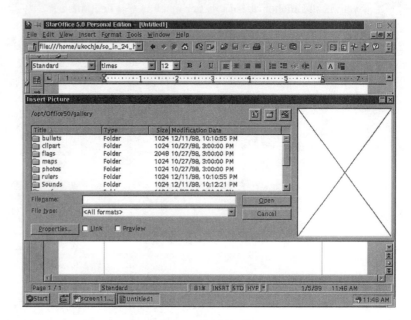

The advantage of using the Insert Picture dialog box (instead of the Beamer) for graphics that aren't in the StarOffice Gallery is that you can select the Preview checkbox (as it is in the figure) and see the graphic before you insert it.

After you find the graphic file that you want to insert, choose OK to close the dialog box and insert the graphic. The graphic appears with the green handles, ready to be edited (as described later in this hour).

Using Other Linux Programs to Convert Graphic Formats

This book isn't all about Linux graphics tools, but it is useful to review a few popular programs that can help you get your graphics into StarOffice.

StarOffice supports a variety of image formats, including GIF, TIFF, BMP, EPS, JPEG, WMF, Mac-pict, PNG, and a few others.

When you have to deal with another image format, however, you can also try one of these tools to convert it to one supported by StarOffice:

1. Start the xv program from an X Window System command line, with the name of a graphic file that you need to convert.

2. Click the right mouse button in the graphic to open the control window.

3. Choose Save to open the Save dialog box.

4. Choose a graphics format in which to save the image.

Use one of the following formats:

- JPG (if you need a small file)
- GIF (if you want to use a graphic on a Web page that can be viewed in StarOffice, save it in GIF format.)
- TIFF

The GIMP is another excellent graphics program for Linux. It's intended as a graphics editor, however, and might seem like overkill if you just need to convert graphic formats.

If you need to convert a large number of files, or need to convert to or from a format that isn't available in StarOffice, XV, or GIMP, you can use the ImageMagick package, which converts between dozens of image formats.

For example, if you need to convert a file from Targa (tga) to Macintosh pict, you can use the following command:

```
$ convert samplepic.tga samplepic.pict
```

Creating New Images in the Image Editor

StarOffice includes a simple bitmapped image editor that can come in handy—not because it's a full-featured editor, but because it's always available.

Suppose you need to insert a graphic of a large colored circle in your document. Rather than creating a StarDraw drawing or opening a separate drawing program such as the GIMP, you can follow these steps in StarOffice:

1. From the Insert menu, choose Picture, and then From Image Editor. The New Image dialog box appears, as in Figure 11.4.

11

FIGURE 11.4

Select a size and color depth for each new image that you create in the Image Editor.

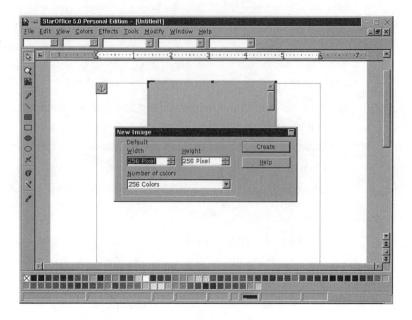

2. Select the size, in pixels, for the image that you want to create.

3. Select the number of color bits per pixel to include in the saved image (this dialog box doesn't consult your system to see how many are available, so disregard the higher numbers if your system doesn't support them).

Note that you can't Cancel the insert operation from here. If you change your mind, choose the Create button and then just delete the graphic by clicking in your document—to end Edit mode—and pressing the Delete key.

4. Choose Create to start editing the graphic. The graphic appears as a blank canvas and the Image Editing toolbar appears (see Figure 11.5).

5. Click on the filled-in circle icon on the Image Editing toolbar on the left of the editing window.

6. Click on a color that you like in the palette at the bottom of the screen.

7. Click in the image editing window and drag to size your circle.

8. Use any other icons to add lines, rectangles, or a variety of special effects to your image.

FIGURE 11.5

You can edit a graphic as part of your text document using the Image Editor.

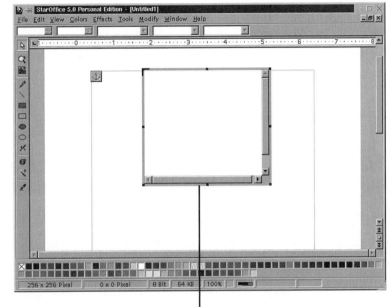

A new, blank graphic

9. When you have finished, click anywhere in your document, outside the image editing window. The image is selected with green handles, but is no longer being edited.

10. Click again in your document to deselect the image and continue editing the text of your document.

To further edit the image that you created in the Image Editor, double-click on the image. You are switched to image editing mode.

> Although the Image Editor is great for creating a quick embedded image, bitmapped graphics take a lot more space (memory and hard disk) than do vector graphics created by StarDraw.

Although the use of the Image Editor is being downplayed here in favor of StarDraw or other programs, following is a list of some of the features of the Image Editor. As you'll see in the next section, these can be used with any bitmapped image you import, as well as with images that you draw from scratch in the Image Editor. All the following features are available from the Image Editing toolbar:

- Independent RGB level controls
- Brightness, contrast, and grayscale controls
- Visual effects, such as solarization, tiling, smoothing, and noise reduction
- Eyedropper for color sourcing
- Airbrush
- Multiple magnification ratios and cropping

Formatting Images in Your Document

After you have an image that looks the way that you want it to graphically, many other issues remain in terms of having the image correctly positioned and displayed within the context of your document. These issues apply whether you've created an image in the Image Editor or StarDraw or imported it from another program.

The following section describes how to set options such as where the image is anchored, how text wraps around the image, and where the image is positioned on the page.

Selecting a Graphic to Edit

To work with any image, you must first select it. This tells StarOffice which image you're referring to. It also changes many of the menus and options in StarOffice, giving you choices that are related to images rather than text.

You can select any image by clicking on it once. You can tell that an image is selected because it has an outline around it and small green squares on each corner and on each side, as in Figure 11.6.

With an image selected, notice that the format menu and the Object toolbar change to show image-manipulating options, as shown in Figure 11.7.

You learn more about these options and icons in the following sections.

StarOffice refers to a graphic that you insert from a file as a Picture; a graphic that you insert from the Image Editor (by drawing it) is called an Object. The Object toolbar and Properties dialog boxes for Pictures and Objects vary slightly. The same operations can be used on both Pictures and Objects, but some operations (such as flip image) are located in different places for Pictures and Objects. After selecting a Picture or Object, check the menus, toolbar icons, and Properties dialog box.

FIGURE 11.6

A selected image has an outline and green handles.

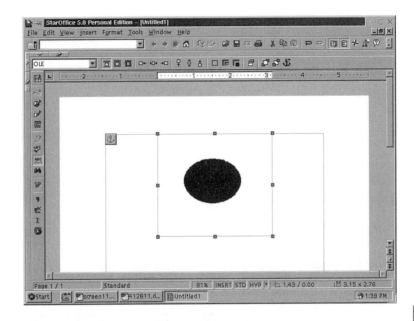

The Format menu and Object toolbar for image editing

FIGURE 11.7

The Format menu and Object toolbar change when you select an image.

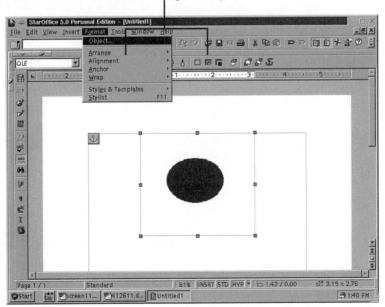

11

Moving and Resizing Images

The first thing you might want to do with an image is to move it to a new location on the page, to position it more precisely after you dragged it from the Beamer.

To move a selected image, click anywhere in the image and drag the mouse. The outline that moves shows where the image is to be placed when you release the mouse.

By default, the text flows around the image, above and below it. You'll learn how to change that setting momentarily.

If you need to resize the image, use the green handles that appear when you select the image.

To resize any selected image, click and drag on any of the green handles. The moving outline shows you the size that the image will be when you release the mouse button.

Notice that you can easily (too easily) alter the ratio of height to width for an image as you resize it. (See Figure 11.8.)

FIGURE 11.8

As you resize an image, hold down the Shift key to prevent the distortion shown here.

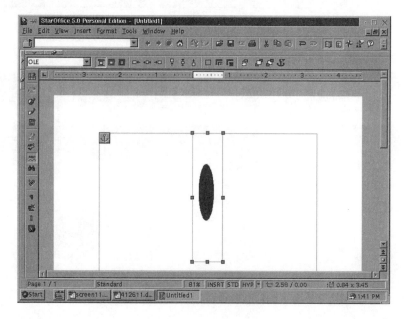

To prevent distortion, hold down the Shift key as you drag on a handle to resize an image. The Shift key makes both directions of the image move in concert so that the image is sized without being distorted.

Setting Alignment and Text Wrapping

The easiest way to set many image options is by clicking the right mouse button on a selected image. The Formatting pop-up menu appears, so you can easily choose an option from a menu or submenu (see Figure 11.9).

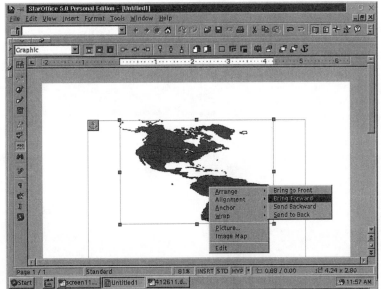

Similar options to most of the pop-up submenus appear on the Object toolbar (just scroll the toolbar over as needed). You can explore the icons on the toolbar by leaving your mouse pointer over an icon for a few seconds. A descriptive message tells you what that icon is used for.

Although you can move an image by dragging it with the mouse, this isn't the most precise method. Instead, you can use the menus to select a left margin, centered, or right margin position for an image. Just follow these steps:

1. Select an image in your document.

2. Click the right mouse button to access the Formatting pop-up, or select Format on the menu bar.

3. Select the Alignment submenu.

4. Choose Left, Center, or Right from the submenu. The image is repositioned horizontally.

The Top, Middle, Bottom alignment options refer to the vertical placement of the image when you have the text wrapping around it.

Text wrapping determines whether the image has blank space to either side of it, or whether the text in your document flows down the sides of the image. Several options are included on the Wrap submenu of the Format menu. The three most useful ones are included on the Object toolbar. They are as follows:

- **No wrap**—Text doesn't flow around the image at all, as in Figure 11.10.

FIGURE 11.10

No wrap forces blank space to either side of your image.

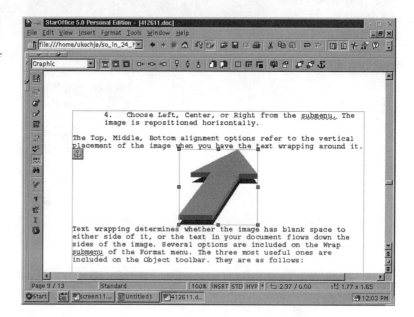

- **Page wrap**—Text flows down either side of the image, around the sized box that contains the image, as in Figure 11.11.
- **Wrap through**—Text flows into the box containing the image; the main background color of the image is considered transparent, and the text forms around the shape of the image, as in Figure 11.12.

Study the Figures to understand the Wrapping terms used by StarOffice. They might differ from what you're accustomed to in other programs.

FIGURE **11.11**

*Page wrap flows text
around the box that
contains the image.*

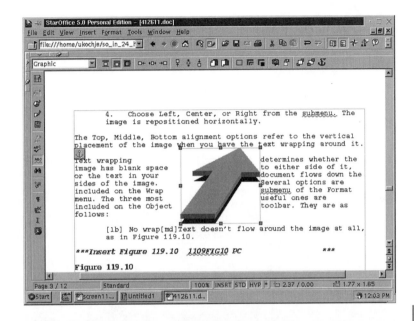

FIGURE **11.11**

*Page wrap flows text
around the box that
contains the image.*

FIGURE **11.12**

*Wrap through treats
the background of the
image as transparent
and flows text into the
image box.*

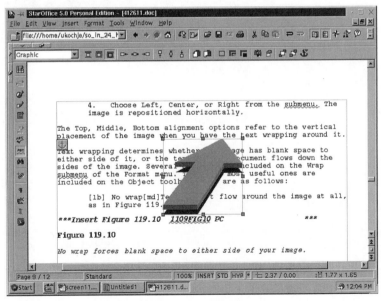

11

Using Layers

If you use a lot of images in your documents, you might need to occasionally layer them on top of each other to get the effect that you want.

By selecting options from the Position submenu of the Format menu, you can raise or lower images as graphical layers in your document. For example, suppose you have two images combined to create an effect, as in Figure 11.13.

FIGURE 11.13

Two images can be overlapped to create an effect.

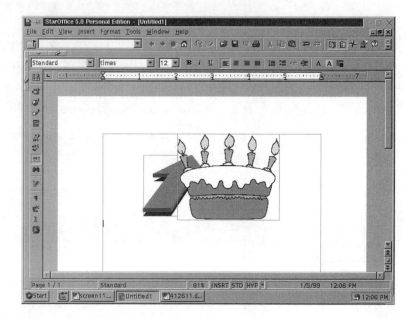

If you select one of the images and choose Send to Back, the other image covers it, as in Figure 11.14.

Adding a Border

Most graphics that you import into your document won't have a border. Within a text document, however, images often need to be set off with a border.

If you have the Object toolbar displayed onscreen, you can add a border with a few mouse clicks. Follow these steps:

1. Select the image to which you want to add a border.

2. Click on the Border icon on the Object toolbar (see Figure 11.15).

FIGURE 11.14

Layers are used to arrange multiple images.

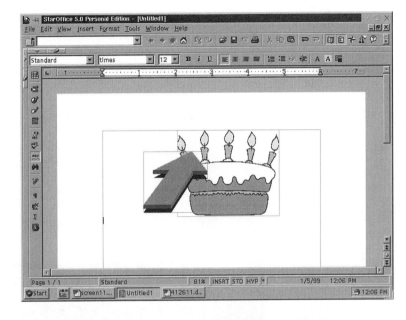

FIGURE 11.15

Use the Border icon on the Object toolbar to add a border to any selected image.

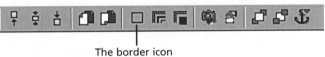

The border icon

3. Choose a border style from the pop-up menu of icons.

4. Click on the Line Style icon on the Object toolbar (see Figure 11.16).

FIGURE 11.16

When an image has a border, you can set the border's line type with this icon on the Object toolbar.

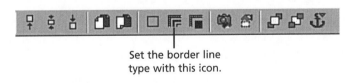

Set the border line
type with this icon.

5. Click on the Line Color icon on the Object toolbar—it's the one on the far right (see Figure 11.17).

11

FIGURE 11.17

You can select any color for the border from the line color icon's pop-up menu.

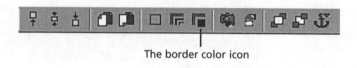

The border color icon

So how does the result look? It looks similar to Figure 11.18.

FIGURE 11.18

A border can be added to an image with the icons on the Object toolbar.

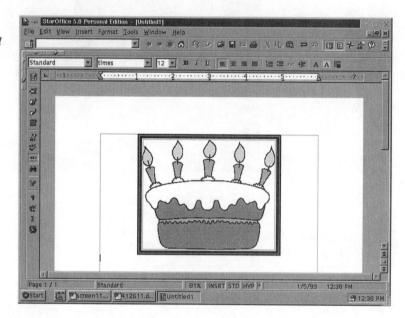

Using the Object Dialog Box

The Formatting pop-up menu and the Object toolbar have been used for all the examples of manipulating images. All these functions, however, including moving an image on the page, can be done from the Object dialog box.

With an image selected, choose Object from the Formatting pop-up menu or from the main Format menu. The Object dialog box appears (see Figure 11.19).

From the seven tabs in this dialog box, you can set all the features described previously, as well as several others that you can explore on your own. For example, you can add an URL link to any image so that clicking on it brings up a Web page in StarOffice.

Most of the image editing you'll do is probably more easily done from the pop-up menus and Object toolbar, but you might choose to use this dialog box for a more methodical approach.

FIGURE 11.19

Every image option and setting can be configured for a selected image from the Object dialog box.

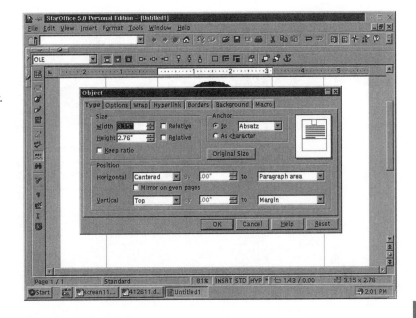

Adding Horizontal Lines

A much simpler graphic element that you can add to your document is a simple horizontal line. These are useful as ruling lines for documents, for example to divide sections of a resume or report.

You can add a variety of horizontal lines by selecting Horizontal Line from the Insert menu. The Insert Horizontal Line dialog box appears, as shown in Figure 11.20.

The collection of horizontal lines in the scrolling list is a little different from similar lists in programs such as WordPerfect. If you want a standard horizontal ruler, choose the top item, Single, and then choose OK.

If you scroll down in the list, you'll see a variety of lines that are more suited to a Web page than to any normal text document that you might print out on paper: rainbows and rabbit feet, airplanes, and marbled textures.

If you use one of these fancy lines, the horizontal line is treated as an image. You can select it, add a border, and so on.

If you choose the Single horizontal line, however, you can't easily select it for editing, so you're stuck with the line that you initially see. In fact, you might have trouble deleting the line if you need to. It's so narrow that clicking on it doesn't often work. Instead, place the cursor just above it, hold down the Shift key, and use the arrows to select it.

11

FIGURE 11.20

From the scrolling list, you can select which type of horizontal line to insert.

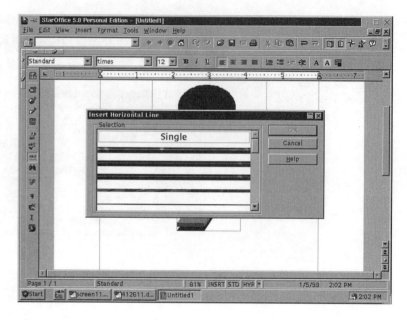

In the Next Hour

In the next hour, "Using Spellcheck and the Thesaurus," you will learn how to use the spellcheck and thesaurus features of StarOffice. Spellchecking includes automatic high-lighting and word correction, and the powerful StarOffice thesaurus enables you to explore word meanings to choose just the right term.

HOUR 12

Using SpellCheck and the Thesaurus

During this hour, you learn to use some of the language tools in StarOffice—specifically, you learn about the most useful ones: the spellchecking features and the associated thesaurus.

You explore features such as AutoCorrect and Auto Spellcheck, as well as learning how to start a regular spellcheck session. You also learn how to use the thesaurus by seeing how to look up words and follow new word options.

Using AutoCorrect

This hour looks first at the AutoCorrect feature of StarOffice spellchecking. The AutoCorrect feature can automatically correct common errors that occur as you enter text.

For example, when you type a period and begin a new sentence, AutoCorrect capitalizes the first letter of the first word of the new sentence if you forget to do it. AutoCorrect also corrects commonly misspelled words as you type.

AutoCorrect looks at all the text that you type, unless you turn off this feature in the Options dialog box. You can also change settings on AutoCorrect to make it fit your style and needs.

Setting AutoCorrect Options

The AutoCorrect feature works automatically, although you can turn it on or off and set up options for how AutoCorrect works on your document.

You can open the AutoCorrect options dialog box by selecting AutoCorrect/AutoFormat from the Tools menu. (See Figure 12.1.)

FIGURE 12.1

The AutoCorrect dialog box enables you to set options regarding how your typing is automatically corrected.

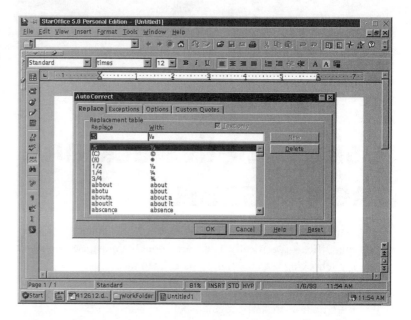

The Replace tab in the AutoCorrect options dialog box contains a list of common typing errors or abbreviations that are automatically replaced. For example, if you type *abbout*, with two *b*'s, the second *b* is removed as you type.

The autocorrection list contains hundreds of entries, but you can also add to the list. Suppose that you always type *regards* as *regrads* at the end of your letters. This autocorrection isn't in the list. To add it, follow these steps in the AutoCorrect options dialog box (in the Replace tab):

1. Enter *regrads* in the Replace field.
2. Enter *regards* in the With field.

3. Press the New button.

4. Choose OK to close the dialog box and continue typing. Now anytime you enter *regrads*, it is replaced with *regards*.

> You can also remove any item that you don't want to have automatically corrected as you type. Just select it from the list, and then choose the Delete button.

The next tab of the AutoCorrect options dialog box is for exceptions to the rules in the next tab: Options. Look there first. The Options tab is shown in Figure 12.2.

FIGURE 12.2

The Options tab of the AutoCorrect dialog box enables you to turn AutoCorrect features on or off.

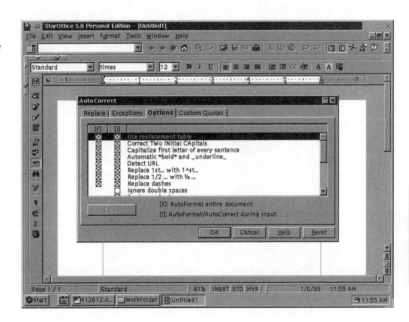

In the Options tab, you can turn features on or off by selecting a check box for each one. These features include the following:

- Start each sentence with a capital letter.
- Correct TWo INitial CApitals (make the second letter lowercase—using two initial capitals is a common typing mistake).
- Ignore double spaces (after periods, for example).

Auto Spellcheck, which underlines in red any word that can't be found in the dictionary, is a separate feature. You learn about it later in this hour.

Now, go back to the Exceptions tab of the AutoCorrect options dialog box (see Figure 12.3).

FIGURE 12.3

In the Exceptions tab of the AutoCorrect dialog box, you can prevent the correction of certain situations.

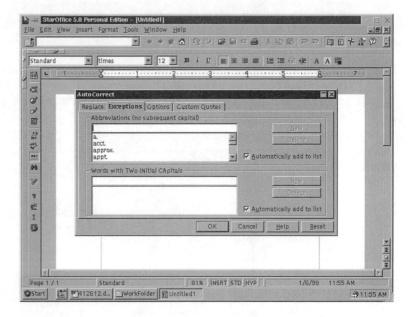

When you use an abbreviation in a sentence, you don't want the next word to start with a capital letter—but the AutoCorrect rules do this. By having a list of exceptions, AutoCorrect leaves some things (such as lowercase letters following abbreviations) just as you type them.

You can add other abbreviations that you use so that they don't have a capital letter added after them.

This hour doesn't cover the Custom Quotes tab of this dialog box. You can use it to set up how smart quotation marks are used in your document.

Using Auto Spellcheck

The Auto Spellcheck feature of StarOffice helps you create correct documents by pointing out misspelled words as you type. It won't guarantee perfect documents, but it can help you catch your errors before someone else does.

When the Auto Spellcheck feature is turned on, any word that you type that can't be found in the spelling dictionary is underlined in red, as in Figure 12.4.

FIGURE 12.4

With Auto Spellcheck, words that can't be found in the dictionary are underlined in red.

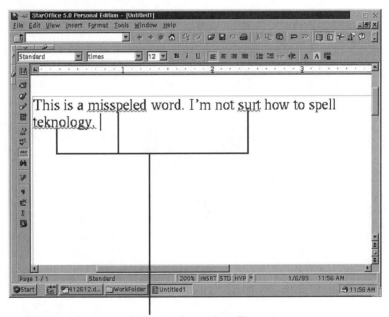

Words with wavy underline to show misspellings.

Turning Auto Spellcheck On or Off

You might not want to use Auto Spellcheck all the time; seeing all those red lines can be annoying.

To turn Auto Spellcheck on or off, select Spelling from the Tools menu. On the submenu that appears, you see Auto Spellcheck as an option. You can select that option to turn on Auto Spellcheck (see Figure 12.5). After a moment, words that can't be found in the dictionary are underlined in red.

12

Figure 12.5

The Auto Spellcheck menu option can be selected to turn this feature on or off.

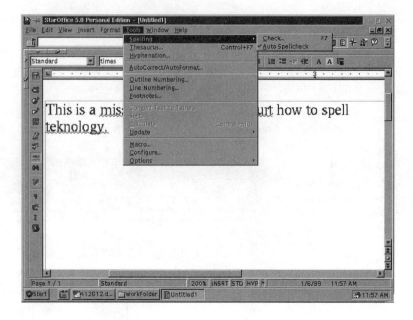

You can also turn on Auto Spellcheck by clicking an icon on the Main toolbar. The icon displays characters underlined in red.

When Auto Spellcheck is on, you see a check by that menu item. Select it again to turn Auto Spellcheck off. All the red underlines disappear.

Be careful about the meaning of red underlines. They don't always mean a misspelled word. Names that aren't in the dictionary are underlined, such as ThinkPad (an IBM laptop).

In addition, misused words that are in the dictionary won't be underlined. For example, using *to* and *too* or *there* and *their* incorrectly won't be marked.

The next section describes how to use the regular spellcheck dialog box to go through your document and check for misspelled words.

Spellchecking Your Document

The AutoCorrect feature is nice, but a traditional spellchecker provides more flexibility. At the same time, the Auto Spellcheck feature can underline words in red that aren't in the dictionary, but it doesn't fix your errors. You might need to run the spellchecker to correct the errors.

Using the Pop-Up Spelling Menu

StarWriter enables you to check the spelling of a document using a special pop-up menu, or with a standard dialog box.

To check the spelling of a single word in a document, position your mouse pointer over a word that has a red underline and click and release the right mouse button. When you do this, a menu similar to the one in Figure 12.6 is displayed.

FIGURE 12.6

The right-click pop-up menu contains different spelling options.

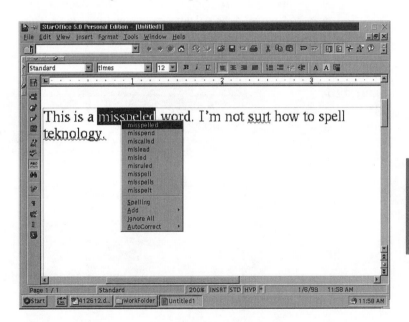

12

If you right-click on a word without a red underline (or with Auto Spellcheck turned off), you'll see a different menu than the one described here.

The pop-up menu is divided into two sections. The top section contains words that StarWriter suggests as possible corrections for the word you right-clicked. If you select one of the words in the top section of the menu, the word you clicked is replaced with the word you selected from the menu.

> If the pop-up menu you see has only four items, starting with Spelling, StarOffice can't determine any suggestions to correct the word that you clicked on. You'll have to use a paper dictionary.

In the bottom part of the pop-up menu, the following four commands are listed:

- **Spelling**—Selecting the Spelling item opens the full Spellcheck dialog box, which is described at length later in this hour. Choosing this option is a good idea if you want to have more help determining how to correct a word.

- **Add**—Selecting Add adds the word to the spelling dictionary that you select from the submenu that appears (see Figure 12.7).

FIGURE 12.7

Add opens a submenu where you can select a dictionary to which to add a word.

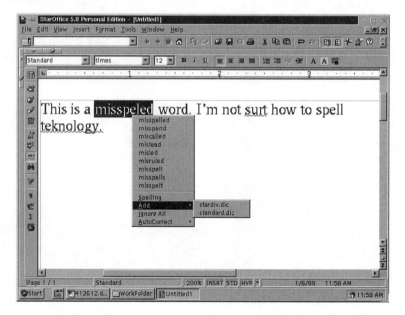

Adding a word to a dictionary means that word won't be marked as mis-spelled any longer. You learn more about this in the next section.

- **Ignore All**—Selecting Ignore All causes the StarOffice spellchecker (including the Auto Spellchecker) to ignore the misspelled word throughout this entire document.
- **AutoCorrect**—Selecting AutoCorrect opens a submenu with suggestions for how this word can be corrected. (See Figure 12.8.) If you select one of the items in the AutoCorrect submenu, that correction is added to the AutoCorrect configuration. This means that any time that you type this word (the one you right-clicked on) in this way, it is corrected to the spelling that you selected in the AutoCorrect submenu.

FIGURE 12.8

AutoCorrect opens a submenu where you can select a spelling correction to add to the AutoCorrect feature.

You can review any item that you add to AutoCorrect via this menu by look-ing it up in the AutoCorrect dialog box, described earlier in this hour.

Don't add every word to the AutoCorrect feature. It can become overbur-dened and sluggish. Just add words that you habitually misspell (as in the previous *regrads* example).

12

Activating the Spellcheck Dialog Box

The traditional method of spellchecking a document also works in StarOffice. You can use a spellcheck dialog box to review misspelled words and choose how to correct them.

The StarOffice spellchecker starts from the current cursor position and pauses at each word that can't be located in a StarOffice dictionary.

To start the spellchecker and check your entire document, move to the top of your document and choose Spelling from the Tools menu; then choose Check from the Spelling submenu. The Spelling dialog box appears when StarOffice finds a word that it thinks is misspelled, as in Figure 12.9.

FIGURE 12.9

The Spelling dialog box enables you to carefully check the spelling of your document.

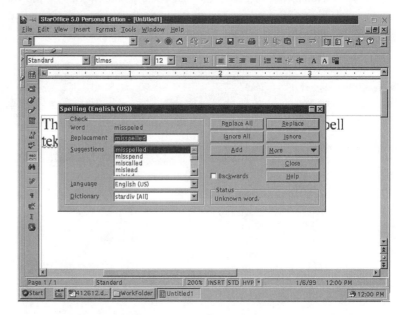

When you start the Spelling dialog box, the first misspelled word (starting from your cursor position) is shown in the dialog box. If a potential correction for the word can be determined by StarOffice, the replacement is shown in the replacement field. Other potential replacements are listed in the Suggestions list that follows.

After you take one of the following actions, the spellchecker looks for the next misspelled word, and you repeat the process. This continues until the document has no misspelled words (words not found in the dictionary), or until you choose the Close option to close the dialog box. The options you can choose for each word include

- **Click Replace**—To replace the word in your document with the word in the Replacement field.
- **Click Replace All**—To replace every occurrence of this misspelled word with the word in the Replacement field.

> If you choose this, the spellchecker does not pause on this word next time—it corrects it and moves on.

- **Click Ignore**—To skip this word without correcting it. (For example, choose this option if the misspelled word is a person's name.)
- **Click Ignore All**—To skip every occurrence of this word in this document. (In other words, don't pause the next time this word is encountered.)
- **Choose Add**—To add this word (as it appears in your document before the correction) to the currently selected dictionary (see the Dictionary field).

> Choosing Add or Ignore All are similar in results; however, choosing Add makes the spellchecker skip the word in other documents, not just in this document.

If StarOffice can't figure out how to correct the word, the word from your document is shown in the Replacement field. In this case, choosing Replace doesn't change anything.

If you don't see the corrected spelling in the list of Suggestions, you can type anything into the Replacement field (by memory or from a dictionary) and then choose Replace, Replace All, or Add to correct the word.

Don't be surprised by some of the words that aren't included in the StarOffice spelling dictionary. For example, neither StarOffice nor Linux is included, for some reason. You might want to add them, especially if you're writing a book about StarOffice for Linux.

12

> You can't click on the document and edit it without closing the Spelling dialog box first. But that's OK because when you restart the Spelling dialog box, it starts from the current cursor position.

Searching the Thesaurus

One final language feature of StarOffice is the Thesaurus. The word *thesaurus* comes from the Latin word for treasure, and you can think of a thesaurus as a treasure chest of words that you haven't yet seen.

Whenever you need just the right word in a document, you can type a word that's close in meaning, but not just right. Then look it up in the Thesaurus to search for related or similar words.

The StarOffice Thesaurus even includes a dictionary definition for thousands of words.

To use the Thesaurus, select a word by placing the cursor in it. Then select Thesaurus from the Tools menu. The Thesaurus dialog box appears (see Figure 12.10).

FIGURE 12.10

Use the Thesaurus dialog box to search for words related to your selected word.

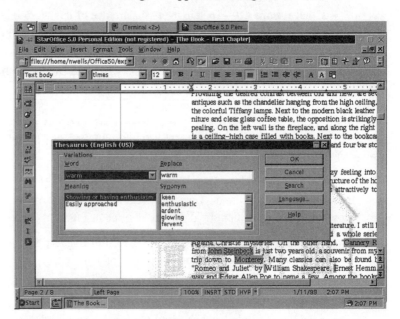

The word that you selected in the body of the text is displayed in the Word field. The various meanings for that word are listed under the Meaning field.

The Replace field contains the word that you selected (the same word as the Word field), but the Synonym list contains a list of possible replacements for your selected word.

Words meaning the opposite of the word you selected are also listed in the Synonyms list, but with the word *antonym* listed after them.

To change your selected word into one of the synonyms, select that synonym from the list and choose OK. The dialog box closes, and your word is updated.

Searching for More Meaning

After you've selected a word in the Synonyms list, you can look up that word in the Thesaurus by clicking the Search button.

The new word appears in the Word field, with its definitions in the Meaning list.

> Choosing an interesting word and exploring its meanings and synonyms in an online thesaurus is a great way to improve your writing.

If you want to see how well the dictionary and thesaurus work, try one of these words: *set, tone, malignant, fix,* or *joy.* They have strong lists of synonyms or long lists of meanings to explore.

A thesaurus with definitions can also help you choose between words such as *effect* and *affect,* or *complement* and *compliment.*

Using the Thesaurus from the Spelling Dialog Box

When you're spellchecking your document, you might want to use the Thesaurus dialog box to review possible word replacements.

From the Spelling dialog box, select the More button, and then choose Thesaurus. The same Thesaurus dialog box appears, with the current word from the Spelling dialog box as its entry. You can use this dialog box to choose a replacement word, and then return automatically to the Spelling dialog box.

In the Next Hour

In the next hour, "Creating Spreadsheets with StarCalc," you start working with StarCalc spreadsheets. You learn how to create a new spreadsheet using the New menu, templates, or the AutoPilot. You also learn how to work with cells, navigate around your spreadsheet, and enter data.

12

PART III

Creating Spreadsheets with StarCalc

Hour

13 Creating Spreadsheets with StarCalc

14 Entering Spreadsheet Data

15 Using Formulas, Functions, and Names

16 Formatting Your Spreadsheet

17 Adding Charts and Graphics to Spreadsheets

18 Using Database Functions

HOUR 13

Creating Spreadsheets with StarCalc

In this hour, you learn how to create, print, and save a new spreadsheet. Although the process is similar to creating a new text document (which you learned in Hour 7, "Creating a New StarWriter Document"), spreadsheets use some different methods of formatting and printing.

In addition, this hour describes other information specific to spreadsheets, such as setting input and calculation preferences and various other spreadsheet options.

Opening a New StarCalc Spreadsheet

StarOffice provides several methods for starting a new spreadsheet, all of which are familiar to you from starting a new StarWriter text document. The sections that follow describe these methods.

Using the Start or New Menus

The easiest way to open a new spreadsheet is to click on the Start button in the bottom left corner of the StarOffice window, and then choose Spreadsheet from the pop-up menu that appears.

You can also open a new spreadsheet by choosing New from the File menu; then choose Spreadsheet from the submenu. (See Figure 13.1.)

FIGURE 13.1

You can open a new spreadsheet from the New submenu of the File menu.

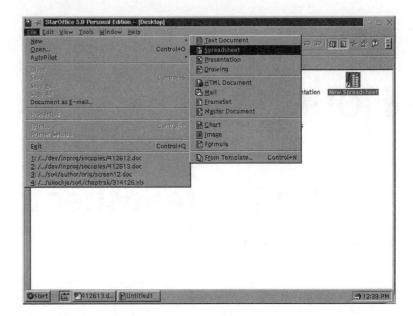

Using the Desktop

The default StarOffice Desktop also includes an icon that you can double-click to open a new spreadsheet. The icon is indicated in Figure 13.2.

You can use the Desktop icon on the Start bar to switch to the Desktop.

Icon for a new
spreadsheet

FIGURE 13.2

When you double-click on the New Spreadsheet icon on the Desktop, a new spreadsheet document opens.

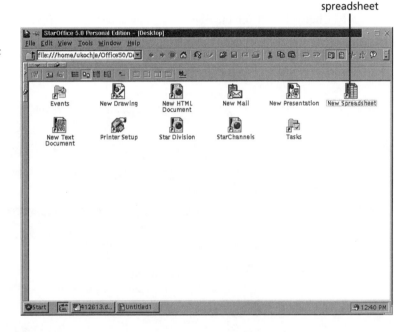

Using a Template

StarOffice includes a collection of templates that you can use as a starting point for several commonly used spreadsheets, such as expense reports and calendars.

When you use a template, the formatting is all set up for you; you just enter the data and print the document.

StarOffice includes spreadsheet templates for things such as

- Yearly/monthly calendar
- Loan calculation
- Amortization schedule
- Inventory
- Schedule
- Timetable

13

To use one of these templates, follow these steps:

1. Choose New from the File menu; then choose From Template from the bottom of the New submenu. The New dialog box appears.

2. Scroll down the list of Categories and click on Financial Documents. A list of templates appears. (See Figure 13.3).

FIGURE 13.3

Choosing From Template on the New submenu opens a dialog box where you can select from a list of financial templates.

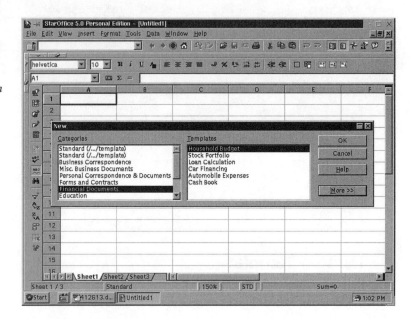

3. Click on the template that you want to try.

4. Choose OK. The template document opens.

5. In many cases, the template starts with a dialog box that asks you questions about the document that you want to create. Answer the questions in the dialog boxes to continue.

6. Choose Save As from the File menu.

7. Enter a name and location to which to save this document; then choose OK.

Opening a template is similar to opening a blank form with only formatting and an outline in which you can enter your own information. Always save the document under a name that you choose as soon as you start entering data in it.

Templates can be very useful for everyday spreadsheets. Following is an example to show you how they work.

Suppose that you need to prepare an expense report after a business trip. You can get out a piece of blank paper and start drawing columns, or you can follow these steps:

1. Choose New from the File menu.

2. Choose From Template from the New submenu. The New dialog box appears.

3. Scroll down in the Categories list and click on Spreadsheet.

4. Click on Travel Expense Report in the Templates list.

5. Click the More button in the lower-right corner. The dialog box expands to show you more about the templates. (See Figure 13.4.)

FIGURE 13.4

The New dialog box can be used to preview a template or to review template descriptions.

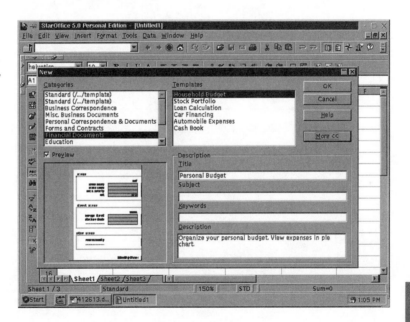

6. Click on the Preview check box to see a graphical image of the Travel Expense Report spreadsheet.

7. Choose OK to open the template. The Travel Expense Report document appears on your screen as in Figure 13.5.

8. Choose Save As from the File menu.

9. Enter a new name for the expense report that you are creating and choose Save.

10. Enter your expense data in the worksheet, saving regularly as you work. All the totals and other calculations are included in the template. All you enter is the detailed information from your trip.

FIGURE 13.5

Templates such as the Travel Expense Report give you a formatted area in which to enter your data.

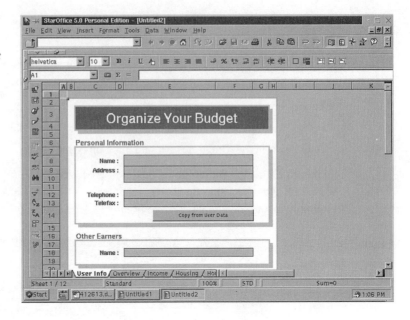

 Although templates can come in handy, it is still recommended that you review the formulas in the spreadsheet before accepting the information in a template as being perfectly accurate. Mortgages, expense reports, and so on deserve careful attention to detail.

Opening an Existing StarCalc Spreadsheet

Opening an existing StarCalc spreadsheet is similar to opening a text document. You can access an existing file in several ways:

- Choose Documents from the Start menu and select a document from the list of recently visited files.
- Choose Open from the File menu. From the Open dialog box, select a StarCalc spreadsheet file and choose OK.

 You can also use the file folder icon on the Function toolbar to view the Open dialog box.

- If you have a spreadsheet stored on your StarOffice Desktop, double-click on its icon.

- Use the Explorer window to browse your Workplace or the Work Folder. When you find the spreadsheet file that you want to open, double-click on it.

When you use any of these methods, the spreadsheet appears on your screen, ready to be edited.

Saving Your Spreadsheet

Saving your spreadsheet is just like saving your text documents, as you learned in Hour 7. The relevant menu items on the File menu are the same for both text documents and spreadsheets.

As soon as you start a new spreadsheet, choose the Save As item from the File menu. The Save As dialog box is shown in Figure 13.6; notice that StarCalc is automatically chosen as the format in which to save.

FIGURE 13.6

The Save As dialog box for a spreadsheet uses the StarCalc format.

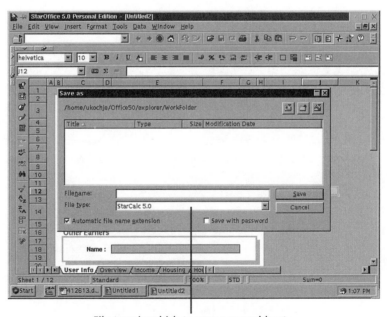

File type in which to save a spreadsheet

Select a directory, if necessary, using the file/directory browsing window; enter a file-name for the spreadsheet.

 Remember, filenames in Linux can be long and can include spaces and most other special characters.

When you press OK, the file is saved. After giving a name to a document the first time you save it, you can update the document on the hard disk by pressing Ctrl+S at any time, or by choosing Save from the File menu.

 You can also click on the disk icon on the Function toolbar to save the current spreadsheet. If the disk icon is gray (disabled), no changes have been made in your spreadsheet since it was last saved (or since it was created).

When you save your spreadsheet, all the sheets of the spreadsheet are saved into a single file.

Printing Your Spreadsheet

Printing a spreadsheet can be a lot more complicated than printing a text document. Instead of just choosing which pages to print, you might need to print a certain block on the spreadsheet, compress its size, turn the grid on or off, or set other printing features. This section explores how to set these options and print your spreadsheet.

Setting the Print Area

When you have a large spreadsheet (several screens of data), you might want to print only a portion of the entire sheet. In StarOffice, you can select an area of your spreadsheet as the Print Area. Then, when you issue a command to print, only the part of the spreadsheet within the Print Area is printed.

You can define a Print Area, and then turn it on or off, so that the Print command prints only the Print Area or the entire spreadsheet, respectively.

To define a print area within a larger spreadsheet, follow these steps:

1. Select a block of cells within the spreadsheet, using either of the following methods:

   - Click and drag the mouse, releasing the mouse button when the desired area is selected.
   - Hold down the Shift key and use the arrows to enlarge the selected area.

2. Choose Print Range from the Format menu.

> If you are not viewing a spreadsheet the Print Range option isn't shown on the Format menu.

3. Choose Set from the Print Range submenu.

After using this procedure, when you select Print, only the cells in the spreadsheet that you selected as the Print Area are printed.

If you want to print the entire spreadsheet again, you can choose the Clear item in the Print Range submenu of the Format menu. Then no Print Area is set, and each `Print` command prints everything.

To explore the Print Area options, select Edit from the Print Range submenu of the Format menu. The Edit Print Areas dialog box is displayed (see Figure 13.7).

FIGURE 13.7

In the Edit Print Areas dialog box, you can set which cells you want to print.

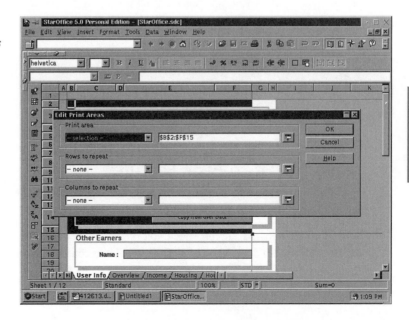

13

When you set a print area using the procedure outlined earlier, you're setting what StarOffice calls the User-Defined Print Area.

In the Print area part of the Edit Print Areas dialog box, you can select from the following three options from the drop-down list:

- **None**—Don't use a Print area selection; print the entire spreadsheet when the `Print` command is issued.
- **User-defined**—Print the area defined as the Print Area when the `Print` command is issued. The range of cells that is defined as the print area is shown in the field next to the drop-down list.
- **Selected**—Print the selected block of cells when the `Print` command is issued. This is like a one-time print area. The range of selected cells is shown in the field next to the drop-down list.

You can use the Edit Print Areas dialog box to specify what you want to print using a few more options. If you choose None from the drop-down list, the entire spreadsheet is printed when you issue a `Print` command, but the User-defined Print area cell range isn't cleared. You can select it again from this list without having to set it again manually by selecting the cells.

If you choose Selected from the drop-down list in the dialog box, a `Print` command prints whatever cells you have selected. This is handy for printing several sections of a spreadsheet without setting and clearing the print area each time.

Be sure to reset your selection in the Edit Print Areas dialog box after you've used the selected setting for whatever you needed to print. Otherwise, you might try to print your spreadsheet later and be surprised to print only a single cell.

Using the Fit-to-Page Feature

One printing feature that always seems to be necessary when working on a spreadsheet is the fit-to-page feature.

When you've prepared a spreadsheet, you often want it to print onto a certain number of pages, scaling both directions to fit. Otherwise, you can end up with a single column or row on a separate page.

To set how many pages a spreadsheet is to print on, follow this procedure:

1. Choose Page from the Format menu (with a spreadsheet open).

2. Choose the Sheet tab in the Page dialog box (see Figure 13.8).

FIGURE 13.8

In the Sheet tab of the Page dialog box, you can fit your spreadsheet onto a fixed number of pages.

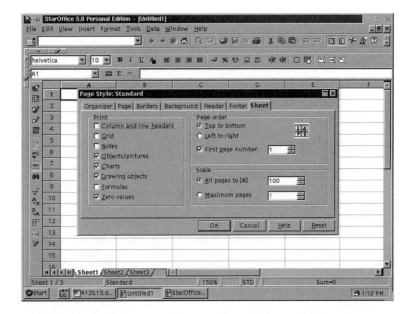

3. In the Scale area of the dialog box, click on the Maximum pages option.

4. Enter the number of pages on which to print in the field provided.

5. Select whether you want the pages printed from top to bottom or from right to left.

Here's an example of how you can use this feature. This hour walks through it without presenting actual spreadsheets, but it should still be clear.

Suppose you had prepared a long expense report with several columns for date, city, descriptions, amount, exchange rate, and so on. When you printed the expense report, the far-right column printed on a separate page. The entire printout was four pages long, two each way, although the two pages on the right (looking at all the pages arranged correctly after being printed) contained only a single column.

Now, if you use the Sheet tab of the Page dialog box, you can choose Maximum pages and enter 2, and then select print Top to bottom. StarOffice compresses the spreadsheet horizontally just enough to fit all the columns onto one page, but still prints two pages (see Figure 13.9).

13

FIGURE **13.9**

The fit-to-page feature squeezes your spreadsheet onto the number of pages that you specify.

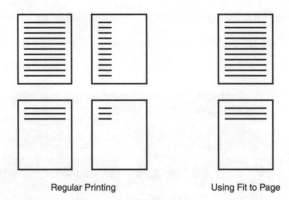

Regular Printing   Using Fit to Page

If you try to squeeze too many cells onto too few pages (I always try for one page), StarOffice does it; however, you can't read the type—it is too small.

Turning Grid Lines On or Off

When you print spreadsheets in StarOffice, you can also choose from other options that define what parts of the spreadsheet are printed.

Each of these are selected individually in the Page dialog box (choose Page from the Format menu while viewing a spreadsheet), in the Sheet tab.

The following options are listed in the dialog box. You can select whether each one prints:

- **Column and Row Headers**—Include the alphanumeric labels on columns (such as column D). When you include these labels, you can troubleshoot your spreadsheet by checking formulas and references to actual cells in the sheet.

- **Grid**—The grid in the spreadsheet is made up of the vertical and horizontal lines that separate cells. If you've turned on shading or other formatting (such as borders on some cells), you might not want the grid labels in the way.

    On the other hand, if you have a complex or busy spreadsheet, the grid lines make it much easier to read.

- **Formulas**—Printing formulas means that instead of printing the results of a formula, the behind-the-scenes instructions are printed. For example, instead of printing

    $23,419

the formula that generated the number is printed—perhaps something similar to the following:

=sum(D7:D28)

If you're reviewing your spreadsheet design or looking for potential errors before you pass on your work, printing the formulas enables you to check how the sheet is put together.

> Printing Formulas works best if you also print Column and row Headers. That way you can see which cells a formula refers to.

- **Notes**—You can add a note to any cell in your spreadsheet (just choose Note from the Insert menu). If you choose to print notes, they are added to your printed pages as footnotes are in a report. If notes are not printed, they are visible only when you view the spreadsheet onscreen.
- **Charts**—Charts that have been imported or created in your spreadsheet can add a lot visually, but they take a lot of time and toner to print. While you're in the draft stages of preparing a spreadsheet, you can choose not to print Charts.
- **Zeros**—Sometimes it's important to distinguish between cells that have values of zero and cells that are just empty (have no data entered). This option enables you to have StarCalc indicate in your printed pages the cells in which a zero value occurs. A zero can be typed in or can be the result of a formula calculation.

After you've chosen which items to print, choose OK in the dialog box to set those options.

Choosing the Page Format

As with text documents, you need to correctly define the overall page layout that you'll be using. This amounts to the following two things above all:

- Landscape or portrait style (long or tall pages)
- Page size

You can decide on landscape or portrait depending on the layout of the spreadsheet that you're preparing. Use whatever fits the shape of the data best.

Both of these options can be set in the Page Style dialog box. Just follow these steps:

1. Choose Page from the Format menu.
2. Click on the Page tab in the Page dialog box. (See Figure 13.10.)

13

FIGURE 13.10

The Page tab of the Page dialog box enables you to set paper size and print orientation.

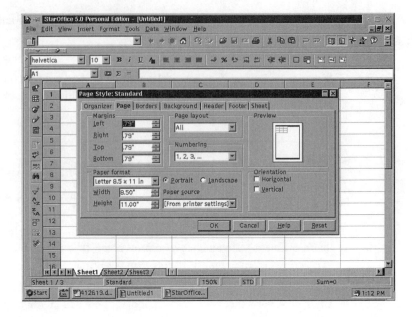

3. In the Paper format part of the dialog box, check that the page size drop-down list displays Letter. (Select Letter if it doesn't.)

4. To the right of the paper size field, click on the Landscape or Portrait buttons to change the print orientation.

> The results of your changes in this dialog box are shown graphically in the Preview area of the dialog box (on the right side). Changes don't take effect, however, until you choose OK.

5. Review other options in this dialog box, such as page margins and page numbering, to see whether you want to make other changes.

6. Choosing OK causes your changes to take effect, and closes the dialog box.

> If the margins that you've set in the page formatting don't seem to match what comes out on your printed pages, you probably have the paper size set to A4 instead of Letter.

Setting Spreadsheet Options

In Hour 4, "Configuring StarOffice," you learned about setting options that apply to everything that you do in StarOffice. You can also set options that apply to how StarOffice works with and formats spreadsheets.

> The options that you set while viewing a spreadsheet are specific to that file and are saved with that file. If you open a new spreadsheet, the default spreadsheet options are used.

To view or set the spreadsheet options, select Options from the Tools menu; then choose Spreadsheet from the submenu. The Spreadsheet Options dialog box appears, as shown in Figure 13.11.

FIGURE 13.11

The first tab of the Spreadsheet Options dialog box, Contents, enables you to set preferences for how spreadsheet information is displayed.

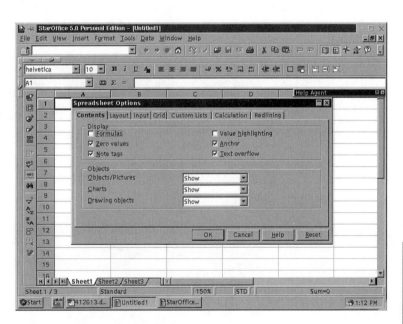

The Spreadsheet options dialog box consists of six tabs where you can set different options. The most important options are described in the following sections.

Choosing What to Display Onscreen

A spreadsheet contains a lot of information behind what you see onscreen. Formulas, charts, values, and notes can be part of different cells.

From the Contents tab of the Spreadsheet Options dialog box, you can select parts of the spreadsheet to be displayed onscreen. In the top part of the dialog box, you can check any item that you want displayed.

> Notice that these display options are similar to the options for printing in the Sheet tab of the Page Style dialog box, described in the previous section. Remember that the options described here affect only onscreen display.

For example, if you want to have formulas displayed instead of the result of the formula calculation, you can check the Formulas check box in the Display field.

By default, any values in your spreadsheet that calculate to zero, or that you enter as a zero, are displayed. Also, any notes that you enter for a cell are visually noted in two ways. A red dot in the corner of a cell indicates that the cell has a note attached. When you leave the mouse pointer over a cell for a few seconds, the note appears in yellow (see Figure 13.12).

FIGURE 13.12

A note can be added to any cell. If the file is configured to view notes, they appear automatically when the mouse is left over a cell.

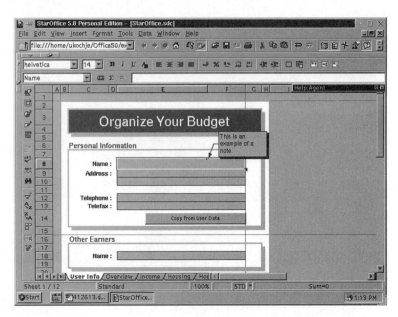

For objects, such as graphic images and charts, you can select from a drop-down list in the bottom part of the dialog box. You can choose to have any of these object types displayed, hidden, or used as a placeholder. (A placeholder appears, showing the size of the object, but without using the processing time or memory to prepare and display the real object.)

You can also select some display options from the Layout tab of the Spreadsheet Options dialog box (see Figure 13.13). The layout options define the display and color or gridlines, and whether screen elements such as the scroll bars, multisheet tabs, and page break lines are displayed.

FIGURE **13.13**

The Layout tab of the Spreadsheet Options dialog box includes some display options.

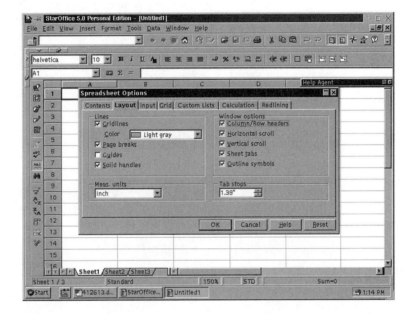

Setting Input Options

In the Input tab of the Spreadsheet Options dialog box (see Figure 13.14), you can set preferences for how you use the keyboard to enter data in your spreadsheet.

When you're entering a lot of data in a spreadsheet, it can help to set where the focus goes when you press Enter, or whether pressing Enter in a cell starts Edit mode for the contents of that cell or just moves to a new cell. All these items can be set with the check boxes in the Input tab.

You can also select whether the row and column headings are highlighted for the currently selected cell.

13

FIGURE 13.14

The Input tab of the Spreadsheet Options dialog box determines how you use the keyboard to enter data in cells.

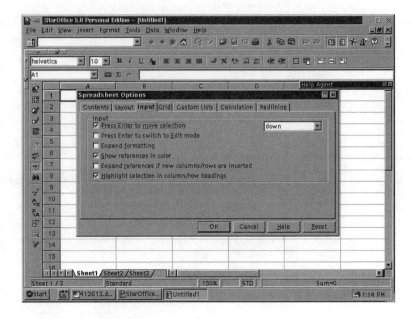

Adding a Grid to a Spreadsheet

When you use a spreadsheet, you probably think of the grid as the lines that divide the cells in the sheet. When you select printing options in the Page dialog box under the Format menu (in the Sheet tab), the grid *does* refer to the lines between cells.

In StarOffice, however, you can also turn on a grid of closely spaced dots to help you create or place charts or other objects within the spreadsheet. This is the grid that you're setting options for in the Grid tab of the Spreadsheet Options dialog box (shown in Figure 13.15).

Most of the time you won't want to use this grid at all. If you do, select the Visible grid check box. Checking the Snap to grid check box forces objects that you create or insert to be aligned on the grid points. A spreadsheet with a visible grid is shown in Figure 13.16.

FIGURE **13.15**

FIGURE **13.15**

The Grid tab of the Spreadsheet Options dialog box enables you to turn on a point grid to help you place objects in your spreadsheet.

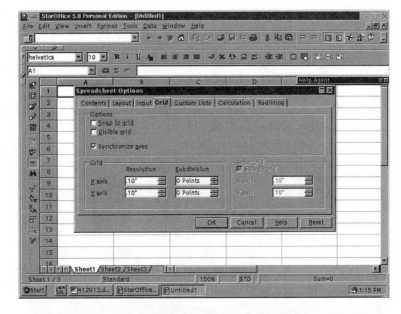

FIGURE **13.16**

A spreadsheet with a graphics grid can help you place objects such as charts and graphics files.

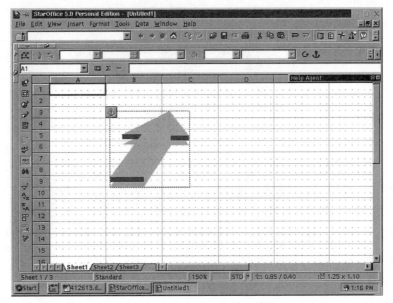

13

Setting Calculation Preferences

The Calculation tab of the Spreadsheet Options dialog box (shown in Figure 13.17) enables you to set how the formulas in your spreadsheet are to be calculated by StarOffice. These options refer to mathematical and alphanumeric operations.

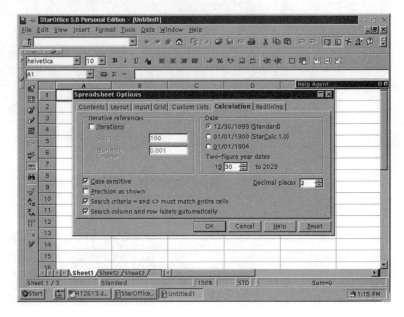

If you want to allow iterative formulas, check the Iterations check box. This enables self-referring formulas that reach a final value by a process of *iterating*—or refining—the cell value. The fields next to the Iterative check box determine how many times the formula iterates.

If the cell value doesn't change at least the amount in the Minimum Change value field, the iteration process stops. This keeps the formula from entering an *endless loop*.

The Date field is provided for compatibility with other programs or processes (including formulas) to which you might be accustomed. The difference in dating methods is only in where the dates begin. In the end, this isn't something that most users need to worry about.

The Decimal places field is the default number of decimal places to display in a cell. Of course, you can increase or decrease the number of decimal places displayed in any cell with a mouse click. This is just the default value for all cells.

Finally, the check boxes in the lower half of the dialog box are used for sorting and searching operations. They define how StarOffice determines the order of sorting, and which items qualify as matches for a search. This is a nice feature for manual searching or sorting.

> When you start doing macros (which are not covered in this book), it's critical that you understand how the sorting and searching operations are done, and that you can adjust them here. Otherwise, your programmed operations might not turn out as you had planned.

In the Next Hour

In the next hour, "Entering Spreadsheet Data," you begin navigating and entering data into your StarCalc spreadsheet. You learn how to cut, copy, and paste information in spreadsheet cells, as well as how to work with multiple named sheets (which are similar to pages) in a single spreadsheet.

13

Hour 14

Entering Spreadsheet Data

In this hour you learn how to enter data in the new spreadsheet you created in Hour 13, "Creating Spreadsheets with StarCalc." You'll learn how to enter numbers, navigate around the spreadsheet with a mouse or keyboard strokes, and select different blocks of cells to work on.

Navigating in StarCalc

If you've used other spreadsheet programs, moving around in StarOffice will be familiar to you. The following sections describe some specifics about how it's done.

Moving with the Mouse or Keyboard

The spreadsheet almost always has a certain cell that has *focus*. The cell with focus has a heavy black outline around it, and is the active cell in which the things that you type are entered.

You can move the focus around by using either the mouse or the keyboard, as follows:

- **With the mouse**—Click on the cell that you want to focus. Most StarCalc operations affect the active cell—the one with focus. You can also use the mouse with the scroll bars to quickly move to a distant point in the spreadsheet.
- **With the keyboard**—You can use the four arrow keys to move the focus to a new cell. This can be quicker than the mouse for small distances, but time-consuming in large spreadsheets. You can also use the PageDown and PageUp keys to move a screen down (to rows with higher numbers) or up, respectively.

As has been said before, some people like to use the keyboard for everything, and some prefer to use the mouse rather than memorize strange key combinations. Use of the mouse with the scroll bars is straightforward. For keyboard fans, however, Table 14.1 shows some additional navigational clues.

Some Linux window managers might not allow the Alt and Ctrl key combinations shown in Table 14.1 to work correctly. See the documentation for your window manager if you have trouble with these.

TABLE 14.1   KEY COMBINATIONS TO NAVIGATE AROUND A STAROFFICE SPREADSHEET

Key combination	Action
Ctrl+PageDown	Go to the next sheet (for example, from Sheet1 to Sheet2)
Ctrl+PageUp	Go to the previous sheet (for example, from Sheet2 to Sheet1)
Alt+PageDown	Go right one screen (increasing the current column from A to K, for example)
Alt+PageUp	Go left one screen
Alt+*any arrow key*	Change the width or height of the current row or column (not all selected areas—you'll see that later)
Home	Go to the far left (column A), but don't move up or down in the sheet
Ctrl+Home	Go to the top left corner (cell A1) of the current sheet

Understanding Cell References

Spreadsheets are basically large electronic worksheets. In order to use them effectively, you need a consistent method to refer to any point on the sheet.

You're probably familiar with the idea of using numbers for rows (down the left edge of the spreadsheet) and letters for columns (across the top edge of the spreadsheet).

It's also important to know how to refer to a cell so that you can work with spreadsheets later in this hour—and later in this book.

A simple cell reference consists of the column and row, as follows (always put the letter first; capital letters are traditionally used):

D13

If you enter this cell reference in a calculation formula, and then move things around, StarOffice updates this cell reference according to where you move things. It can be complicated, but that's the basic idea.

On the other hand, if you enter the following cell reference

D13

StarOffice never updates the reference, even if you insert columns or rows, move blocks of cells, and so on. For this reason, using the dollar signs within a cell reference makes this an *absolute* reference.

> You can also use an absolute reference for just one part of the reference, such as $D13. This way, the row can change if you have to move things down, but the column remains as D.

You can refer to a block of cells by placing a colon between two cell references:

D13:Z45

Finally, you can refer to different sheets by placing the sheet name, followed by a period:

$sheet1.$F$15

You'll learn more about using multiple sheets a little later in this hour.

Naming a Cell or Range

If you're working on a large spreadsheet, even the mouse and keyboard navigation can be less than precise. By naming a cell or a range of cells, you can jump to a precise location in your spreadsheet with one click.

The idea behind naming a cell is to assign human-readable words to a location such as the top of the balance sheet; you can then go directly to Balance Sheet instead of fumbling through thousands of cells looking for it.

14

The following steps show you how to name a cell or block of cells and then jump to them at any time:

1. Select a cell to be the named point to which to jump, or select a group of cells.

> Selecting a range of cells is described in the next section, but it's often just as easy to select the cell in the upper left corner of the area to which you want to jump.

2. Select Names from the Insert menu. Choose Define from the Names submenu. The Define Names dialog box is shown in Figure 14.1, with the cell or cells that you selected listed in the Refers to field.

FIGURE 14.1

In the Define Names dialog box you can assign names to cells or blocks of cells for easy reference.

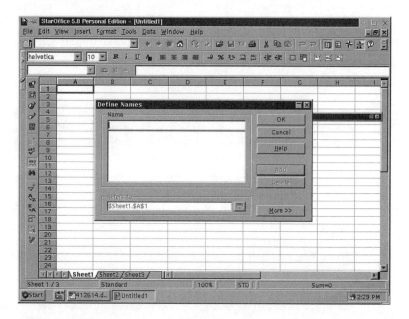

3. In the Name field, enter a name such as Balance Sheet or Summary for the area to which you want to jump.

4. Choose OK. You've now defined a name for the cell or cells that you selected in Step 1.

5. Press Ctrl+Home to jump to the top left corner of the spreadsheet (so that you can test the Name you just created).

6. From the Edit menu, choose Navigator (or press F5). The Navigator window appears, as shown in Figure 14.2.

FIGURE **14.2**

The Navigator window can be used to select a named area to which to move.

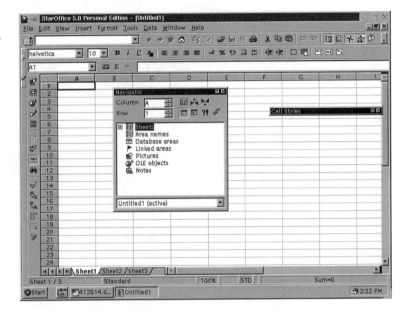

7. Click on the plus sign (+) next to the Area Names item in the Navigator window. The name that you enter appears on the list.

8. Double-click on the name in the Navigator window. The focus jumps to the cell or cells that you entered for that name.

9. Click in the spreadsheet. Notice that you can leave the Navigator window open while you work in the spreadsheet.

In the next section, you'll see some tricks for selecting parts of the spreadsheet.

Selecting a Range of Cells

As you work with a spreadsheet in StarOffice, you'll often want to select a large block of cells in order to print it, give it a name, format it, or perform some other operation on it.

The easiest way to select a block of cells is to click on one corner of it with the mouse and drag the mouse to the other corner. All the cells in that area are highlighted in black, indicating that they are selected (see Figure 14.3).

14

FIGURE 14.3

When you select a block of cells by dragging the mouse, they're highlighted in black.

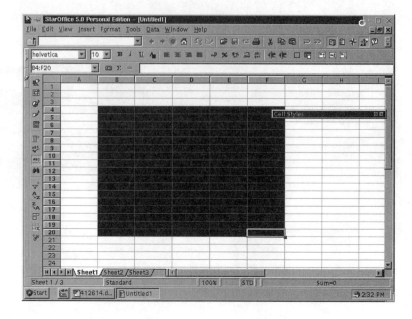

You can also use the keyboard to select a block of cells. Whether the mouse or the keyboard is faster depends on how large the block is and how well you type.

To select a block with the keyboard, hold down the Shift key while using other keys to expand the selected area. Keys that you can use while holding down Shift include

- All four arrow keys
- PageUp and PageDown
- Alt+PageUp and Alt+PageDown

Selecting Rows or Columns

Sometimes you'll want to select an entire row or an entire column. For example, if you have a long list of figures that you want to format as currency (with dollar signs), the easiest way to do it is to select the entire column and then choose a formatting option.

You can select an entire row by clicking on the row label. You can select an entire column by clicking on the column label. Any actions that you take (formatting, changing width, and so on) apply to every cell in the row or column that you've selected (see Figure 14.4).

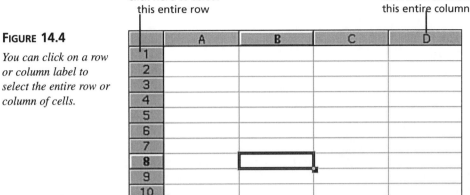

FIGURE 14.4

You can click on a row or column label to select the entire row or column of cells.

Click here to select this entire row

Click here to select this entire column

Working with Sheets

Although you've seen how to move rapidly all over your spreadsheet, it can still make more sense to split your information across several sheets that are part of a single spreadsheet file.

For example, suppose you're preparing a company budget. All the information is related, but rather than scroll all over a large spreadsheet to find items and check formulas, you can place each division's expected revenues and expenses on a separate sheet. The first sheet can be used to summarize the information on all the other sheets.

StarOffice provides this capability. The default new spreadsheet that opens includes three sheets. You can rename these sheets or add additional sheets as needed.

In addition, you can use features such as hiding sheets to arrange and protect the information on each sheet.

Naming a Sheet

When you start a new spreadsheet, the three sheets are named Sheet1, Sheet2, and Sheet3. This is straightforward, but not very descriptive. If you want to change the name of a sheet, follow these steps:

1. Go to the sheet that you want to rename by either clicking on its tab (see Figure 14.5) or pressing Ctrl+PageDown.

14

FIGURE 14.5

Each sheet has a tab that you can use to view that sheet.

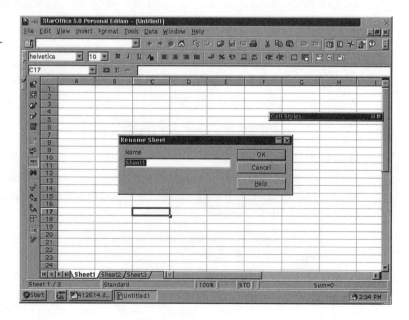

> If the sheets' tabs aren't visible, choose Options on the Tools menu, and then choose Spreadsheet options. In the Layout tab of the dialog box, check Sheet Tabs in the Window options area.

2. From the Format menu, select Sheet.

3. From the Sheet submenu, choose Rename. The Rename Sheet dialog box appears (see Figure 14.6).

FIGURE 14.6

The Rename Sheet dialog box enables you to assign a name to any sheet in your spreadsheet.

4. Enter the name that you want to use for this sheet.

5. Choose OK.

The name that you enter appears on the sheet tab at the bottom of the spreadsheet.

Adding Another Sheet

On many occasions, you'll want to add another sheet beyond the three provided by default. StarOffice enables you to add more sheets, as long as you have enough system resources to work with them.

To add another sheet to the spreadsheet you're viewing, follow these steps:

> If you have Document protection turned on (in the Protect Document sub-menu under Tools), you can't insert a sheet. Turn it off so that the insert sheet menu item is available.

1. Choose Sheet from the Insert menu. The Insert Sheet dialog box appears as in Figure 14.7.

FIGURE 14.7

The Insert Sheet dialog box enables you to add another sheet to your spreadsheet.

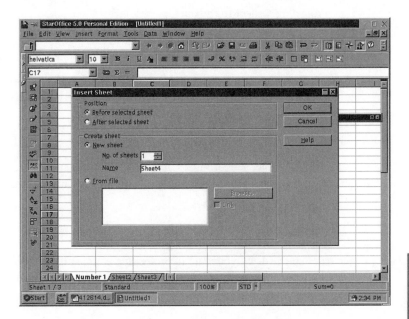

14

2. Enter a name for the new sheet in the Name field.

 If you have another spreadsheet file that you want to insert in this spreadsheet, choose From file and then click the Browse button to select a file from the file browsing dialog box.

3. Choose OK.

The new sheet appears to the left of the currently active sheet, with the name you entered shown on the sheet tab.

Protecting a Sheet

The security features of StarOffice enable you to protect your information both from prying eyes and from accidents caused by user error (for example, if you accidentally delete or change something).

You can protect information in your spreadsheet in several ways, including

- Hiding a sheet from view without password protection
- Protecting a sheet from being altered
- Protecting specific cells in a sheet from being altered
- Preventing certain cells from being printed when the spreadsheet is printed

You can easily hide a sheet from view. Choose Sheet from the Format menu, and then choose Hide from the Sheet submenu. The current sheet immediately disappears.

To see that sheet again, choose Show from the same submenu and select the sheet that you hid.

As another example, suppose that you have a spreadsheet containing sales figures. Those sales numbers are reality, but you want to experiment with a formula to see how certain actions will affect future sales.

All the cells in a StarOffice spreadsheet are marked as read-only by default. That is, when you turn Sheet Protection on, you can't modify any cells in the spreadsheet. For your sales spreadsheet, you want to protect the entire spreadsheet so that you don't alter the sales figures, but you want to leave a few cells unprotected so that you can experiment with a formula or two.

Follow these steps to unprotect a few of the cells in your spreadsheet so that they can be modified even when the Sheet Protection is On (to protect the rest of the sheet):

1. Start by entering information in several cells of your spreadsheet.

2. Select the cells that you want to modify when Sheet Protection is turned On.

3. Choose Cells from the Format menu and select the Cell Protection tab (see Figure 14.8).

FIGURE 14.8

The Cell Protection tab provides several options for protecting your data.

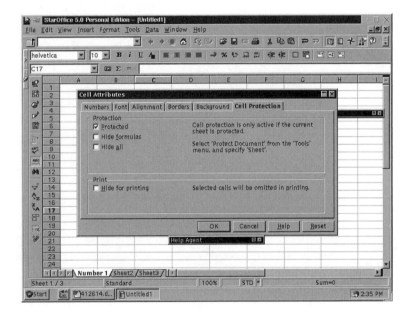

4. Uncheck the Protected checkbox.

5. Choose OK.

6. Under the Tools menu, select Protect Document, and then choose Sheet from the submenu that appears. The Protect Sheet dialog box appears (see Figure 14.9), where you can enter a password for the sheet.

When you enter a password, the same dialog box appears a second time. You must reenter the password to confirm that you have typed it correctly.

14

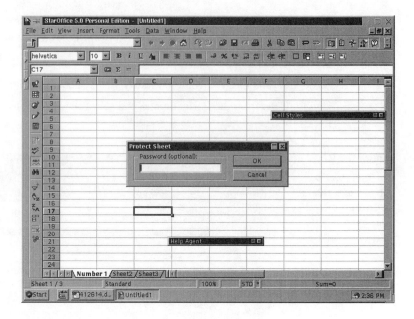

FIGURE 14.9

You can password protect a sheet, or you can choose to use no password.

7. Notice that the password is optional. If you don't want to use a password, just press Enter.

The entire spreadsheet is now protected (that is, it is read-only), except for the cells that you selected and unprotected. You can enter data in those cells, but you can't alter any other cells in the spreadsheet; a message tells you that you can't alter a protected cell (see Figure 14.10).

Think of Cell Protection (from the Cell Attributes dialog box under the Format menu) as an attribute of each cell that can be turned on or off. It's on by default for all the cells of a spreadsheet. You can activate protection for all the cells that have that attribute by choosing Sheet Protection from the Tools menu.

With the cells protected, you won't accidentally alter them.

| If you used a password to protect the sheet, you have to enter that password before you can turn off sheet protection. |

FIGURE 14.10

*StarOffice prevents you
from altering protected
cells.*

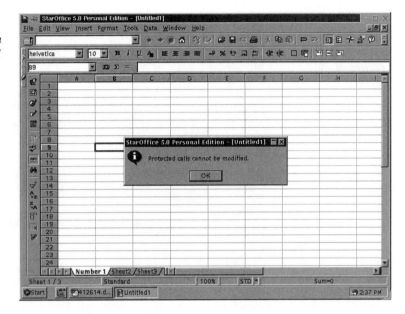

FIGURE 14.10

*StarOffice prevents you
from altering protected
cells.*

Use a password for sheet protection when several people are working with or viewing your file. This prevents them from changing things when they don't know any better, or from changing things on purpose to make the numbers look better.

Hiding Cells

You can even use protection to hide information in your spreadsheet so that it isn't visible onscreen.

Suppose your spreadsheet has everyone's salary as part of the expenses categories. You want everyone to review the spreadsheet, but they don't need to see the salary information.

From the Cell Protection tab of the Cell Attributes dialog box under the Format menu, you can select the Hide All checkbox to make cells invisible (see Figure 14.11). This assumes that the spreadsheet isn't already protected, in which case you can't even use this dialog box.

If you hide information, be sure to use a password when you turn on sheet protection; otherwise, everyone can turn off sheet protection and view the hidden information!

14

FIGURE 14.11

You can hide cells so that they don't appear onscreen at all.

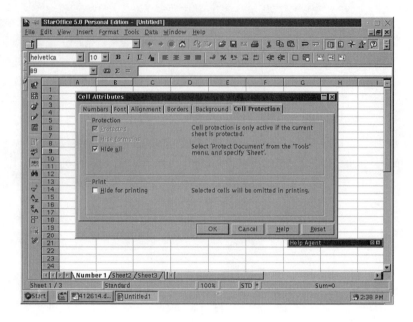

 If you need to use cell and sheet protection, experiment a little before handing out proprietary information to others.

Entering Data in Your Spreadsheet

Hours 15, "Using Formulas, Functions, and Names," and 16, "Formatting Your Spreadsheet," provide more detailed information on entering spreadsheet data. In this hour, however, you'll being entering basic numbers and dates, and you'll see how text can be formatted.

Entering Numbers, Dates and Text

You can enter information in a StarOffice spreadsheet just as you do in a word processor; the only difference is that you enter it one cell at a time.

Each time you type information into a cell, StarOffice examines what you enter and determines what type of data it is. Hour 15 provides more information about formulas; to begin, though, here are a few rules that you'll see StarOffice following as you enter data:

- If you enter text, StarOffice capitalizes the first letter and uses left justification within the cell.

You can turn off Capitalization as part of the AutoCorrect feature. See Hour 12, "Using Spellcheck and the Thesaurus."

- If you enter a number, StarOffice displays it right-justified with the default two digits after the decimal, if they are present.
- If you enter a date—or anything that StarOffice can recognize as a date— StarOffice displays it in a standard format and marks the cell as containing a date (this affects the operations that can be done on that cell).

There is one important point about entering numbers: Although the display formatting constrains how numbers are shown in the spreadsheet, the cell actually stores the full number that you enter. Try the following experiment:

1. Open a new spreadsheet so that the default settings apply.
2. Click in a cell so that you can enter a number.
3. Enter the following number (or another one with several decimal places):

   `45.149874`
4. Press Enter. The focus moves to the next cell down, but notice how the number in the cell is rounded to two decimal places:

   `45.15`
5. Press the up arrow key once to return the focus to the cell where you entered the number.
6. Look at the input line above the cells and notice that it still contains the full number you entered (see Figure 14.12).

The Input line shows
the complete contents
of the current cell.

FIGURE 14.12

Numbers are displayed according to formatting rules, but they are stored with their full precision.

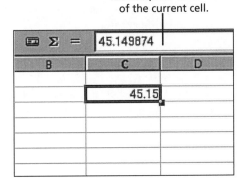

14

This is the important point: When you refer to a cell in a formula, the full number is used in calculations—not the rounded number that might be displayed on screen. This means that your calculations are accurate no matter how you format cells. (Cell formatting is described in Hour 16.)

Cutting, Pasting, and Moving

As with information in a word processor, information in spreadsheet cells can be deleted, copied, and pasted. The difference is that data in spreadsheets is more structured, and therefore has more rules and possibilities attached to it.

When you're working in a spreadsheet, you can use several methods to delete things. When you have a block of cells full of information, you can

- Delete the contents of the cells, so that they are all empty. Use the Delete key or the Delete Contents item on the Edit menu. You can also use the Undo item from the Edit menu to reverse a delete operation.

- Delete the contents of the cells by pressing the backspace key. This method doesn't use a confirmation dialog box; it simply clears the cell contents.

- Delete the contents of the cells and place them in the paste buffer, as if you were using cut and paste in a word processor. Use the Cut item on the Edit menu, or press Ctrl+X.

- Delete the cells from the spreadsheet so that other cells, which might have other numbers in them, move up or over to fill the space in the spreadsheet left by the deletion. Use the Delete Cells option on the Edit menu.

If you want to copy information, you can use Copy from the Edit menu, or the Ctrl+C key combination. This is similar to the Cut operation, except that the cell contents are not deleted.

Spreadsheets contain different types of information, such as labels (text), numbers, and formulas that resolve (calculate) into numbers (values). Because of this, you can paste information into cells using several different rules.

When you paste cells that you have cut or copied, you can decide exactly which pieces of the structured spreadsheet information you want to place in the new location.

To see how this works, select some cells and press Ctrl+C to place them in the buffer. Then select Paste Special from the Edit menu. The Paste Special dialog box appears (see Figure 14.13).

FIGURE 14.13

Pasting information can take many forms in the Paste Special dialog box.

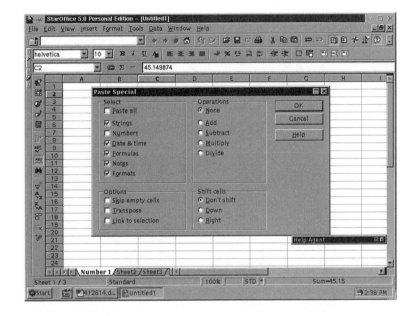

Notice that you can select which types of information are to be pasted into the cells at the current focus point in the spreadsheet.

> If you use Ctrl+V or the regular Paste item on the Edit menu, everything is pasted—without regard to the type of data being pasted.

The Paste Special command gives you control over what is pasted, how existing cells are shifted around, and other operations that can be performed during the paste operation.

In the Next Hour

In the next hour, you'll learn how to use formulas to calculate basic information in your spreadsheet. In addition, you'll learn about the functions available in StarOffice and see examples of using a few of the most popular ones.

14

HOUR 15

Using Formulas, Functions, and Names

In this hour you will learn about using formulas and functions to add useful information to your StarCalc spreadsheets. This hour explains the different functions available in StarOffice, as well as how to use calculation preferences to determine how those functions are used by StarOffice.

The formulas in a spreadsheet are what make it more useful than a pencil and paper. This hour demonstrates how to use simple formulas, and it shows several functions that you can use for regular and specialized applications.

Labels and Formulas

Every cell in a spreadsheet can contain one of the following three types of data:

- A number (digits that you enter in the cell)
- Text (called a label)
- A formula (something that requires computation by StarOffice to reach a value that is displayed)

Most of this hour discusses using formulas. *Formulas* are entered into a cell to make StarOffice calculate something. They're what gives a spreadsheet its real power.

Entering Cell References

In Hour 14, "Entering Spreadsheet Data," cells in a spreadsheet are defined as a letter-number combination that refer to a row and column in the spreadsheet. For example, one cell is

D13

or, using an absolute reference (of which you'll see an example in this hour), the same cell is

D13

A range of cells (a rectangular block) is referenced as follows:

D13:R55

Hour 14 also describes how to assign a name to a cell or a block of cells (a range). You'll use ranges later in this hour.

Entering Numbers and Labels

How does StarOffice determine what type of information a cell contains? A few simple rules are all it takes:

- If a cell contains only numbers (digits), it's a number.
- If a cell contains anything else (letters), it's a label.
- If a cell starts with an equal sign (=), it's a formula, and it needs to be evaluated to reach a value.

Open a new spreadsheet and enter some information to see how all this works:

1. Click on cell B5 to place the focus on that cell.
2. Type the word Sale and press Enter. Notice as you type that the information you type appears both in the cell (B5) and above all the cells on the Input Line (see Figure 15.1).
3. When you press Enter, the cursor moves to the cell below.

FIGURE 15.1

Information that you type is shown in the cell and on the Input Line.

You can change which direction the focus moves when you press Enter. Go to the Spreadsheet Options dialog box (choose Options under the Tools menu); the Input tab contains this option.

4. Now type the number 2450 (in cell B6, where you now are) and press Enter.

5. Repeat this process, selecting any numbers you want, to enter numbers in the next four cells. The spreadsheet looks similar to Figure 15.2, with a total of five numbers entered in a column.

FIGURE 15.2

A new spreadsheet with a label and a few numbers entered.

By starting with this type of information, you can experiment with some formulas. First, however, you need to know how to edit a cell.

Editing a Cell

Often, you'll need to return to a cell in which you've previously entered information and make a change.

If you move the focus to a cell and start typing, you'll erase the contents of the cell and replace them with what you're typing. This can be a waste of time if you want to preserve most of the cell's contents.

You have to tell StarOffice that you want to edit the cell contents instead of replacing them. To do this, press the F2 key. You'll see that the focus outline around the current cell disappears, and a cursor appears in the cell.

You can also double-click on a cell to begin editing its contents.

When you've finished editing the cell contents, press Enter or click the mouse pointer in another cell.

In the next section you start using formulas. When you press F2 to edit a cell that contains a formula, the formula, rather than the number that was calculated from the formula, is displayed for you to edit.

Entering Formulas

A *formula cell* is any cell in which StarOffice must do some calculation before displaying a numeric or text value.

To place a formula in a StarOffice cell, start your entry in the cell with an equal sign (=). A formula can be simple math, such as the following:

=4*5

The cell that contained this formula displays

20

Of course, that formula doesn't serve much purpose in a spreadsheet because it is much easier to just enter the result. To make a formula useful, another cell is usually referred to, as follows:

```
=4*C55
```

The value displayed in the cell containing this formula depends on the value stored in cell C55. Because of the formula, the value of one cell is updated as the value in another cell changes. This is the power of a spreadsheet.

> The four basic math operations—addition, subtraction, multiplication, and division—can be used in any formula. In fact, you'll probably use them regularly as part of your formulas.

An example of a basic formula is to add the values of several cells. Click on cell B11 if it doesn't already have focus. Type the following:

```
=B6+B7+B8+B9+B10
```

When you press Enter, StarCalc adds together the four numbers that you entered in your sample spreadsheet and displays the total in cell B11.

Using Functions

Spreadsheets also provide a set of tools that make calculations a lot easier. These are called *functions*. A function takes a cell or a set of cells as a parameter, and does some calculation on those cells to produce a value.

The value produced by a function can be combined with other functions to reach a final cell value. All the calculation is done instantly by StarOffice.

Using Functions to Simplify Formulas

For example, look at the column of sales numbers and the sample formula that you just entered. The formula you entered is shown again here:

```
=B6+B7+B8+B9+B10
```

This works fine, but it's not ideal. What if you had a list of 50 numbers to add? Instead of listing all the cell references, you can use a StarOffice function called sum(), which adds together all the cells referred to as parameters of the function. That formula looks like the following:

```
=sum(B6:B10)
```

Using either formula, changing one of the values in cells B6 through B10 changes the total shown in cell B11. The recalculation is automatic. Using the sum() function, however, has advantages that will become apparent—advantages beyond being easier to type in.

Following is another example to show how useful functions can be.

Suppose you have prepared a spreadsheet of sales figures. Each time you open the spreadsheet for review and printing, you want it to contain a date and time stamp at the top of the spreadsheet. This indicates when that sheet was updated and printed.

You can enter a new date and timestamp each time you open the spreadsheet, or you can place the following formula in a cell somewhere in the spreadsheet:

=now()

Now, each time you open or recalculate the spreadsheet, the now() function inserts the current date and time into that cell (see Figure 15.3).

FIGURE 15.3

The now() *function can be used to insert the current date and time in a cell each time you open or recalculate the spread-sheet.*

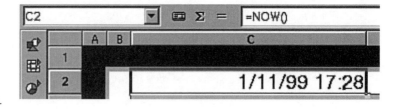

> If your columns are too narrow to display the complete result of a formula, you'll see something such as ####. Click on the border of the column heading and drag the column so that it's a little wider, and you can view the result.

Finding Functions

When you begin using StarOffice to create complex spreadsheets, you might not know which functions are available to get the results you want. The sum() function is probably the most used function, but beyond that, how do you find and use the right function?

The answer is the StarOffice Function AutoPilot. By using this tool, you can review a list of functions by category, choose the one that you think fits your needs, and then review what the function does and be guided to enter the correct parameters to make it work correctly.

15

For example, suppose you are working with the list of sales figures that you entered previously. You want to know some information beyond the sum of the column of figures.

If you want to know the average daily sales (assuming each cell was a day's sales), for example, you can use the following procedure to find and use the correct formula:

1. Click on cell A12 and type Daily Average.

2. Click on cell B12 (where you want the Average figure stored).

3. Choose Function from the Insert menu. The Function AutoPilot dialog box appears (see Figure 15.4).

FIGURE 15.4

The Function AutoPilot dialog box helps you choose and then enter parameters for any StarOffice function.

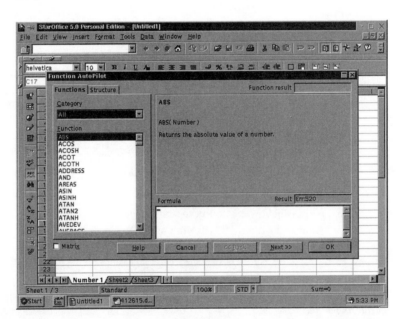

4. Select a category for the function that you want to use. You won't always know immediately, but assume that the averaging functions are part of the statistical category.

With Statistical selected in the Category list, only the statistical functions are displayed in the Function list.

If the cell with focus was empty when you launched the Function AutoPilot, a description appears to the right of the Function list when you click on a Function name (see Figure 15.5).

FIGURE 15.5

The Function AutoPilot shows a description of any function that you select.

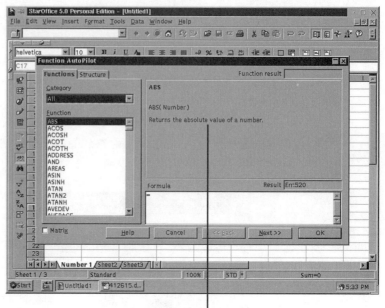

Function description

5. Sometimes you'll need to review several descriptions to see which function best fits your needs. This time the answer is obvious: Click on the AVERAGE function.

6. With AVERAGE selected in the Function list, click on the Next>> button. The parameter entry dialog box for the AVERAGE function appears (see Figure 15.6).

FIGURE 15.6

The Function AutoPilot guides you in entering all the parameters needed to make the selected function work correctly.

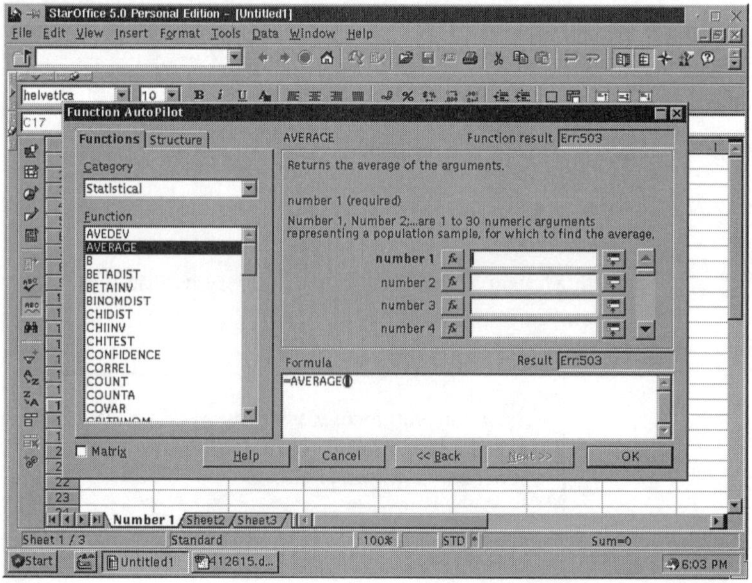

Notice that the description in the dialog box above the field names includes information about the current parameter field. When you move to the next parameter field, the description is updated to tell you about it.

7. You want to calculate the average of a single range of numbers. In the first field, number1, type

   b6:b10

Notice that the Result field shows you what the result will be as you enter the cell range in the number1 field. Refer to this area to see that the results you're programming with the selected function don't leave common sense behind.

8. Because you don't have any other numbers to add to this average, press OK to close this dialog box and insert the completed function into the spreadsheet at the current cell location.

Each of the functions listed in the Function AutoPilot dialog box includes the descriptive information and parameter fields to help you use the functions correctly.

Editing a Function

You already learned how you can press F2 or double-click on a cell to edit the contents of that cell, including cells that contain a formula you've entered.

The Function AutoPilot has a partner dialog box called the Edit Function dialog box that can help you edit any function.

Suppose that you entered the AVERAGE function example described previously, and now you need to update the cell references to include a second block of cells.

If you've forgotten the format of the function parameters, you can click on the cell containing the AVERAGE() function, and then choose Function from the Insert menu.

StarOffice detects that the cell already contains a function. The Function AutoPilot dialog box is opened and the function is displayed, as in Figure 15.7.

FIGURE 15.7

When started in a cell containing a function, the Function AutoPilot dialog box helps you update a function that you've already entered.

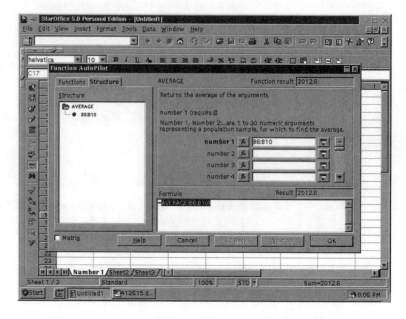

The cell references that were part of the selected formula are contained in the first field. You can enter other cell references and read the helpful description of how the function is used.

When you're finished, choose OK to close the dialog box with the updated function.

Using the Mouse to Enter Cell References

StarOffice provides another handy way to enter function information, instead of typing in cell references or using the Function AutoPilot dialog box. You can also use the mouse to drag across an area of cells that you want to use in a function.

Using the mouse can be confusing at first, but it's a very convenient feature after you're comfortable with it. The following example uses the same list of sales figures that you worked on for the previous examples, but erase the sum and average formulas that you entered previously before trying this example:

1. Click on cell B11, where the column total is displayed.

2. Type this much of the sum( ) function in the cell, but don't press Enter:
   =sum(

3. Click and hold the mouse button on the bottom cell in the list of sales figures (B10).

15

4. Drag the mouse pointer up to the top of the list of sales figures (cell B6). Notice that the block of cells is outlined in red, and that the cell range reference appears in the sum() function shown in cell B11 (see Figure 15.8).

Outline shows cells selected
for use in the formula

FIGURE 15.8

You can use the mouse to drag around a block of cells that you want to use as a parameter in a function.

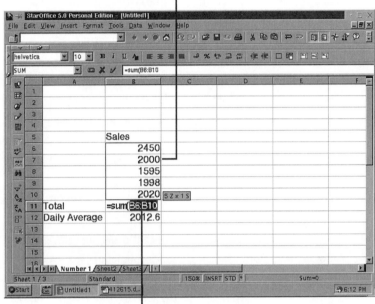

Formula updated to
show selection

5. Release the mouse button and end the operation by pressing) to close the sum() function.

6. This formula is finished, so press Enter. The cell value is calculated. You can add other things to this formula instead of pressing Enter if you need to.

You can also use the keyboard arrows with Shift to select a block of cells while entering a formula, but it's a little more confusing than using the mouse.

You can use this mouse-dragging technique for any function that uses a cell reference as a parameter, or even for regular math operations in a formula. You can either click on a cell to enter a single cell reference, or click and drag to enter a range of cells.

Recalculating Your Spreadsheet

When you enter formulas in your spreadsheet, the values that are calculated from those formulas can change continually as you enter new information in the other cells of the spreadsheet.

StarOffice automatically recalculates everything in your spreadsheet as you enter new or revised numbers in cells. StarOffice determines which cells need to be recalculated by watching which cells you enter numbers in.

If you've entered a large spreadsheet, however, with many complex formulas, you might find that the constant recalculation slows down your work with StarOffice. This is especially true if you use a lot of financial or mathematical functions with large numbers of cells.

You can turn the auto-calculate feature off so that StarOffice waits for explicit instructions before recalculating the spreadsheet.

To turn off the auto-calculate, select Cell Contents from the Tools menu, and then choose AutoCalculate from the Cell Contents submenu. This feature is unchecked, and the spreadsheet is no longer recalculated until you explicitly request a recalculation.

With AutoCalculate turned off, you can give the command to recalculate by choosing Recalculate from the Cell Contents submenu (under the Tools menu).

Press F9 at any time to recalculate the spreadsheet.

Using More Advanced Functions

In this section, you'll see an example of a financial function provided by StarOffice. The functions that are part of StarOffice include specialized scientific and complex mathematical functions that will meet almost any calculating need that you might have in a spreadsheet. (When was the last time you needed to calculate an arctangent?)

Many of the advanced functions require that you have a spreadsheet set up with certain information as background. A less-involved function is used as an example to show you the power of these functions.

Using a Financial Function

15

Suppose you want a little mortgage calculator spreadsheet to help you decide how much you can afford for a house that you want to purchase.

Set up a few fields to fill in for principal, number of years in the loan, and annual interest rate. The payment field has been left so that you can calculate it using a spreadsheet function.

You can arrange this in several different ways. For this example, keep changing the principal and interest rates until you see a payment that you can handle. The cell information that you'll enter will look similar to Figure 15.9. The numbers shown here were actually typed in, not computed using any formulas.

FIGURE 15.9

The fields for a sample financial calculation include principal, interest rate, and time.

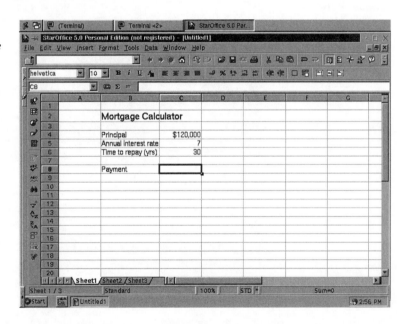

 You'll learn how to do the currency and boldface formatting in Hour 16, "Formatting Your Spreadsheet."

Use a principal amount of $120,000 for the loan. This example estimates that you can get the loan for 7.0 percent annual interest, and assumes that you're planning for a 30-year loan.

Now you can use a function to calculate the payment:

1. Click on cell C8, to the right of the Payment label.

2. Choose Function from the Insert menu.

3. Select Financial from the Category list in the Function Autopilot dialog box.

4. Select PMT from the Function list.

5. Choose the Next>> button. The dialog box containing the required fields appears (see Figure 15.10).

FIGURE 15.10

The fields for the PMT function can be entered in this screen of the Function AutoPilot dialog box.

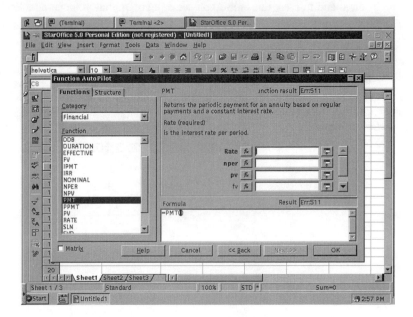

6. Move the dialog box to a place on your screen so that you can see the cells you've already entered (as in the previous figure).

7. The description of the Rate field tells us that this is the rate per period, which means monthly because you're making monthly payments. Type this in the Rate field (changing the cell number of the Interest rate value, if necessary, to match your screen). Don't press Enter yet or the Function AutoPilot will close prematurely.

(C5/100)/12

Dividing by 100 makes the interest rate (7) into a percentage (.07). Dividing by 12 makes it a monthly rate instead of an annual rate.

15

8. Move to the nper field of the dialog box. This is the number of payments. Because you have a 30-year mortgage planned, this is 30*12. But to make it interesting, click on the cell in your spreadsheet that contains 30 (C6). The cell reference appears in the nper field. Now add *12 to the cell reference so that it says something similar to the following:

C6*12

9. Move to the PV, or principal value, field of the dialog box.

10. Click on the principal value cell in the spreadsheet (on the number 120,000, cell C4). The cell reference appears in the field.

11. Move to the FV, or Future Value, field and enter 0 (the bank wants the loan paid off at the end of this exercise).

12. Choose OK to close the Function Autopilot dialog box, with the function completed. The payment, computed by the function, appears next to the Payment label, in cell C8 (see Figure 15.11).

FIGURE 15.11

The PMT function provides the mortgage payment based on other information in the function.

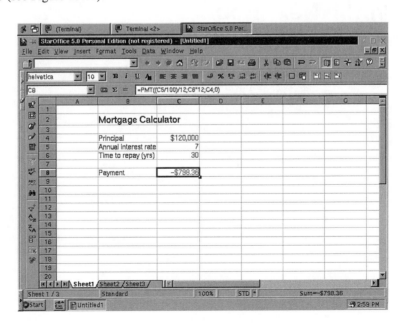

In mortgage calculations, the principal value and the payment always have opposite signs (one negative and one positive) to indicate that you receive one and pay the other. Therefore, the PMT value is a negative number.

13. Try changing the principal value and see how the Payment changes.

 If you've switched automatic recalculation off, remember that you'll need to manually recalculate each time you make a change in order for the correct result to appear.

 From the fields in this example, it's obvious that you have to know something about how to use a complex function before it can work well, even with the Function AutoPilot to guide you. Be careful using functions until you understand them well.

In the Next Hour

Now you know how to enter lots of useful data in a StarCalc spreadsheet. The next hour describes how to make the spreadsheet look attractive. Formatting cells is described, both for type format and numerical format. You'll learn how to adjust sizes of rows and columns, and even to insert or delete rows and columns as you edit spreadsheets that you've created.

HOUR 16

Formatting Your Spreadsheet

In this hour, you will learn how to change the formatting of your spreadsheet.

The look of a StarCalc spreadsheet is almost as flexible as a StarWriter document. This hour describes how to set text attributes such as boldface, colors, and currency style. In addition, you'll learn how to add and delete rows and columns, and to use some other StarOffice features that make viewing and arranging your spreadsheet more convenient.

Changing Fonts and Sizes

When you write a report, you use headlines, special fonts, and italic and bold text to help get your point across. A spreadsheet is no different. The information that you are communicating needs to be easy to access and appealing—even attractive.

The best way to start making your spreadsheet attractive is to set up the fonts and text attributes that make information easier to locate and read.

When you're viewing a spreadsheet, most of the text formatting options you'll use are included in the Object Bar (see Figure 16.1).

The Object Bar has the formatting options that you'll use the most.

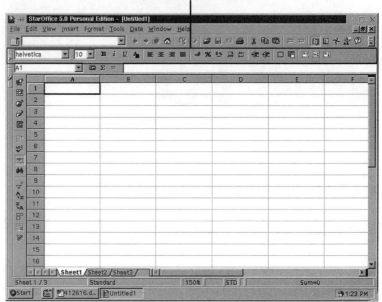

Included in the Object bar are the following text formatting options:

- Font name
- Font size
- Bold/Italic/Underline
- Justification (Center, Left, Right)
- Vertical alignment (Top, Center, Bottom)
- Number format (common options; others are selected via menu options)
- Border type and background colors
- Decimal places

All these formatting options can be set using menu items in the Format menu, but the Object toolbar provides a quick shortcut. In the sections that follow, you'll learn how to work with these formatting options.

Formatting Cell by Cell

Formatting in a text document can be for a word, a paragraph, a page, or an entire document. Different formatting options apply to different areas of the document.

In Hour 13, "Creating Spreadsheets with StarCalc," you learned about printing a spreadsheet and setting options such as margins and page headers.

Almost everything else in a spreadsheet is formatted on a cell-by-cell basis. That is, all the choices that you make apply to one or more individual cells. When you select a column and apply a formatting option, you're really applying that option to each cell in the column, and not to the column itself.

16

> There isn't much time to talk about it here, but cells can also use Styles, as described in Hour 9, "Using Advanced Formatting Tools." This means that you can apply several formatting options to a cell at one time by assigning it a named style.

Setting a Font and Size

Suppose that you want to make headlines for the main column headings in your spreadsheet. You might have a spreadsheet similar to the one in Figure 16.2.

FIGURE 16.2.

A spreadsheet often needs its column headings highlighted for easy reading.

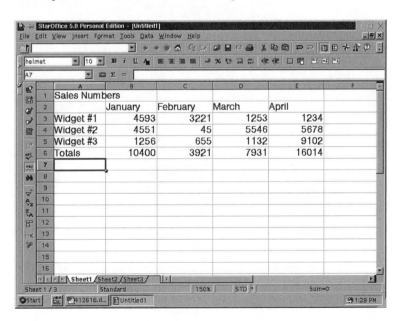

You can use your own spreadsheet for this example. To make the column headings more readable and attractive, follow these steps:

1. Click on the far left column heading, hold the mouse button down, and drag right to select the entire block of column headings (see Figure 16.3).

Figure 16.3

All the column headings can be formatted at one time by selecting the cells before selecting a formatting option.

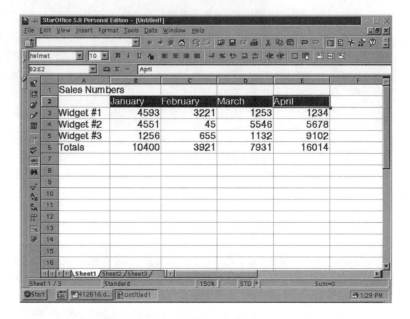

 You can also use the keyboard arrows while holding down the Shift key to select a block of cells.

2. In the Format menu, choose Cells.... The Cell Attributes dialog box appears. Choose the Font tab (see Figure 16.4).

3. Select a font from the list under the Font field in the dialog box.

4. Select a style from the list under the Style field.

5. Select a size from the list under the Size field. If you're viewing text in point sizes (you can set this in the Options dialog box), the common sizes for headlines range from 12 to 24 points.

6. Choose OK to close the dialog box and apply your choices to all the cells that were selected when you opened the dialog box (see Figure 16.5).

FIGURE 16.4.

Cell formatting options can be set in the Cell Attributes dialog box.

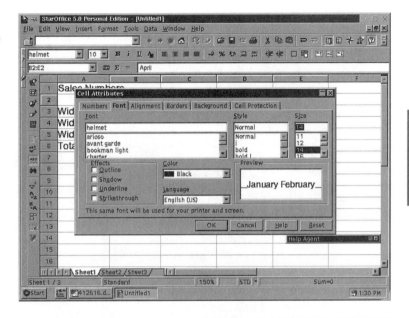

16

In the Preview window of the dialog box, the font you define by your choices is shown for your review.

FIGURE 16.5

A 14-point Helmet font is used for these head-lines.

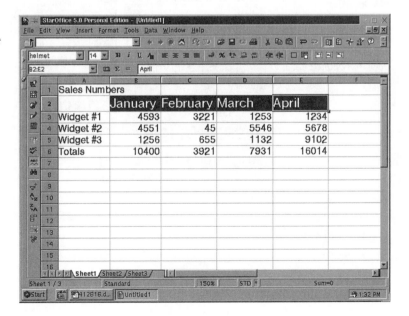

You can set all sorts of things in the Cell Attribute dialog box, as you'll see in a minute. But after you're familiar with what you can do, it's usually easier to use the Object toolbar. You can still format a group of cells at the same time by selecting them before choosing a formatting option. With the cells selected, you can use the Object toolbar for any of the following operations:

- Select a font from the drop-down list (see Figure 16.6).

FIGURE 16.6

A font can be chosen for selected cells from the drop-down list on the Object toolbar.

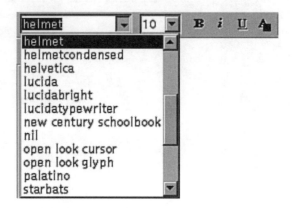

- Select a font size from the drop-down list (see Figure 16.7).

FIGURE 16.7

A font size can be chosen for selected cells from the drop-down list on the Object toolbar.

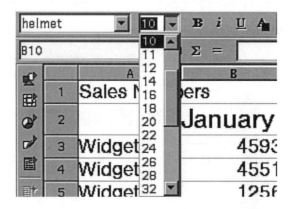

- Set a font as bold, italic, or underlined by clicking on the corresponding button (see Figure 16.8).

FIGURE 16.8

Bold, Italic, and Underline buttons are applied to any selected cells, or just to the cell with current focus.

Italic

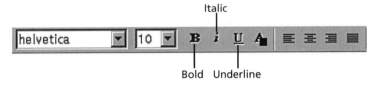

Bold Underline

16

- Set the justification for the selected cells to make them centered, right-, left-, or full- justified (both right- and left-justified). See Figure 16.9. You can also make them top, vertical center, or bottom aligned (see Figure 16.10).

FIGURE 16.9

Selected cells can be left-, center-, or right-justified using buttons on the Object bar.

Left   Center

Right   Full

FIGURE 16.10

Selected cells can also have their contents placed against the top or bottom of the cell border, or vertically centered in the cell.

Center

Top   Bottom

Knowing how to set justification on cells is important because StarOffice sets justification automatically to the right side for words and to the left side for numbers, which might not fit how you want them to look.

Remember, if you leave the mouse pointer over a button for a couple of seconds, a small pop-up help dialog box tells you what the button is used for.

Setting Number Formats in Cells

Formatting cells involves more than just the font and size of the numbers. Formatting also determines how numbers in cells are arranged according to the information they represent. For example, sales figures, scientific data, and baseball scores are all numbers. But they all look quite different.

Setting a number format for a cell determines how the number entered in that cell is displayed. StarOffice provides several convenient ways to select common formats, as well as more advanced features for less-used formats.

Using the Object Bar to Set Number Formats

For example, suppose you need to enter a set of sales numbers. You can enter a column of figures like the one shown in Figure 16.11.

FIGURE 16.11

A column of sales figures can be entered to represent dollar volumes.

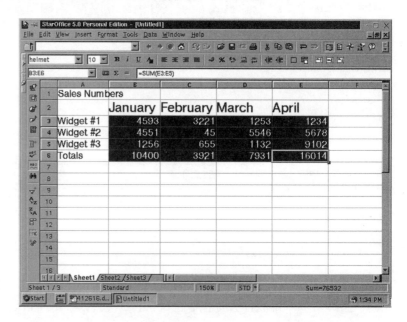

But these don't look much like sales figures. Select the cells in which you entered the sales numbers. Now press the "money" button (StarOffice calls it the Currency button, but we like our name better). It looks like a little stack of coins on the Object Bar (see Figure 16.12).

FIGURE 16.12

The Currency button formats cells as dollar amounts.

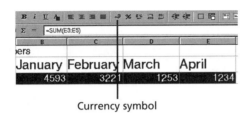

Currency symbol

The selected cells are immediately formatted with a dollar sign and two decimal places (see Figure 16.13).

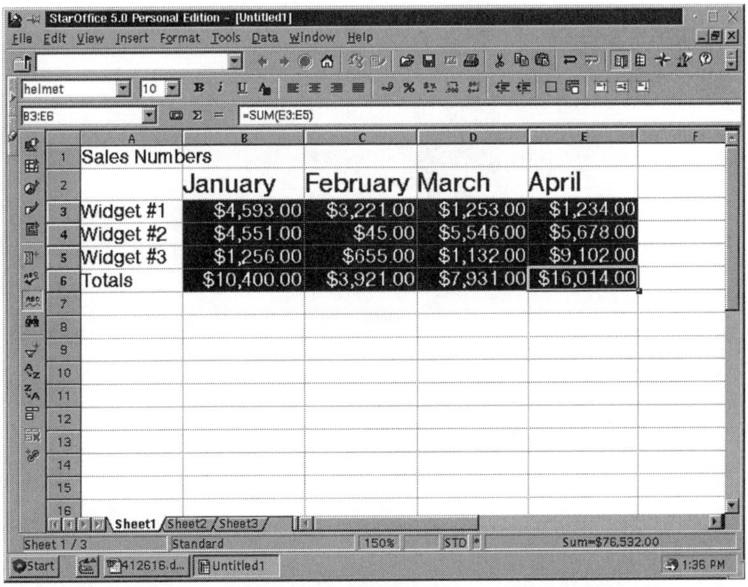

FIGURE 16.13

A column of numbers can be formatted as dollar amounts with the currency button on the Object bar.

16

A similar button, next to the Currency button, formats numbers as percentages (for example, .56 is displayed as 56.00%).

Adjusting Decimal Places

One feature of number formatting that you might want to adjust for many types of figures is how many decimal places are displayed.

Two buttons on the Object Bar increase or decrease the number of decimal places on all selected cells. These buttons are shown in Figure 16.14.

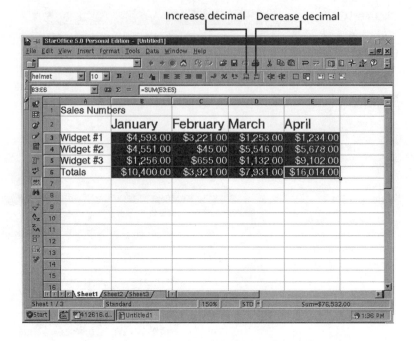

FIGURE 16.14

The number of decimal places can be increased or decreased from these buttons on the Object Bar.

For example, enter this number in a cell, press Enter, and then click on the cell to give it focus again:

45

Now press the Increase decimal button (the one on the left in Figure 16.14) three times. The cell displays

45.000

Now type this number in the cell, press Enter, and click on the cell to give it focus again:

45.724

When you press Enter, the cell immediately displays

45.72

because the default cell setting is for two decimal places. If you press the Decrease decimal button twice, the cell displays

46

Notice that the number is rounded, not just cut off. Pressing the Decrease decimal button again has no effect because these buttons only round below the decimal point.

Using the Number Formatting Dialog Box

All these number formatting operations on the Object bar are actually shortcuts for things you can do from the Cell Attributes dialog box.

Open the Cell Attributes dialog box by selecting Cells... from the Format menu, and then selecting the Numbers tab (see Figure 16.15). From this dialog box you can set many options for how numbers are displayed.

16

FIGURE 16.15

Numbers can be formatted in many different ways within the Numbers tab of the Cell Attributes dialog box.

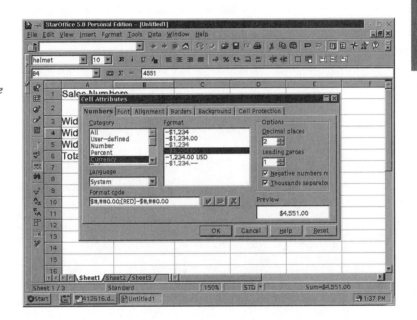

These options are as follows:

- The category field determines the overall characteristics of how the number in a cell is formatted, such as whether a percentage sign or dollar sign is included, or whether scientific notation is used.

- The Format field determines how digits and decimal places in that category are formatted, for example, how many decimal places are displayed, and how negative numbers are displayed.

- The Options section includes a field in which you can set the number of decimal places explicitly.

- A checkbox enables you to select whether negative numbers are displayed in red onscreen (and on a color printer if you have one).

As with other StarOffice dialog boxes, a Preview window shows you how the current cell looks when formatted with the current selections in the Numbers tab.

Adjusting and Inserting Rows and Columns

If you're like the rest of us, creating spreadsheets often includes discovering that you didn't leave enough space for your data, or that you left too much space between sections of your information.

Setting row height and column width enables you to fit the spreadsheet to the data that you've entered.

Inserting and removing rows and columns enables you to add or remove unused space to make your data fit the spreadsheet.

Adjusting Row Height and Column Width

Row height adjusts automatically to the tallest characters on the row. You can also adjust the height if you choose, however.

Column width, on the other hand, always has to be adjusted manually to accommodate longer numbers or text labels.

First, play with the row height. If you want to change the row height from the height that's automatically chosen, follow these steps:

1. Choose Row from the Format menu, and then Height from the Row submenu. The Height dialog box appears (see Figure 16.16).

2. Selecting default value changes the row height to the default of 0.19 inches.

3. Enter a new height value in the Height field.

4. Choose OK to apply the new height to the current row.

The Optimal Height dialog box enables you to add a little extra space to the automatic height of rows (based on font size). Choose Optimal Height from the Row submenu under the Format menu.

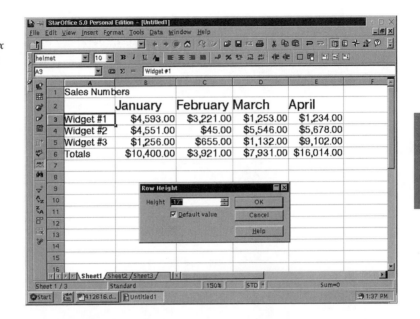

FIGURE 16.16

The Height dialog box enables you to adjust the row height as needed.

16

Setting column width to match the width of lines of text or numbers is more useful than setting new row heights. By setting the width to match your data, you can keep your spreadsheet looking good while also keeping track of how it will be printed (by using the Print Area and Fit to Page features).

If your columns aren't wide enough for the text that you enter in a cell, the text is simply cut off, often mid-character.

If your columns aren't wide enough for the numbers that you enter, or that are calculated from the formulas that you enter, StarOffice displays these characters in the cell:

###

The numbers are still stored in the cell, but you can't read them (onscreen or on paper) until you make the column wider. To see the value contained in an undersized cell, you must select that cell and read the Input line above the spreadsheet.

The easy method of adjusting the column width is to use the mouse. Follow these steps:

1. Move the mouse pointer to the right edge of the column letter label (see Figure 16.17).

FIGURE 16.17

Click on the right edge of the column label to adjust column width.

Click here to adjust the width of column B

	A	B	C	D	E	F
1	Sales Numbers					
2		January	February	March	April	
3	Widget #1	$4,593.00	$3,221.00	$1,253.00	$1,234.00	
4	Widget #2	$4,551.00	$45.00	$5,546.00	$5,678.00	
5	Widget #3	$1,256.00	$655.00	$1,132.00	$9,102.00	
6	Totals	$10,400.00	$3,921.00	$7,931.00	$16,014.00	

2. When the mouse pointer changes to a side-by-side double-headed arrow, click the mouse button and move it to the right for a wider column, or to the left for a narrower column.

A pop-up message tells you the width of the column as you resize it.

3. Release the mouse button.

If you select several columns before resizing, all the selected columns are resized to the same size.

Row height can be set in the same way by clicking and dragging on the row labels on the left edge of the screen.

Of course, using the mouse to adjust row and column size are only shortcuts. If you want to be precise, you can use the sizing dialog boxes under the Format menu. Choose either Row or Column and then Height (for Rows) or Width (for Columns). See Figure 16.18.

FIGURE 16.18

The Column Width dialog box enables you to reset the default width of a column or enter a specific numeric value for a column width.

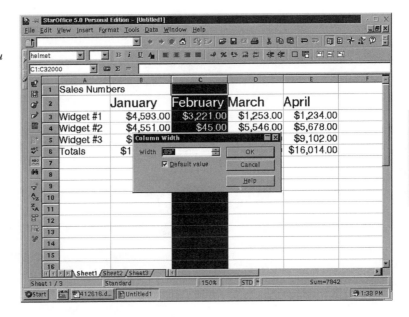

16

In the Height and Width dialog boxes, you can reset the size to the default value with the checkbox, or you can enter a specific numeric value for the size of the row or column.

As with the mouse-driven procedure, all the selected rows or columns are affected when you use these dialog boxes.

Inserting and Deleting Rows

Although you can use copy and paste functions to move data around in a StarCalc spreadsheet, sometimes the easiest thing to do is to insert a row or column, rather than try to move everything to a new location.

Inserting a row is basically like using Cut and Paste to move the entire spreadsheet down one line. But it's a lot easier to just insert a row. In fact, you can insert several rows in one operation to give yourself more room in a section of your spreadsheet.

This example uses the spreadsheet shown in Figure 16.19. This Figure shows the Movie3 file from the samples/spreadsheets folder in the Explorer. You can load it and follow along.

FIGURE 16.19

A spreadsheet like this one might need extra rows inserted to accommodate additional data.

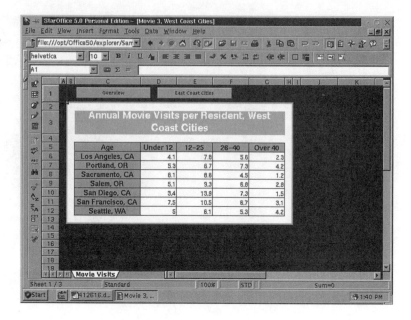

Suppose that you need to add information about several other cities to this table of movie statistics. You can insert additional rows by following these steps:

1. Click on the row label for row 9 (click on the 9).

2. Drag the mouse downward until three rows are selected (see Figure 16.20).

> You can also select a cell in each of three rows, such as cells C9, C10, and C11. But selecting the entire row makes the data easier to keep track of.

3. Choose Rows from the Insert menu. The bottom half of the table moves down to add three rows in the middle (see Figure 16.21).

Notice a couple of things about this operation:

- Formatting for the cells was maintained. This isn't always the case, but StarOffice tries to make the new rows look similar to the old rows.

- The row numbers changed for the lower part of the table. Any formulas you entered in the lower part of the table (in row 9 or higher) were automatically updated by adding three to the row number.

FIGURE 16.20

You select the number of rows that you want to insert.

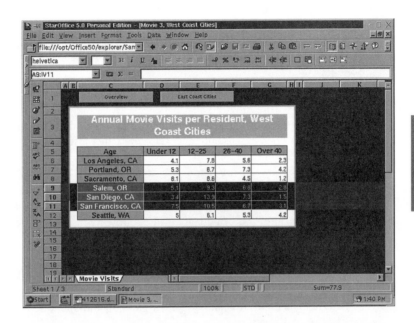

16

FIGURE 16.21

A table with three new rows inserted to accommodate additional information.

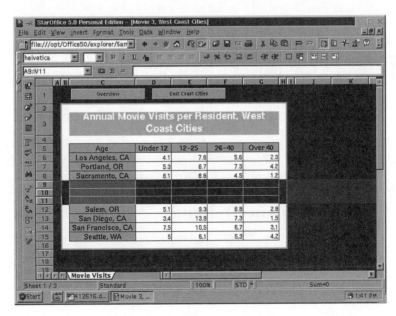

If you used an absolute row reference (with a dollar sign on the row, such as C$15), it won't be updated, and the formula might not calculate correctly.

If you select Rows from the Insert menu without doing anything else first (such as selecting other cells), StarOffice inserts one row above the current row.

Deleting rows is a little more complicated. Some of the details were covered earlier in this hour. Basically, you can do any of the following in a StarOffice spreadsheet:

- Delete the contents of a block of cells (clear the cells).
- Delete a block of cells, moving other cells up to fill in the space left by the cells you deleted (and updating formulas as needed).
- Delete an entire row, moving other rows up and updating formulas.

Here, you'll just learn how to delete a complete row. Just follow these steps:

1. Select a complete row by clicking on the label for that row (on the far right of the row).

2. Choose Delete Cells from the Edit menu. The entire row is deleted and other cells are moved up and renumbered.

If you use Cut on the Edit menu, or the delete key, the cells are cleared but the empty cells remain in your spreadsheet.

Inserting and Deleting Columns

Inserting columns is done using the same procedure as inserting rows.

Some areas of a spreadsheet, for example where cells have been merged together, don't allow you to insert or delete rows or columns because doing so creates an ambiguous situation.

To insert a single column, choose Columns from the Insert menu. A single column is added to the left of the current cell.

You can also insert multiple columns by selecting several cells across a row. New columns are always inserted to the left of the currently selected cells.

As you probably suspect by now, deleting a column is similar to deleting a row:

1. Select the column to be deleted by clicking on the column label (the letter above the cells).

2. Choose Delete Cells from the Edit menu. The columns are removed.

16

 You can choose Undo from the Edit menu if you delete information and then change your mind.

In the Next Hour

In Hour 17, "Adding Charts and Graphics to Spreadsheets," you'll learn how to create charts within a spreadsheet by selecting cells in the spreadsheet and using the StarOffice charting tools. After the chart is created, you'll learn how to format and arrange the information on the chart to best suit your needs.

HOUR 17

Adding Charts and Graphics to Spreadsheets

This hour guides you through creating graphics and charts from the data in your spreadsheet, and then inserting those graphics into your spreadsheet or exporting them for other uses.

StarOffice includes many types of chart options. You'll learn how to use the most popular ones in this hour. You'll also see how to modify and format charts after they're created and inserted into your spreadsheet.

Adding a Graphic to a Spreadsheet

After formatting your spreadsheet with the options presented in Hour 16, "Formatting Your Spreadsheet," you can add graphic images of your data (charts) to further spruce up the look of your spreadsheet.

Importing a Graphic File

Hour 11, "Adding Graphics to Documents," described how to add a graphic to a text document. The process is identical for adding a graphic to a spreadsheet. Just follow these steps:

1. Move to the cell in which the upper left corner of the graphic image is to be positioned.

> You can move or resize the image after you import it, but it's helpful to have the graphic near the location at which you want it.

2. Choose Picture from the Insert menu. Then choose From File from the Picture submenu. The Insert Picture dialog box appears (see Figure 17.1).

FIGURE 17.1

Select a graphics file to insert from the Insert Picture dialog box.

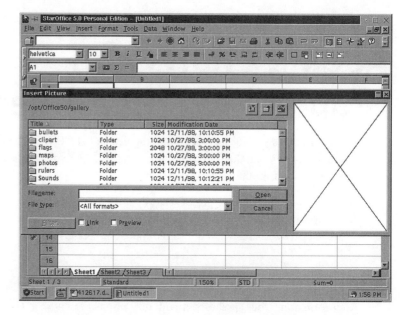

> You can also create a picture in the Image Editor or StarDraw and insert it into your spreadsheet. Using the Image Editor is described in Hour 11. The use of StarDraw is described in Hour 6, "Creating Graphics with StarDraw."

3. Browse through the filesystem until you find the graphics file you want to insert.

4. Select the Preview checkbox and click on a listed filename once to view it in the Preview window; double-click the filename to choose and load it.

Importing a graphic file can make your spreadsheet file very large. If you're concerned about this, or if the graphic file might change, use the Link checkbox in the Insert picture dialog box so that the picture is reloaded from the original graphic file each time you open the spreadsheet. Note that if the graphic file is later moved or the spreadsheet file is copied to another machine, this method might loose the image, displaying an empty box instead.

17

5. The graphic is loaded into the spreadsheet and appears as a selected item (with green handles and an anchor icon). See Figure 17.2.

FIGURE 17.2

A newly-imported graphic is selected, ready to edit using the procedures in the following section.

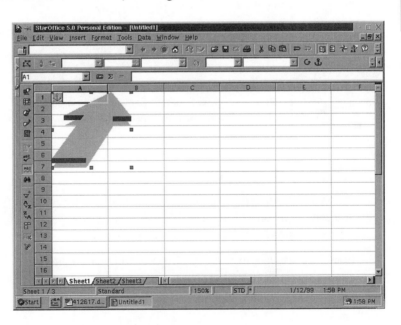

Editing an Imported Graphic

After you load a graphic file into your spreadsheet, you can move and edit it in many ways. Although this is covered in detail in Hour 11, Table 17.1 shows you the most important things that you can do with an imported graphic.

TABLE 17.1 EDITING IMPORTED GRAPHICS

Action	Steps
Select the graphic	Click once anywhere on the image.
Move the graphic	Select the image. Click and drag the image to a new location.
Resize the graphic	Select the image.Click and drag on a green corner handle. (Hold down the Shift key while dragging to maintain the aspect ratio)
Do bitmap editing on an image	Double-click on the image to open it within an Image Editor window
Arrange the image within several layers	Right click on a selected image and select an item from the Arrange submenu

Because a spreadsheet isn't arranged in paragraphs and pages, you can't use the justification and alignment settings for a graphic in a spreadsheet.

Creating a Chart

A powerful feature of StarOffice is the capability to create charts from the information you enter in the spreadsheet cells. Charts are a great way to highlight your information for presentations and to quickly see trends onscreen.

StarOffice provides many types of charts, with many options. The chart feature is flexible, but it can take some experimentation to get your data to look just right.

Mark Twain was right when he said, "There are lies, damn lies, and statistics." Check your charts to be sure that they reflect an accurate visual message.

The sections that follow walk you through creating a few basic charts and editing those charts. You'll learn the steps that you can use to create a chart with your own data. You'll be using a set of simple sales data as the basis for your chart samples.

The words chart and graph are used interchangeably in this discussion.

Selecting a Data Set

The first step in creating any chart is to select the data that you want to graph. Use the mouse to click and drag over a block of cells, or use the keyboard to select an area.

The area that you select can be as small or large as you need. It needs to include all the numbers and labels that you want to be part of the graph.

The labels are the headings that you typed in to identify your data. Include these in the cells that you select. The charting feature uses these to place labels on the chart that it creates.

A sample set of data is shown selected, with its labels, in Figure 17.3.

17

FIGURE 17.3

A selected set of data, ready to be charted.

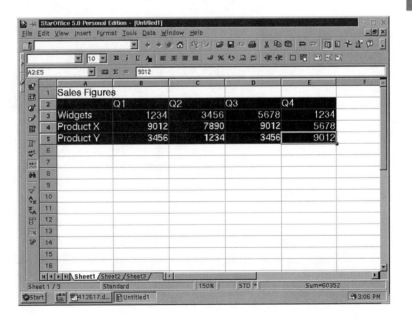

Creating a useful chart in StarOffice involves several steps. First, you answer questions in a series of dialog boxes. After the chart is created, you can edit the chart to make it look just as you want it to.

The following sections step you through this process.

Starting a Chart

With a data area selected in your spreadsheet, choose Chart from the Insert menu. The AutoFormat Chart dialog box appears, as shown in Figure 17.4.

FIGURE 17.4

The first part of the AutoFormat Chart dialog box enables you to set up the location of the chart.

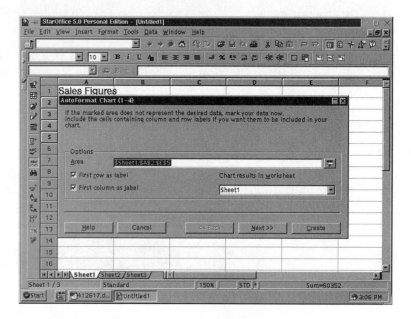

The name in the title bar of the dialog box includes the following: (1–4). Notice the button in the bottom of the dialog box labeled Next>>. You'll use the Next>> and <<Back buttons to look at four different parts of the AutoFormat Chart dialog box, filling in information as you go. You can go to any or all the different parts of the dialog box before pressing the Create button to create the chart that you've defined.

The options in the first part of the dialog box enable you to indicate the location of the chart. Specify both where the data for the chart are being taken from and where the finished chart is to be placed. The options in the first part are as follows:

- **The Area field**—Uses cell reference notation to describe the block of cells that you selected before opening this dialog box. The sheet name and corner cells define the block of information being charted. You don't have to do anything in this field.

- **The location where the chart will be placed**—This field is labeled Chart, and results in a worksheet. From this drop-down list, select the sheet in which to place the chart. The default is the sheet where the selected cells are located. The chart will be placed to the right of the selected cells.

> You're inserting this sample chart on Sheet2 so you can enlarge it and edit it later. If you leave this field set to Sheet1, the chart is inserted next to the cells that you selected.

- **Label checkboxes**—StarOffice tries to determine whether you've included labels in the block of selected cells. It does this by checking the data type of the cells. StarOffice uses this information to set the checkboxes for the first row or first column being used as chart labels, rather than as numerical data. Make sure the checkboxes are selected correctly to get a correctly-configured graph.

Selecting a Chart Type

To continue setting up your chart, select the Next>> button to move to the second part of the AutoFormat Chart dialog box, shown in Figure 17.5.

FIGURE 17.5

In the second part of the AutoFormat Chart dialog box, you select which type of chart to use.

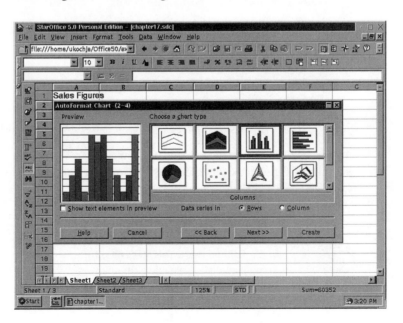

You select the type of chart that you want to use from the set of 12 small pictures in the dialog box (scroll down to see the last four). StarOffice tries to pick an appropriate chart type based on your data, but you might want to change the selected chart type.

> Note that some chart types are intended for certain types of data. For example, a pie chart is intended for percentage data, where the total is 100 percent (a full pie).

The available chart types include the following. This list uses the names that StarOffice uses, followed by explanation as needed:

- Lines (horizontal)
- Areas (horizontal lines filled in underneath)
- Columns (vertical bar graph)
- Bars (horizontal bar graph)
- Pies (pie chart)
- XY diagram (requires that X-axis values be sorted, which is done for you automatically after StarOffice checks with you)
- Net (graphed in polar coordinates)
- Lines (three dimensional)
- Areas (three dimensional)
- Bars (three dimensional horizontal bar graph)
- Columns (three dimensional vertical bar graph)
- Pies (three dimensional pie chart)

The Preview window on the left side of the dialog box shows you how the data appears as a chart of the selected type. The preview image changes as you select different chart types.

> The color of the charts might not appear correctly in the Preview window or in the finished chart. This makes it difficult to judge the data in the chart. In the next section, you'll learn how to edit the colors to make your chart readable.

It is recommended that you select the Show text elements in preview checkbox. It makes the graphic part of the chart preview smaller, but it helps you to visualize how the final chart will look. In the third and fourth parts of the dialog box, it also helps to determine the effect you are having with your selections.

For this sample data, a vertical bar graph (columns) has been selected, as shown in the previous figure.

Selecting a Chart Variant

To continue the process of defining your chart, choose the Next>> button. The screen that you see next depends on which chart type you selected in the second screen. The one you see (after choosing the Columns chart type) is shown in Figure 17.6.

FIGURE 17.6

In the third part of the AutoFormat Chart dialog box, select a chart variant and choose whether to display the grid lines.

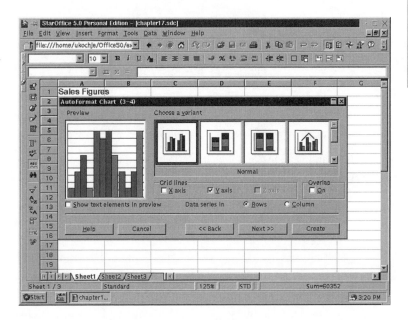

You can always move back and forth between the sections of this dialog box and change any selections that you've made. To see this, use the following steps:

1. Press the <<Back button. The second part of the dialog box is shown.

2. Select the Pie chart type.

3. Press the Next>> button. The third part of the dialog box is shown again, but the chart type variants from which you can choose are all pie charts instead of column charts (see Figure 17.7).

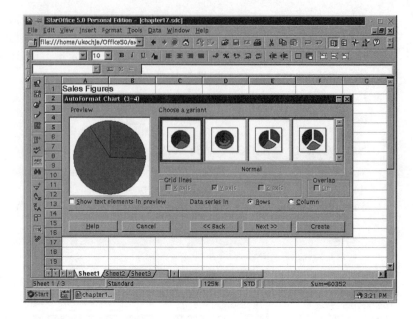

FIGURE 17.7

The variants in the third part of the AutoFormat Chart dialog box depend on which chart type is selected.

We'll continue with the columns type for this example if you want to go back and choose the columns chart type before going on.

Following is a look at the chart variants for the columns chart that was selected. You might want to look back at the data in the cells to see how it can be represented in different ways.

- The first variant is normal, and matches the chart pictures in the second part of the AutoFormat Chart dialog box.
- The second variant is a stacked column (or bar graph). This is appropriate if you want to graphically represent the total of a group of figures, as well as their individual values.
- The third variant is also a stacked column, but uses percentages instead of actual values. Thus, all the columns are the same height. This is useful when you want to judge the relative weights of the data points in your cells.
- The fourth variant uses a horizontal line for one set of data, plus the columns for the others. This might be used for data sets that include a line of totals that run above the individual bars.

You can see why a bit of experimentation is suggested to get your graph just right.

Because we're more interested in developing an attractive chart than in teaching Statistics 101, we'll select the Normal chart variant.

The checkboxes in the third section of the dialog box are used to turn the grid lines on or off. You can see the gridlines in the preview window as you select or deselect the checkboxes.

> All the checkboxes in this part of the dialog box might not be available. For example, the Z axis checkbox is only available if you selected a three-dimensional chart type.

You can continue to the final part of the AutoFormat Chart dialog box by pressing the Next>> button.

Labeling Your Chart

In the fourth and last section of the AutoFormat Chart dialog box (shown in Figure 17.8), you can set options for how the chart is labeled and which text elements are included on it.

FIGURE 17.8

In the fourth part of the AutoFormat Chart dialog box, you determine which text labels are included on the chart.

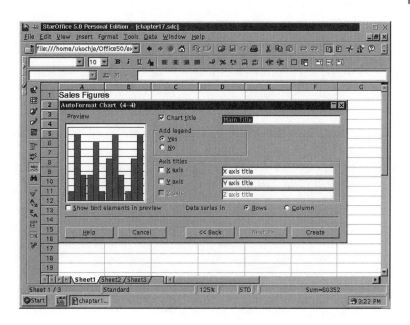

If you want to include a title at the top of your chart, leave the Chart Title checkbox selected and enter the name of the chart in the text entry field (where Main Title is entered by default).

You won't always want a title, depending on what other information is nearby in your spreadsheet.

If you want to include a legend on your chart, leave the Yes button selected in the Add legend section. It is recommended that you include a legend as you develop your chart. You can turn it off after you've seen that the chart is appropriate to your needs.

A *legend* is a mini-chart that coordinates the graphical information on the chart to the labels that give them meaning, for example, a red box to indicate first quarter profits.

If you want titles on the axes, select the X axis or Y axis checkbox. These are useful if you're not certain that readers will know which side of the graph corresponds to which part of the data.

If you've selected the checkbox to display text elements in the preview, you can see these labels being added as you select the checkboxes.

Finally, you can select a checkbox to indicate whether the data series that you're graphing are in rows or in columns. This needs to be on the first part of the dialog instead of the fourth, but you can back up if you need to change chart types.

To understand this option, here's a look at the sample data that has been used for this chart. It includes four columns, one for each quarter of a year, and three rows, for three different sources of revenue. (An additional row and column are for labels, but that was indicated in the first part of the dialog box.)

If you use rows as the data series (which StarOffice selected by default), you have three sets of data with four pieces of data in each set (one for each quarter). This is displayed as four sets of chart columns, with each set containing three pieces—one for each source of revenue. This graphic is shown in Figure 17.9 as it appears in the Preview window.

This can be described as follows: "Each quarter's revenue is shown separately, broken down into its three sources of revenue."

Now click on the columns button in the dialog box, and the preview chart changes. StarOffice is seeing the column of three figures as a series of data points, with four data points for each (from four different columns). This graphic is shown in Figure 17.10 as it appears in the Preview window.

FIGURE 17.9

Using rows as the data series, you see four sets of data with three items in each set.

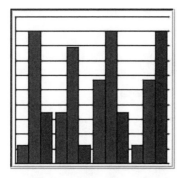

FIGURE 17.10

Using columns as the data series, you see three sets of data with four items in each set.

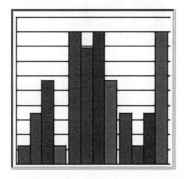

17

This can be described as follows: "Each source of revenue is shown together, with the year's revenue broken down by quarter for that source." Looking from left to right in the figure, you see the sets of data for Domestic Direct, Domestic Retail, and International revenue.

You can see a couple of things from this example:

- You need to understand both your data and what you want to communicate with a chart before the charting tools are of much use to you.
- It can help to have text on the chart to explain things to readers (or to you later on).

With all these selections made, you're ready to create your chart. Choose the Create button. The dialog box closes and the chart you defined appears on the sheet that you selected (see Figure 17.11). The chart is selected and ready to edit, which is covered in the next section.

FIGURE 17.11

The chart you define is inserted into the sheet, ready to be edited as needed.

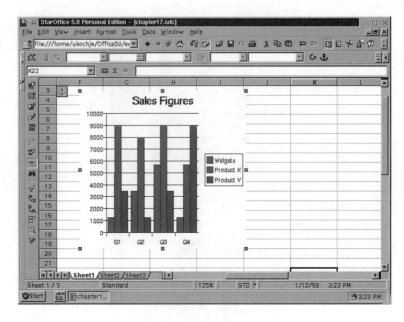

Charts in your spreadsheet are dynamic. If you change the value of a cell that has been charted, the chart changes immediately to reflect the new data.

A chart that you insert into a spreadsheet doesn't fill the cells. It covers them up. You can still have (and lose track of) data in cells behind a chart.

Modifying and Formatting a Chart

After you have a chart inserted into your spreadsheet, you're ready to edit it to make it fit your needs precisely. StarOffice charts are easy to edit.

The following sections describe the main editing options that you'll want to use. Not all the editing options are described in detail, but the same methods are used to access editing for all parts of a chart.

To explain the editing tasks, we'll build on the chart that was created in the previous section.

Selecting a Chart to Modify

When you click on a chart, it becomes a selected object. (It has green handles around it.)

When a chart is selected, you can use the handles to resize the chart, or click and drag in the middle of the chart to move it anywhere in the spreadsheet.

To modify the chart itself, you must have the chart in edit mode. To do this, double-click on a chart. You can tell that a chart is ready to edit because it has a heavy line around it (see Figure 17.12), and the toolbar on the left of the screen contains icons to edit the chart (those are described in a moment).

FIGURE 17.12

A chart that's ready to edit has a heavy line around it and a chart editing toolbar visible to the left of the spreadsheet (depending on the toolbar options you've selected).

The main toolbar changes to show chart editing tools

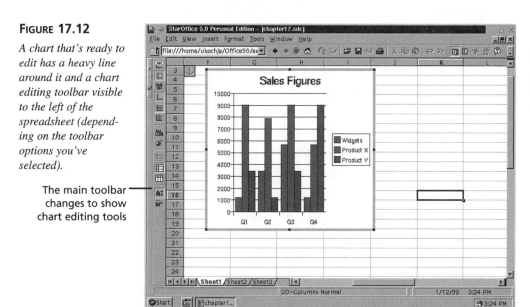

Reviewing the Edit Options on a Chart

After you've created a new chart, you can edit any part of it, and even make it look completely different if you choose to.

You can access a piece of the chart to format it in one of three ways:

- Double-click on a part of the chart when it's in edit mode (with a heavy line around it).
- Click on a part of the chart to select it and then click the right mouse button to select from a submenu of editing options. The Object Properties item is usually the most comprehensive.
- Click on one of the buttons on the Main toolbar to use a chart editing tool.

At first glance, all the buttons on the chart editing version of the Main tool-bar look alike. Leave the mouse pointer over an icon for a couple of seconds to see a pop-up description of what it does.

The following items can all be edited by double-clicking on the chart or using a toolbar button. You can tell exactly what you're editing by the title of the dialog box that opens:

- Scale text in the chart (use a toolbar button)
- Edit the chart's title (double-click on the title)
- Change the grid layout (vertical or horizontal)
- Edit a data point for color or labels (by double-clicking)
- Set the color of the chart area
- Select rows or columns as the data series (with a toolbar button)
- Change the cells that make up the chart (in a little pop-up mini-spreadsheet; use a toolbar button)
- Turn the vertical or horizontal grid on or off
- Turn axis labels on or off (use a toolbar button)
- Turn the legend on or off (use a toolbar button)
- Turn the title on or off (use a toolbar button)
- Set the color, position, and character type of the legend (double-click on it)
- Turn on labels for individual data points
- Set the scale, number style, and line and color style for each axis

Just a couple of the editing options are used in the following sections to show you how to set some features of the sample chart.

Changing a Color in the Chart

The first edit you'll make on your chart is to alter the colors used for a data set.

With the chart selected for editing, follow these steps:

1. Double-click in the top color box within the legend (see Figure 17.13).

FIGURE 17.13

Double-clicking on an item in the legend enables you to edit a data row or column, depending on how the data series are arranged.

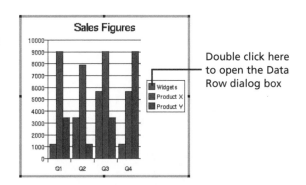

Double click here
to open the Data
Row dialog box

2. The Data Row dialog box appears. Choose the Area tab (see Figure 17.14).

FIGURE 17.14

The color for the area within a bar is set from the Data Row or Data Column dialog box, in the Area tab.

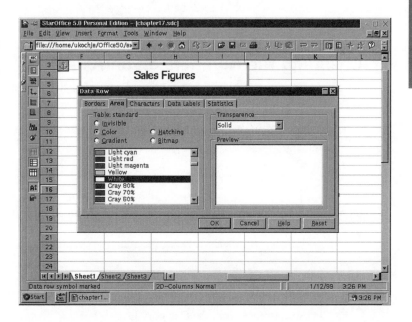

17

3. From the transparence drop-down list, choose 75 percent. The Preview area shows the changes in color.

If you are going to print this chart, choose the Hatching button and select a hatching pattern from the list.

4. Choose OK to apply your changes. The data set (each of the corresponding columns) on the chart is updated as shown in Figure 17.15 (notice that the item you double-clicked on is still selected).

FIGURE 17.15

The color for the data set is updated based on the selections you made in the Data Row dialog box.

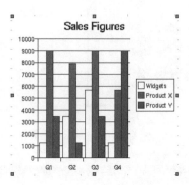

Changing the Numbers on an Axis

As an additional example, make the numbers on the Y axis of this chart into dollar amounts instead of plain numbers:

1. Double-click on the vertical axis in the chart, right on the line, between two numbers.

> Sometimes it's hard to double-click in just the right spot. If you single click and use the right mouse button to select Object Properties, it can be more precise.

2. The Y Axis dialog box appears (check the Title Bar). Choose the Numbers tab (see Figure 17.16).

3. Choose Currency from the Category list.

4. Choose a format from the Format list (the default is probably fine).

5. Choose OK to apply your changes. The numbers on the Y axis are all shown as dollar amounts.

With so many editing possibilities, you are now left to experiment with others to see how you can arrange your chart for the best visual presentation.

FIGURE 17.16

You can edit the style of the numbers used on the axis within the Numbers tab of the Y Axis dialog box.

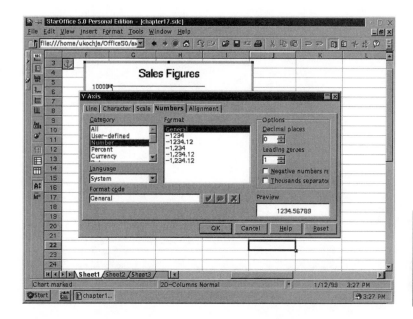

Both graphics and charts in a spreadsheet can be hidden or displayed as placeholders. Select the setting you want from the Contents tab of the Spreadsheet Options dialog box in the Charts field.

In the Next Hour

Charting is a special feature of spreadsheets beyond entering and calculating numbers. In the next hour, "Using Database Functions," you'll learn about another set of specialized functions within a StarOffice spreadsheet: database tools.

Database tools enable you to work with rows of data in a spreadsheet as if they were *tuples* (records) in a database, using features such as sorting and filtering.

HOUR 18

Using Database Functions

In this hour you will learn about the database functions of StarOffice. Database functions enable you to operate on a set of spreadsheet data as if it were records in a database. The data in spreadsheet cells is examined using spreadsheet functions in formulas that provide useful tools for manipulating your data.

The database features that you'll learn about include using data validity checking to help guide you in entering data in your sheet, plus sorting and filtering features to organize large amounts of data.

Defining Database Terms

Before describing the database features of StarOffice, some database terms are outlined to ensure that we're all starting from the same point.

Loosely defined, a *database* is a collection of organized information. A database can contain multiple tables or specific sets of information. For example, an Orders database might contain a table of customer information and a table of product information. You'll often hear a single table referred to as a database when it's not part of a larger dataset—that's what is done in this hour.

Each table consists of records, with each record being a data set, or *tuple*, if you're familiar with some of the more formal database terminology.

Each record is made up of fields, and each field is a distinct piece of information.

Because a spreadsheet is being used as a database management program in this hour, the following generalizations can be made about what you'll be shown here:

- A record is a row or part of a row in the spreadsheet.
- A field is a column in the spreadsheet.
- A spreadsheet cell is a single field within a single record of the table or database.

Here's a look at the sample data that is used to show you about databases in StarOffice. Figure 18.1 contains a table, organized as rows and columns, with a label at the top of each field.

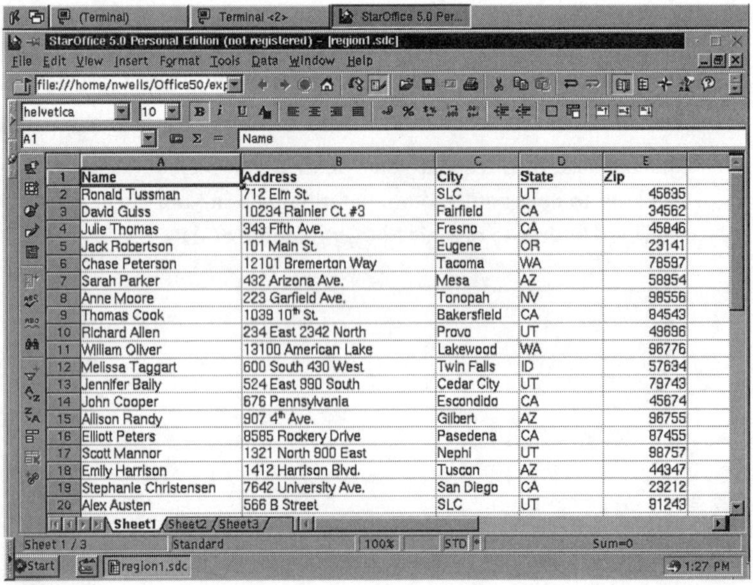

FIGURE 18.1

The sample data, organized in rows (records) and columns (fields).

From this sample, you can see that each record contains the name and address of a person.

The fields that make up each record are

- Name
- Address
- State
- Zip Code

Many other database terms are used when you work with a more formal database program such as Informix or Microsoft Access.

Terms such as *primary key* and *outer join* apply to relational databases, but not to the less formal, flat-file databases that you can create and manage in a StarOffice spreadsheet.

Using Data Validation

Data validation enables you to control what information is entered in each field of your database, and provide feedback messages as data is entered.

You can use the data validation procedures outlined in this section for single cells within a spreadsheet, but using them for fields within a database-style table of information is described here.

18

Using data validation assumes two things:

- You are working within a structured table that needs information to fit certain patterns in order to be useful.
- Several people might be entering data in the table, or you want to be reminded of the restrictions that will make the data valid and useful.

Looking at the sample table, you can immediately see two fields that require data of a certain format:

- Information in the State field must be letters only (no numbers) and must be two characters (to match the standard U.S. state codes).
- Information in the Zip field must be numbers only, and must be at least five characters (someone might enter a Zip+4 code, however).

Data validation can be used to make certain that anyone entering data in these fields follows these rules to maintain the integrity of your database table.

Setting up Data Validation Criteria

To set up *criteria*, or rules, for how your data must be structured, you first must select the cells to which the data validation rules are to apply.

For this example, the entire spreadsheet is dedicated to a names and addresses table, so you can select the entire column to define a field to which you want to apply a data validation rule.

1. Click on the column heading for column C to select the entire column of state information (see Figure 18.2).

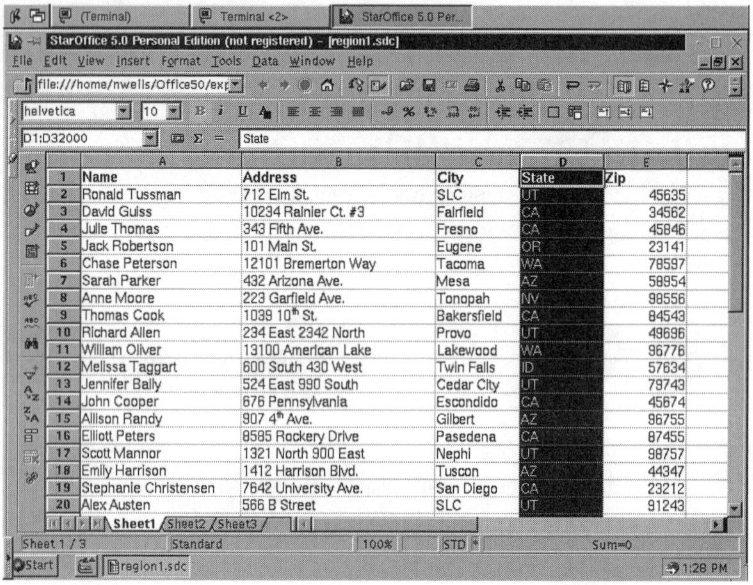

FIGURE 18.2

FIGURE 18.2

With the State field selected, you can set validation criteria for that field in all records.

2. Select Validity from the Data menu. The Data Validation dialog box appears (see Figure 18.3).

3. Choose the Values tab.

4. Select Text Length from the Allow field drop-down list.

   The Allow field defines what type of data can be contained in the selected cells (the States field in this case).

5. Select Equal from the Data field drop-down list.

   The Data field defines how the cell entry is examined compared to a fixed value. (For example, all numbers must be greater than zero.)

6. In the Value field, enter 2.

The State field must have exactly two characters. This is shown by selecting Text Length Equal 2.

7. Before choosing OK, select the Input Help tab (see Figure 18.4).

FIGURE 18.3

Data validation rules and feedback are set up in the Data Validation dialog box.

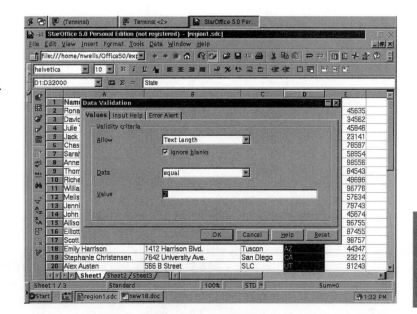

FIGURE 18.4

The Input Help tab enables you to define a message to guide users in entering correct data.

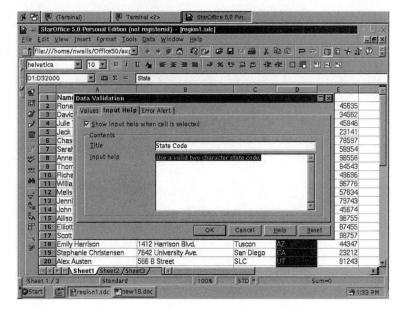

Normally, you might not use this feature for a full column of fields like this, but it is included in this example so that you can see how it works.

8. Select the checkbox for Show input help when cell is selected.
9. Enter State Code in the Title field
10. In the Input help text area, enter Use a valid two character state code.

You can use Input help in the data validation dialog box for a single cell to help someone enter a correct value to recalculate a spreadsheet or to try different scenarios.

11. Finally, select the Error Alert tab (shown in Figure 18.5). This tab defines what StarOffice is to do if the data entered in a cell doesn't match the rules you specified in the Values tab (in this case, if something besides two characters were entered).

FIGURE 18.5

The Error Alert tab defines how to respond to incorrect data entry.

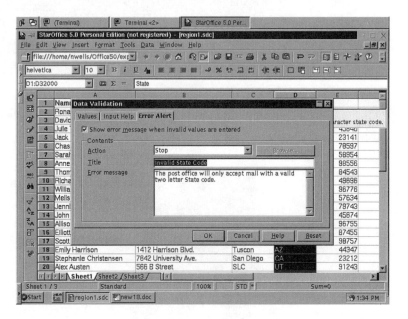

12. Select the Show error messages when invalid values are entered checkbox. If this box is not checked, the options you define in this section of the dialog box are not active.

13. Select Stop from the Action drop-down list. Stop clears data from the cell if it doesn't match the rules set in the Values tab.

> You can choose Information or Warning to leave the bad data as the user entered it, after displaying a message. You have to decide how important it is to follow the data rules for your situation.

14. In the Title field, enter Invalid State Code.

15. In the Error Message field, enter The post office only accepts mail with a valid two letter State code.

16. Choose OK to close the Data Validation dialog box and apply your settings to the selected cells.

Now you can try entering some state codes and see what happens. Follow these steps:

1. Move the cell focus to the first empty cell below the list of states.

2. Notice that the yellow pop-up window describes what to enter in that cell (see Figure 18.6).

18

FIGURE 18.6

Input help can guide users as they enter data in cells.

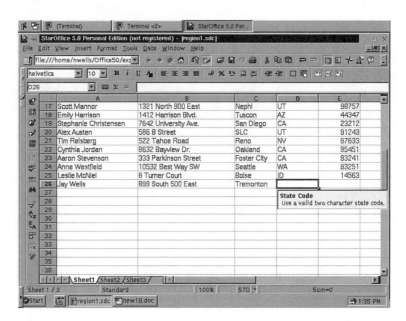

As was mentioned earlier, Input help is better suited to a single cell. It can get annoying when you see it for every cell in the column, as it is applied here.

3. Type UT and press Enter.

This is a valid state code by the rules that were set, so it is accepted without comment and the cell focus moves down one line.

You can't use the data validation dialog box for rules such as "Only allow the following 50 state codes," but see the note at the end of this section regarding macros.

4. Now type 12345 and press Enter.

A message box appears, containing the error message that was entered (see Figure 18.7).

FIGURE 18.7

An error message explains to users why the data that was entered cannot be accepted.

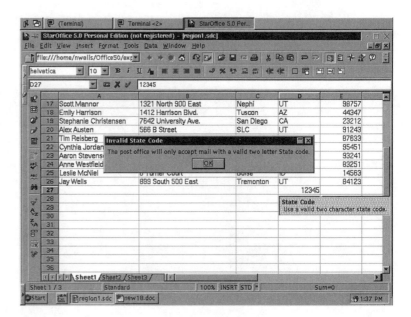

5. Choose OK to close the message dialog box. The cell focus moves to the next cell down, but the cell data that was entered, 12345, is cleared from the cell.

You can see how useful this feature can be when you're using StarOffice for lists or tables of information. With data validation, all the information in the table is valid and useful. Typing or knowledge errors can be greatly reduced by using simple rules to control what is entered in each cell.

Data validation in StarOffice is a useful feature, but it isn't like the data validation that is available if you use a full-featured relational database.

Still, if you want to have more fine-grained control over the data validation process (for example, to check that the state code matched one of the actual codes in a list), you can create a macro program and check the data each time it is entered.

Macro is one of the options in the Error Alert tab of the Data Validation dialog box—but you're not going to learn how to write StarOffice macros during this 24 Hours.

Sorting Database Records

Another of the truly useful database features in StarOffice is the capability to sort lines of information.

You can choose which field to sort on, and set other sorting options to fit your data arrangement.

The same sample list of names and addresses is used to show how sorting works.

Selecting Data to Sort

The first step in sorting data is selecting the area that you want to sort. This area consists of a block of cells, including the field names at the top of the block. Figure 18.8 shows the selected cells that you want to sort.

Remember these two dangers as you select the area to be sorted:

- If you don't select all the rows in the table, they are left at the bottom of the table, unsorted. This problem can be solved by selecting the entire table and resorting.
- If you don't select all the columns in the table, the sort operation rearranges the first part of each row, leaving the mismatched last part of each row (record). You can fix this by choosing Undo from the Edit menu if you recognize the problem immediately.

After you have selected the cells to be sorted, choose Sort... from the Data menu. The Sort dialog box appears (see Figure 18.9).

18

FIGURE 18.8

The full table, with field names, is selected for the sort operation.

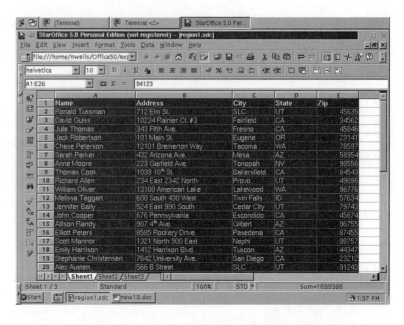

FIGURE 18.9

The Sort dialog box enables you to choose options for how a block of records is sorted.

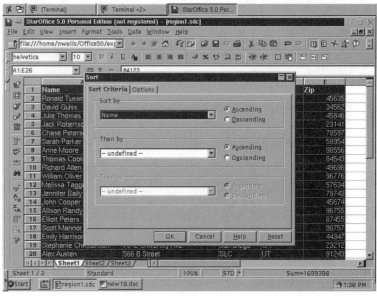

Setting the Sort Criteria

The method used to sort a list of records in StarOffice is based on two things:

- Which column is to be sorted (used as the key to the sort)
- Are the highest values or the lowest values listed first

The first field in the Sort dialog box is Sort by. Click on the drop-down list and notice that it contains the names of the fields from your sample data. It's a good idea to include the field names in the block of cells that you select for sorting.

> The field that you sort on is sometimes called the sorting KEY.

Suppose that you want the list sorted by state, and then alphabetically within each state. Follow these steps:

1. From the Sort by drop-down list, select State. (If you're using different sample data, the items in the list are different.)
2. Choose the Ascending button (so that AL is listed first and WY last).
3. Now that the first Sort by field is defined, you can select a second field from the next field down, labeled Then by. Choose Name from this drop-down list.
4. Also choose the Ascending button next to this field (so that Allan is listed first and Zoe last).

With the sort criteria set, you can choose OK, and the records are sorted.

Reviewing Sorting Options

Sorting in StarOffice provides many other options, however, in addition to setting up the sort criteria.

Select a block of cells and choose Sort from the Data menu. Then choose the Options tab (see Figure 18.10).

The following sections describe each of the items in the Options tab:

- When the Case sensitive checkbox is selected, all alphabetic sorting is based on upper- or lowercase letters, instead of all letters being treated the same.
- When the Area contains column headers checkbox is selected, the Sort criteria window uses the words in the first row to help you identify which sorting method you want to use.

18

Figure **18.10**

The Sort dialog box includes an Options tab in which you can set up many variations in how StarOffice sorts records in your tables.

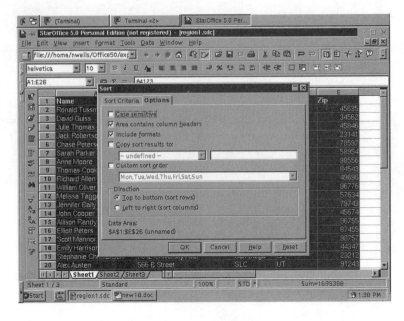

 You can uncheck this box and choose the Sort Criteria tab to see that the drop-down list contents change to Column B, Column C, and so on.

- When the Include formats checkbox is selected, the format of each cell is moved with it during the sorting process. If this checkbox is not selected, the values are moved, but the formatting remains as it was before the sort.

  For example, some lines might be highlighted in bold. The bold format can follow the sorted line, or remain on the same row as new data is sorted into that position.

- The Copy sort results to checkbox indicates that the sorted table is to be copied to another location in the spreadsheet, rather than replacing the selected cells that are being sorted.

  The drop-down list shows any names that you have defined within your spreadsheet (defining names was described in Hour 14, "Entering Spreadsheet Data").

  If you don't have names defined, or prefer to use another area of your spreadsheet, you can enter cell references in the text entry field to the right of the drop-down list below the Copy results checkbox.

- The Custom sort order checkbox enables you to define an ordered list that is used to sort information, rather than the alphabet or numerical sequence.

  Some ordered lists are already defined in StarOffice, such as days of the week and months of the year.

- Finally, you can change the sorting so that one column is considered a record and each row is a field. Instead of rearranging the rows, a sort rearranges the columns from left to right.

Filtering Data Records

The final StarOffice database feature that is described here is data filtering. *Data filtering* is used to select a subset of records based on a rule.

For example, when you're looking at all the records in your sample data, suppose you want to review all the names from California. You can sort the table and scroll to that point, but sometimes you can't rearrange the table; you'd have to find all the California records manually.

Filtering provides a way to auto-select these records so that you can work on them.

StarOffice provides an automatic filter that examines all values in the table, or you can enter the specific values that you want to filter for viewing.

Filtering is a feature that you turn on to work with certain records, and then turn off to view the entire table again. Be sure to save your spreadsheet after you complete your edits!

Using Automatic Filtering

Using the sample data from the previous examples, you can select Filter from the Data menu, and then select AutoFilter from the Filter submenu. AutoFiltering is turned on, and the filtering drop-down lists appear at the top of your columns of data for each field (see Figure 18.11).

To select all the records from California, click on the drop-down list on the State field, and select CA (see Figure 18.12).

FIGURE **18.11**

*By turning on
AutoFiltering, you can
select a filtering crite-
ria from the drop-
down lists.*

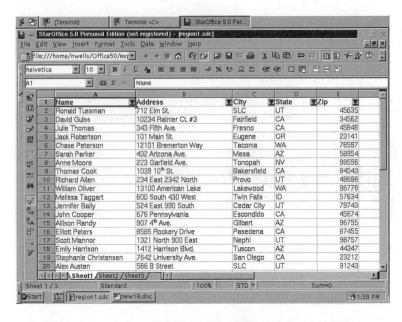

FIGURE **18.12**

*Select a value (such
as CA) from the drop-
down list to see only
records that match
that value for that
field.*

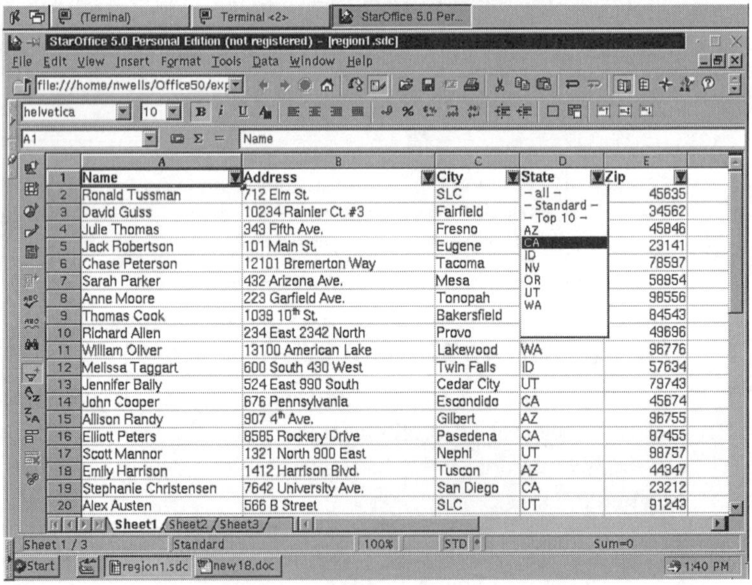

The records that are displayed are those that have CA in the State field (see
Figure 18.13).

FIGURE 18.13

AutoFiltering makes it easy to view only the records that match a selected value for a certain field.

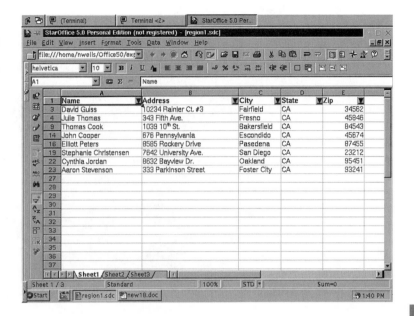

With the California records showing, you can easily review or edit them as a group. Notice that the row numbers shown match the true row numbers in the unfiltered spreadsheet.

When you're done working with the California records, select Filter from the Data menu, and then uncheck AutoFilter by selecting it again from the Filter submenu. All the records in the table are displayed again.

Using the Standard Filter

You can also define filter criteria yourself. This can save time if you have a field that contains many types of data.

For example, if you have hundreds of records for California, and you only want to view those that are in Fairfield, you can use a Standard filter to set both City and State criteria at the same time. The AutoFilter doesn't allow this flexibility.

To set a Standard filter, select Filter from the Data menu, and then choose Standard filter from the Filter submenu. The Standard Filter dialog box appears (see Figure 18.14).

18

FIGURE 18.14

The Standard filter dialog box can be used to select multiple values on which records are to be filtered.

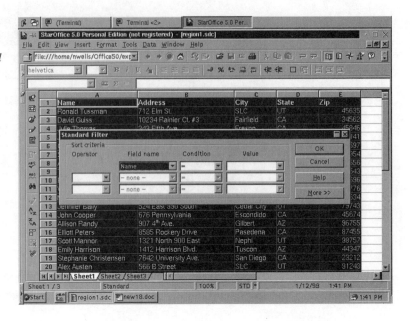

You can choose up to three fields to filter. This is similar to choosing three fields to sort, except that with filtering, only records matching a certain value are displayed.

For example, you can choose State as the Field name, equals (=) as the Condition, and CA as the Value.

Then you choose an Operator to define the interaction between the multiple criteria. Choose AND from the drop-down list.

Next choose City as the field value, greater than or equal to (>=) as the Condition, and a city name near the middle of the alphabet as the Value.

The dialog box with your selections appears in Figure 18.15.

After choosing OK to apply the Standard filter, the list of records looks similar to Figure 18.16. Notice that only California records with names greater (later in the alphabet) than your criteria are listed.

FIGURE 18.15

The Standard Filter dialog box with field names and values chosen.

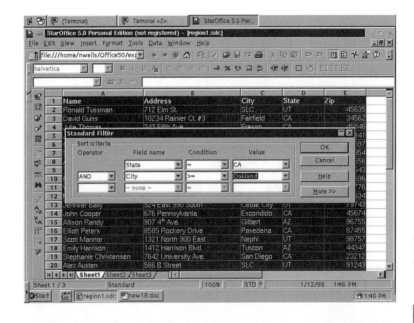

FIGURE 18.16

Records selected with a standard filter are shown without the drop-down lists at the top of each column.

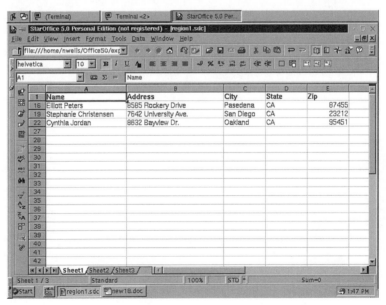

18

Notice also that the field names at the top of the columns do not have drop-down lists. To alter the filtering, you must go back to the Standard filter dialog box.

After you've finished editing the filtered records, you can remove the filter so that all the records are displayed. To do this, open the Standard filter dialog box and select none from the Field name list. All the filtering fields are cleared. When you choose OK, all the records are displayed.

In the Next Hour

Hour 19, "Creating Presentations with StarImpress," begins Part 4, which moves on from spreadsheets to presentations. You'll learn how to start and format a new StarOffice presentation using a built-in template, the StarOffice AutoPilot, or a complete design that you create yourself.

Part IV
Working with Presentations

Hour

19 Creating Presentations with StarImpress

20 Adding Graphics and Charts to Your Presentation

21 Formatting and Giving Your Presentation

Hour **19**

Creating Presentations with StarImpress

In this hour, you learn how to create a new presentation using the StarImpress features of StarOffice. You see how to use templates and the AutoPilot to help you get started, as well as how to add text and to format the information on your presentation slides. You also learn how to save your presentation to graphic formats or to HTML, for viewing in a Web browser.

Creating a New StarImpress Presentation

A presentation is usually a little more theatrical than a spreadsheet, and a little less verbose than a document. StarOffice gives you the tools to create professional presentations that can be presented live within your Linux system.

To start a new presentation in StarOffice, you can use any of the methods that are now familiar to you:

- Choose New from the File menu, and then choose Presentation from the New submenu.
- Double-click the New Presentation icon on the Desktop.
- Choose Presentation from the Start menu.

When you use any of these methods, the first slide appears in the viewing area, as does the Modify Slide dialog box. In this dialog box, select the auto-layout for the first slide in your new presentation. The view that you're seeing is called the Drawing view. (See Figure 19.1.) Other views are explained in Hour 21, "Formatting and Giving Your Presentation."

FIGURE 19.1

A blank slide appears and the Modify Slide dialog box opens when you start the creation of a new presentation.

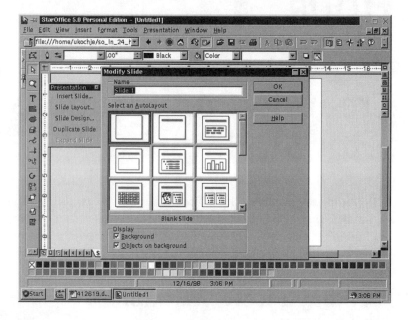

Slides and Pages

StarImpress is like a combination of PowerPoint and CorelDRAW. StarImpress can create multiple-slide presentations with transitions, embedded links, and slide templates (all explained in later hours).

Each slide also has a full set of drawing tools, multiple layers, color capabilities, and so forth. In fact, you'll notice a lot of similarities between the StarDraw tools that you learned about in Hour 6, "Creating Graphics with StarDraw," and the drawing tools that you can use within a StarImpress Presentation.

You can use StarDraw to create a flyer, card, or brochure, or you can use similar tools within a slide to develop a traditional slide presentation.

Making Use of Presentation Templates

Most people are not creative enough to start with a blank slide and create a presentation worthy of the name. Instead, they prefer to use templates that professional designers at StarDivision have created to guide their efforts.

If you're like most people, you might want to use one of the nine presentation templates and more than two dozen background templates that StarOffice includes to start creating your slides.

To start a presentation from a StarImpress template, follow these steps:

1. Choose New from the File menu.
2. Choose From Template... from the New submenu. The New dialog box appears, listing templates that you can use for your new presentation.

> You can also press Ctrl+N to open the new dialog box to select a Template.

3. Scroll down the Categories list until you find Presentations. Click on it to see a list of presentation templates in the right side of the dialog box (see Figure 19.2).
4. To see more information about the selected template, including a preview, choose the More button to expand the dialog box.
5. Double-click on the name of the presentation template that you want to use (the Annual Report template is used for this example).
6. The presentation appears onscreen, ready for your text. (See Figure 19.3.)

With the presentation template onscreen, you can see that a lot of your work is done for you. The flow of the presentation, with information that you need to include, is already entered on the slides.

> Use the PageUp and PageDown keys to move between slides. Other navigation methods are described in Hour 21.

19

FIGURE 19.2

*You can select from
nine presentation
templates in the New
dialog box.*

FIGURE 19.3

*A presentation tem-
plate includes sample
text on a formatted
slide for each topic.*

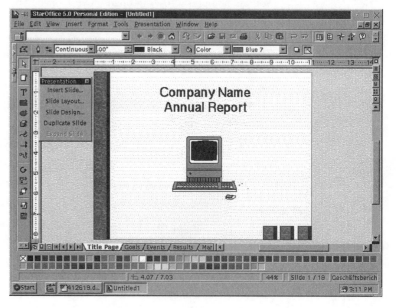

Using a Slide Layout

Presentation layouts are similar to the slides in a presentation template, but layouts are less complete. They include a background and predefined text or graphics areas, but no sample text. To use a presentation layout, follow these steps:

1. Choose New from the File menu.

2. Choose From Template… from the New submenu. The New dialog box appears, listing templates that you can use for your new presentation.

3. Scroll down the Categories list until you find Presentation Layouts. Click on it to see a list of layouts in the right side of the dialog box (similar to Figure 19.2).

4. Decide on the layout that you want to use and double-click on it in the New dialog box.

5. Select a slide layout for your first slide from the dialog box that appears. When you choose OK, the first slide in a new presentation appears, as shown in Figure 19.4.

FIGURE 19.4

A slide layout includes a background graphic, but not the format of multiple individual slides.

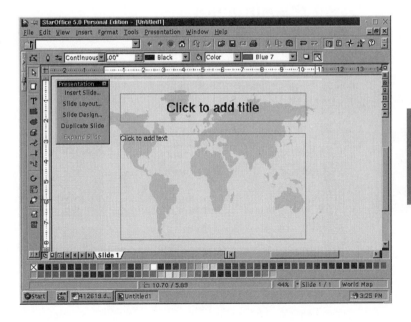

19

Table 19.1 explains the similarities and differences between a presentation and a presentation layout.

TABLE 19.1 PRESENTATIONS VERSUS PRESENTATION LAYOUTS

Presentations	Presentation Layouts
Applies a graphical background to each slide.	Applies a graphical background to each slide.
Consists of multiple slides, one for each topic in a subject (such as "Finance Report").	Includes only a single slide when opened, to hold the background graphics.
Includes sample text in a set of formatted slides.	Doesn't include any text. Formatted areas for text and graphics are provided to match the layout's background.
Best when your presentation built need some basic presentation templates.	Best when you just fits one of the nine pre-structure and a nice graphic to get you started.

Using the AutoPilot

If you want to create a personalized presentation as rapidly as possible, try the *AutoPilot* feature. The AutoPilot, which has been described for other types of documents, is similar to the *wizards* supplied with other programs. It asks you questions, and then creates a document outline based on your answers.

To use the AutoPilot to create a new presentation, follow these steps (you don't have to have a document already open to use the AutoPilot):

1. Choose AutoPilot from the File menu, and then choose Presentation from the AutoPilot submenu. The AutoPilot dialog box for a presentation appears (see Figure 19.5).

2. Click the Next>> button to advance to the first data entry screen of the AutoPilot dialog box (shown in Figure 19.6).

3. Enter your name or company name in the first field. For example

   `Thomas Travel Corp.`

4. Enter a single line topic for your presentation in the second field. For example

   `Employee briefing: 1999 Cruise Season`

5. Enter topics that you want to cover. Type each topic on a separate line, pressing Enter after each. The box scrolls down as you enter each line. For example, you might enter

```
Changes in industry law
New competitors for travel agencies
Popular areas this year
New information sources for clients
Promotions to watch for
```

FIGURE 19.5

The AutoPilot guides you through questions about your presentation, and then creates an outline for you.

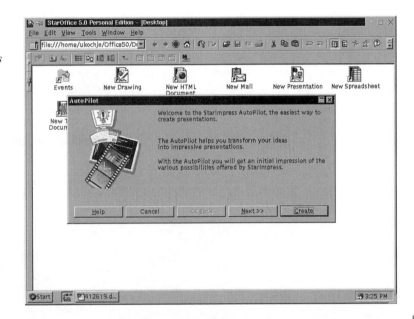

FIGURE 19.6

The first information requested by the Presentation AutoPilot is your name, the company name, and the topic information for the presentation.

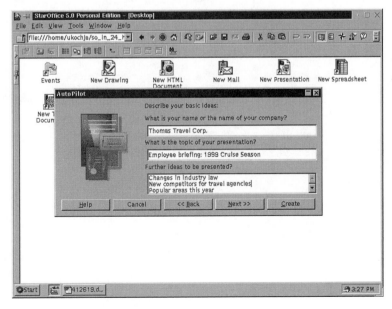

19

The lines that you enter as topics are part of the Agenda, and also headlines on individual slides, depending on the type and length of presentation that you specify.

6. Click the Next>> button to advance to the next screen in the dialog.

7. Choose the type of presentation that you want to make by selecting a radio button on this screen. Note that a description is provided on the left side of the dialog box. The description changes when you select different items in the list. (See Figure 19.7.)

FIGURE 19.7

Select a type of presentation so that the AutoPilot can assign certain features to the presentation that it creates for you.

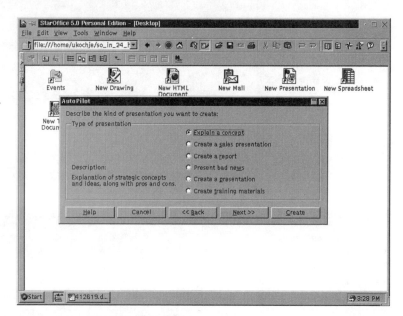

8. Click the Next>> button to continue. In the next section, shown in Figure 19.8, select a design style and a duration for your presentation.

FIGURE 19.8

Select a design style and a duration for your presentation.

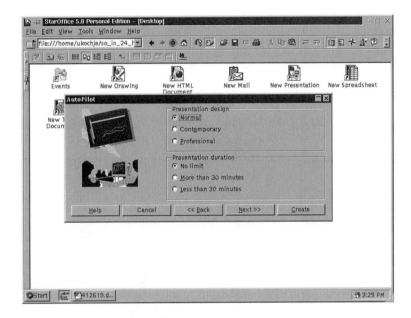

9. Click the Next>> button to continue. In the next section, shown in Figure 19.9, select a presentation medium: paper, overhead transparency, or 35mm slide. The medium that you select determines which types of graphics are used in the presentation.

FIGURE 19.9

Choose a medium for your presentation so that graphics and pages are sized optimally.

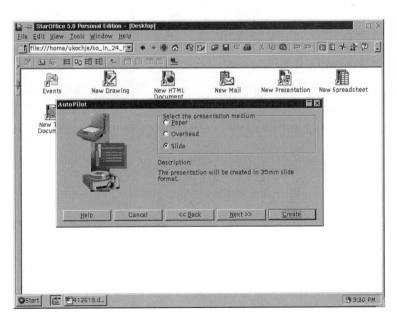

19

If you intend to use your presentation directly from your computer (running a slide show as described in Hour 21), choose Overhead as the medium.

10. Click Next>> to continue, and then click Create to finish the presentation. After a moment, the first slide appears onscreen, as shown in Figure 19.10.

FIGURE 19.10

A presentation set up by the AutoPilot includes slides for each of your topics.

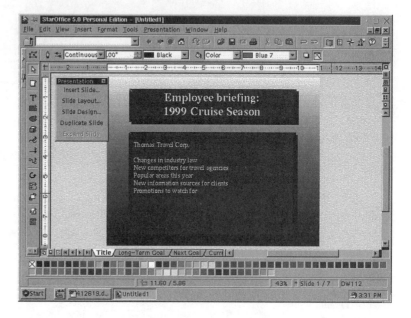

 You might not always like the results of an AutoPilot presentation, but they can be edited normally after they're first created—and it's a very fast way to get started.

Creating Individual Slides

After you have a layout or presentation template onscreen, you're ready to enter the information that you actually want to present.

StarOffice uses a layout for each slide to simplify and organize the placement of text and objects on the slide. You can add information in other locations, but the layouts make basic text entry much easier.

Adding a Layout to a Slide

If you used either the New Presentation icon or a background layout from the set of Presentation Layouts, your screen shows a blank or graphical slide with no indication of how to proceed. Choose Slide Layout from the Format menu. The Modify Slide dialog box appears. (See Figure 19.11.)

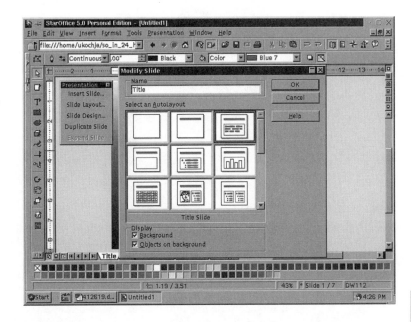

From the set of AutoLayout pictures, click on the one that matches how you want the current slide to look. For example, if you want a single headline with bullets underneath (a common choice), click on the middle picture in the second row.

Other choices indicate slides that include text in columns, charts, graphics, tables, and every combination of these elements. Completely empty slides (totally or in part) can be used to provide space for other creative things that you want to do with imported objects or with the drawing tools (see Hour 20, "Adding Graphics and Charts to Your Presentation").

When you've selected the best layout, click OK. The current slide now includes the layout that you selected (see Figure 19.12).

19

FIGURE 19.12

FIGURE 19.12

An AutoLayout applied to a slide provides guided areas for you to enter information on a slide.

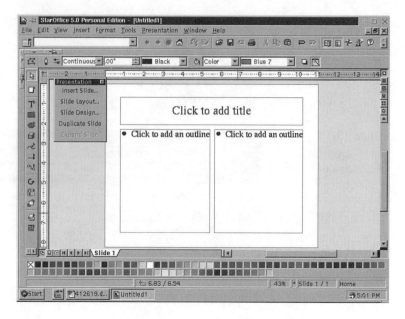

The AutoLayout areas show you what to do next. Each block in the layout includes an instruction to Click and add a title, double-click to add a document or chart, or something similar.

If you don't use one of the areas in the AutoLayout, the instructions and outlined boxes that you see onscreen do not appear in your slide presentation. They are only there as a reference while you enter information.

You can use the Slide Layout dialog box at any time to change the layout of the current slide. StarOffice tries to fit any existing text into the areas on the newly-selected layout.

Inserting a New Slide

As you create your presentation, you'll need to add new slides for each topic. Even if you used the AutoPilot or a presentation template, you might need to insert an additional slide or two.

To add a slide, choose Slide from the Insert menu. The Insert Slide dialog box appears. In this dialog box, select the layout of the slide that you want to insert. (This dialog box looks just like the one used to modify the layout of an existing slide.)

New slides are always inserted after the current slide.

After a slide is inserted, you can add and edit text on it just like any other slide in your presentation.

Entering Text on a Slide

With the helpful hints scattered throughout the slide layouts, entering information on a slide isn't very challenging. The large-type instructions such as Click to add title, for example, don't leave much to the imagination.

After you have entered text, you can click on any block of text to select that block and begin editing it. A cursor in the block of text indicates that it can be edited. (See Figure 19.13.)

FIGURE 19.13

Text within a slide can be edited by clicking on the text. The block is selected, and an editing cursor appears.

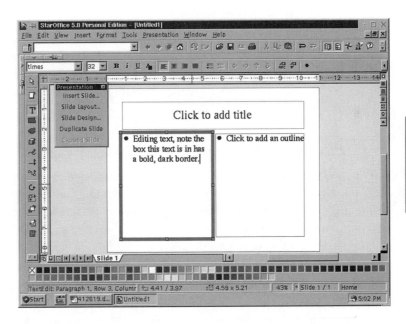

19

The green handles around the text block can be used to adjust the block in which the text sits. You can do any of the following:

- Click in the center of the text box and drag it to a new location.

> The layouts have all the text boxes centered and aligned. Dragging them to a new location on the slide might not work well with graphics or background elements on the slide.

- Click on any green handle to expand or contract the size of the text box.

  The size of the text box doesn't affect the size of the font used for text. It does, however, affect how much text is visible on the slide and how the text is arranged. For example, making a title text box longer allows more letters to fit on one line before the title wraps to a second line.

Adjusting Paragraphs

Each slide within a presentation is almost like a separate document. Text doesn't flow from slide to slide like pages in a word processing document. Instead, text is arranged in individual paragraphs. Each paragraph is one of the blocks of text that you click on to add or edit text. If the paragraph is too long for the slide, the extra text is cut off and won't appear in your presentation.

For example, in many slides the title of the slide is one paragraph and the bulleted list that follows is a second paragraph.

Because these paragraphs reside in text boxes that can be moved or adjusted with the green handles described in the previous section, paragraphs in a presentation don't have margins. You just move and resize the text box to the location on the page where you want the text.

You can, however, set up some features of each paragraph of text. With a block of text selected (with a heavy outline and green handles around it), select Paragraph from the Format menu. The Paragraph dialog box appears (see Figure 19.14), but with three tabs instead of the eight tabs that appear when you're working in a StarWriter word processing document.

In the Indents and Spacing tab, you can set up automatic indents for lines in the selected block of text. You can also define if text is single- or double-spaced. These options are useful for larger blocks of text, which don't frequently occur within slides.

In the Alignment tab (see Figure 19.15), you can define the current block of text as center-, left-, or right-justified. This is very useful for titles and some summary information.

FIGURE **19.14**

Each block of text on a slide can be edited from the Paragraph dialog box.

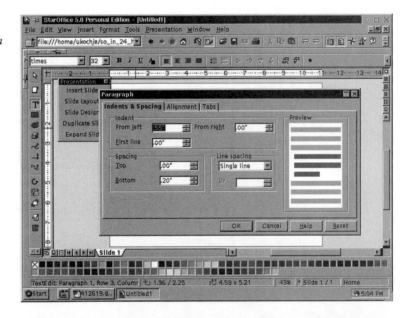

FIGURE **19.15**

The Alignment tab enables you to center-justify text in the current paragraph.

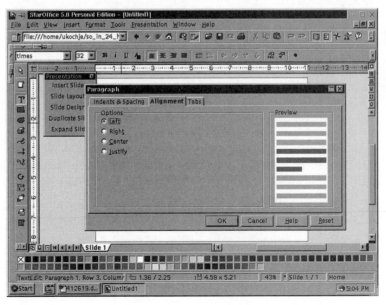

19

Finally, in the Tabs tab (see Figure 19.16) you define tab stops for each of the lines of text in the paragraph. This is used for setting up columns of figures or tables within a block of text.

FIGURE 19.16

Tab stops can be used to set up table-like formats or columns, figures, or names. An embedded spreadsheet can often replace these options, however.

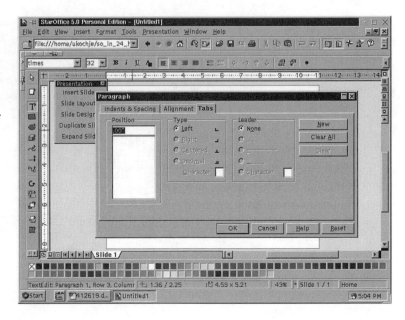

Because StarOffice enables you to import charts from spreadsheets and to include mini-spreadsheets, setting a lot of tab stops won't often be necessary.

Setting Font Options

Reasonable font choices are part of the pre-defined layouts and templates in StarOffice. However, if you want to change fonts or add effects as you do in a word processing document, it's easy to do.

To select a block of characters that you want to format, first select the entire paragraph that contains the characters. With a paragraph selected and a cursor in that paragraph, you can use the arrows keys with the Shift key, or drag your mouse pointer, to select words that you want to reformat.

With characters selected within a paragraph, choose Character from the Format menu. The Character dialog box appears (see Figure 19.17).

FIGURE 19.17

Individual characters or words can be formatted within a slide using the Character dialog box.

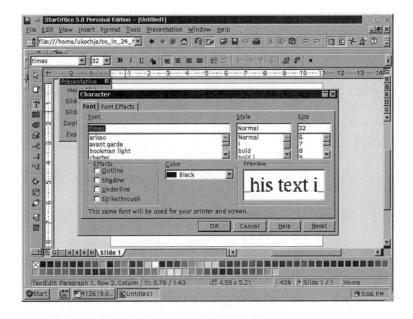

Using this dialog box, you can choose a font and font size, and standard or advanced font effects.

You remember from previous hours that most of the character formatting tools appear on the Object toolbar whenever you start editing text. For example, when text is selected within a slide, you can perform any of the following actions from the Object toolbar:

- Set bold, italic, or underlined text.
- Choose a font and font size.
- Set justification for the text (for example, centered text).
- Set single- or double-spaced text.
- Choose a color for the selected text.

Using the Object toolbar is often the most convenient way to format text, but not everything can be done from the toolbar. Some formatting, such as indents and superscripts, are generally done in the Character dialog box.

Saving Your Presentation

Although this topic is listed last in this hour, you need to save your presentation with a unique name before you enter the first line of text on the first slide.

19

To save a presentation, use the Save As item on the File menu. The now-familiar Save As dialog box appears. (See Figure 19.18.)

FIGURE **19.18**

The Save As dialog box enables you to choose a new name for the presentation that you're creating.

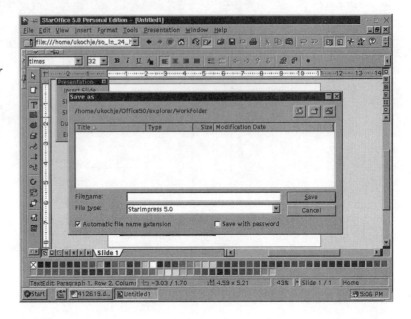

Enter a name for your file and select the directory to which it will be saved. Then choose the Save button.

After you save your presentation with a name, you can quickly update your saved presentation on disk at any time with a keystroke: Ctrl+S.

StarImpress 5.0 is the default format. If you need to read this presentation in another program, export it to another format, as described in the next section.

Exporting Slides in Graphics Formats

Despite our interest here, StarImpress is not a well-known presentation format. If you need to work with your presentation in another program, plan to export your presentation in another format.

For both text documents and spreadsheets, the StarOffice Save As dialog box includes several formats from which you can choose. For example, a text document can be saved as a Word 97 or an RTF file.

Presentations use the Export dialog box instead of the Save As dialog box. Exporting in a graphics format such as GIF, BMP, or JPEG creates a single graphics file for the currently-displayed slide.

To create a graphic version of a slide, follow these steps:

1. Choose Export from the File menu. The Export dialog box appears; this dialog box looks just like the Save As dialog box except for the default directory and the file types available.

2. Select a graphics format from the File Type drop-down list.

3. Enter a filename for the slide that you are exporting as a graphic (by default, the correct graphics file extension is added automatically).

4. Choose Save. For most formats, another dialog box appears and asks questions specific to the selected graphics format. For example, Figure 19.19 shows the BMP-specific dialog box.

FIGURE 19.19

Exporting a slide as a BMP graphic opens a dialog box with graphics-specific questions.

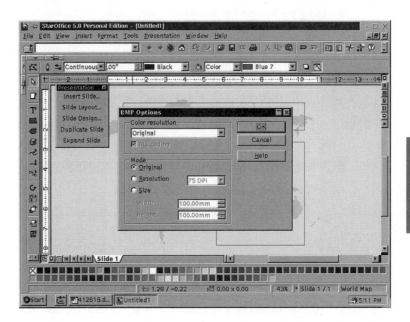

5. Answer the questions in the dialog box (if one appears) and choose OK to complete the export process.

Exporting a graphic can take several seconds. Don't worry if StarOffice seems to pause for a while.

Exporting as a Web Presentation

Although StarOffice can't export presentations in PowerPoint format, it can export in HTML format, so your presentation can be viewed in any Web browser.

Exporting in HTML creates a set of files with names based on the name you enter as an export filename. To export a presentation in HTML format, follow these steps:

1. Choose Export from the File menu. It doesn't matter which slide you're viewing when you choose Export in this case because the entire presentation is exported.

2. In the Export dialog box, choose HTML from the File Type drop-down list.

3. Enter a filename for the HTML document.

 Make the first part of the filename that you enter recognizable. Because each slide is a separate HTML file, StarOffice creates many filenames based on the name that you enter, chopping off part of it and adding numbers to the end of each filename.

4. Choose Save. The HTML Export dialog box appears (see Figure 19.20).

5. Choose a resolution for the graphic part of the HTML pages (the slides themselves). The higher the resolution, the larger the graphic image files are.

6. Choose OK to finish exporting to HTML.

When you have finished exporting, you can use a browser, or StarOffice, to read the first file of the set of HTML documents for your presentation.

For example, if you name your exported file Travel, StarOffice names the Contents page Travel_0. The first slide is Travel_1, which you can load as shown in Figure 19.21. Notice that a Continue link takes you to the next slide. (Low resolution has been used for these files so that they fit onscreen in StarOffice.)

FIGURE 19.20

Exporting an HTML version of a presentation enables you to choose from several options.

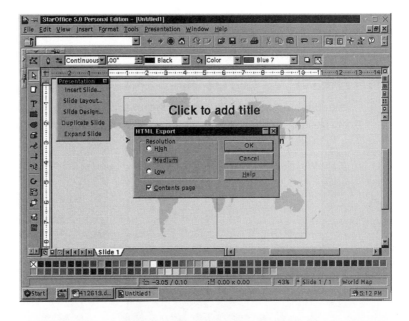

FIGURE 19.21

Each slide in a presentation exported to HTML includes a Continue link to go to the next slide.

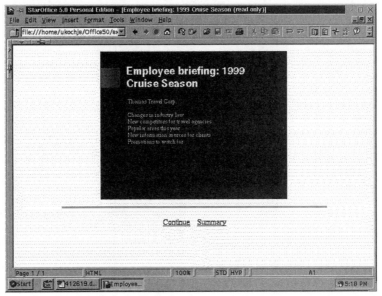

19

If you use a longer filename, StarOffice might cut off the end of the filename as each slide graphic file is created.

In the Next Hour

Hour 20 is a detailed description of how to add graphics and charts to your slides, either from existing graphics files or from spreadsheet charts that you've created in StarOffice.

Hour **20**

Adding Graphics and Charts to Your Presentation

In this hour you learn how to add additional graphical elements to your StarOffice presentations, beyond those provided by the StarOffice presentation templates.

Within a StarOffice presentation, you can add clip-art graphics, draw your own graphics, import graphics files, or use charts created in a StarCalc spreadsheet. In this hour you learn how to do each of these things.

Importing and Editing Graphic Files

Graphics are an important part of any slide presentation. With only bulleted lists, any presentation rapidly becomes a chore for both presenter and audience. With colorful graphics that illustrate your points, however, everything becomes more interesting.

StarOffice uses graphics in slides much as it does in word processing documents and spreadsheets. The sections that follow describe how to use the basic graphics features within your presentation slides.

Importing an Existing Graphic File

Any graphics file can be imported into a slide by following these steps:

1. Move to the slide on which you want to insert a graphic.
2. Set the viewing mode to Drawing (from the Master View submenu under the View menu).
3. Select Picture under the Insert menu, and then choose From File on the Picture submenu. The Insert Picture dialog box appears. (See Figure 20.1.)

FIGURE 20.1

A graphic can be imported into a slide from the Insert Picture dialog box.

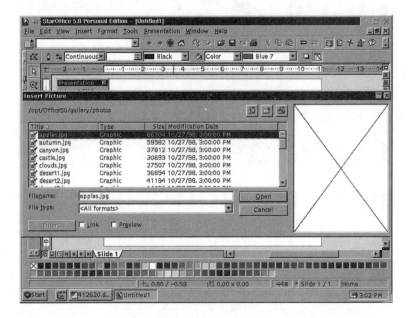

 You can also use StarDraw or Image Editor tools to draw a separate picture within a slide. Use of these drawing tools is described later in this hour.

Moving and Resizing an Imported Graphic

Any image that you import into a StarImpress presentation can be moved and sized to fit the slide you're creating.

To work with an image, it must first be selected. Select an image by clicking on it; green handles appear around the object when it is selected.

> If you don't see a regular arrow-shaped mouse pointer, you can't select objects on a slide. Choose the Arrow icon on the Main toolbar (usually on the left side of the screen).

After an object is selected, you can manipulate it in several ways:

- Click on the middle of the object and drag it to a new location.
- Click and drag a corner of the object (on a green handle) to change the size of the object (up or down). Hold down the Shift key as you do this to keep the ratio correct (to avoid distorting the image).
- Click the right mouse button or go to the Format menu to see all the formatting options available for the imported image, including 3D effects and slide show actions.

Editing an Imported Graphic File

For most bitmapped graphics that you import into a StarImpress presentation (in formats such as TIFF, GIF, and BMP), you can use the Image Editor to edit the imported graphic directly.

To use the Image Editor, right-click on a selected graphic and choose Image from the pop-up menu. Choose Edit from the Image menu that appears.

When you choose Edit from the Image menu, the bitmapped image appears in a heavy border and a different set of image manipulation tools appears in the Main toolbar (see Figure 20.2). The resolution of the image might also change so that you see only a portion of the graphic.

20

FIGURE 20.2

Bitmapped graphics within a slide can be edited in the Image Editor.

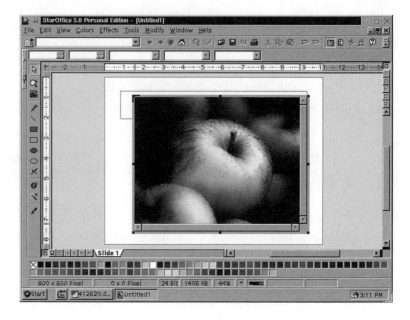

Table 20.1 describes the image manipulation tools provided on the Main toolbar when you start to edit a bitmapped image.

TABLE 20.1 IMAGE MANIPULATION TOOLS ON THE MAIN TOOLBAR

Tool name and icon	Description
Select tool; an arrow	Clicking the mouse cursor selects an object.
Zoom tool; a magnifying glass	Change the amount of theimage being viewed, or reset to a full-size view of the image.
Image tool; a small desert	Rotate or invert the landscape image by a set amount (45 degrees, 90 degrees, and so forth).
Pen tool	Select the tip of the drawing tool to determine what the line you create will be like (thick, thin, and so on).
Line tool	Enables you to draw a line; click to start the line, click again to end it.
Rectangle tool; a filled rectangle	Click and drag to form a filled square or rectangle.

Tool name and icon	Description
Rectangle frame tool; an unfilled rectangle	Click and drag to form an unfilled square or rectangle.
Ellipse tool; a filled ellipse	Click and drag to form a filled circle or ellipse.
Ellipse frame tool; an unfilled ellipse	Click and drag to form an unfilled circle or ellipse.
Airbrush tool; a pen with ink around it	Draw freehand lines with an airbrush effect.
Color tool; a rainbow circle	Set colors in your image by RGB channel, black and white, or other methods (using the fly-out menu).
Effects tool	Add effects to your image, such as charcoal, tile, embossed, and so on.
Eyedropper tool	Select an existing color in your image as the current palette color for new drawing actions.

If you click and hold on some of the image manipulation tools in the Main toolbar (Zoom, Image, Color, or Effects), a fly-out set of icons appears; you can then select options related to that tool. Hour 6, "Creating Graphics with StarDraw," describes these fly-out menus in more detail.

You can resize the image by using the mouse in the corner of the window. Changing the size of the Image Editing window doesn't make the image larger after editing, it just gives you more space to view the image during editing.

When you are done editing a graphic in the Image Editor, click the mouse somewhere else on the slide (not in the image window). The Image Editor closes, leaving the edited image in place on your slide.

Adding Actions to Graphics

Graphics in presentations have a special linking feature that makes them especially useful. A slideshow is often viewed on-line, whereas a spreadsheet or word processing document is almost always viewed on paper.

When you add a graphic to a slide, the graphic can be *live*. That is, it can have an action associated with it so that when you run a slide show, clicking on the graphic causes a certain action to occur in the slide show. This is similar to having a programmable button that you define on a slide.

20

To use this feature, follow these steps:

1. Import a graphic into your slide.

2. Select the imported graphic by clicking on it so that you can edit its properties.

3. Choose Interaction from the Presentation menu. The Interaction dialog box appears. No action is selected, so the dialog box isn't much to look at right now.

4. Click on the drop-down box and select an action to associate with clicking on this graphic. The choices include the following:

   - Play a sound.

   - Start another Linux program.

   - Go forward or backward in the slide show.

   - Go to another StarOffice document (for example, a full spreadsheet that explains the overview on the slide).

   - Go to a specific slide in the presentation.

   For example, if you choose Go to page or object, the dialog box changes to show the options from which you can select (see Figure 20.3).

FIGURE 20.3

When you select an Interaction for a graphic on a slide, you must define the parameters of that action.

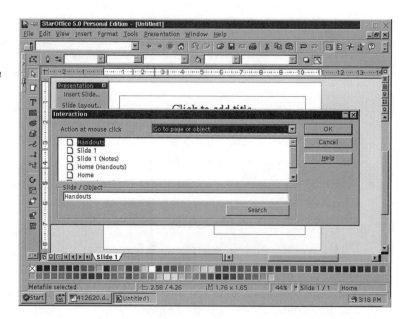

The slide titles in a presentation can be listed so that you can choose which slide to go to when the selected graphic is clicked.

Some of the choices in the Interaction dialog box are only relevant in the Windows version of StarOffice, even though they are still listed in the Linux version.

5. Choose OK to close the Interaction dialog box.

When you start a slide show (see Hour 21, "Formatting and Giving Your Presentation"), you can click on the graphic that you imported to execute the action that you selected in the Interaction dialog box.

Drawing Your Own Graphics

Adding graphics that you've created in a spreadsheet or other drawing program is a big part of most presentations. A slide is similar to a picture, though, and sometimes you need to add a feature specific to one slide.

StarOffice drawing tools enable you to do this. The basic drawing tools are always visible on the Main toolbar—on the left of the screen—as you edit slides in Drawing mode (a single slide fills the screen in this mode). The toolbar is shown in Figure 20.4.

FIGURE 20.4

The Main toolbar on the left side of a slide in Drawing mode contains a complete set of drawing tools.

20

The drawing tools shown on the Main toolbar are vector-based drawing tools, like those used in StarDraw (see Hour 6). Bitmap (raster) drawing tools are available by choosing Picture from the Insert menu, and then selecting From Image Editor.

Adding Lines and Rectangles

Simple shapes such as lines and boxes are easy to add and edit with the drawing tools. The steps that follow take you through a series of additions to a basic slide from a StarOffice template.

Start with a slide in Drawing mode, as shown in Figure 20.5. (This is the first slide of the New Employee Introduction presentation from the templates.)

FIGURE 20.5

This slide is used as the basis for these examples of drawing lines and shapes.

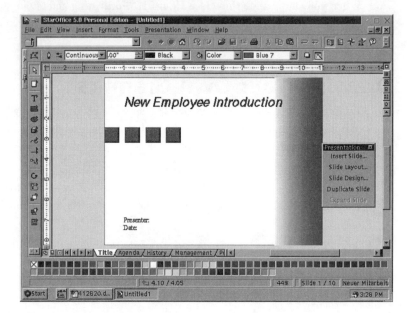

1. Click on the Lines and arrows icon on the Main toolbar on the left side of the screen.

2. Move the mouse pointer over the slide and notice how it changes from an arrow to crosshairs.

3. Click and drag the mouse pointer across the middle of the screen to make a long horizontal line.

4. Press the Shift key to constrain the line to vertical, horizontal, or a 45 degree angle.

5. Release the mouse button to finish drawing the line. The mouse pointer changes back to an arrow (the select object mode), but the line you drew remains selected (with a green handle on each end). The screen looks similar to Figure 20.6.

FIGURE 20.6

After drawing a line, the mouse pointer changes back to an arrow for object selection but the line object you drew remains selected.

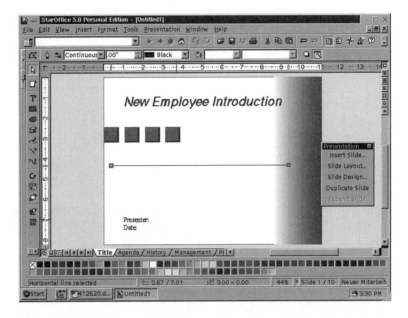

6. Move the mouse pointer over the line you drew and press the right mouse button. A pop-up menu appears.

7. Choose Line from the pop-up menu. The Line dialog box appears, as in Figure 20.7.

FIGURE 20.7

Lines and other shapes are formatted for color and style in the Line dialog box.

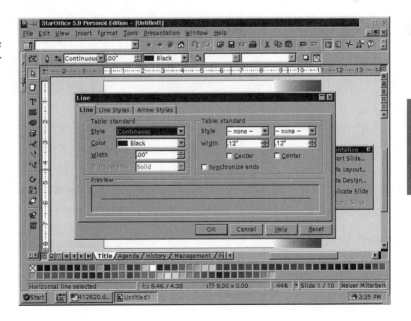

20

After an object is selected, you can usually use either the Format menu or the pop-up menus (accessed through the right mouse button) to choose formatting options for the object.

8. Choose a line style from the Style drop-down list. (See the Preview area in the dialog box to see how it will look.)

9. Increase the line width in the Width field.

10. Choose the Arrow Styles tab. (See Figure 20.8.)

FIGURE 20.8

The Arrow Styles tab defines how the ends of lines appear.

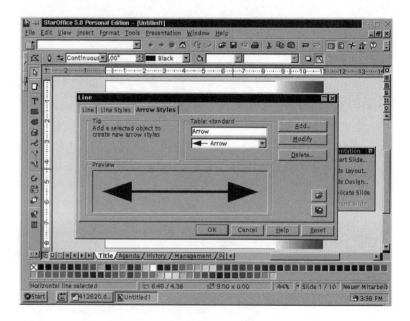

11. Select a style for the ends of the lines from the drop-down list.

You can import or save arrow styles as graphics by using the Folder or Diskette icons in the bottom right corner of the Arrow Styles tab.

12. Choose OK to close the Line dialog box. Your slide now looks somewhat similar to Figure 20.9.

FIGURE 20.9

A line can be added anywhere on a slide to separate sections of the slide.

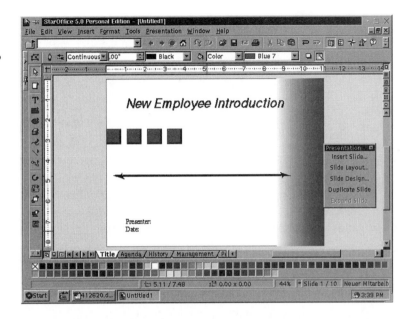

Now add a rectangle using another of the drawing tools as follows:

1. Click and hold on the 3D Rectangle icon on the Main toolbar on the left side of the window. A pop-up set of icons appears next to the Rectangle icon. (See Figure 20.10.)

FIGURE 20.10

Icons that have a small arrow include several options that you can see by clicking and holding the mouse button.

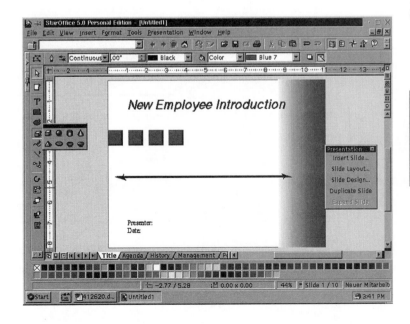

20

2. Move to the 3D Cylinder icon and release the mouse button.

3. Click and drag the mouse pointer within the slide to form a 3D cylinder. The new object remains selected.

4. Click in the middle of the cylinder and drag it to cover the text in the lower left corner of the slide.

5. Click and drag the green arrow in the middle, right side of the cylinder to make it wider.

6. Right-click on the cylinder. A pop-up formatting menu appears.

7. Choose Send to Back on the Arrange submenu. The slide text now appears on top of the cylinder.

 You can also use the Line menu item to control the thickness and color of the object borders.

The slide now looks similar to Figure 20.11.

FIGURE 20.11

Lines and shapes can be added to any slide with the drawing tools.

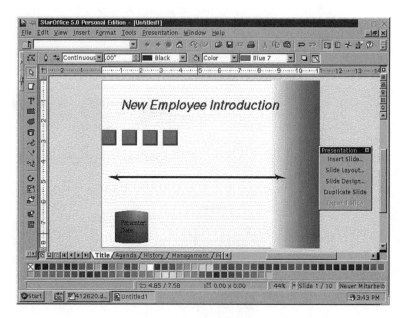

Other drawing tools from the Main toolbar on the left side of the screen can be selected to add polygons, circles, blocks of text, and other graphic elements to your slide.

Using Charts from Spreadsheets

Using charts within a presentation can be a powerful tool of persuasion. A good chart combines the visual impact of a graphic with the facts that you convey through the details of the chart.

StarOffice makes it easy to combine a chart with your presentation because the charting tools are part of the same program.

Importing a Chart

The easiest way to import a chart from a spreadsheet is to use the standard copy and paste functions. Follow these steps:

1. Go to the spreadsheet that contains a chart that you want to use in your presentation.
2. Click on the chart to select it (so that it has green handles on all sides).
3. Choose Copy from the Edit menu.
4. Switch to the presentation you're working on by selecting it from the Window menu.
5. Move to the slide on which you want the chart inserted.
6. Choose Paste from the Edit menu. The chart appears in the slide as an object that you can resize or move. (See Figure 20.12.)

FIGURE 20.12

Charts can be added to a presentation by using Copy and Paste from a spreadsheet.

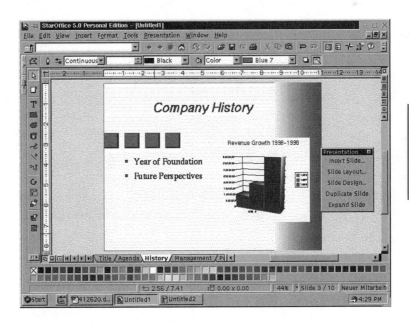

20

Charts that you copy from a spreadsheet and paste into a presentation slide are not linked to the spreadsheet. That is, they do not update instantly if the numbers in the spreadsheet change.

Inserting a spreadsheet

If the chart isn't enough, you can add a mini-spreadsheet to a slide in your presentation. The mini-spreadsheet functions like a regular spreadsheet in StarOffice, but it's surrounded by a presentation slide.

A spreadsheet within a slide provides a good structure for presenting tables of figures. Be careful, however, not to place too much in the spreadsheet, or the slide won't be legible.

To insert a spreadsheet into your slide, choose Spreadsheet from the Insert menu while viewing a slide in Drawing mode. A miniature spreadsheet appears in the slide, ready to have numbers entered (see Figure 20.13).

FIGURE 20.13

A spreadsheet can be inserted into a slide within a presentation.

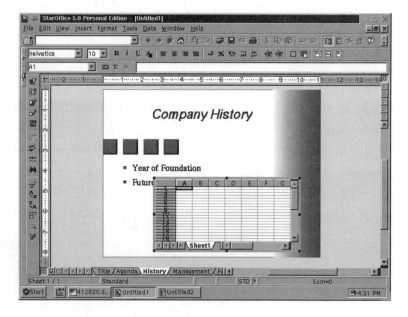

During editing of spreadsheet data, the slide might appear distorted. The slide appearance is restored when you click outside the spreadsheet to end editing mode.

In the Next Hour

In Hour 21, you'll move from preparing a single slide to working with your entire presentation. You'll learn how to format and arrange your slides using the slide sorter and outline view. You'll learn how to use the spell checker. Finally, you'll cover slide transitions and how to actually run your slide show.

20

HOUR 21

Formatting and Giving Your Presentation

In the last two hours you learned how to format and work with individual slides. This hour explains how to arrange and work with all the slides in a presentation: arranging them, defining transitions, and so on.

This hour describes how to set up and run your presentation as a slide show and how to prepare printed handouts of various styles to accompany or replace a stand-up slide show presentation.

Arranging Your Slides

As you prepare a presentation, you often want to rearrange the slides that you've prepared into a different order, or to at least get a feeling for their overall order and flow.

StarImpress provides several master views that make it easy to see all your slides, and to rearrange or sort them as needed.

The templates provided by StarImpress use Arial and Times New Roman fonts (leftovers from the Windows version of StarOffice). These are mapped to bitmapped fonts in Linux, which look terrible onscreen—especially if you increase their size. To fix this problem, change Arial fonts to Helmet and Times New Roman fonts to Timmons. (Other scalable fonts include charter, arioso, chevara, conga, and helmet condensed.)

Choosing a Master View

When you start a new presentation, StarImpress displays it in Drawing view. This view shows a single slide that fills the working area. All the drawing tools are available, and all the graphics, text, and other components of a slide are displayed as they will appear during a slide show. (See Figure 21.1.)

FIGURE 21.1

The default view for slides is the Drawing view, showing one slide with all its graphics and text.

The advantage to the Drawing view is that what you see onscreen is how the actual slide will look.

If you're using StarOffice to create a single graphical project such as a flyer or invitation, you'll probably only need the Drawing view. The other views described in this section are intended for multi-slide presentations.

Moving Between Slides

When you have multiple slides in your presentation and you're using the default Drawing view, you can use any of several methods to move between slides.

The easiest way to move to the next slide is to press Page Down. Pressing Page Up moves you to the previous slide.

Two other methods are also available for selecting which slides to view. At the bottom of the viewing area, StarOffice displays a tab for each slide, as well as navigation arrows. Either of these can be used to change which slide you are viewing.

The tabs at the bottom of the screen each contain the name of a slide. Clicking on one of these tabs displays the named slide. (See Figure 21.2.)

FIGURE 21.2

You can use slide tabs to move the Drawing view to a different slide.

Slide tabs

The navigation arrows can be used to move to the next slide in either direction by clicking on one of the middle two arrows, right or left. Or, you can click on the far left or right arrow to move to the first or last slide, respectively. (See Figure 21.3.)

FIGURE 21.3

The navigation arrows enable you to move to the previous or next slide, or to the first or last slide in your presentation.

Next slide Last slide

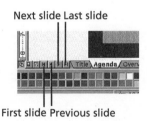

First slide Previous slide

Don't confuse these navigation arrows to the *left* of the slide tabs with the scroll bars on the *right* side of the slide tabs. The scroll bars and accompanying arrows only adjust the view of the current slide.

21

Using the Background Mode

While viewing slides in the Drawing view, you can choose to view just the text and graphics that you've entered, or you can view the background description of what the slide contains.

For example, the background mode contains bulleted items that you click to fill in or outlines of areas that are intended for graphics.

Background mode is useful if you're just learning how information is arranged on a template. Figure 21.4 shows how the background mode displays a slide in the Drawing view.

FIGURE 21.4

Background mode displays the areas in which text or graphics can be placed. The words that you see are not part of the slide—they only act as guides during data entry.

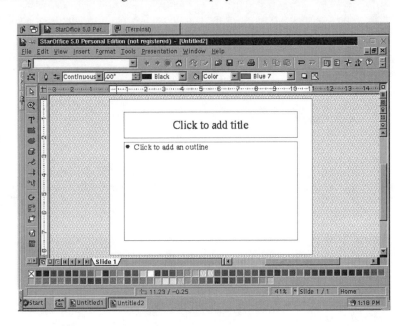

You can choose background mode by selecting Background from the View menu, and then choosing Drawing from the Background submenu. Return to the regular slide mode by selecting Slide from the View menu.

You can also use the buttons below the slides and to the left of the navigation arrows to choose slide mode or background mode. These are shown in Figure 21.5. (Another button, used to display Layers, is next to these buttons. It operates independently of them, but using layers is not described in this book.)

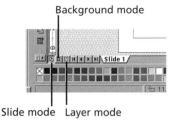

Background mode

Slide mode   Layer mode

FIGURE 21.5.

The Slide mode and background mode can be quickly selected from the buttons below a slide in the Drawing view.

Selecting Other Views

Four other Master views are available to help you prepare and visualize your presentation. Any of these Master views can be selected by choosing Master View from the View menu and making a selection from the Master View submenu. The Drawing view was described in the previous section; following is a description of each of the other views:

- **Outline view**—The outline view shows only the text on your slides, as if it were an outline in a word processor. (See Figure 21.6.) Slide titles and bullet points for all slides are shown in a single text flow. This helps you examine all the ideas in the presentation to see how they relate to each other.

FIGURE 21.6

Outline view displays all the titles and text of your slides in a single text flow, like an outline in a word processor.

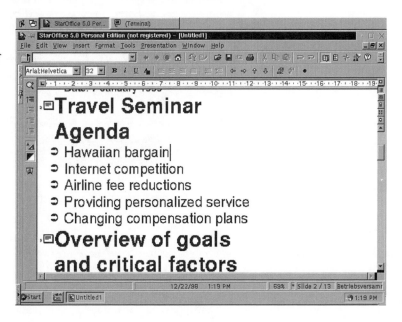

The outline view also makes it easier to edit your text because you can access text on all your slides without jumping from one slide to another.

21

Remember that graphics on your slides are not displayed in the Outline view. Be certain that you view the slides full-screen in Drawing view or a practice slide show to see how your edits have affected the slides.

• **Slide sort view**—The Slide Sort view displays all or most of the slides in your presentation, graphically and in a single view. (See Figure 21.7.) The size of the slides is adjusted to fit as many as possible onscreen at one time, but they don't shrink beyond a certain point. You can use the page up and page down keys or the navigation arrows as needed to reach other slides.

FIGURE 21.7

The Slide Sort view displays as many slides as possible on a single screen. This view is ideal for rearranging slides.

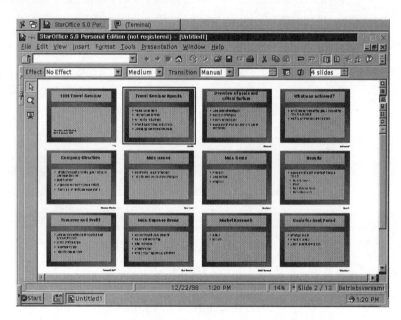

The Slide Sort view is ideal for arranging slides in your presentation (described in the next section).

• **Notes view**—When you've added notes to your presentation, sometimes called *presenter's notes*, you might want to view those notes at the same time that you view your slides. The Notes view enables you to do this (see Figure 21.8).

The Notes view displays only one slide at a time onscreen. As with the Drawing view, you can use the tabs, page up/page down, or navigation arrows to move between slides.

- **Handout view**—When you give a presentation, it's common to hand out paper copies of your slides as a reference for your audience. The handout view enables you to see how those handouts will look by displaying four slides at once on a single page-sized view. (See Figure 21.9.)

FIGURE 21.8

The Notes view shows your slide with presenter's notes below.

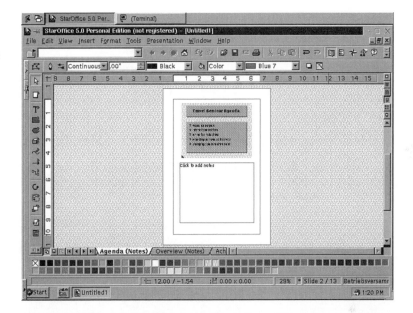

FIGURE 21.9

The Handout view enables you to see how your slide handouts will look.

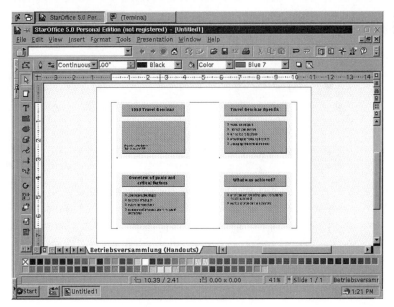

21

You can also select from among these viewing options by using the buttons on the right edge of the screen above the vertical scroll bar. The icons are small, but if you leave the mouse pointer over an icon, a pop-up description tells you which view is selected. Click on any of these icons to select a view. (See Figure 21.10.)

FIGURE 21.10

You can select a view by clicking on one of the view buttons located on the right edge of the display.

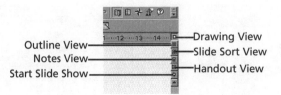

Outline View
Notes View
Start Slide Show

Drawing View
Slide Sort View
Handout View

Rearranging Slides Using the Slide Sorter

The Slide Sort view is ideal for rearranging slides after you've created a presentation. With the Slide Sort view, you can work with all the slides at once, seeing how they relate to each other in the presentation.

While working with slides in the Slide Sort view, you can double-click on any slide to switch to the most recently used full-screen view of that slide (Drawing, Notes, or Handouts view is used, depending on what you were viewing before selecting Slide Sort view).

To select a slide in the Slide Sort view, click on it once. You'll see a heavy black outline around the slide to indicate that it's been selected.

Moving Slides

The most useful feature of the Slide Sort view is the way it enables you to move slides around.

Suppose you have a presentation with many slides and you decide to move a slide to another position in the presentation.

While in the Slide Sort view, you can move the slide by clicking, dragging, and dropping the slide in a new location. As you drag the slide, an outline of the slide moves around the screen and a bar appears between the two slides where the slide you are dragging will be inserted when you release the mouse button (see Figure 21.11).

FIGURE 21.11

Moving slides in the Slide Sort view is guided by the slide outline and insertion bar.

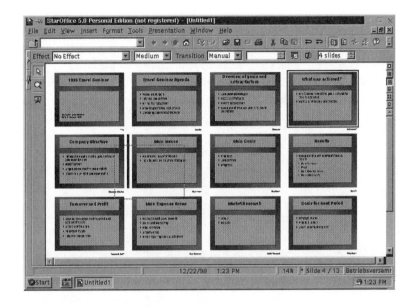

Copying and Pasting Slides

In Hour 19, "Creating Presentations with StarImpress," you learned how to insert new slides into your presentation using the Slide... item on the Insert menu.

You can't directly insert slides in the Slide Sort view, but you can easily copy and paste slides. Using copy and paste enables you to duplicate a slide and then make modifications to it, saving time when the slides are similar in layout or content.

To copy and paste a slide in the Slide Sort view, follow these steps:

1. Click on the slide that you want to copy to select it.
2. Press Ctrl+C to copy the selected slide.
3. Press Ctrl+V to paste the selected slide.

> You can also use the Cut, Copy, and Paste items from the Edit menu. The keyboard shortcuts are used to show how quickly you can work with slides in the Slide Sort view.

21

After you have used Paste to insert a copy of a slide, you can drag that slide to a new location if necessary.

Deleting Slides

As with moving and copying slides, deleting slides is best done in the Slide Sort view because the slide sorter enables you to see how the entire presentation is affected by the deletion of a slide. As the other slides fill in the space of a deleted slide, you can see how the topics flow and the presentation improves (hopefully).

To delete a slide in Slide Sort view, follow these steps:

1. To select the slide that you want to copy, click on it.
2. Press Ctrl+X to cut the slide from the presentation. Other slides move in to fill its place.

You can also use the Delete key or the Cut item from the Edit menu to delete a slide in the Slide Sort view.

If you realize you've made a mistake after deleting a slide, choose Undo from the Edit menu.

Defining Transitions Between Slides

Transitions are the visual movement from one slide to the next in your presentation. The transitions between slides can add or take away from the effect that you are trying to create.

For example, you can add to the excitement of a sales team presentation with varied and interesting transitions, or you can damage your image of professionalism by using wild transitions with strange sounds during a presentation to a key client.

StarOffice provides dozens of slide transitions from which you can select. The Slide Sort view is used to apply transitions to slides. You can use other views if you prefer, but with the Slide Sort view you can set all the transitions at once and see that they all fit together nicely.

To begin choosing slide transitions, choose Slide Transition from the Presentation menu. The Slide Transition window appears. (See Figure 21.12.) Use this window to select slide transitions, apply them to slides, and preview the results.

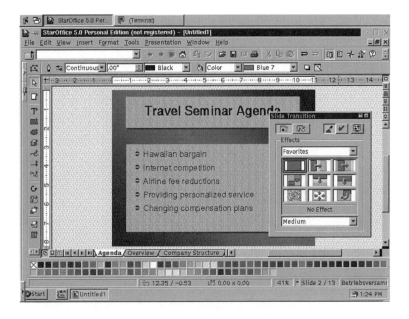

FIGURE 21.12

The Slide Transition window contains dozens of options for setting up transitions.

Notice that the Slide Transition window isn't like a dialog box—it can stay open as you work on the slides. Just choose the transition that you want to use at any time. You can close the window by choosing Slide Transition again from the Presentation menu (or by clicking the Close button in the upper right corner of the window).

All the transition options are not going to be explained here (including timed automatic transitions and adding a sound to a transition). You can experiment with these on your own by selecting the Extras button in the Slide Transition window.

Several parts of the Slide Transition window require an explanation. The main part of the window contains two drop-down lists.

From the top list, you select which set of transition effects are displayed in the boxes below the list. Favorites is selected by default. Other choices include Fade, Spiral, Stretch, and Uncover. If you select any of these the set of diagrams below the list changes.

The second list is the speed of the transition. Medium is selected by default. You can choose Slow or Fast from the list to change how rapidly the slide transition you define occurs.

21

Across the top of the Slide Transitions window are several buttons. From left to right they are

- **Effects**—Displays the set of transition effects from which you select, as previously described (this button is selected by default when you first open the Slide Transition window).
- **Extras**—Displays a set of other options that are not described here, but that you can experiment with on your own.
- **Update**—When this button is selected (toggled on), clicking on a slide selects the transition of that slide in the Slide Transition window.
- **Apply**—Applies the transition to the currently selected slide.
- **Preview**—Opens or closes the Preview window. When the Preview window is open, you can view a miniature transition for any slide by clicking the Apply button.

To apply a transition to a slide, follow these steps:

1. Open the Slide Transition window by selecting Slide Transition from the Presentation menu.
2. Click on the slide to which you want to apply a transition. (Make sure that the Update button is not selected.)

> When you apply a transition to a slide, you are defining what transition is displayed to arrive *at* that slide—not *from* that slide to the next slide. This is apparent as you use the Preview window.

3. Select a transition type from the drop-down list.
4. Select a transition by clicking on one of the small graphic images below the list.
5. Select a speed from the drop-down list.
6. Click on the Apply button (the green check-mark) to apply the selected transition to the current slide. A transition tag appears below the slide. If the Preview window is already open, the transition is also previewed as you select the Apply button.

> You can see if a slide has a transition applied to it by noting whether a transition tag appears below it in the Slide Sort view (see Figure 21.13).

FIGURE 21.13

The Slide Sort view displays a small tag or icon below each slide that has a transition applied to it.

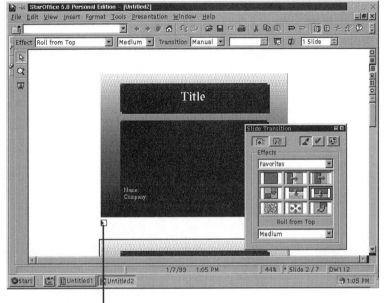

Indicates that a transition has
been applied to the slide

7. Click on the Preview button to open the Preview window (see Figure 21.14). The current slide appears in miniature in the Preview window.

FIGURE 21.14

The Preview window enables you to review how the slide transitions will actually look while still in the slide sorter view.

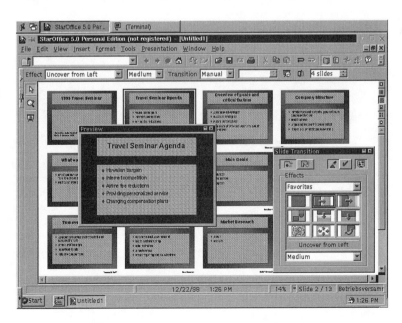

21

8. Click in the Preview window to see a demonstration of the transition that you have selected.

The transition Preview shows the transition to the current slide from a black background, rather than from the previous slide. It's still a good idea to review the entire presentation as a slide show (with all transitions in place) before showing it publicly.

9. Click on another slide in the slide sorter and repeat the process of assigning a transition to it.

In the Slide Sort view, you can click and drag a box around several slides, or you can hold down Shift while clicking on several slides at once. With several slides selected, you can apply a transition to all of them at once.

SpellChecking Your Presentation

Hour 12, "Using SpellCheck and the Thesaurus," already provided the lecture on the importance of spellchecking your document. Now imagine your misspelled word spread across a screen in 18 inch letters before 250 people. Follow the easy steps that follow to spellcheck every presentation.

You can run the StarOffice spellcheck from any slide view; however, the Outline view might be the fastest and most convenient because each slide doesn't have to be graphically drawn during spellcheck.

The spellcheck options for a presentation are the same as those for a document (as described in Hour 12):

- The AutoCorrect option fixes many simple typing errors, such as transposed letters.
- The AutoCheck option can be selected under the Spelling submenu on the Tools menu. This provides red underlining as a warning for any word that can't be found in the spelling dictionary.
- The Spelling window, with its replacement and ignore options and the thesaurus, is available to check the text of your presentations.

Adding Speaker Notes

Speaker notes (also called *presenter notes*) can guide you in making a presentation. They help you cover all the relevant points, in the correct order. They can also provide additional information in case questions arise during your presentation.

Speaker notes can be printed out on paper (described later in this hour) or displayed onscreen in the Notes view, as described earlier in this hour. Speaker notes are not intended for distribution to the audience; they provide information for the presenter.

Speaker notes can also be useful if you're preparing a presentation but not giving it. The speaker will appreciate the additional information and guidance on the topics as preparation for what the audience might ask or want to hear.

To add notes to a slide, you must be in the Notes view of your slides. Choose Master View from the View menu, and then Notes from the Master View submenu.

With the Notes view onscreen, you can add notes by double-clicking on the bottom half of the page that is displayed. A heavy line surrounds the notes area and a cursor appears.

Type the notes that you want to add to the slide. You can format the text as you do any paragraph of text in a StarOffice document. You can

- Change the font size of the text to fit more in the Notes window or to make it easier to read. (You only have the half page shown for each slide—no running over like a multi-page footnote.)
- Use bold, italic, or underline to emphasize points in the notes.
- Set justification to center or align paragraphs.
- Make the spacing between paragraphs wider or narrower (single- or double-spaced). Double-spaced is a good idea if you're using a smaller font size.

All these formatting options are available from the Format menu, from the toolbar, or by right-clicking in the notes area and selecting from the editing pop-up menu that appears (see Figure 21.15).

The slide itself is generally where you include graphics to assist in your presentation, but you can also include them in the notes area so that they are only visible to the speaker.

With the notes area selected, you can choose Picture from the Insert menu, and then select From File... from the Picture submenu. The now-familiar Insert Picture dialog box appears, and you can select an image file to insert into the Notes area (see Figure 21.16).

21

FIGURE 21.15

A pop-up editing menu appears when you click the right mouse button in the Notes area of a slide.

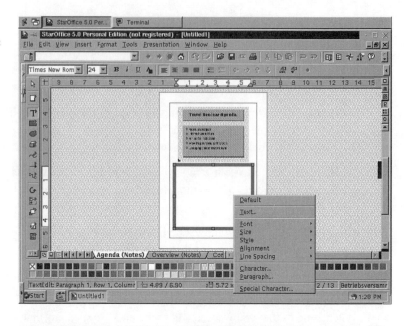

FIGURE 21.16

You can insert a picture in the Notes area, just as you can in the Slide itself, by using the Insert Picture dialog box.

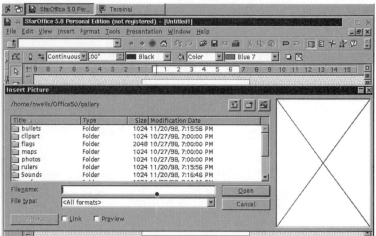

You can also use the built-in StarOffice Image Editor or the StarDraw tools on the Main toolbar to sketch graphics in the Notes area.

Setting Presentation and Slide Show Options

StarOffice provides many different settings for preparing and running a presentation. You can choose from among these options using two dialog boxes: one for general presentation settings and one for slide show options.

Setting Presentation Options

You can open the Presentations Options dialog box by selecting Presentations on the Options submenu under the Tools menu. This dialog box, shown in Figure 21.17, includes settings for what is displayed and how graphic snap and grids function, and for various layout and measurement options.

FIGURE 21.17

The Presentation Options dialog box includes settings for display choices, drawing with graphics tools, and measurement options.

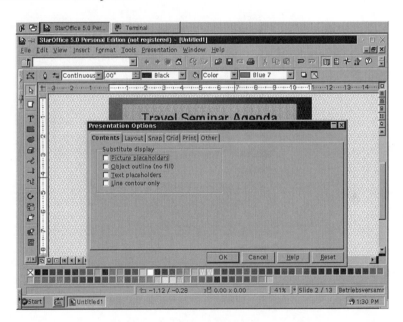

The Contents tab contains options for how objects are displayed in slides as you create them. You can select a checkbox to make any of the following substitutions in the slide display:

- **Picture placeholders**—These are of the same size and shape as the picture, to save time redrawing graphic images.
- **Object outlines**—To save time redrawing objects.
- **Text placeholders**—To see where text goes on a slide without displaying it.
- **Line contours**—Contours, without filling in the complete curve and details of the line, again to save time in drawing the line.

21

In the Layout tab (shown in Figure 21.18), you can set which items to display to assist you with slide layout:

FIGURE 21.18

In the Layout tab, select which tools are displayed to assist with slide layout and how measurements are calculated.

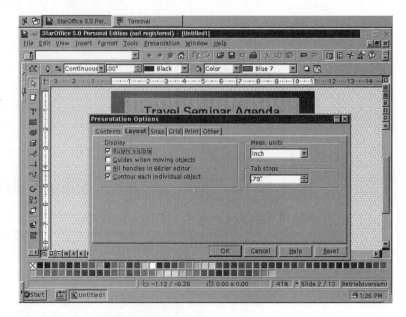

- Rulers that show vertical and horizontal position of objects on a slide. A line in the ruler tracks the mouse pointer position as you work.
- Guides when moving objects, to show you the location that objects are being moved to.
- All handles on a Bezier object (default is to display only a few of the handles on these objects).
- The complete contour of each object (you can de-select this option to limit the contours shown and speed up the display).

In addition to these display options, in this tab you can set the distance between tab stops and choose a measurement unit such as inches, picas, or centimeters.

The Measurement units drop-down list includes Miles and Kilometers in addition to inches, millimeters, and picas. Who knows how they ended up on the list, but they're not much help in building a slide.

The Snap tab (shown in Figure 21.19) and the Grid tab (which is the same as the Grid tab in the Spreadsheet Options dialog box) are both used to assist in precisely positioning graphics and objects within a slide.

FIGURE 21.19

The Snap tab defines how snap-to functions operate when creating objects that need to be aligned with other items (such as the grid or page margins).

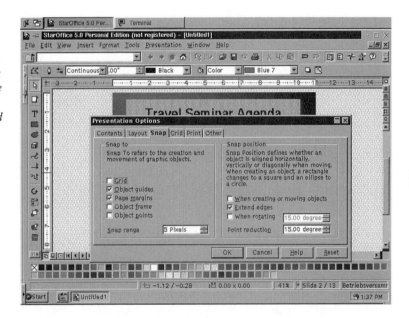

For example, you can use the Snap tab to define that when an object is moved to within 5 pixels of the page margin, it is automatically *snapped* to the page margin. This helps you line up all the objects on your slides.

> The Print tab is described later in this hour. It can also be accessed from the Options... button on the Print dialog box (which is opened from the File menu).

Setting the Slide Show Options

The options that apply to running a slide show are not part of the Presentation Options dialog box. Instead, you can find them by selecting Presentation Settings from the Presentation menu. The Slide Show dialog box appears (see Figure 21.20).

21

FIGURE 21.20

In the Slide Show dialog box you can select settings that define how your slide presentation will be run.

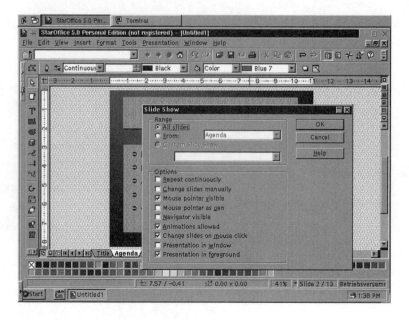

The following list describes each of the features that you can select in the Slide Show dialog box (most of the default settings will be acceptable):

- **Range**—You can select the All slides radio button to include all slides in the slide show, or you can select the From radio button and choose a slide title from the drop-down list. If you choose the From button, the slide show starts from the selected slide.

> An item on the Other tab of the Presentation Options dialog box (in the Options submenu under the Tools menu) enables you to choose to start a slide show from the current slide. This option is not selected by default.

- **Repeat continuously**—If this checkbox is selected, the slide show is repeated continuously, linking from the last slide back to the first slide, until the Esc key is pressed to end the show.

- **Change slides manually**—This checkbox works in conjunction with an option in the Slide Transition window (which was described earlier in this hour). The Slide Transition window, under the Extras button, enables you to choose Automatic or Manual advance for the current slide, and to enter a delay in seconds (see Figure 21.21).

FIGURE 21.21

You can select automatic slide advance with a timed delay in the Slide Transition window.

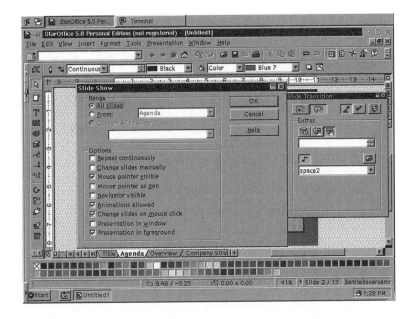

The Change slides manually checkbox forces you to manually advance slides even if an automatic setting is part of any slide transition.

- **Mouse pointer visible**—If this checkbox is not selected, the mouse pointer is not visible during the presentation. However, not all Linux systems are configured in a way that allows this feature to work properly, so you might just have to move the mouse pointer to the edge of the screen as you give your presentation.

- **Mouse pointer as pen**—If you select the Mouse pointer visible checkbox, you can also select the Mouse pointer as pen checkbox, which changes the mouse pointer from an arrow to a small pen. This looks better than having the familiar arrow floating around the screen as you speak.

- **Navigator visible**—During a slide show, the Navigator window contains a list of all the slides in the presentation. If you select this checkbox, the Navigator window is visible over the top of your presentation at all times. Figure 21.22 shows how this window looks during a presentation.

The Navigator window is helpful if you are moving to different slides a lot because you are reviewing your presentation. For a public presentation, the Navigator window might be in the way.

21

FIGURE 21.22

The Navigator window can be displayed during a presentation to help you move among the slides in your presentation.

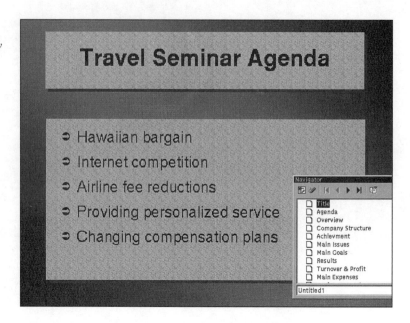

- **Animations allowed**—If this checkbox is selected, any animations that you have defined within your slides are executed as each slide is displayed. Uncheck this option if you're concerned about speed, or if you just want to try the presentation without animations running.

- **Change slides on mouse click**—With this checkbox selected, you can use the mouse to advance to the next or previous slide during a presentation. If this checkbox is not selected, you must use the keyboard to advance the slides.

- **Presentation in window**—If this checkbox is selected, the slide show appears within the StarOffice window, looking as it did when you were editing the slide in the Drawing view.

After you select options for your slide show, choose OK in the Slide Show dialog box to apply your settings and close the dialog box.

Running a Slide Show

As you develop a presentation in StarOffice, you'll probably want to run it as a slide show many times to see how it looks.

To start a slide show do any of the following:

- Choose the slide show icon on the right edge of the StarOffice window.
- Select Slide Show from the Presentation menu.
- Press Ctrl+F2 (this might not work within some window managers, however).

After a few seconds, the first slide appears full-screen (see Figure 21.23).

FIGURE 21.23

The slide show appears full-screen, enabling you to advance the slides with the mouse or keyboard.

You might notice a menu item called Display quality below the Slide show item on the View menu. This item only affects how the slides appear during editing. (A lower quality setting can improve system performance if you have graphic images in your slides.) The slide show is always presented in full color.

You can control the slide show using the mouse or keyboard, depending on the settings that you selected in the Slide Show dialog box (described in the previous section). For example, if you've deselected Change slides on mouse click, none of the mouse events listed in the table that follows will function.

Table 21.1 describes how to interact with the slide show while it is running.

21

TABLE 21.1 SLIDE SHOW INTERACTION VIA MOUSE OR KEYBOARD

Action	How to do it
Advance to the next slide	*Mouse*: Click the left mouse button once.
	Keyboard: Press spacebar, the Enter key, or the right arrow key.
Return to the previous slide	*Mouse*: Click the right mouse button once.
	Keyboard: Press the left arrow key.
Go to the first slide	Press the Home key.
Go to the last slide	Press the End key.
End the slide show	Press the Esc key.

Some people have a habit of double-clicking on everything. Double-clicking during a slide show advances two slides. If you happen to make this mistake, click the right button once to back up, and then click the left button once to advance the slide when you're ready.

Preparing Hardcopy Slides

For many presentations, you'll want to have paper handouts of your slides for your audience. StarOffice has several options for how those handouts can be printed. The following section describes how to set up and print the handouts that you need.

Setting the Page Size

The default size setting for a presentation is the computer monitor. When you print the slides to paper, you need to select the correct paper size to which you want to print.

To set the page size, follow these steps:

1. Choose Page from the Format menu. The Page dialog box appears. (See Figure 21.24.)

2. From the Paper format drop-down list, select 8.5 x 11 in.

3. Choose the Landscape option to print slides or handouts. Choose the Portrait option to print Speaker Notes or a presentation outline.

4. Choose OK to apply these settings and close the dialog box.

FIGURE 21.24

In the Page dialog box, you can set up margins and paper size to print your presentation.

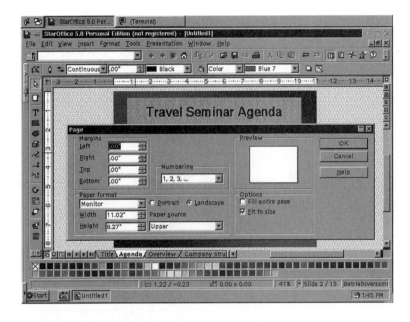

Defining Printing Options

To print a presentation, choose the Print item from the File menu. The Print dialog box appears (see Figure 21.25).

FIGURE 21.25

The Print dialog box is used to print a paper copy of your presentation. First, however, choose Options... to select what to print.

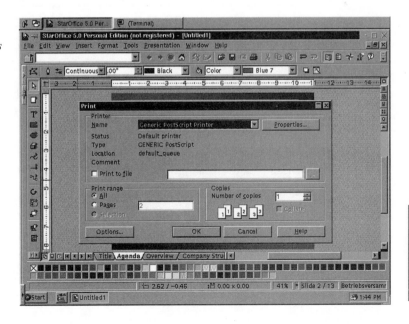

21

The presentation printing options are linked to this standard printing dialog box. You can access them by choosing the Options… button. The Printer Options dialog box appears, and you can select how and what to print. (See Figure 21.26.)

FIGURE 21.26

Select what to print and which other printing options to apply in the Printer Options dialog box.

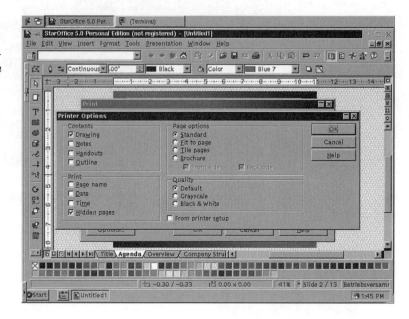

The Printer Options dialog box can also be viewed as the Printing tab in the Presentation Options dialog box.

In the Contents area of the Printer Options dialog box, you can choose what you want to print. The four options correspond to the four Master Views that you can use while preparing your slides. They are

- **Drawing**—Print one slide per page. This choice is suitable for copying onto transparencies for an overhead projector.
- **Notes**—Print one slide on the top half of a page with the speaker notes on the bottom half.
- **Handouts**—Print four slides per page for handouts to your audience.
- **Outline**—Print the text of the slides without formatting it into slides. The text is printed like a continuous outline in a word processor document.

Note that these options are checkboxes, not mutually-exclusive radio buttons. If you check all the boxes, StarOffice prints four sets of pages, one after another.

The Print area of the dialog box defines what information is included on each printed page. You can include

- The page name, which corresponds to the slide name
- The date
- The time
- Any hidden pages (which aren't displayed during a slide show)

The Output quality area enables you to choose the default, Grayscale, or Black & White setting for printing. If you choose Grayscale or Black and White, your printing time can be significantly reduced. If you aren't using a color printer to prepare transparencies, you can use the grayscale option in most cases.

Finally, if you've selected a non-standard paper size—instead of Letter—you can use the Page options to select how pages will be arranged on paper (from the printing options that you selected).

Choose OK to close the Printer Options dialog box.

With the options selected, you can choose OK in the Print dialog box to begin printing your presentation handouts.

In the Next Hour

Hour 22, "Creating Internet Documents with StarOffice," guides you through setting up the basic Internet features of StarOffice and starting to use StarOffice to browse the Web. It also teaches you about using Web documents (importing and creating them) and linking to the Web from your other StarOffice documents.

21

PART V

Using Internet and Scheduling Features in StarOffice

Hour

22 Creating Internet Documents with StarOffice

23 Using StarOffice Email and Newsgroup Features

24 Using StarSchedule

Hour **22**

Creating Internet Documents with StarOffice

This hour describes how to use key Internet features of StarOffice to integrate the documents that you create with StarOffice with those that you find or want to provide on the Internet.

StarOffice is the most completely integrated Office suite available. Whereas the rest of this book has described how to use the basic features of StarOffice, in this hour you'll learn how to integrate many of those features into an Internet environment.

Setting Internet Options

In order to use StarOffice as an Internet-aware office suite, you must be connected to the Internet. If you are not connected, you can still create HTML pages (described later in this hour) but you can't browse the Web or send and receive email as described in Hour 23, "Using StarOffice Email and Newsgroup Features."

If you are connected to the Internet and have a correctly configured Linux system, the browser features of StarOffice will work correctly without any additional action on your part. This hour provides a review of the Internet options to help you understand a little more about how StarOffice interacts with the Internet.

The technical descriptions are kept to a minimum as the Internet options are described, but you might find that you need more information to set up the Internet connection properly. Contact your system administrator or, if you are the system administrator, pick up a copy of *Sams Teach Yourself Linux in 24 Hours* or *Special Edition Using Linux, 4th Edition*. Either of these books can teach you more about the protocols and Internet server tools of Linux—things that are only touched on here.

Using StarOffice with the Internet involves three separate sets of option settings within StarOffice:

- Basic Internet connectivity information (servers, proxy, and so on)
- Internet Browser configuration (caching, display sizes, and so on)
- HTML Document settings (source text and table options, content display, printing, and so on)

The following section describes the Internet options that allow your connection to the Internet to work correctly. The browser and HTML options are described later in this hour.

Choosing Internet Server Options

StarOffice provides many Internet capabilities, but you have to set them up before you can use them all. This setup is done in the Internet Options dialog box, which you can open by selecting Options from the Tools menu, and then selecting Internet... from the Options submenu. (See Figure 22.1.)

The first tab, Proxy, defines the proxy server that you're using for your Internet connection. If you have no proxy server, you can leave this set to None. If you are using a proxy server, choose Manual and enter the server name and port number for each protocol that uses the proxy.

For example, the server might be something such as gw.thomastravel.com, and the port might be something such as 3260. The server and port are often the same for all the protocols in the list.

FIGURE 22.1

*The Internet options
dialog box controls the
configuration of
Internet servers and
protocols within
StarOffice.*

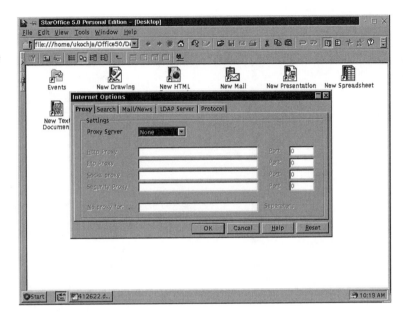

22

If you thought you had an Internet connection, but the browser functions
(described later) don't work, your network might require a proxy to access
Internet protocols such as HTTP. Check with your network administrator for
more information.

Email and newsgroups are the subject of Hour 23; however, setting up the connection to
use them is part of this dialog box, so it is described here.

In the Mail/News tab (see Figure 22.2), enter the server names and user information
required to retrieve and send email messages and newsgroup postings.

The Outgoing and Incoming mail servers are often different. The Outgoing mail server
might be the name of the system on which you are running StarOffice, if your Linux
system is running a mail server program such as Qmail or Sendmail.

The Incoming mail server can also be your Linux system, but might be another server on
your network or the Internet. StarOffice can use several different mail protocols to send
and receive email, depending on how your network is configured and how you set up an
email account (described in Hour 23). The User ID and Password that you enter in this
dailog box are used mainly to retrieve POP3 email from a POP mail server.

FIGURE 22.2

*In the Mail/News tab,
enter the server names
and usernames needed
to access your email
and post to news-
groups.*

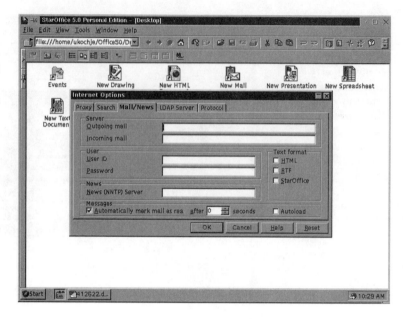

The News server is the computer that contains the newsgroups that you want to read and
post to. Unless you have a large system and a lot of expertise, your desktop Linux computer is probably not the news server (they are difficult to set up and are not set up by
default like mail servers are).

Enter the name of the nearest news server on your network, or the news server at your
ISP location.

Finally, the Text Format area defines how incoming messages for email and news are
formatted. You can save a message in any of these formats as you view it, so the choice
is not restrictive.

The other server option that might need some attention is the LDAP Server tab (see
Figure 22.3).

LDAP is a *directory service protocol* that enables you to access worldwide
listings of people and resources through your Web browser. LDAP is growing
rapidly in popularity. Linux is developing strong LDAP support, so you might
be able to use LDAP for these directory services soon.

FIGURE 22.3

The LDAP server tab lists directory servers that StarOffice can use as you access the Internet.

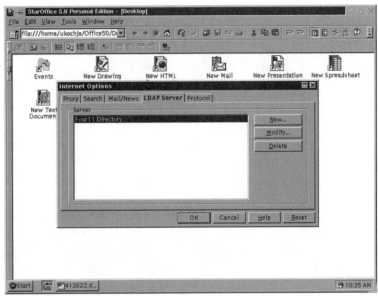

The name of each LDAP server is listed in the Server list. You can define a new Internet LDAP server that you want to access by pressing the New... button. You can also select any of the servers listed and choose Modify... to see or update the information related to that LDAP server. (See Figure 22.4.) Note that the standard port for the LDAP protocol is 389. If you choose another port number, you might not be able to access the LDAP server.

FIGURE 22.4

Each LDAP server can be set up with a server and port number.

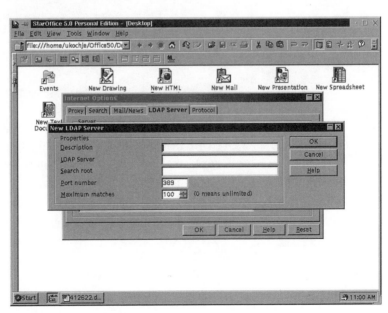

Four11, a master LDAP directory server that is available to everyone on the Internet, is already included in the LDAP Server list.

Setting up Internet Searching

The Web is becoming much more friendly to those who don't know their way around. Directories, search engines, and other portals provide guidance as you seek information on a particular topic.

StarOffice integrates access to seven of the most popular search sites (or *portals*) as part of its browser capabilities. In the Search tab (see Figure 22.5), you can review the search options that are set by default, or you can alter the list as needed.

FIGURE 22.5

In the Search tab, you can review or alter how popular search engines are used to retrieve information on topics for which you search.

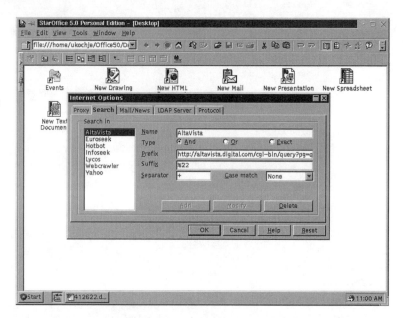

For example, Yahoo! is shown in the list of search engines. When you click on Yahoo, the Prefix field shows the URL that StarOffice uses to send a search query to Yahoo. Words that you enter as subjects to search for are added to the information shown so that you can receive a list of search hits.

Unless you discover that one of the seven nationwide search engines has altered their searching format, you won't need to change anything in the Search tab.

Setting up Internet Protocols

Internet connectivity for your Linux system is not set up in StarOffice. You can use commands such as `route` and `ifconfig` at a Linux command line to examine your networking (if you're logged in as root).

Within StarOffice, however, you can set a couple of networking options. These are included on the Protocol tab of the Internet Options dialog box. (See Figure 22.6.)

FIGURE 22.6

In the Protocols tab, you can define settings for HTTP, FTP, and DNS.

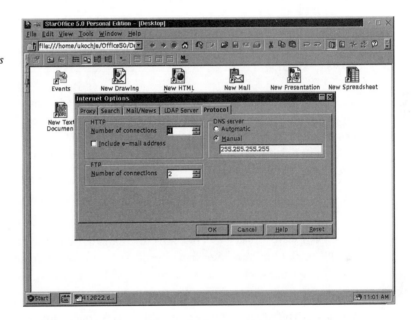

In the HTTP area, you can define how many connections are used at the same time to retrieve a document. For example: If you request an HTML document which in turn contains ten small graphics, StarOffice can request several of them at the same time instead of requesting one, waiting for a reply, and then requesting the next one.

If you have a fast Internet connection (such as a 56K modem or faster), you can increase this number from the default of four. If you are using a slow modem, increasing the connection won't improve the speed of document downloads.

The Include email address checkbox determines whether your email address (as entered in the General Options dialog box, described in Hour 4, "Configuring StarOffice") needs to be included as part of each request that is sent to a Web server. If this checkbox is selected, Web servers can log your email address and use it to send you information (such as advertising). Most people probably prefer to leave this unchecked (the default setting).

> Not all Web servers can or do track email addresses submitted with page requests. Most of those who track them for statistical purposes will never use them for unsolicited advertising—but why give them the chance?

Connections for FTP servers are handled like those for Web servers (HTTP servers). You can choose to have multiple connections at the same time to speed up the retrieval of files. However, using an FTP server usually involves only a single interaction. An FTP site doesn't include multiple graphics that are downloaded at the same time to create a page.

The default setting of two FTP connections will be fine, even if you're using a fast Internet connection.

In the DNS server area, you define how the Domain Name Service is used within StarOffice. *Domain Name Service* is the network system that maps from an Internet IP address to a name such as www.cnn.com.

The DNS server area works independently of the settings within your Linux system; that is, it can. If you select Automatic, StarOffice uses your Linux settings to find a DNS name server. If you prefer to use a different name server while browsing with StarOffice, you can select Manual and enter the IP address of another DNS name server.

> The DNS name server on your network might work in conjunction with a proxy server (see the Proxy section earlier in this hour). Choosing a different name server might not be possible.

When you have finished setting options in the Internet Options dialog box, choose OK to apply your changes and close the dialog box.

Using the StarOffice Browser

With the Internet access options set, you can use StarOffice as a Web browser as easily as you use it to create documents.

Opening a Web Document

Viewing a document from the Web in StarOffice is as easy as entering the URL. Make sure that the Function toolbar is visible, and then enter the URL that you want to view in the URL field (see Figure 22.7) and press Enter.

URL Field

FIGURE 22.7

Enter the URL for the Web page that you want to view in the URL field on the Function toolbar.

In the drop-down list below the URL field, you can see a list of other URLs for the documents that you've been working on. The URLs in this list usually start with file:/// to indicate that they are locally-stored documents. This list is similar to the history list in a Web browser, or to the list of recently opened files on the bottom of the File menu.

When you press Enter after typing something in the URL field, the Web page or file is retrieved and displayed in the working window as if you had used the Open item on the File menu. (See Figure 22.8.)

If your network connection appears to be working in Linux, but not in StarOffice, check that the Online button on the function toolbar (a small globe) is toggled to On.

FIGURE 22.8

A Web page address entered in the URL field causes that page to be retrieved and displayed in StarOffice.

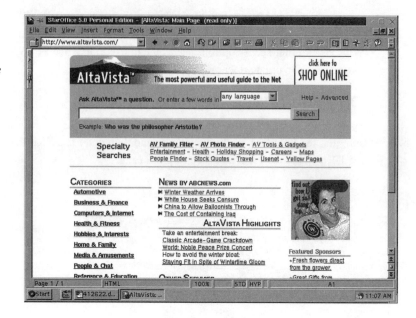

After you have retrieved a Web document, you can treat it as you do in a regular Web browser—click on links to view other pages, print it, and so on. However, you can also treat the Web document as you do any other StarOffice document—edit it, save it, or copy and paste parts of the document into other StarOffice documents.

The formats of the Web and StarOffice are not the same, so some formatting features (such as footnotes) don't transfer exactly between the two; but StarOffice is intended to be used with the Web, making the Web just like an extension of your local workspace.

If you have sufficient permissions and a Web server that supports it, you can also upload, or PUT, documents to a Web server from within StarOffice; check the StarOffice online help for more information.

One of the great advantages of the Web is its capability to easily hyperlink to other documents. StarOffice builds on that feature in several ways, as the next section describes.

Inserting Automatic Links in StarWriter Documents

As you work with documents in StarOffice that you've loaded from the Web, you probably click on a lot of links. StarOffice enables you to add links to any StarOffice document. This can be done in two ways: automatic or manual links. When either type of link

22

is added to a StarOffice document, anyone who reads that document (within StarOffice) can click on the link and jump to that page.

To see an automatic link created, open a StarWriter word processing document and enter an URL or an email address as text. For example, in the middle of a document, type the following:

```
http://www.linuxjournal.com
```

Notice that StarOffice automatically creates a link to the URL that you entered. The link is usually blue and underlined. (See Figure 22.9.) Immediately after you enter the sample URL, click on it with your mouse. The document—in this case, the Web home page for the Linux Journal magazine—appears in StarOffice.

FIGURE 22.9

An URL entered in a StarOffice document is immediately converted to a live Web link.

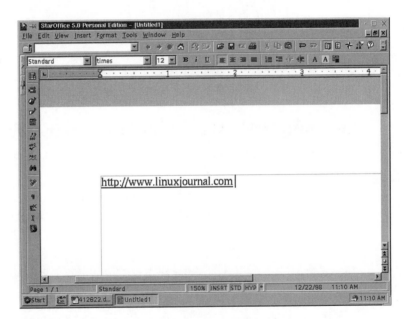

Email addresses function in the same way. Enter an email address such as the following:

```
nwells@xmission.com
```

StarOffice immediately makes it into a `mailto:` link; therefore, clicking on the words that you just entered causes StarOffice to initiate an email message to this email address, as shown in Figure 22.10. (See Hour 23 for details on configuring and sending email within StarOffice.)

FIGURE 22.10

Email addresses also create automatic links; when you click on the links, they initiate email to the named person.

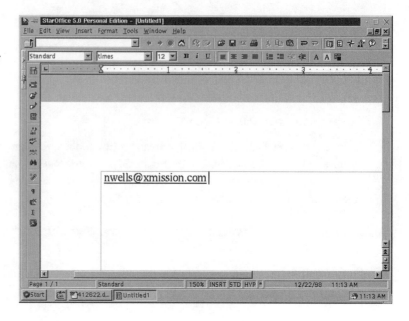

nwells@xmission.com

Inserting Manual Links in StarWriter Documents

Sometimes, of course, you don't want to enter the URL to a piece of information—you just want to click on a reference that links to another Web page.

Any piece of text in a StarOffice document can be linked to an URL, just as you might mark a piece of text as bold or italic. This can be done in a StarWriter word processing document, not just in a document written in HTML or intended for direct viewing on the Web.

To manually mark a word or phrase with an URL link to a Web page, follow these steps:

1. Select the text that you want to link to a Web page.
2. Choose Character... from the Format menu. The Character dialog box appears.
3. Select the Hyperlink tab (see Figure 22.11).
4. In the URL field, enter the URL to which you want to link the selected text. (The other fields aren't used in this example.)
5. Choose OK to close the dialog box. The selected text is now hyperlinked to the URL you entered.
6. To see the hyperlink, move the mouse pointer over the underlined words and leave it there for a second. A pop-up box with the linked URL appears (see Figure 22.12).

FIGURE 22.11

Hyperlinks can be added to any block of text by specifying a link address in the Character dialog box.

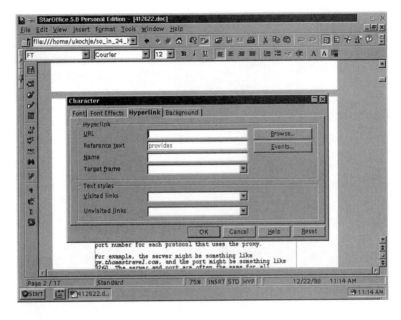

FIGURE 22.12

Hyperlinks within text are shown in pop-up boxes whenever you move over a hyperlinked phrase.

Hyperlinked phrase

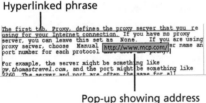

Pop-up showing address

You can also enter a file:/// link to hyperlink the selected word or phrase to one of your own documents, sort of like a mini-Web site without the server.

Inserting Links in Spreadsheets and Presentations

In the preceding example, you created a hyperlink with a phrase in a word processing document. You can also enter links in spreadsheets and presentations, but not with as much flexibility.

When you type an URL within any spreadsheet cell or presentation slide, the URL is immediately converted to a hyperlink that you can click on to go to that page. (See Figure 22.13.)

FIGURE 22.13

You can enter an URL in a spreadsheet cell to create an automatic hyperlink.

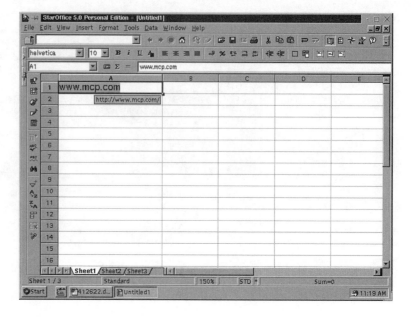

However, you can't select a word in a cell or on a slide and attach a hyperlink to it. The Format menu for a spreadsheet or presentation doesn't include the hyperlink option.

Saving URLs in the Explorer

The Explorer window and the Bookmarks folder were described at the beginning of this book; now you're ready to use them.

Anytime you view a file or a document on the Internet, you can save the location of that document in the Bookmarks folder. To save the location of any document, follow these steps:

1. Open the Explorer window by selecting Explorer from the View menu. Click the Show arrow in the corner of the Explorer window if the Explorer is selected but hidden.

2. Click on the Bookmark icon, drag it to the bookmarks folder, and release the mouse button. (The link icon is shown in Figure 22.14.)

You can make use of the links in the Bookmark folder in a couple of ways.

To view the contents of the Bookmark folder, click on the Start menu below the document window. The Bookmarks submenu contains all your bookmarks. You can also open the Beamer window (select it from the View menu) and click on the Bookmarks folder in the Explorer window to view the bookmarks in the Beamer.

FIGURE 22.14

The Bookmark icon represents the URL of the current document. Drag it to the Bookmarks folder to save a link to the current document.

The Bookmark icon

22

> An HTML document in the Bookmark folder is listed by its HTML title, which appears in the title bar of any browser when you view the file. Local files are listed by their filenames.

To open a bookmark, select it from the Bookmarks submenu of the Start menu. If you're viewing bookmarks in the Beamer window, you can either

- Drag the bookmark from the Beamer window and drop it in the current document to place a link at the current cursor location.
- Double-click on the bookmark in the Beamer window to open that document.

The advantage of using bookmarks is that they make a document easy to access, but take up almost no space (only a few bytes each).

Working with Web Documents

StarOffice enables you to view and link to Web documents, but it also enables you to create them. New Web documents can be created from existing Web documents that you download, or they can be started from scratch with nothing but an idea.

> If you want to use downloaded pages as the basis for your own Web pages, ask for permission and check the legal statements on the site. Generally it's best to learn from other sites—even studying the HTML code from their pages—but to create your own Web page from scratch.

Saving Existing Documents for the Web

Hour 5, "Importing and Exporting StarOffice Documents," describes how you can use the Save As feature of StarOffice to export HTML documents for use on the Web or as an interchange format for others who aren't using StarOffice.

HTML—HyperText Markup Language—is a tagging system used to create documents for display on the Web. It's a simple format, but it's tedious to enter the codes by hand.

Although all the features of a StarOffice document can't be converted to HTML for Web display, the primary ones can. Saving an existing document in HTML format is a quick and easy way to create a Web page. Tables, graphics, and all standard text formatting is included in the exported Web page.

To export a document in HTML, follow these steps:

1. Open an existing StarOffice document.

2. Choose Save As... from the File menu.

3. In the drop-down list of file formats, select HTML. (See Figure 22.15.)

FIGURE 22.15

Select HTML as the file format in which to save your existing StarOffice documents for use on the Web.

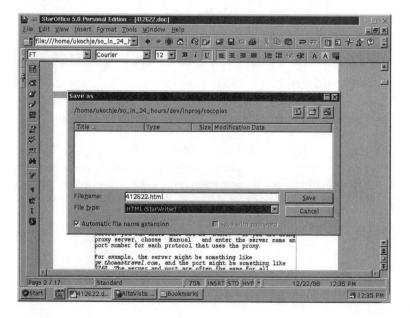

4. Enter a new name for the file (html is added automatically).

5. Choose OK.

6. Reopen the newly-saved HTML file in StarOffice or in another browser to see how well the formatting converted to HTML.

> Presentations and spreadsheets can also be saved in HTML format for immediate viewing in a Web browser; use the preceding procedure.

Creating New HTML Documents

If you don't already have a document prepared that you want to move to the Web but you know that the Web is the target for the document that you want to create, the best option is to create it from the beginning as an HTML document. That way, you'll know how it will look in a browser when you're finished.

StarOffice enables you to create native HTML documents. To start a new HTML document, select New from the File menu, and then select HTML document. You can also choose New HTML Document from the StarOffice Desktop, or click the Start menu and choose More, and then HTML document.

A new blank document appears that looks similar to the word processing documents that you're familiar with. However, you'll see that the menus and toolbars are slightly different when you create an HTML document.

Create a small HTML document now and see where the differences lie. Use the following steps:

1. Enter a headline on the first line of the new document.

2. Enter a paragraph of descriptive text.

3. Enter three bullet items after the paragraph. If you start each line with a hyphen, StarOffice converts the hyphens to bullets.

4. Choose Picture from the Insert menu and pick a graphics file to insert.

> You cannot use the Image Editor to create an image within an HTML document. The image must exist in a separate file.

Your file will look somewhat similar to the one in Figure 22.16.

FIGURE 22.16

An HTML file with a few lines of text and a graphic included.

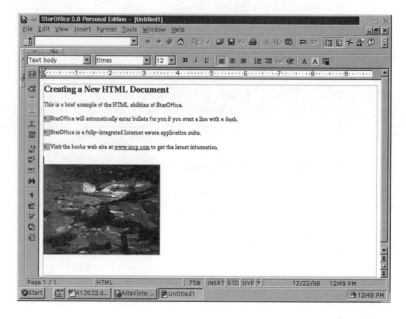

Now try the following:

- Click in the headline to place the cursor there, and then click on the drop-down list of paragraph styles in the Object toolbar and choose Heading 1. The text of the headline changes to a headline font.

> Remember that the headline might look different in another browser if you use this document on the Web. The browser settings determine, for the most part, how a document looks; StarOffice can't control that in all cases.

- Click and drag to select all the bulleted lines, and then click on the Numbering icon in the Object toolbar (see Figure 22.17).
- Click on the figure in the document to select it, and then try to drag it to another location on the page. It returns to its original location. Basic HTML tags that you're using here don't allow graphics to be located as precisely as a word processor does.

FIGURE 22.17

Choose the Numbering icon on the Object toolbar to change selected paragraphs to a numbered list.

The numbering icon

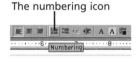

22

With the figure selected, press the right mouse button and move down to the Wrap item. Notice that several of the options are gray—not available (see Figure 22.18). This reflects the more limited formatting capabilities of HTML.

FIGURE 22.18

The Wrap submenu doesn't include as many available options when creating an HTML document.

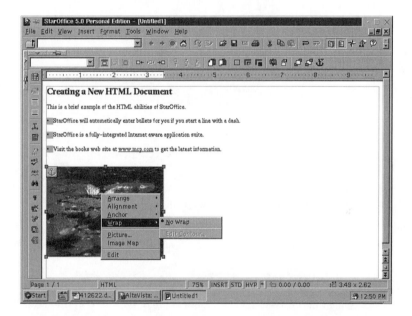

Now—for the really startling part of this exercise—choose HTML Source from the View menu. The HTML codes that StarOffice is creating for you are displayed (see Figure 22.19).

HTML keywords and automatically generated information are shown in red text. You can directly edit the HTML source in this window—if you know what you're doing. When you close this window, StarOffice interprets whatever changes you've made and redisplays the document as it will appear in a browser.

FIGURE 22.19

The HTML Source window shows you the HTML codes for the HTML document that you are creating.

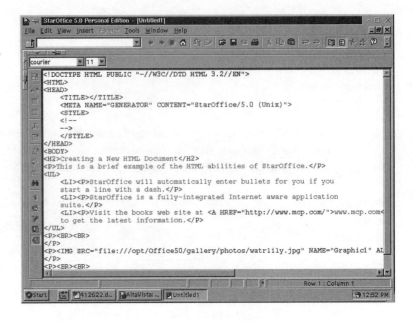

For example, if you locate the IMG tag in the HTML Source window, you can change the name of the graphic file. If you enter a name that cannot be found, the HTML code is accepted but StarOffice shows a small box that says Read Error when you return to the browser view, just as any browser might if an error occurred reading a graphics file.

To return to the browser view of the HTML document, choose HTML Source from the View menu.

Adding Other HTML Elements

Using StarOffice to create the home page for your corporation is not recommended because the editing and graphics tools aren't sophisticated enough to make a really nice looking site. For creating basic Web pages or making other documents available on the Web, however, StarOffice is great.

One reason that StarOffice isn't perfect for creating other Web pages is the limited set of features. Some HTML features that many people like to use, such as frames and client-side image maps, cannot be added using automated tools when you create an HTML page in StarOffice (although they are supported when viewing Web pages that you download into StarOffice).

The following list shows some features that you can include in your StarOffice HTML documents:

- **Horizontal Lines**—Insert a horizontal line (HTML tag <HR>) by selecting Horizontal Line… from the Insert menu. A dialog box appears (see Figure 22.20) in which you can select from many different horizontal rules.

FIGURE 22.20

Insert a horizontal rule in an HTML document from the Insert Horizontal Line dialog box.

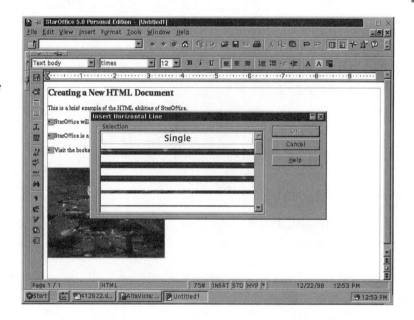

Only the first choice listed in the dialog box inserts a regular <HR> tag. The other choices insert an <IMG> Tag with a line-shaped graphic. This type of rule does not appear (or at least doesn't look good) if users turn off graphics in their browser.

- **Tables**—Complete HTML table functionality is provided in StarOffice. Choose Table from the Insert menu. With the cursor placed in the table, or with one or more table cells selected, the Format menu includes all the formatting options for HTML tables.

- **Javascript**—You can insert Javascript into a Web page by selecting Script… from the Insert menu. The Insert Script dialog box appears (see Figure 22.21); here you can either type in the actual script or enter an URL for the script (this is normally a file on your Linux system where you created the script).

FIGURE 22.21

Javascripts can be included in your HTML pages using the Insert Script dialog box.

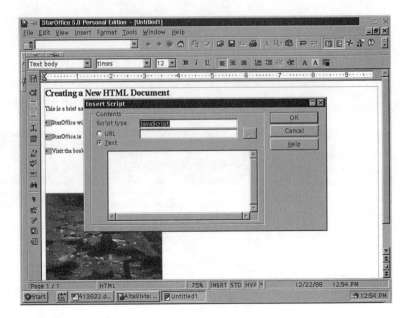

- **Hyperlinks**—Because of the importance of hyperlinks in an HTML documents, Hyperlink is included as a separate item on the Insert menu when you are creating an HTML document.

  Select the text that you want to link and choose Hyperlink from the Insert menu. The dialog box that appears is the same as the Hyperlink tab of the Character dialog box.

- **Comments**—HTML code, as you viewed it in the HTML Source window, can include comments that are not seen when using a browser to view the HTML page. They are only visible when viewing the HTML source text. (These comments are similar to comments in a programming language).

  To insert a comment in your HTML page, choose Note… from the Insert menu. In the Insert Note dialog box (see Figure 22.22), enter the text that you want to include as a comment.

  You can view the comment by opening the HTML Source window. Comments are shown between special characters that identify them as comments. For example

```
<!--This table needs to be updated before end of
➥ the year.-!>
```

FIGURE 22.22

The Insert Note dialog box inserts a comment in the HTML code. None of the text you enter is visible in a browser.

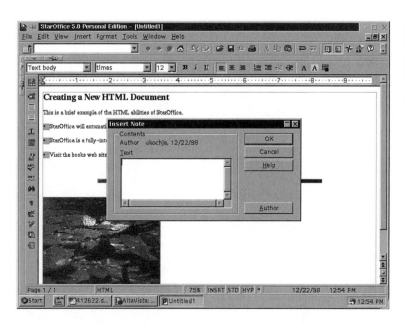

HTML includes a tag called <NOTE>, which inserts a visible, indented comment similar to this one. Don't confuse this with the use of the term Note in StarOffice. A StarOffice Note is really an HTML Comment.

In the Next Hour

In Hour 23 you'll continue to learn about using StarOffice with the Internet by configuring email and newsgroup reading accounts, and you'll learn how to read and send email messages in StarOffice. You'll also become familiar with using StarOffice to to read and post to Internet newsgroups.

Hour 23

Using StarOffice Email and Newsgroup Features

In this hour you'll learn how to use other Internet-aware features of StarOffice. Specifically, you'll learn how to configure your email system within StarOffice to send and receive email, and how to read and post to Internet newsgroups.

The features described in this hour go beyond working with Web documents, as described in the previous hour. Using email and reading newsgroups are two other important sources of information sharing on the Internet. StarOffice provides access to these resources for anyone with an Internet connection. This hour describes how to use those features.

Configuring Email Accounts

Before you can send and receive email in StarOffice, you must configure the incoming and outgoing email accounts so that your email can be located and routed properly.

The mailboxes that you set up in this section define specific email accounts. You can create multiple inboxes for different accounts you have, as well as multiple outboxes to hold messages sent through those accounts. Each of these accounts can use any of several protocols, such as POP3, VIM, or IMAP. To use an account, you must define the server on which the account resides.

Don't confuse these accounts with the default SMTP servers for outgoing and incoming mail that you define in the Internet Options dialog box (opened from the Tools menu). For example, you can have a separate POP3 account through an ISP, in addition to the email arriving on your local SMTP mail server.

Email accounts can use any of several formats, including POP3 and IMAP. Check with your ISP or system administrator to see which protocol you need to use to retrieve email.

As you work with email accounts in StarOffice, you'll see VIM as an option in several places. VIM is a protocol used by cc:Mail and Lotus Notes. This option isn't discussed in this book, however.

Setting up a POP3 Account

Before you can work with your email, you must create both an incoming (POP3 or IMAP account) and an outgoing mail account. These two accounts can refer to the same server or to different servers, but StarOffice requires both.

To set up a POP3 incoming email account, follow these steps (the steps to create an IMAP account are almost identical; just choose IMAP instead of POP3 on the menu):

1. Make the Explorer visible by clicking the Hide/Show icon or selecting Explorer in the View menu.

2. Right click on the word Explorer, the top icon in the Explorer window. A pop-up menu appears.

3. From the pop-up menu, select New, and then POP3 Account. The Properties of POP3 Account dialog box appears (see Figure 23.1).

FIGURE 23.1

The Properties of POP3 Account dialog box enables you to define an email account.

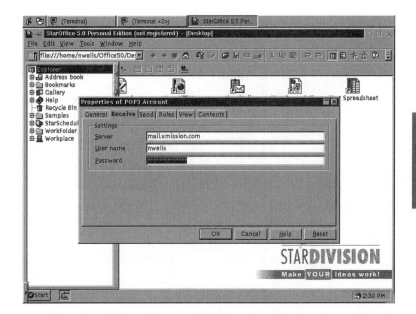

23

4. On the Receive tab, enter the server name, username, and password to be used to retrieve email from your POP email account.

   For example, if you have a PPP connection to the Internet and your email address is nwells@ix.netcom.com (NetCom is a popular nationwide ISP), your POP3 server is popd.ix.netcom.com. The name varies, however, depending on the ISP.

5. On the General tab of the Properties of POP3 Account dialog box, enter a name for the incoming email account. This might be something such as Netcom Email or Incoming mail.

   The name that you enter in the General tab is the name you'll select to read your email after setting up the email accounts.

6. Next, choose the Send tab in the Properties of POP3 Account dialog box.

7. In the Private box, choose SMTP as the Default Protocol.

8. Select the User-defined Settings radio button.

9. Choose the User Defined Settings button. The Properties of Send Protocols dialog box appears (see Figure 23.2).

FIGURE 23.2

The Properties of Send Protocols dialog box enables you to define how email messages are sent from this POP3 account.

10. Enter the mail server for outgoing email messages from your Linux computer. (This might be the same server name as for the incoming POP3 email in the Receive tab mentioned previously.)

11. Enter the username and password of the account on the server listed here, if required.

12. Choose OK to close the Properties of Send Protocols dialog box.

> You can explore the Rules, View, and Contents tabs if you want. They pro-vide options for managing your email account. These include filtering, mark-ing and updating your mailbox, and can be very helpful tools if you receive a lot of email.

13. Choose OK to close the Properties of POP3 Account dialog box.

After you finish defining a POP3 Account, StarOffice checks to see if you have an out-box already set up. If you don't, a message prompts you to create one, as described in the next section.

The email account icon for your POP3 Account as it appears in the Explorer is shown in Figure 23.3.

FIGURE 23.3

An email account icon in the Explorer indicates that StarOffice has been configured to use your Internet email account.

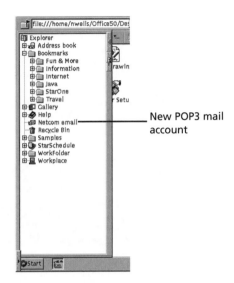

New POP3 mail account

23

After you've created an email account, you can drag the POP3 Account icon to a folder in the Explorer, if you want to.

With an email account icon in the Explorer, you can begin using email immediately by clicking on that icon. An email window appears with your messages ready to read. The use of this window is covered later in this hour.

Setting up a Separate Email Outbox

If you need to specify an outgoing email account that is different from the incoming email account, you can create a separate Outbox for sending email. For example, you might have a sendmail mail server running on your Linux computer, so you can use your own hostname as the outgoing SMTP email server.

To create a new Outbox, follow these steps:

1. Make the Explorer visible by clicking the Hide/Show icon or selecting Explorer in the View menu.

2. Right click on the word Explorer, the top icon in the Explorer window. A pop-up menu appears.

3. From the pop-up menu, select New, and then Outbox. The Properties of Outbox dialog box appears (see Figure 23.4).

FIGURE 23.4

The Properties of
Outbox dialog box
enables you to define
a separate outgoing
email account.

4. On the SMTP tab, enter the server name, username, and password to be used for sending email from your computer.

   For example, if you have a PPP connection to the Internet and sendmail running on your Linux computer, the server might be `localhost` or your machine's hostname. Or, the server might be something such as `popd.ix.netcom.com` if you're using a popular ISP account for outgoing email.

5. On the General tab of the Properties of Outbox dialog box, enter a name for the outgoing email account. This might be something such as `local account` or `ISP Outgoing mail`.

Activating Your Email Settings

After you have defined an email account in the Explorer, you have to tell StarOffice to use it because you can have multiple email accounts set up in the Explorer, each using a different server, username, email filters, and so forth.

As part of the Internet options, you define which server to use for incoming and outgoing email messages. StarOffice then uses that server to send out messages. This enables you to use the New Mail icon on the Desktop or Start menu to quickly send a new email message.

To define an email server, follow these steps:

1. Choose Options from the Tools menu, and then choose Internet from the Options submenu. The Internet Options dialog box appears.

2. Choose the Mail/News tab (see Figure 23.5).

FIGURE 23.5

In the Mail/News tab of the Internet Options dialog box, you define the servers to be used for email.

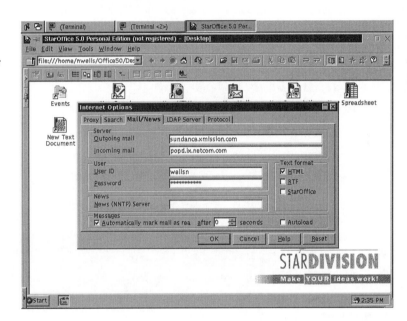

3. Enter a server name in the Outgoing mail field.

4. Enter a server name in the Incoming mail field. (This might be the same server as the Outgoing mail field.)

5. Enter the User ID and Password for the servers that you entered.

You'll also need to define an NNTP protocol News server before you can use Internet newsgroups. This is described later in this hour, but you can enter the NNTP server name immediately in this dialog box.

Finally, you must have your personal email address entered in the StarOffice configuration before you can create email messages. Because an email address is required as part of the StarOffice installation process, you have probably done this already.

You can review your email address by choosing Options under the Tools menu, selecting General, and viewing the User Data tab.

Sending Emails

If you're accustomed to using StarOffice to write documents, it's natural to use StarOffice to send email as well. After you have email configured (as just described), you can send email directly from within StarOffice—including attaching StarOffice documents and linking from documents to new email messages.

The sections that follow describe how to prepare and send email messages using StarOffice.

Starting an Email Message

You can open a new email message in one of several ways:

- From the Start menu below the Desktop, choose Mail.
- From the New submenu of the File menu, choose Mail.
- From the Desktop, double-click on the New Mail icon.

In any case, a new email message window appears, as shown in Figure 23.6.

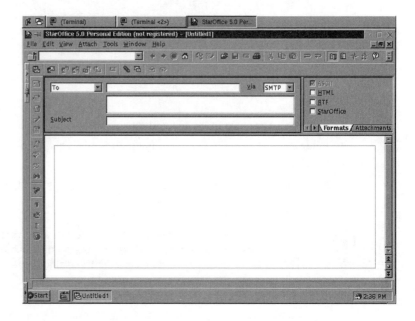

If you try to start an email message without configuring an outbox, a message warns you that you can't proceed. Return to the previous sections in this hour to learn how to configure StarOffice email.

The email message window consists of three sections:

- The message window, where you enter the text of your email
- The headers section, where you define who will receive the message and other information about the message
- The attachments section, where any attached files are listed, as well as the formats in which the email will be in

To prepare your email, follow these steps. Some of the steps can be skipped if they don't apply to the email that you're sending:

1. A drop-down list indicates the word To: when you start the email. In the empty field next to the To: field, enter the email address of the person (or persons) who are to receive your email. Then press Enter.

   The line

   ```
   To: <email address>
   ```

   appears in the box below the field in which you entered the email address.

2. Click on the drop-down list in which To: appears and select Copy: from the list.

3. Enter your own email address in the empty field next to it. Press Enter. This sends a copy of the message to your email account for reference or archiving.

   The line

   ```
   Copy: <your email address>
   ```

   is added to the box below the field in which you entered the email address.

4. In the empty field next to Subject, enter a subject for the email message.

5. Click the Extras tab in the top right part of the message window.

6. If you want an email message returned to you, confirming receipt of this message, check the Confirm receipt checkbox.

> Not all email systems issue return receipts.

7. Choose a priority from the Priority drop-down list. The default of Normal is fine for most messages.

8. Click in the message body area and start typing:

   ```
   This is the message
   ```

Your screen now looks somewhat similar to Figure 23.7.

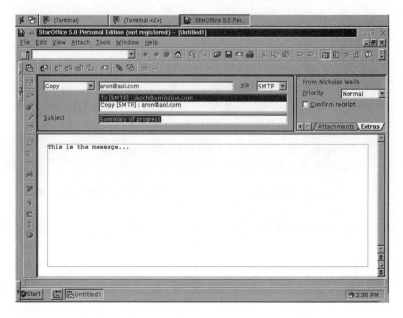

When you click in the message body area and start typing your message, the menus and toolbars change to reflect text entry capabilities. For example, when you click on the message body, the Object toolbar changes to include

- The font and font size drop-down lists
- Bold, italic, and underline icons
- Justification icons for right, left, center, full
- Numbered list and bulleted list icons

Many email systems that receive your message won't recognize any formatting that you add to an email message (for example, bulleted lists and bold text). Using plain text with no formatting beyond asterisks and spaces is the safest way to create an email.

Including Attachments in an Email

After you've entered the text of your email message (or before, if you prefer), you can attach a file to the email message. The file is encoded and sent with the message.

Some email systems don't allow attachments that are larger than a certain size. Either your email server or the receiver's email server might reject the message if you attach a large file or several files to your email message. Common limits are 100K, 1MB, or 10MB. If this occurs, you'll have to figure out a way to split up attached files into multiple smaller email messages, or call the system administrator for help.

23

To attach a file to an email, choose File... from the Attach menu or click on the Attach icon (a paperclip—see Figure 23.8).

FIGURE 23.8

You can open a dialog box and select files to attach to your email message by clicking the paperclip icon.

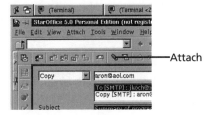

Attach

If the Attach menu and paperclip icon are not visible, click on the header section of your email window. When the body of the email message is active, different icons and menus are displayed.

The Attach File dialog box is the same as the Open File dialog box with which you're already familiar (see Figure 23.9). The only difference is that when you select a file and choose OK, the filename is listed in the Attachments section of the email window.

When you have attached files to your email, click on the Attachments tab in the upper right area of the message window to see a list of attached files. The Attachments tab is to the right of the headers section. If it isn't visible, click and drag the border between sections to reveal the tab.

Several browsers that include email capabilities send the email message in plaintext (ASCII) and in HTML text, so that if the message is read within another browser, the text looks nicer. You can define any of four formats in which your email message can be sent:

- **ASCII**—The plaintext default, standard on the Internet for all email readers and checked by default
- **RTF**—Useful for viewing text in any word processor because formatting information is included

- **HTML**—Nice if your message will be read within a browser
- **StarWriter**—Useful only if someone using StarOffice is going to receive your message

FIGURE 23.9

Select a file to attach in the Attach File dialog box. The name of the selected file is listed in the Attachments section of your email window.

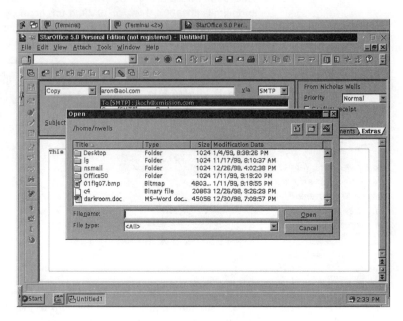

To choose to include any or all of these formats, go to the Formats tab and select the checkboxes for the formats that you want.

Sending the Email Message

When you're typing in the message window, the toolbars and menus reflect text editing features.

In order to send the email message, you must have the correct toolbar visible, so you can click on the Send icon. If you click on the headers section, the text editing menus and toolbars disappear, and the email-specific toolbar appears.

> You must use the icon on the toolbar to send your email message. No menu item is available for this function.

Click on the Send icon to send your email message (see Figure 23.10).

FIGURE 23.10

Send your completed email message by clicking on the Send icon.

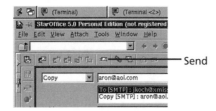

Send

23

> If you attempt to close an email message that you've entered by choosing Close from the File menu, StarOffice prompts you to see if you want to send the message.

Sending a Document as Email

In addition to creating an email message from scratch, you can use a document that you've written as the email and send it directly from StarOffice, rather than starting an email and adding the file as an attachment.

If you're viewing a StarOffice document, spreadsheet, or presentation, you can choose Send from the File menu, then choose Document as Email from the Send submenu. The Send Mail dialog box appears (see Figure 23.11), where you can choose how to send the current file.

FIGURE 23.11

The Send Mail dialog box enables you to send the current document, spreadsheet, or presentation as an email without first opening a new Mail message window.

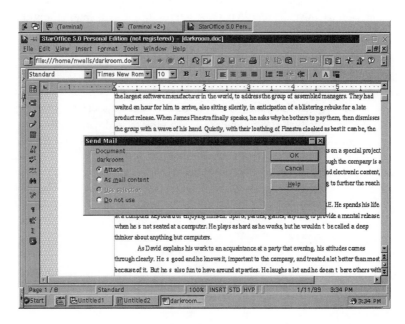

When you choose OK, the new mail message window appears. The option that you select in the Send Mail dialog determines how the document is included:

- If you choose Attach, the file is listed in the Attachments tab.
- If you choose Content, the file is inserted into the message body (use this option for documents, not for spreadsheets).

You can then enter other details of the email message and press Send to finish it.

Using Other StarOffice Internet Functions

The rest of this hour describes how to use the other Internet capabilities of StarOffice. To access most of these features, you must create a new icon in the Explorer window, just as you created a POP account to access email. New icons in the Explorer are created by right-clicking on the word Explorer at the top of the Explorer window.

The Internet functions available within the Explorer include

- Reading email via POP or IMAP protocols (described in the previous section)
- Browsing FTP servers
- Reading newsgroups
- Adding Internet links and searches as icons on your Desktop

Most of these services require that you set up certain configuration options. In particular, server names and networking information (such as proxy server or username and password) must be entered in the configuration for an Internet option that you want to make use of.

Browsing an FTP Site

FTP sites are Internet archives. They don't include graphics and sound like Web sites, but they do have files that you can download for use on your computer. Most publicly available FTP sites allow any user to log in to download files by using the username anonymous or ftp, and a complete email address as a password.

To browse an FTP site within StarOffice, start by right-clicking on the word Explorer in the Explorer window. From the New submenu, choose FTP Account. The Properties of FTP Account dialog box appears (see Figure 23.12).

FIGURE 23.12

*You can create a refer-
ence to an FTP server
so that you can easily
browse the files on
that server.*

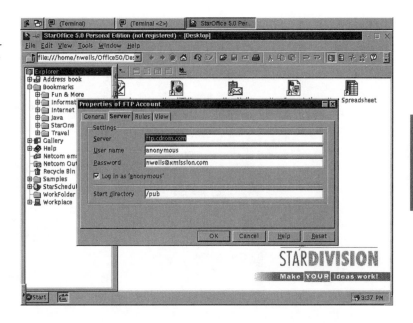

In this dialog box, follow these steps:

1. Choose the Server tab, if it isn't already selected.

2. Enter a server name in the Server field (for example, `ftp.cdrom.com`).

3. If you don't have an account on this server, but are just accessing it as a public
   server, click on the Log in as anonymous checkbox.

4. If you do have a personal account on this server, enter your username and password for the server in the corresponding fields.

5. If you know the directory structure of this FTP server, you can enter a subdirectory
   with which to begin your FTP session. (A common choice is `/pub`)

6. Choose the General tab, shown in Figure 23.13.

7. Enter a name to refer to this FTP Account. For example, the server `ftp.cdrom.com`
   might be called `Walnut Creek CDROM`. This name appears in the Explorer window
   so you can open this FTP Account.

8. Choose OK to close the dialog box. A new FTP Account icon appears in the
   Explorer window.

Now you can access the new FTP Account by double-clicking on the FTP icon in the
Explorer. When you do, an FTP browsing window opens, as shown in Figure 23.14.

FIGURE 23.13

Each FTP Account is assigned a name.

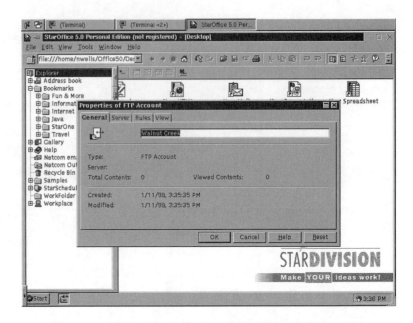

FIGURE 23.14

Opening an FTP Account icon starts an FTP browsing window.

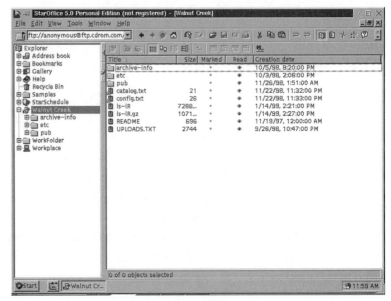

The sections that follow describe configuring a news account, and reading and posting newsgroup messages. These news features are all accessed in the Explorer window, like the email and FTP accounts just described.

Configuring the Newsgroup Reader

Newsgroups are subject-oriented group discussions across the Internet. They're sort of like email, except everyone's messages are posted in a common place for everyone to read and respond to. You can also compare them to a chat session on the Internet, except that they don't occur in real time. Newsgroup messages can be delayed several hours from the time that they are *posted* or sent, to the time that you see them listed on your newsgroup reader.

Newsgroups cover every subject imaginable, from the scholarly to the mundane to the obscene (there are lots of those). Newsgroups are organized in a tree, with a broad category listed first, followed by a more specific subject.

For example, the sci.physics group discusses physics; the soc.religion.muslim discusses issues for Muslims, and comp.os.linux.announce contains announcements relevant to Linux users (it stands for computers/operating systems/linux/announcements). There are thousands of different newsgroups. The newsserver that you connect to for reading newsgroup postings probably receives more than 100MB of data each day from new postings.

Although other word processors might have email capability, none that we've seen include the capability to browse Internet newsgroups. Normally you must use your Web browser to read newsgroups. StarOffice integrates these features.

Creating a News Icon

The first step in reading newsgroups is to create and configure a news server item in the Explorer window. With the news server item in place, you can select it to read and post messages to newsgroups.

To create a news server icon in the Explorer, follow these steps:

1. With the Explorer window open, right-click on the word Explorer on the top line of the Explorer window. A pop-up menu appears.

2. From the New submenu, choose News. A Properties of News dialog box appears, where you can define the properties of the news server that you want to access (see Figure 23.15).

3. Make sure that the Receive tab is selected.

4. Enter the name of the news server in the Server field. You'll need to get the name of this server from your ISP or system administrator.

5. Enter a username and password for this server if these are needed to access it (usually you won't need to fill in these fields).

6. Change to the General tab and enter a name for this news server icon. The name that you enter is listed in the Explorer window next to the new icon.

7. You can use the other tabs in the Properties of News dialog box to define other information about this news server:

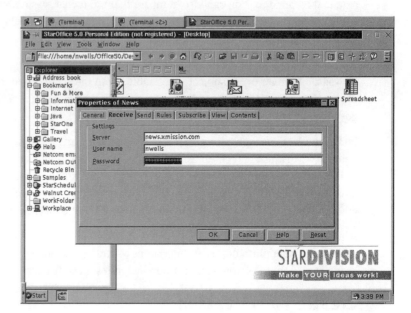

- **The Rules and View tabs**—Define which newsgroups and which messages in those newsgroups are shown onscreen. For example, you can list all newsgroups (a long list) or only those to which you have subscribed, or you can automatically delete postings from a person who always makes offensive remarks.

- **The Subscribe tab**—Enables you to predefine the names of the newsgroups for which you want to view message postings. (See the next section.)

- **The Contents section**—Defines how messages are updated and stored, locally and on the POP server from which they were retrieved.

When you finish setting up these properties, choose OK to close this dialog box. Another message asks if you want to create an Outbox.

As you read newsgroup postings, you can reply publicly, posting your message back to the newsgroup for everyone to read; or you can reply privately, using email to send a note to the author of a news message. Creating a separate Outbox for this news server enables you to separate email that you send while reading mail from other messages that you send. If you decide to create another Outbox, follow the steps given earlier in this hour for defining an email outbox.

After creating an Outbox (or immediately if you answered No to the Outbox question), a news server icon with the name you entered appears in the Explorer window.

Choosing Newsgroups to View

Of all the newsgroups on the Internet, you probably only want to review a few at a time. Newsreaders enable you to subscribe to a newsgroup. Subscribing to a newsgroup doesn't affect anything on the Internet (for example, it doesn't send your name to the news server). Subscribing to a newsgroup just adds that newsgroup to a list kept within the newsreader to keep track of which newsgroups are to be displayed for you.

A list of subscribed newsgroups defines those newsgroups from which you want to regularly read messages. In the Subscribe tab of the Properties of News dialog box, you can view all the newsgroups that are available on your selected news server, and then mark, or subscribe to, those that interest you. Depending on the settings in the View tab, only those newsgroups that you subscribe to are listed in the news browsing window described in the next section.

Reading Newsgroup Postings

To read news messages, double-click on the news server icon that you created in the Explorer. A news reader window appears; you can select a message to read from the message subject lines shown (see Figure 23.16).

FIGURE 23.16

Newsgroup messages are read within a StarOffice newsgroup browsing window.

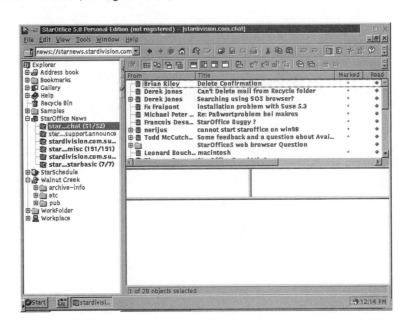

Reading newsgroup messages is a little like reading email. But instead of viewing multiple email subject folders, the message titles in the current folder, and the text of one message, with news you view the list of newsgroups (like folders), the titles of news messages (like email messages), and the text of the selected news message.

Posting a New Message to a Newsgroup

As you read newsgroup postings, you'll probably want to reply to some of them. Posting a message to a newsgroup is similar to sending an email message, with these important differences:

- Newsgroup postings are read by thousands of strangers around the world.
- Newsgroup postings can take longer to appear in the newsgroup than email takes to reach a recipient (though they usually don't).
- Newsgroup postings in some newsgroups can be rejected if the moderator who controls the group feels the posting is off-topic or inappropriate.
- In some newsgroups, strangers who don't like what you say might respond with various levels of verbal abuse. Ignore it.

With these differences in mind, a few rules of Internet etiquette (*netiquette*) might be helpful. These are generally accepted rules of behavior within newsgroups and the Internet generally:

- Read postings in a newsgroup for a few days before posting anything yourself. Try to sense the tone of the messages (social, friendly, scholarly, antagonistic) so you can match it.
- Look for a message in the newsgroup that contains a list of Frequently Asked Questions (a FAQ) and read it before posting to the newsgroup. The FAQ answers a few dozen questions that everyone with an interest in the subject of the newsgroup asks. They all want you to read the answer in the FAQ instead of asking it again.
- When people say something offensive in retaliation to a comment with which they didn't agree (this is affectionately called a *flame war*), don't add fuel to the fire. Take the high ground and change the subject.

With these ideas in mind, you can reply to any message in a newsgroup, either by replying privately via email, or by replying publicly back to the newsgroup (see Figure 23.17).

23

FIGURE 23.17

Responses to news-group messages can be private (via email) or public (back to the newsgroup).

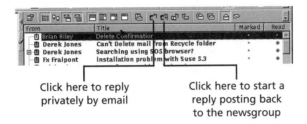

Click here to reply
privately by email

Click here to start a
reply posting back
to the newsgroup

Updating Explorer Icons

You've seen how to create several types of Internet-related icons in your Explorer window. These icons are the only way that you can access these features in StarOffice.

If you need to fix or update the information in any of the Internet icons on your Desktop, right-click on the icon and choose the Properties item in the pop-up menu that appears.

The other menu items shown can be used to set options for that Internet account. For example, you can change which messages are shown in an email or news account. Not all items shown, however, apply to all the Internet-related icons.

In the Next Hour

The next hour, "Using StarSchedule," describes the StarSchedule features of StarOffice, where you can define calendar events and appointments and maintain lists of contacts and friends. The scheduling information can even be coordinated with other StarOffice users to set up meetings or check the availability of a coworker.

HOUR 24

Using StarSchedule

In this hour you'll learn how to use the StarSchedule features of StarOffice. StarSchedule is new to StarOffice 5. It enables you to track to-do lists and calendar events, and integrate those events and tasks with others on your network to schedule meetings, share ideas, and so forth.

To make full use of the features of StarSchedule, you need to have other users using StarOffice on your network. If you're a single user on StarOffice, however, you can still use the task lists and calendar to track your own time.

In the sections that follow, you'll learn how StarSchedule tools are organized, and how to work with the task list, events calendar, and address book.

How StarSchedule is Organized

To use StarSchedule, you'll work within two different screens of information: the Events screen and the Tasks screen. You can view either of these screens by either double-clicking on the Events or Tasks icon on the StarOffice Desktop, or selecting Events or Tasks within the StarSchedule folder of the Explorer.

As with many of the Internet features in StarOffice, you must use the icons in the Explorer to set some options for Events and Tasks. For that reason, the Explorer is used for the examples. Using the Desktop icon and leaving the Explorer closed leaves you more space for the events or tasks, of course.

StarSchedule also works with servers and users on your network. You can select other computers on the network and view the calendar schedule for users on that computer. You must have permission, and you can only view public events, however.

All the StarSchedule components are shown in Figure 24.1 as they appear in the Explorer. You can right-click on any of these components to set various options, as the sections that follow describe. In particular, the Properties item on the pop-up menus open a dialog box where you can review how that component is set up.

FIGURE 24.1

StarSchedule components are best accessed from the Explorer, where you can right-click on an item to see a pop-up menu of options.

If you right-click on the Events or Tasks icon on the StarOffice desktop, the pop-up menu you see refers to the link to Events or Tasks, and not to the actual component of StarSchedule. That's why the Explorer is being used for the examples.

Using the Task List

The StarSchedule task list is really just a computerized to-do list. But if you have a lot of things to do, StarSchedule provides some features that you'll find helpful.

You can view the task list by double-clicking on the Tasks item under StarSchedule in the Explorer. A simple default Task List is shown (see Figure 24.2).

FIGURE 24.2

The default Task List shows two items that StarDivision wants you to complete.

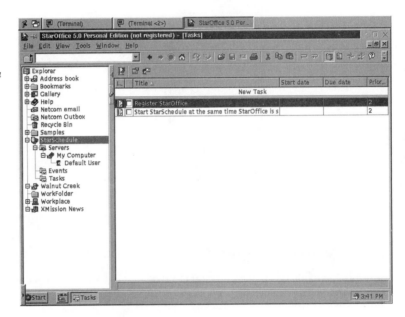

The following sections describe how to create new tasks, modify the details of those tasks, and filter the task list.

Creating New Tasks

To create a new task in the Task List, just click under the Title field on the New Task line above the currently displayed tasks. A cursor appears in the Title field, where you can enter a brief description of the task that you're defining. When you've typed in the description, press Enter.

Now you can set the start and due dates for this task. Click in the Start date field, and then click on the drop-down arrow to see a calendar where you can click on a start date (see Figure 24.3).

FIGURE 24.3

A pop-up calendar enables you to choose start and due dates for a task.

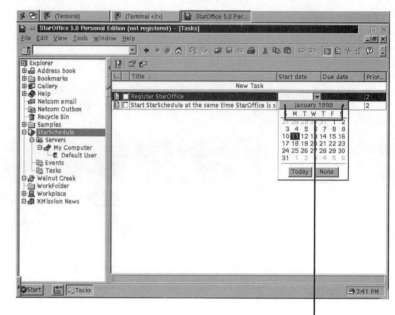

Click here or here to change
to the previous or next month

Set the priority for the task in the priority field (numbers 1–5 are available).

Click outside of the new task line to indicate that you've finished entering information in it. Enter a few more tasks in the list if you have some in mind.

Reviewing Task Details

Starting with a basic task list, you can review other details about each task. To view task details, click on the Details icon in the Object toolbar (see Figure 24.4). You can also select Details from the View menu.

FIGURE 24.4

Click on the Details icon to open the Details section of the Task list screen.

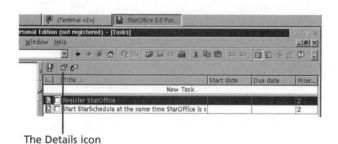

The Details icon

The Details section of the task list screen shows more information for the currently selected task in the task list. Where many StarOffice dialog boxes use tabs to show sets of information, the Details section of the task list has buttons on the left side of the screen. You can choose different buttons to show different details for the selected task.

You can view the first part of the Details section by choosing the Contents button (see Figure 24.5).

FIGURE 24.5

The Contents button shows further descriptive information about the selected task.

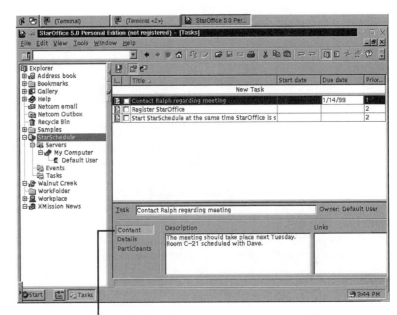

Click the contents button to
show this information.

With the contents button selected, you can enter more information about the selected task by typing in the Description field. This field can contain many lines of text to further define the task.

Choose the Details button next (see Figure 24.6).

FIGURE 24.6

*The Details button
shows fields for many
task details.*

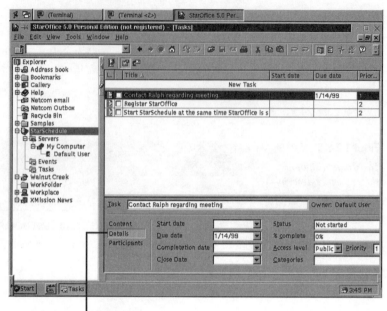

Click the Details button to
show this information.

Some of the information in the Details area is already shown in the single-line task summary above the Details area. You already entered a start and due date, for example. Each of the drop-down boxes in this area defines something about the selected task. Each of these items is described here:

- **Start date**—The date the task is to be started.

- **Due date**—The date the task is to be completed.

- **Completion date**—The date the task was completed (not always the same as Due date for most of us).

- **Close date**—When the task was closed. This can be used separately from the completion task because of other actions taken on this task. Also, the closed field can be used to filter tasks, as described later in this hour.

- **Status**—Enables you to define how the task is progressing or if it's been deferred or put on hold. Five options are given in this field.

- **% complete**—Enables you to define in 10 percent increments how the task is progressing.

- **Access Level**—Can be public, private, or confidential. The access level is used when you work with others on a network who can view your task and calendar. Only tasks marked public are available for others to view.

- **Priority**—As described previously, this enables you to assign a priority level from one to five to each task.
- **Categories**—Enables you to group tasks by things such as family, work, and hobbies, or by project or group name as you choose. You'll learn how to add or change the categories list in the next section.

Finally, the Participants list can be viewed by choosing the participants button (see Figure 24.7).

FIGURE 24.7

The Participants button shows which users are marked as participants for the selected task.

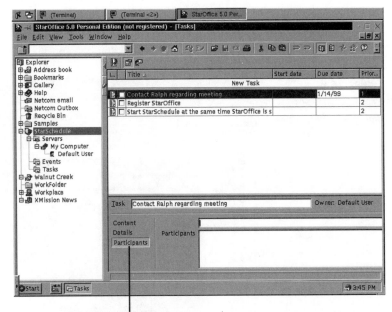

24

Click the Participants button
to show this information.

You can select which users on your system are involved in the selected task by choosing them from the drop-down list. Each selected user appears in the Participants field below the drop-down list.

At first, only Default User is listed as an available user. You must add other users to your StarSchedule system to be able to add them as participants. Adding users is described later in this hour.

Setting up Task Categories

The default task categories of Personal, Ideas, Vacation, and Job are a good start, but you'll probably want to define others. Categories are assigned to each user individually, so you must edit the Default User properties (or those of another user that you establish) to change the categories.

Follow these steps to add or change task categories:

1. In the Explorer, open the StarSchedule item, the Servers item, and then the My Computer item. The Default User icon is shown.

2. Right-click on the Default User icon and choose Properties from the pop-up menu that appears. The Properties of User dialog box appears (see Figure 24.8).

FIGURE 24.8

The Properties of User dialog box defines how a user works with StarSchedule.

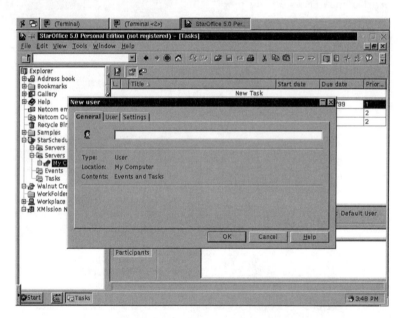

3. Choose the Settings tab in the Properties of User dialog box. The category list is shown.

4. To delete a category, select it from the list and choose Delete.

5. To add a new category, choose New and enter the category name in the New Category dialog box that appears (see Figure 24.9).

FIGURE 24.9

*The New Category
dialog box enables
you to define task
and event categories.*

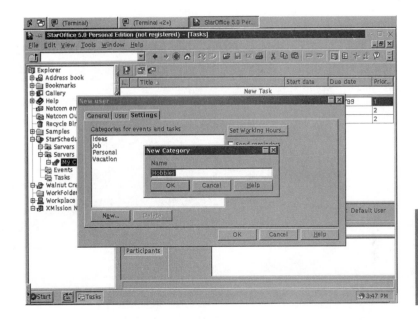

6. Choose the OK button in the Properties of User dialog box to finish defining categories.

All the categories that you defined appear as options in the Categories drop-down list of the details area for tasks or for events (described later in this hour).

You can also set working hours from this dialog box. Working hours define which hours on the event calendar are available for job-related tasks assigned by others.

Setting up Other Users

To add a new user to your StarSchedule system so that multiple users can participate in tasks or work in the event calendar, follow these steps:

1. In the Explorer, open the StarSchedule item, and then the Servers. The My Computer icon is shown.

2. Right-click on the My Computer icon and choose New User from the pop-up menu that appears. The New User dialog box appears (see Figure 24.10).

FIGURE 24.10.

The New User dialog box defines another user who can partici-pate in StarSchedule tasks and events.

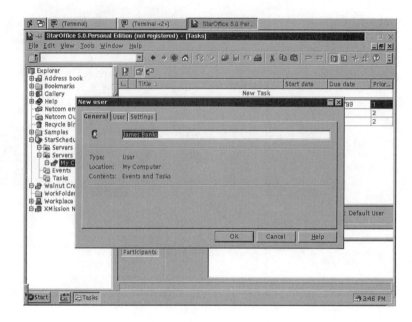

3. Enter a name for this user in the General tab.

4. In the User tab (see Figure 24.11), enter the login name (system username) and password for the Linux user to which this StarSchedule user is to be tied.

FIGURE 24.11

The User tab of the New User dialog box defines which system user is tied to this StarSchedule user.

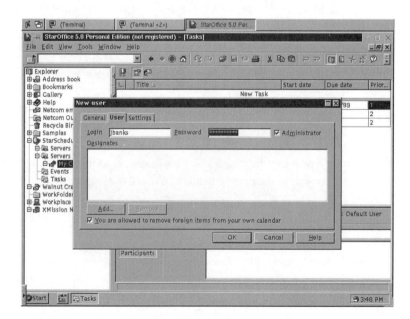

5. If you want to, choose the Settings tab and define categories and other options for this user, as described in the previous section.

Changing the Task List Layout

The look of the task list can be altered to fit your needs. The easiest way do this is by right-clicking on the column names in the task list. From the pop-up menu that appears, you can select items in the Displayed Columns submenu to define which task details are shown on the one-line task list.

> The task list screen won't scroll right and left. If you add several columns to the single line display of tasks, each column is very narrow. You can adjust column width by dragging on the column title, but you can't see them all at once unless you have a very large display.

24

From the pop-up menu, you can also open dialog boxes for Sorting, Grouping, Layout, and Filtering. The same dialog boxes are available from the View menu.

From the View menu, choose Define Task Layout. The Task Layout: Define Layout dialog box appears (see Figure 24.12).

FIGURE 24.12

The Task Layout: Define Layout dialog box enables you to define which task information is displayed and how tasks are grouped.

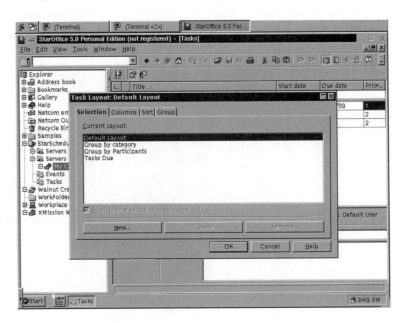

In the Columns tab, you can define which columns of detail information are included in the single-line task line screen. This has the same effect as selecting items from the pop-up menu that was just described.

In the Selection tab, you define how to *group*, or arrange, the tasks on the list. You can use any of these four options:

- **Default Layout**—List tasks as they are entered (still applying sorting and filtering).
- **Group by Category**—Group tasks by the categories defined for each user (such as Job, Personal, Vacation).
- **Group by Participants**—Arrange tasks so that all of one user's tasks are listed together.
- **Tasks Due**—Arrange tasks by their due date.

> The grouping in the Selection tab works with the Filtering described in the next section. Only those tasks remaining after filtering are grouped for display according to the selection you make here.

You can further refine how tasks are grouped together using the Group tab (see Figure 24.13). Select a task detail from the Group by drop-down list, and then choose sub-groupings from the next drop-down list as needed.

FIGURE 24.13

The Group tab of the Task Layout: Define Layout dialog box enables you to define how tasks are grouped together.

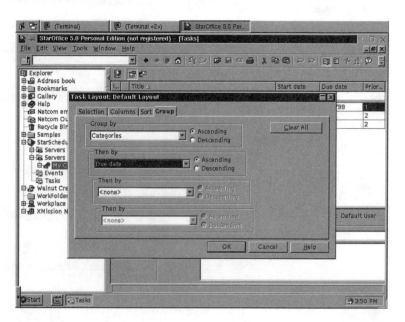

In a similar way, you can sort all the tasks within each group that you define (or all tasks, if no groupings are defined). The Sort tab enables you to choose from the same list of task details.

Sorting and grouping work together, with grouping occurring first. For example, you can have tasks grouped by category, and then sorted by due date within those categories.

Filtering the Task List

You can also filter the task list so that only certain tasks are shown in the list for your review. Default filters such as Only tasks due today are already defined. You can define other filters with any criteria you choose.

You can turn any filter on or off by using the right-click pop-up menu on the main task list screen. To start defining a filter, choose Define Task Filter from the View menu. The Task Filters dialog box appears (see Figure 24.14).

24

FIGURE 24.14

The Task Filters dialog box enables you to define a filter for which tasks are shown onscreen.

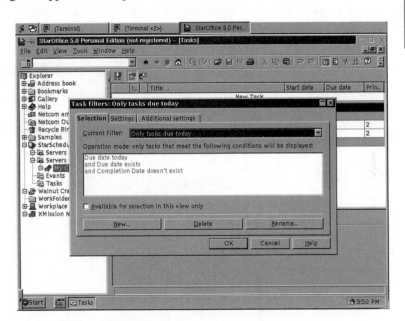

From the Selection tab, you can start defining a new filter. Default filters are shown in the Current Filter drop-down list. Choose the New button and enter a filter name to start a new filter.

The Settings tab enables you to define the criteria used to select which tasks to display when this filter is chosen. Specific categories, priorities, or status settings can be selected.

The Additional Settings tab also enables you to define other features of a task filter. You can select any field in the task details and define the value that it must have to be included in this filter.

> You can select by name any filter that you create by right-clicking on the task list screen and selecting from the Current Filter submenu.

Using the Event Calendar

The StarSchedule event calendar enables you to arrange your appointments and tasks on a visual calendar, and coordinate that calendar with other users and with the task list that you define. (See the first half of this hour.)

The Events calendar is best accessed from the Explorer. Open the StarSchedule item and double-click on the Events icon to view the Events screen as shown in Figure 24.15.

FIGURE 24.15

The Events screen shows a calendar where your events are displayed.

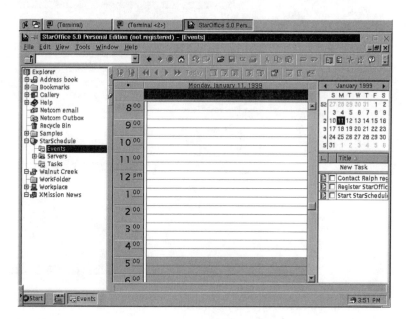

Changing the Events View

The Events screen includes a dizzying array of viewing options. These viewing options are selected either by using the icons on the Object menu or by using the pop-up right-click menu.

To begin with, you can move from the current day (the default starting place in the calendar) to any day, week or month. Use the arrows on the Object toolbar to move to the next period in the calendar (see Figure 24.16)

FIGURE 24.16

The arrows on the Object toolbar enable you to move to the next or previous calendar period.

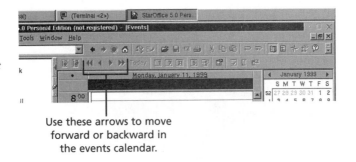

Use these arrows to move
forward or backward in
the events calendar.

The amount that the arrows move depends on whether you're viewing a day, a week, or a month.

You can also change how many days are shown in the onscreen event calendar. Use the buttons in the Object toolbar to select one day, a five or seven day week, or a full month. The buttons are labeled 1, 5, 7, and 31, respectively.

With any of these time frames shown in the event calendar, you can select how time is divided onscreen. While viewing a single day, for example, if you right-click the Select from the Time Scale menu, your time during the day can be broken down into one hour blocks, or into smaller blocks if you prefer.

One of our favorite options is the Colors item on the pop-up menu. It enables you to assign colors to different task/event categories so that they appear color coded on your event calendar.

The event calendar also has other sections that can be displayed or hidden. You'll want a big screen to use them all (as the figures show).

The sections that you can turn on for display include

- **The details area**—Shows the details for the selected event, much like the details described for tasks earlier in this hour.

- **The task list**—Can be displayed in a separate window. This enables you to drag tasks to spots on the event calendar so that you can plan when to work on them.

- **A calendar**—Not the event calendar, but a small calendar to find or track dates.

- **The Address book**—You can drag and drop peoples' names or companies into time slots on your event calendar.

All these display options can be turned on using the icons on the Object toolbar (see Figure 24.17).

FIGURE 24.17

These icons on the Object toolbar enable you to open other tools to help you plan your event calendar.

Click to open event details   Click to display the task list

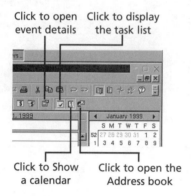

Click to Show a calendar   Click to open the Address book

These icons open or close the indicated screen area, except the Address book. To close the Address book, deselect Beamer from the View menu.

Figure 24.18 shows the event calendar with all these areas open (but the Explorer closed to leave more room).

FIGURE 24.18

The Event calendar with other screen areas displayed.

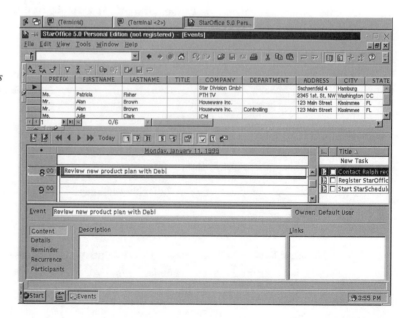

Adding items to the Calendar

Adding items to the Event calendar can be done whenever it's visible. You can either double-click on a time slot, or single-click on a time slot and then choose the New Event icon on the Object toolbar (the far left icon).

The time slot displays a cursor where you can enter text describing the event for that time slot. Press Enter when you've completed the description.

If you want to indicate that a task lasts longer than a single time division on your calendar, click on the border of the text entry area while typing an event description, and then drag the border down to fill in the time you want the event scheduled for: one hour, two hours, or whatever it takes.

If you have the Details section of the Event calendar displayed, you can select any event by clicking on it, and then edit the details of that event, including priority, category, participants, and so on.

24

Filtering the Calendar Events

Calendar events can be filtered just like the task list. Filter criteria can include other items, however, such as out-of-office events.

To define an event filter, choose Define Event Filter from the View menu. The Event Filter dialog box shown in Figure 24.19 appears. The filter definition follows the same procedure as the Task list filter definition described earlier in this hour.

FIGURE 24.19

Defining event filters is just like defining task list filters.

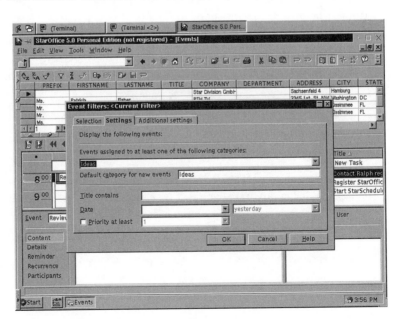

Additional layouts can also be defined for the Event calendar screen by choosing Define Event Layout from the View menu.

From the Event Layout dialog box you can set how a workweek is defined, which colors to assign to event categories, and how the display of events in the calendar is autosized for easy reading.

Setting up Reminders and Recurring Events

When you have an important event coming up, it can be helpful to have a reminder to get you to the event on time. StarSchedule enables you to define pop-up dialogs or email messages as a method for receiving a reminder about an important event.

Not all events require a reminder, of course, so you'll have to explicitly set the reminder option for events that warrant it.

To set a reminder for a calendar event, follow these steps:

1. Enter the event in your calendar.

2. Turn on the Details area of the screen. Notice that the Details for an event includes additional buttons compared to Details for a task.

3. Click the Reminder button to display Event Reminder options.

4. Choose Dialog to display a pop-up dialog box before the event time (you select how far in advance from the drop-down list).

5. Choose the Play sound checkbox to play a tune as the dialog box appears (this helps if you might not be in front of your computer).

6. If you prefer an email reminder (this is a good idea for recurring events—see the next section), choose the Email button.

7. Define the amount of time before the event to send the email (allow time for your email server to deliver the message).

8. Define the email address to which to send the reminder.

9. Click on another time slot to indicate that you've finished setting up details for this event.

If StarSchedule is not started automatically when StarOffice begins (this is the default case), a dialog box warns you that reminders require StarSchedule to be started with StarOffice. You can select a button to make this happen.

If you haven't defined any email settings, including an email Outbox, the email reminder features can't function. See Hour 23, "Using StarOffice Email and Newsgroup Features," for information on setting up email in StarOffice.

Some events assigned to a particular day or week occur at regular intervals. StarSchedule enables you to mark those recurring events so that they appear automatically in your event calendar. To set up a recurring event, follow these steps:

1. Enter the new event in your calendar.

2. Click the Recurrence button to display recurring event options. None is selected by default.

3. Choose the radio button that matches how often this event is to be automatically scheduled in your event calendar: daily, weekly, monthly, or yearly. The options to the right change according to your selection (see Figure 24.20).

FIGURE 24.20

Recurring events can be defined precisely in the Details for any calendar event.

4. Choose the appropriate settings for when you want the recurring event to be scheduled.

5. Click in another time slot in the calendar to indicate that you've finished defining the details for this event.

 A recurring event is often a good place to use an event reminder. Weekly or monthly events are often easily forgotten.

Congratulations

Congratulations! You've learned enough about StarOffice in the last 24 hours to make it a productive part of your Linux environment. With what you've learned about how StarOffice operates, you can continue to explore the additional features that StarOffice provides.

INDEX

Symbols

displayed in cells, 280
$ (dollar sign), cell references, 259
& (ampersand), xterm window, command line, 27
+ (plus sign), Explorer, 46
- (minus sign), Explorer, 46
.TXT extension, 95
3D Cylinder icon, 384
3D object icon, torus object, 114
3D Rectangle icon, 383
= (equals sign), formula cells, 278

A

abbreviations, AutoCorrecting, 222
absolute references, 259
Accelerator keys, 61
    Ctrl+B, 146
    Ctrl+I, 146
    Ctrl+S, 135
    Ctrl+U, 146
actions, graphics in presentations, 377-379
Address book, 41, 48
addressing, email messages, 451
aligning
    images, 211
    paragraphs, 151
Alignment tab, 151, 365
All slides radio button, 408
Alt key, keyboard shortcuts, 61
Ami Pro, 95

ampersand (&), xterm window, command line, 27
anchoring graphics, 203
animations, presentation options, 410
Annual Report template, 353
Applied Styles, 91
Apply button, 400
Arrange submenu, 120
Arrow icon, 116
Arrow Styles tab, 118, 382
Attach File dialog box, 453
attachments (email messages), 452-453
attributes, spreadsheet text, 296
Auto numbering
    footnotes, 165
    outlines, 197-199
Auto Spellcheck, 78, 223-224
AutoCalculate, 286

AutoCorrect, 81-84, 219
  overriding, 81
  settings, 220-222
AutoFiltering, 343-345
AutoFormat Chart dialog box
  chart types, 317-319
  label options, 321-323
  placing charts, 316-317
  variant, selecting, 319-321
AutoLayout, 361-362
automatic links, inserting in StarWriter documents, 428-429
AutoPilots
  Function, 280
  new documents, 131-132
  presentations, 356-359
Autosave, 75
autostart folder (KDE), 29
autostarting StarOffice, KDE, 28
AVERAGE function, 282

B

Back arrow, 35
background mode, slides, 392
backgrounds
  paragraphs, 154
  presentations, 353
backups
  Excel spreadsheets, 101
  Save options, 74
  Word formatted documents, 91
Based on style option, 180
bash shell, 27
BASIC, 66

Beamer window
  navigating directories, 203
  Recycle Bin contents, 51
  saving URLs, 432
  viewing, 41, 47
bitmaps, Image Editor, 207
block references, 259
.BMP graphics, 108
  saving presentations as, 369
bold text attribute, 145-148
Bookmark icon, 433
Bookmarks (Explorer), 41
Bookmarks folder, 49
  saving URLs, 432
borders
  images, 214-216
  paragraphs, 154
Browser, viewing documents, 427-428
browsing FTP sites, 456-458
bullets, 50
  numbering, 199
Bullets icon, 50
buttons, Function toolbar, 35

C

Calculation tab, 254
Caldera Linux, 8
calendar. *See* event calendar
capitalization, cell data, 271
Categories list, Templates dialog box, 130
Cell Attributes dialog box, 269
Cell Protection, 268
cells
  block references, 259
  converting text to tables, 184

  data types, 275
  deleting contents, 272
  editing, 278
  formatting, 293
  formulas, 278-279
  naming, 259-261
  navigating, 185, 257-258
  number formats, setting, 298
    decimal places, 299-300
    Number Formatting dialog box, 301
    Object bar, 298-299
  pasting data into, 272
  references, 258-259, 276
    functions, 284-286
  selecting ranges, 261-262
  selecting rows/columns, 262-263
  splitting/merging, 187-189
chapters, footnote numbering, 166
Character dialog box, 145, 172, 366, 430
  Effects tab, 146
  Font Effects tab, 146
  fonts, 144
  Hyperlink tab, 149
  Style list, 145
character styles, 143, 171
  bold, 145-148
  fonts, 144
  hyperlinks, 148-150
  italic, 145-148
  underline, 145-148
Chart command (Insert menu), 316
charts, 314-315
  axis, changing numbers, 328
  color, 318
    changing, 326-328

data set, selecting, 315-316
edit mode, 325
edit options, 325-326
inserting, 316-317
labeling, 321-323
legends, 322
presentations, 385
previewing, 318
printing spreadsheets, 247
selecting, 325
sizing, 325
titles, 321
types, 318
   selecting, 317-319
variant, selecting, 319-321
Check spelling. *See* **spellchecking**
clients
network installation, 20
StarOffice installation, 6
clip art, 202
color
changing, 119
charts, 318
   changing, 326-328
columns (spreadsheets), 170, 332
adding, 186
adding to existing document, 169
defining, 167-169
importing documents, 99
margins, 168
selecting, in blocks, 294
sizing, 302-305
spreadsheets, selecting, 262-263
Columns command (StarCalc Insert menu), 309
command line, starting StarOffice, 27

commands
Data menu (StarCalc)
   Filter, 343
   Sort, 339
Edit menu (StarCalc)
   Cut, 308
   Delete, 308
   Delete Cells, 309
File menu
   New Mail, 450
   Send, 455
Insert menu, Chart, 316
Insert menu (StarCalc)
   Columns, 309
   Rows, 306
menu items, 66
PUT, 428
Start menu, Mail, 450
Commands list, 67
comments, Internet documents, 440
components
not installing, 13
viewing properties, 58-59
compression, raster images, 110
Configuration dialog box, 67
configuring
AutoCorrect, 81-84
document settings, 138
   default fonts, 139
   layout displayed, 139
   parts displayed, 138
   printing options, 140
   table options, 141
email accounts, 443-444
   Outbox, 447-448
   POP3, 444-447
keyboard shortcuts, 79
language options, 77-79
newsgroup reader, 459-461

printers, 87
status bar display preferences, 80
toolbar contents, 68-71
Connect dialog box, 87
connectivity, 425
Contents tab, 138
Convert Text to Table dialog box, 185
copy and paste, charts, importing into slides, 385
Copy icon, 36
copying, slides, 397
Corel Presentations, 106
Ctrl Accelerator key, 61
Ctrl+B Accelerator key, 146
Ctrl+I Accelerator key, 146
Ctrl+S Accelerator key, 135
Ctrl+U Accelerator key, 146
custom installation, 15
Custom Installation option, 15
Customize Toolbars dialog box, 70
customizing
footnotes, 164
   positioning, 165
menus, 66
styles, 177
   creating by example, 178-180
Cut command (StarCalc Edit menu), 308
Cut icon, 36

D

Data Interchange Format (DIF), 102
Data menu (StarCalc)
Filter command, 343
Sort command, 339
Data Row dialog box, 327
data sets, 332
data validation, 333, 339
criteria
setting up, 334-335
testing, 337-338
error alert options, 336-337
input help, 336
databases. *See also* **spreadsheets**
data validation, 333, 339
criteria, setting up, 334-335
criteria, testing, 337-338
error alert options, 336-337
input help, 336
defined, 332
filtering, 343
AutoFiltering, 343-345
criteria, defining, 345-348
sorting, 339
options, 341-343
selecting data, 339
sort criteria, 341
tables. *See* tables
date and time, status bar, 37
De-Install button, 23
decimal places, adjusting (spreadsheets), 299-300
Define Names dialog box, 260

Delete Cells command (StarCalc Edit menu), 308-309
Delete Cells option, 272
deleting
cell contents, 272
columns (spreadsheets), 309
files from Recycle Bin, 42
footnotes, 163
graphics, 206
rows (spreadsheets), 308
single horizontal line, 217
slides, 398
undeleting, 51
deleting StarOffice, 23
Desktop, 32
adding documents, 55-56
deleting files directly, 57
Explorer, 45-47
Address book, 48
Beamer, 47
Bookmarks folder, 49
Gallery, 49-51
Recycle Bin, 51
Samples folder, 51
Work folder, 52
Workplace, 53
Explorer window, 40
Beamer, 41
icons, 41-43
File menu, New submenu, 128
Function toolbar, 34-36
icons, 55
item properties, 58-59
layout of, 33
Main toolbar, 39
menus, 60
keyboard shortcuts, 61-62
new documents, 130

Desktop
New Drawing icon, 111
New Presentation icon, 352
New Spreadsheet icon, 236
removing documents, 57
startup, 54
status bar, 36, 39
switching between documents and Desktop, 59
toolbars, 39
versus Work folder, 54
diagrams. *See* **graphics**
dialog boxes
Attach File, 453
AutoCorrect, 220
AutoCorrect Replace, 82
AutoFormat Chart
chart types, 317-319
label options, 321-323
placing charts, 316-317
variant, selecting, 319-321
Cell Attributes, 269
Character, 145, 172, 366, 430
Configuration, 67
Connect, 87
Convert Text to Table, 185
Customize Toolbars, 70
Data Row, 327
Define Names, 260
Edit Function, 283
Edit Print Areas, 243
Event Filter, 481
Export, 107
presentations, 369
Footnote Options, 164
Function AutoPilot, 281
HTML Export, 370
Insert Columns/Insert Rows, 186

Insert Footnote, 161

Insert Horizontal Line, 217

Insert Index, 195

Insert Index Entry, 194

Insert Note, 441

Insert Picture, 204, 312, 374

   speaker notes, 403

Insert Script, 439

Insert Sheet, 265

Insert Table, 182

Interaction, 379

Internet Options, 420, 449

Keyboard Configuration, 79

Line, 117, 381

Memo AutoPilot, 131

Menu Configuration, 67

Modify Slide, 352, 361

New Category, 472

New Image, 205

New User, 473

Number Formatting, 301

Numbering/Bullets, 197

Object, 216-217

Open, 133

Open Directory Window, 30

Optimal Height, 302

Page, 154

   columns, 167

   slides, 412

Paragraph, 150-151, 364

Paragraph Style, 176

Paste Special, 273

POP3 Account, 444

Presentations Options, 405

Print, 137

Print Setup, 137

Printer Options, slides, 414

Properties of FTP Account, 456

Properties of News, tabs, 460

Properties of Outbox, 447

Properties of Send Protocols, 445

Properties of User, 472

Rename Sheet, 264

Save As, 134

   file formats, 97

Select Filter, 101

Send Mail, 455

Slide Layout, 362

Sort, 339

Spelling, 228-229

Split Cells, 188

Spreadsheet Options, 249

Standard Filter, 345

Style Catalog, 92

Table Format, 190

Task Filters, 477

Task Layout, Define Layout, 475

Templates, 130

Text Document Options, 138-140

Thesaurus, 231

dictionary, adding words to, 229

DIF spreadsheets, importing, 102

directories

Installation, 14

navigating

   Open dialog box, 134

   with Beamer, 203

paths, 76

directory service protocols, 422

Display Details icon, 56

displaying

cell contents, 271

menu items, 66-68

StarCalc settings, 249-251

toolbars, 71

DNS servers, 426

documents

adding bullets, 50

adding to Desktop, 55-56

Auto Spellcheck, 223-224

AutoCorrect, 219

   settings, 220-222

backup copies, Save options, 74

Bookmarks, 49

columns, adding, 169

entering text, 134

existing, opening, 133-134

exporting, 96-97

   reviewing, 98-99

footnotes, 159

frequently used, 54

horizontal lines, 217-218

images, text wrapping, 211-213

inserting graphics, 202-204

inserting indexes, 195-196

Internet

   adding HTML elements, 438-440

   creating new, 435-437

   saving existing, 434

menus, 61

MS Word, 90

new, 127

   AutoPilot, 131-132

   Desktop, 130

   New submenu, 128

   templates, 130

page format, default settings, 158

page headers, footers, 156-158
page margins, 154
page numbering, 155
pages, layout, 155
paper size, 154
paths, Work Folder, 76
printing, 136-137
Recycle Bin, 51
removing from Desktop, 57
saving, 134
  file location, 135
  frequency, 135
  resaving with new name, 136
setting options, 138
  default fonts, 139
  layout displayed, 139
  parts displayed, 138
  printing options, 140
  table options, 141
spellchecking
  pop-up menu, 225-227
  Spelling dialog box, 228-229
Start menu, 60
styles, applying, 174
switching to Desktop, 59
URLs, 429
viewing multiple, 60
viewing properties, 58
Work folder, 52
dollar signs ($), cell references, 259
drawing
graphics in presentations, 379-384
Main toolbar, 379
Drawing view, 390
background mode, 392
Drawing view mode, 374

drawings, StarImpress, 352
drop caps, 154

E

Edit Function dialog box, 283
Edit icon, 36
Edit menu
adding Update Indexes item, 68
Delete Cells option, 272
StarCalc
  Cut command, 308
  Delete Cells command, 309
  Delete command, 308
Edit Print Areas dialog box, 243
editing
cells, 278
charts, 325-326
  axis, 328
  color, 326-328
footnotes, 163
functions, 283-284
graphics in presentations, 375-377
slide text, 363
StarDraw objects, 116-119
  grouped objects, 121
text, StarDraw, 122
effects, transitions, 400
Effects tab, 146
email
activating settings, 448-449
configuring accounts, 443-444
  Outbox, 447-448
  POP3, 444-447

formatting, Internet options, 422
Internet settings, 426
mailto: link, 429
message window, 451
messages
  addressing, 451
  attachments, 452-453
  creating, 450-452
  documents as, 455-456
  formats, 453-454
  priority, setting, 451
  receipts, 451
  sending, 454-455
  subject, entering, 451
  text entry capabilities, 452
servers, defining, 449
embedded images, 207
End of Document position (footnotes), 166
endnotes, 160
footnote options, 165
entering data (StarCalc), 270-271
environment variables, 6
PATH, 26
EPS, 108
equal sign (=), formula cells, 278
event calendar, 478
accessing, 478
adding items, 481
filtering events, 481-482
recurring events, 483
reminders, 482
viewing options, 478-480
Event Filter dialog box, 481
Events screen (StarSchedule), 465
viewing options, 478-480

Excel spreadsheets
   importing, 100-101
   reviewing, 104-106
Existing Printers list, 86
Explorer, 40, 45-47
   Address book, 48
   Beamer, viewing, 41, 47
   Bookmarks folder, 49
   Gallery, 49-51
   icons, 41-43
      updating, 463
   Recycle Bin, 51
   Samples folder, 51
   saving URLs in, 432-433
   Work folder, 52
   Workplace, 53
Export dialog box, 107
   presentations, 369
exporting
   documents to HTML, 434
   documents, 96-97
      reviewing, 98-99
   graphics, 107-108
   presentations, 106
      to graphics formats,
      368-370
      to Web, 370-372
   spreadsheets
      for other programs,
      103-104
      reviewing, 104-106
extensions, .TXT, 95
Extras button, 400

F

Field Shadings
   index markers, 195
   outlines, 199
fields (databases), 332

file formats
   graphics, 108
   HTML, 96
   importing non-supported,
   94
File menu, 61
   New submenu, new docu-
   ments, 128
   New Mail command, 450
   Send command, 455
   spreadsheets, creating, 236
**file permissions, installing
   StarOffice, 7**
file:// descriptor, 34
filenames, spreadsheets, 242
files
   attaching to email,
   452-453
   document locations, saving, 135
   importing
      MS Word, 90-91
      styles, 91-92
   moving to Desktop, 56
   sizes, vector graphics, 111
   text, 95
**filesystem, save as file loca-
   tion, 135**
**filling, StarDraw objects,
   119**
**Filter command (StarCalc
   Data menu), 343**
filtering
   event calendar events,
   481-482
   tasks, 477-478
**filtering databases/spread-
   sheets, 343**
   AutoFiltering, 343-345
   criteria, defining, 345-348
filters, 98
   DIF files, 102
   Excel spreadsheets,
   100-101

   exporting spreadsheets,
   103
   Lotus 1-2-3 spreadsheets,
   101-102
   non-supported formats, 94
financial functions, 287-290
financial templates, 238
finding, functions, 280-283
First line indent, 151
**Fit-to-Page printing,
   244-246**
floating windows, 60
focus, spreadsheet cells, 257
folders
   Bookmarks, 49
   Samples, 51
   Work, 52
Font Effects tab, 146
fonts
   character styles, 171
   choosing, 144
   defined, 144
   document default, 139
   importing documents, 99
   points, 144
   printer configuration, 87
   setting on slides, 366-367
   spreadsheet text, 293-296
   templates, 390
Fontworks item, 123
Footer tab, 157
footers, 156-158
**Footnote Options dialog
   box, 164**
footnotes, 159-163
   customizing options, 164
      positioning, 165
   deleting, 163
   editing, 163
   locating marker, 163
   markers within columns,
   170
   numbering, 165

printing spreadsheets, 247
renumbering, 163
Format menu
Character option, 366
Fontworks item, 123
Position option, 214
Styles & Templates sub-
menu, 173
Table options, 186
formats
graphic, converting with
other tools, 204-205
presentations, 369
formatting
cell ranges, 262
cells, 293
displaying contents,
271
character styles, 143
bold, 145-148
fonts, 144
hyperlinks, 148-150
italic, 145-148
underline, 145-148
columns, 170
adding to existing doc-
ument, 169
defining, 167-169
email messages, 422
footnotes, 159-163
customizing options,
164
deleting, 163
editing, 163
positioning, 165
pages
default settings, 158
headers/footers,
156-158
margins, 154
numbering, 155
paper size, 154

paragraph styles, 150
alignment, 151
indents, 151
line spacing, 151
tabs, 152-154
slides, 361
spreadsheet options, 249
styles, 170
applying, 174
attributes, 176-177
custom, 177-180
reviewing, 174-176
Style command, 171
Stylist window, 173
tables, 185, 189-191
text, spreadsheets,
291-292
**Formatting pop-up menu,
211, 216**
formula cells, 278-279
formulas
recalculating, 286
simplifying with func-
tions, 279-280
spreadsheet cells, 275
frames
styles, 176
within columns, 170
FTP servers, 426
**FTP sites, browsing,
456-458**
Function AutoPilot, 280
Function toolbar, 34-36
Link icon, 49
Stylist icon, 173
functions, 279
cell references, 284-286
editing, 283-284
financial, 287-290
finding, 280-283
simplified formulas,
279-280

G

**Gallery (Explorer), 42, 49,
51**
General Options
Linguistic options, 77
paths, 75
Save options, 73-75
user data, 72
**General Options dialog box,
User Data, 72**
generating indexes, 192
GhostScript, 84
GIFs, 108
**GIMP (GNU Image
Manipulation Program),
205**
graphics
adding to documents, 50
aligning, 211
converting with other
tools, 204-205
deleting, 206
displaying spreadsheets,
250
editing objects, 116-119
exporting/importing,
107-108
Gallery, 49
horizontal lines, 217-218
image manipulation tools,
376
importing, 201
importing documents, 99
inserting into documents,
202-204
inserting objects, 114-115
new images in Image
Editor, 205-207
presentations, 373
adding actions,
377-379

drawing, 379-384
editing, 375-377
importing, 374
moving/resizing, 375
printing documents, 140
raster images, 110
saving presentations, 368
slides, outline view, 394
spreadsheets
bitmap editing, 314
importing, 312-313
layering, 314
moving, 314
selecting, 314
sizing, 314
StarDraw
adding text, 121-124
arranging objects, 120
changing colors, 119
grouping objects, 121
vector images, 110-111
within columns, 170
graphs. *See* **charts**
green handles, 209
Grid tab, 139, 253, 407
**gridlines (spreadsheets), dis-
playing, 246-247, 252**
grouping
objects (StarDraw), 121
tasks, 476

H

handles, graphics, 203
Handout view, 395
handouts, presentations, 414
hard disk space
network installation, 22
StarOffice installation, 13

hardcopy slides
page size, 412
printing, 413-415
Header tab, 156
headers, 156-158
Help menu, 61
hidden files, 26
hiding cells, 269-270
history list, 35
Home button, 35
horizontal lines, 217-218
Internet documents, 439
single, selecting, 217
**HTML (Hypertext Markup
Language)**
elements, 438-440
exporting documents
to, 434
exporting presentations as,
370
files, saving spreadsheets
to, 102
interchange format, 96
**HTML documents icon
(Desktop), 55**
**HTML Export dialog box,
370**
HTML Source window, 438
**HTTP (Hypertext Transfer
Protocol), 425**
**Hyperlink status (status
bar), 37**
Hyperlink tab, 149, 430
hyperlinks. *See* **links**
hyphenation rules, 78

I

icons
Desktop, 55
Explorer, 41-43
updating, 463
Function toolbar, 35
Recycle Bin, 42
Image Editor
creating new images,
205-207
editing slide graphics, 375
importing/exporting, 107
opening graphics into, 314
ImageMagick, 205
images
alignment, 211-213
borders, 214-216
creating new in Image
Editor, 205-207
editing objects, 116-119
green handles, 209
height/width ratio, 210
inserting objects, 114-115
layers, 214-215
manipulation tools, 376
moving/resizing, 210
new in StarDraw, 111-113
Object dialog box,
216-217
raster, 110
selecting, 208-209
StarDraw
adding text, 121-124
arranging objects, 120
changing colors, 119
grouping objects, 121
text wrapping, 211-213
vector, 110-111
viewing in StarDraw,
113-114
IMG tag, 439

importing
 documents, reviewing,
  98-99
 graphics, 107-108, 201
  to presentations, 374
  to spreadsheets,
   312-313
 HTML files, 96
 non-supported file for-
  mats, 94
 presentations, 106
 spreadsheets
  DIF, 102
  Excel, 100-101
  Lotus 1-2-3, 101-102
  reviewing, 104-106
 text files, 95
 WordPerfect files, 93
Incoming mail server, 421
indenting
 outlines, 199
 paragraph, 151
**Indents and Spacing tab,
 364**
indexes, 192-193
 configuring menu items,
  67
 inserting into documents,
  195-196
 inserting markers, 193-195
 markers within columns,
  170
 updating, 197
**input filters, MS Word
 6/95/97, 90-91**
**input help (spreadsheets),
 336**
**Insert Columns/Insert Rows
 dialog box, 186**
**Insert Footnote dialog box,
 161**
**Insert Horizontal Line dia-
 log box, 217**

Insert Index dialog box, 195
**Insert Index Entry dialog
 box, 194**
**Insert indicator (status bar),
 37**
Insert menu
 Chart command, 316
 Footnote option, 161
 Slide option, 362
 Spreadsheet option, 386
 StarCalc
  Columns command,
   309
  Rows command, 306
Insert Note dialog box, 441
**Insert Picture dialog box,
 204, 312, 374**
 speaker notes, 403
Insert Script dialog box, 439
Insert Sheet dialog box, 265
Insert Table dialog box, 182
Insert Table icon, 69
inserting
 columns (spreadsheets),
  308-309
 graphics, 202-204
 horizontal lines, 217
 index markers, 193-195
 indexes, 195-196
 rows (spreadsheets), 305
 sheets into spreadsheets,
  265
Installation directory, 14
installing
 finishing, 16
 minimizing, 15
 modifying, 23
 network, 17
  client user, 20
  server side, 18
 repairing, 24
 single user setup, 9-10

 custom installation, 15
 installation options, 13
 license agreement, 11
 user information, 17
 system requirements, 5
  environment variables,
   6
  file permissions, 7
  Linux versions, 8
  user/network installa-
   tion, 6
 uninstalling, 22
 updating, 23
Interaction dialog box, 379
Internet. *See* **email; newsgroups**
Internet documents
 adding HTML elements,
  438-440
 creating new, 435-437
 exporting presentations to,
  370-372
 inserting automatic links
  into StarWriter docs,
  428-429
 inserting links, into
  spreadsheets and presentations, 431
 inserting manual links into
  StarWriter docs, 430
 saving existing, 434
 setting options, 419
  Internet protocols,
   425-426
  Internet searching, 424
  Internet server,
   420-424
 URLs, saving in Explorer,
  432-433
 viewing on Desktop, 34
 viewing, 427-428

Internet Options dialog box,
420, 449
IP addresses, mapping to
domain names, 426
italic text attribute, 145-148

J - K

JavaScript, 439
joining cells, 188
JPEG, 108
justifying
paragraphs, 152
text, spreadsheets, 297

KDE (K Desktop
Environment)
autostarting StarOffice, 28
Control Center, 60
installing StarOffice, 16
Start menu, 60
key assignments, 80
keyboard
controlling slide shows,
412
navigating spreadsheets,
257-258
Keyboard Configuration
dialog box, 79
keyboard shortcuts, 61-62
menu items, 66
setting up, 79

L

labels, spreadsheet cells, 275
landscape printing, 154
spreadsheets, 247
language options, 77, 79

laptops, battery life,
Automatic save, 75
layering
graphics, 314
StarDraw objects, 120
layers (image), 214-215
layout, 155. *See also*
columns
adding to slides, 361-362
document settings, 139
presentation options,
355, 406
Layout tab, 139
LDAP, 422
legends (charts), 322
library versions, installing
StarOffice, 7
license agreement, 11
license keys, 8
Line dialog box, 117, 381
line spacing, 151
lines
drawing in slides, 380
gridlines (spreadsheets),
246
horizontal, 217-218
Lines & Arrows icon, 115
Linguistic options, 78
Link icon, 34, 49
links
as text attribute, 148-150
automatic, inserting into
StarWriter documents,
428-429
inserting in spreadsheets
and presentations, 431
manual, inserting into
StarWriter documents,
430
Linux
navigating spreadsheet
cells, 258
printers, 84

system requirements, 5
environment variables,
6
file permissions, 7
user/network installa-
tion, 6
versions, 8
Looking Glass, 29-31
Lotus 1-2-3 spreadsheets,
importing, 101-102
lp print queue, 86

M

macros, 66
Mail command (Start
menu), 450
mail servers, 421
Mail/News tab, Internet
servers, 421
mailto: link, 429
Main toolbar, 39
3D Cylinder icon, 384
3D Rectangle icon, 383
adding Insert Table icon,
69
drawing, 379
Open File icon, 133
Printer icon, 136
Save icon, 134
StarDraw, 112
text tool, 121
manual links, inserting in
StarWriter documents,
430
margins, 154
colums width, 168
printing spreadsheets, 248
markers, footnotes, 162
Master documents, footnote
numbering, 166

Master view, 393
  speaker notes, 403
math operations
  cell formulas, 279
  StarCalc settings, 254
Meaning list, 231
Memo AutoPilot dialog box, 131
Menu Configuration dialog box, 67
menus, 33, 60
  customizing, 66
  document types, 61
  keyboard shortcuts, 61-62
  selecting items to display, 66-68
  Start, 60, 128
Merge operation, 188
message windows, 451
messages
  email
    addressing, 451
    attachments, 452-453
    creating, 450-452
    documents as, 455-456
    formats, 453-454
    message window, 451
    priority, setting, 451
    receipts, 451
    sending, 454-455
    subject, entering, 451
    text entry capabilities, 452
  newsgroups
    posting, 462
    reading, 461-462
    replying to, 460
MET (OS/2), 108
Minimum Installation button, 14
minus sign (-), Explorer, 46

misspellings, 82
  Auto Spellcheck, 224
  checking documents, 228
Modified indicator (status bar), 37
Modify Slide dialog box, 352, 361
mortgage calculator, 287
mouse
  cell references, functions, 284
  controlling slide shows, 412
  Desktop icons, 34
  footnote markers, 163
  navigating spreadsheets, 257-258
  presentation options, 409
  saving documents, 136
moving
  cells, 272-273
  graphics, 314
  graphics in presentations, 375
  images, 210
multi-users, installation, 6

N

naming
  cells, 259-261
  spreadsheets, 263-265
navigating
  slides, 391
  spreadsheets, mouse/keyboard, 257-258
Navigator window, 38, 261
  presentation options, 409
netiquette, 462
network installation, 6, 18

New Category dialog box, 472
New documents icon (Desktop), 55
New Drawing icon, 111
New Employee Introduction presentation, 380
New Image dialog box, 205
New Presentation icon, 352
New Spreadsheet icon, 237
New Style by Example icon, 179
New submenu
  new documents, 128
  Text Document, 128
New User dialog box, 473
news servers
  configuring, 459-461
  Internet settings, 422
newsgroups, 459
  configuring newsgroup reader, 459-461
  messages
    posting, 462
    reading, 461-462
    replying to, 460
  netiquette, 462
  selecting, 461
New Mail command (File menu), 450
non-PostScript printers, 84
notes, presentation speaker, 403
Notes view, 394, 403
now() function, 280
Number Formatting dialog box, 301
numbering
  bullets, 199
  footnotes, 165
  outlines, 197-199
Numbering icon, 437

numbering pages, 155
Numbering/Bullets dialog
    box, 197
numbers, spreadsheet cells,
    276-278

O

Object bar
    number formats, setting,
        298-299
        decimal places,
            299-300
    text formatting options,
        292
Object dialog box, 216-217
Object toolbar
    Border icon, 214
    character formatting, slide
        fonts, 367
    character styles, 146
    Display Details icon, 56
    icon descriptions dis-
        played, 211
    images, 208
    paragraph alignment, 152
    StarDraw, 112
    Styles, 174
objects, StarDraw, 120-121
Open dialog box, 133
    navigating filesystem, 134
Open Directory Window
    dialog box, 30
Open icon, 36
opening
    existing documents,
        133-134
    spreadsheet files, 240-241
OpenLinux, Looking Glass,
    StarOffice icon, 29

Optimal Height dialog box,
    302
options
    AutoCorrect, 221
    StarCalc, 249
        items to display,
            249-254
orientations, printing
    spreadsheets, 248
Outbox, configuring,
    447-448
Outgoing mail server, 421
outline view, 393
Outline view, spellchecking,
    402
outlines
    auto numbering, 197-199
    changing indents, 199
Overhead presentations, 360

P

page count indicator (status
    bar), 37
Page dialog box, 154
    columns, 167
    slides, 412
page format, printing
    spreadsheets, 247-248
Page layout drop-down list,
    156
page orientation, 155
Page Style dialog box
    Footer tab, 157
    Header tab, 156
    Page tab, 155
Page tab, 155
Page View, 137
pages
    default settings, 158
    headers/footers, 156-158

layout, 155
    margins, 154
    numbering, 155
    paper size, 154
    StarImpress, 352
    styles, 176
paper format, 154
paper size, 154
Paragraph dialog box,
    150-151, 364
    Alignment tab, 151
    Tab tab, 152
Paragraph Style dialog box,
    176
Paragraph Styles window,
    Word documents, 91
paragraphs
    adjusting on slides,
        364-366
    backgrounds, 154
    borders, 154
    styles, 150, 171, 176
        alignment, 151
        indents, 151
        line spacing, 151
        MS Word, importing,
            91
        tabs, 152-154
passwords, protecting
    spreadsheets, 269
Paste icon, 36
Paste Special dialog box,
    273
pasting
    into spreadsheet cells, 272
    slides, 397
PATH environment vari-
    able, 26
paths
    editing, 76
    troubleshooting, 75-76
PBM, 108

permissions, StarOffice
   installation, 7
PGM, 108
PICT, 108
pictures. *See* graphics
pixels, raster images, 110
plus sign (+), Explorer, 46
PMT function, 288
PNG graphics format, 108
points, 144
POP3, configuring account,
   444-447
POP3 Account dialog box,
   444
portals, 424
Portrait, 154
portrait printing, spreadsheets, 247
Position submenu, 214
positioning
   footnotes, 165
   images, 210
posting messages (news-
   groups), 462
PostScript printers, 84
PowerPoint,
   exporting/importing, 106
PPM, 108
Presentation menu, Slide
   Transition window, 399
presentations, 351
   arranging slides, 389
      choosing master view,
         390
   AutoPilots, 356-359
   charts, 385
   exporting to graphics for-
      mats, 368-370
   exporting to Web presenta-
      tion, 370-372
   exporting/importing, 106

graphics, 373
   adding actions,
      377-379
   drawing, 379-384
   editing, 375-377
   importing, 374
   moving/resizing, 375
hardcopy slides
   page size, 412
   printing, 413-415
inserting hyperlinks, 431
layout, 406
navigating, mouse clicks,
   412
options, 405-407
   slide show, 407-410
running slide shows,
   410-412
saving, 367
slide layouts, 355-356
Slide Sort view
   copying/pasting slides,
      397
   deleting slides, 398
   moving slides, 396
slides, 352
   adding layouts,
      361-362
   background mode, 392
   entering text, 363-364
   fonts, 366-367
   inserting new, 362
   moving between, 391
   paragraphs, adjusting,
      364-366
   views, 393-396
speaker notes, 403
spell checking, 402
spreadsheets, 386
templates, 353
transitions, 398-402

Presentations Options dialog box, 405
presenter notes, 403
Preview area, 155
Preview button, 400
previewing
   charts, 318
   printing documents, 137
Print Area (spreadsheets),
   242
Print dialog box, 137
Print icon, 36
print queues, 86
Print Setup dialog box, 137
Printer Options dialog box,
   slides, 414
printers
   adding printer types, 86
   changing print queue, 86
   configuring, 87
   default printer, 86
   psetup utility, 84
   setting up, 84
printing
   documents, 136-137
      previewing, 137
      printing options, 140
   hardcopy slides, 413-415
   page layout, 154
   paper size, 154
   spreadsheets, 242-244
      Fit-to-Page, 244-246
      gridlines, 246-247
      page format, 247-248
productivity, save options,
   73
profile script, adding PATH
   variable, 26
Programs icon (Desktop), 55
Properties dialog box, 58-59
Properties of FTP Account
   dialog box, 456

Properties of News dialog
  box, 460
Properties of Outbox dialog
  box, 447
Properties of Send Protocols
  dialog box, 445
Properties of User dialog
  box, 472
protocols
  Internet settings, 425-426
  proxy servers, 420
Protocols tab, 425
proxy servers, 420
psetup utility, 84
PUT command, 428

Q - R

ranges of cells, 261-262, 276
RAS, 108
raster images, 110
records
  filtering, 343
    AutoFiltering, 343-345
    criteria, defining,
      345-348
  sorting, 339
records (databases), 332
  sorting
    options, 341-343
    selecting data, 339
    sort criteria, 341
rectangles, drawing in
  slides, 380
recurring events (event calendar), 483
Recycle Bin (Explorer),
  42, 51
red wavy lines, Auto
  Spellcheck, 223

references, spreadsheet
  cells, 259
Reload icon, 36
reminders (event calendar),
  482
removing StarOffice, 23
Rename Sheet dialog box,
  264
Repair button, 24
Replace dialog box, 82
Replace tab (AutoCorrect),
  220
replacing misspellings, 229
resizing
  graphics in presentations,
    375
  images, 210
Rich Text Format (RTF), 95
right-click menus, 47
rows (spreadsheets), 332
  adding, 186
  deleting, 308-309
  inserting, 305, 308-309
  sizing, 302-305
  spreadsheets, selecting,
    262-263
Rows command (StarCalc
  Insert menu), 306
RTF files, 95
  saving presentations as,
    368
rulers, StarDraw, 112
running StarOffice, 25
  command line, 27
  PATH environment vari-
    able, 26

S

Samples folder, 51
Samples folder (Explorer),
  42
sans-serif, 144
Save As dialog box, 134
  file formats, 97
Save icon, 36
Save options, Autosave, 75
save settings, 73-75
saving
  documents, 134
    file location, 135
    frequency, 135
    resaving with new
      name, 136
  presentations, 367
  spreadsheets, 241-242
  spreadsheets in different
    formats, 102
search engines, 424
searching, Internet settings,
  424
security, spreadsheets, 266
Select Filter dialog box, 101
selecting
  cell ranges, 261-262
  charts, 325
  columns, in blocks, 294
  graphics, 314
  images, 208-209
  newsgroups, 461
  rows/columns, 262-263
  StarDraw objects, 116
Send command (File menu),
  455
Send icon, 36
Send Mail dialog box, 455
sending
  documents as email,
    455-456
  email messages, 454-455

Separator option (columns), 168

serif, 144

servers

DNS, 426

email, defining, 449

FTP, 426

incoming mail, 421

LDAP, 423

network installation, 18

news, 422

configuring, 459-461

settings, AutoCorrect, 220-222

setup

De-Install, 23

network installation, 17

client user, 20

server side, 18

single user installation, 9-10

custom installation, 15

installation options, 13

license agreement, 11

user information, 17

uninstalling StarOffice, 22

setup utility, 23

shapes, drawing in slides, 380

Sheet Protection, 266

shell startup, adding PATH variable, 26

shortcuts

keyboard, 61-62

menu items, 66

single horizontal line, selecting, 217

single users

network installation, 20

setup, 9-10

custom installation, 15

installation options, 13

license agreement, 11

user information, 17

sites, FTP, browsing, 456-458

size indicator (status bar), 37

sizing

charts, 325

columns (spreadsheets), 302-305

graphics, 314

rows (spreadsheets), 302-305

text, spreadsheets, 293-296

Slide Layout dialog box, 362

Slide Sort view, 394

copying/pasting slides, 397

deleting slides, 398

moving slides, 396

Slide Transition window, 398

slides, 352, 377

adding layouts to, 361-362

arranging, 389

choosing master view, 390

background mode, 392

entering text, 363-364

fonts, 366-367

hardcopies

page size, 412

printing, 413-415

inserting new slides, 362

layouts, 355-356

moving between, 391

navigating, 391

paragraphs, adjusting, 364-366

running slide shows, 410-412

slide show options, 407-410

Slide Sort view

copying/pasting slides, 397

deleting slides, 398

moving slides, 396

testing, 411

transitions, 398-402

views, 393-396

small caps, 147

Snap tab, 407

soft-formatting, 170

Sort command (StarCalc Data menu), 339

Sort dialog box, 339

sorting, 339

options, 341-343

selecting data, 339

sort criteria, 341

tasks, 477

Source window, 438

spacing, 151

columns, 167

speaker notes, presentations, 403

spellchecking

Linguistic options, 77

pop-up menu, 225-227

presentations, 402

Spelling dialog box, 228-229

Spelling dialog box, 228-229

Split Cells dialog box, 188

Spreadsheet Options, 407

Spreadsheet Options dialog box, 249

spreadsheets. *See also* **databases**

adding, 265-266

cell references, 258-259, 276

cells
    formatting, 293
    number formats, set-
        ting, 298-300
charts, 314-315
    axis, changing num-
        bers, 328
    color, 318, 326-328
    data set, selecting,
        315-316
    edit mode, 325
    edit options, 325-326
    inserting, 316-317
    labeling, 321-323
    legends, 322
    previewing, 318
    selecting, 325
    sizing, 325
    titles, 321
    types, selecting,
        317-319
    variant, selecting,
        319-321
columns
    deleting, 309
    inserting, 308-309
    sizing, 302-305
creating, 236-237
data validation, 333, 339
    criteria, setting up,
        334-335
    criteria, testing,
        337-338
    error alert options,
        336-337
    input help, 336
editing cells, 278
entering data, 270-271
exporting, 103-104
    reviewing, 104-106

filtering, 343
    AutoFiltering, 343-345
    criteria, defining,
        345-348
financial functions,
    287-290
formula cells, 278-279
formulas, 275
functions, 279
    cell references,
        284-286
    editing, 283-284
    finding, 280-283
    simplified formulas,
        279-280
graphics
    bitmap editing, 314
    importing, 312-313
    layering, 314
    moving, 314
    selecting, 314
    sizing, 314
hiding cells, 269-270
importing, 100-101
    DIF, 102
    Lotus 1-2-3, 101-102
inserting hyperlinks, 431
labels, 275
moving cells, 272-273
naming, 263-265
naming cells, 259-261
navigating, mouse/key-
    board, 257-258
numbers, 276-278
opening existing, 240-241
presentations, 386
printing, 242-244
    Fit-to-Page, 244-246
    gridlines, 246-247
    page format, 247-248
protecting, 266-269
recalculating, 286

rows
    deleting, 308
    inserting, 305
    sizing, 302-305
saving, 241-242
selecting ranges, 261-262
selecting rows/columns,
    262-263
settings, 249
    items to display,
        249-254
sorting, 339
    options, 341-343
    selecting data, 339
    sort criteria, 341
templates, 237-240
text
    attributes, 296
    fonts, 293-296
    formatting options,
        291-292
    justifying, 297
    size, 293-296
**Standard Filter dialog box,
    345**
Standard Fonts tab, 140
Standard Installation, 13
StarCalc
    adding sheets, 265-266
    Alt key shortcuts, 61
    cell references, 258-259,
        276
    cells
        formatting, 293
        number formats, set-
            ting, 298-300
    charts, 314-315
        axis, changing num-
            bers, 328
        color, 318, 326-328
        data set, selecting,
            315-316

edit mode, 325
edit options, 325-326
inserting, 316-317
labeling, 321-323
legends, 322
previewing, 318
selecting, 325
sizing, 325
titles, 321
types, selecting,
    317-319
variant, selecting,
    319-321
columns
    inserting, 308-309
    sizing, 302-305
data validation, 333, 339
    criteria, setting up,
        334-335
    criteria, testing,
        337-338
    error alert options,
        336-337
    input help, 336
editing cells, 278
entering data, 270-271
existing spreadsheets,
    opening, 240-241
exporting for other pro-
    grams, 103-104
filtering records, 343
    AutoFiltering, 343-345
    criteria, defining,
        345-348
financial functions,
    287-290
formula cells, 278-279
formulas, 275
functions, 279
    cell references,
        284-286
    editing, 283-284

finding, 280-283
simplified formulas,
    279-280
graphics
    bitmap editing, 314
    importing, 312-313
    layering, 314
    moving, 314
    selecting, 314
    sizing, 314
hiding cells, 269-270
importing Excel spread-
    sheets, 100
labels, 275
moving cells, 272-273
naming cells, 259-261
naming spreadsheets,
    263-265
navigating cells, 257-258
new spreadsheets, 236-237
numbers, 276-278
printing, 242-244
    Fit-to-Page, 244-246
    grid lines, 246-247
    page format, 247-248
protecting sheets, 266-269
recalculating, 286
rows
    deleting, 308
    inserting, 305
    sizing, 302-305
saving spreadsheets,
    241-242
selecting ranges, 261-262
selecting rows/columns,
    262-263
settings, 249
    items to display,
        249-254
sorting records, 339
    options, 341-343
    selecting data, 339
    sort criteria, 341

templates, 237-240
text
    attributes, 296
    fonts, 293-296
    formatting options,
        291-292
    justifying, 297
    size, 293-296
StarDraw
    adding text, 121-124
    arranging objects, 120
    changing colors, 119
    editing objects, 116-119
    exporting, 107
    grouping objects, 121
    inserting objects, 114-115
    new images, 111-113
    raster images, 110
    vector images, 110-111
    view, 113-114
StarImpress, 351
    adding slides to presenta-
        tions, 361-362
    arranging slides, 389
        choosing master view,
            390
    AutoPilots, 356-359
    charts, 385
    exporting to graphics for-
        mats, 368-370
    exporting to Web, 370-372
    exporting/importing, 106
    graphics, 373
        adding actions,
            377-379
        drawing, 379-384
        editing, 375-377
        importing, 374
        moving/resizing, 375
    inserting new slides, 362
    options, 405-407
        slide show, 407-410

running slide shows,
410-412
saving presentations, 367
slide layouts, 355-356
Slide Sort view
copying/pasting slides,
397
deleting slides, 398
moving slides, 396
slides, 352
background mode, 392
fonts, 366-367
inserting text, 363-364
moving between, 391
paragraphs, adjusting,
364-366
vies, 394-396
views, 393
speaker notes, 403
spellchecking, 402
spreadsheets, 386
templates, 353
transitions, 398-402
StarOffice BASIC, 66
StarSchedule
event calendar, 478
accessing, 478
adding items, 481
filtering events,
481-482
recurring events, 483
reminders, 482
Events screen, 465
viewing options,
478-480
interface, 465-466
multiple users, 473-475
task list, 467
categories, defining,
472
creating tasks, 467-468
filtering tasks, 477-478

grouping tasks, 476
layout, changing,
475-477
reviewing task details,
468-471
sorting tasks, 477
Tasks screen, 465
**Start button, spreadsheets,
new, 236**
Start menu, 60, 128
Mail command, 450
starting, 25
**starting StarOffice, Looking
Glass, 29-31**
StarView metafile, 108
StarWriter
Auto Spellcheck, 223
AutoCorrect, 219
existing documents, open-
ing, 133-134
footnotes, formatting, 165
inserting automatic links,
428-429
inserting manual links,
430
new documents, 127
AutoPilot, 131-132
Desktop, 130
New submenu, 128
templates, 130
Thesaurus, 230-231
Status bar, 33, 36, 39
status bar
components, 36
display preferences, 80
StarDraw, 112
Zoom selection menu, 37
Stop sign, 35
Style by Example, 178
Style Catalog, 177
Style Catalog dialog box, 92
Style command, 171

**style indicator (status bar),
37**
styles, 170
applying, 174
attributes, 176-177
character, 143
bold, 145-148
fonts, 144
hyperlinks, 148-150
italic, 145-148
underline, 145-146,
148
custom, 177
creating by example,
178-180
editing attributes, 176
importing Word docu-
ments, 91
importing Word formats,
91-92
paragraph, 150
alignment, 151
indents, 151
line spacing, 151
tabs, 152, 154
reviewing, 174-176
Style command, 171
Stylist window, 173
**Styles & Templates sub-
menu, 173**
Stylist icon, 173
Stylist window, 173
sum() function, 279
SVM, 108
**switching, between docu-
ments and Desktop, 59**
Synonyms list, 231
system requirements, 5
environment variables, 6
file permissions, 7
Linux versions, 8
user/network installation,
6

T

Table Format dialog box, 190
Table Insert icon, 183
Table tab, 141
tables, 182, 332
  adding columns, 186
  adding rows, 186
  Address book, 48
  converting to text, 184
  document options, 141
  fields, 332
  formatting, 185, 189-191
  inserting new, 182-184
  Internet documents, 439
  navigating cells, 185
  records, 332
  splitting/merging cells, 187-189
  within columns, 170
tabs, 152-154
  slide paragraphs, 366
tags, IMG, 439
Task Filters dialog box, 477
Task Layout, Define Layout dialog box, 475
task list, 467
  categories, defining, 472
  layout, changing, 475-477
  multiple users, 473-475
  tasks
    creating, 467-468
    filtering, 477-478
    grouping, 476
    reviewing details, 468-471
    sorting, 477
Tasks screen (StarSchedule), 465

templates
  Annual Report, 353
  financial, 238
  fonts, 390
  new documents, 130
  Samples folder, 51
  spreadsheets, 237-240
  StarImpress, 353
Templates dialog box, 130
text
  adding to StarDraw images, 121-124
  attributes, spreadsheets, 296
  bold, 145
  converting to tables, 184
  fonts, 144
    spreadsheets, 293-296
  formatting, spreadsheets, 291-292
  hyperlinks, 148, 150
  inserting on slides, 363-364
  italic, 145
  justifying, spreadsheets, 297
  paragraph styles, 150
    alignment, 151
    indents, 151
    line spacing, 151
    tabs, 152-154
  size, spreadsheets, 293-296
  small caps, 147
  underline, 145
  wrapping around images, 211-213
Text Animation tab, 123
text boxes, presentation slides, 364
Text Document command, 128

Text Document Options dialog box, 138-140
text documents, 138
text files, 95
Thesaurus, 230-231
  dialog box, 231
  Synonyms list, 231
TIF, 108
titles, charts, 321
to-do list. *See* **task list**
toolbars, 33, 39
  configuring contents, 68-71
  displaying, 71
  drawing, 379
  Function, 34
  Main, 39
  viewing, 39
Toolbars Configuration window, 69
tools. *See also* **AutoPilots**
  Auto Spellcheck, 223
  AutoCorrect, 219-220
  image manipulation, 376
  Thesaurus, 230-231
Tools menu
  AutoCorrect, 82, 220
  Convert Text to Table option, 184
  Footnote Options, 164
  General option, 72
  Page Numbering, 155
torus (ring), 114
  editing, 118
transitions, 398-402
Travel Expense Report template, 239
troubleshooting, paths, 75-76
tuples. *See* **data sets**
.TXT extension, 95

U

underline text attribute,
145-148
Undo, Save options, 75
uninstalling, 23
Update button, 400
Update Indexes item, inserting into Edit menu, 68
URL field, 427
URL history arrow, 35
URL window, 35
URLs (Uniform Resource
Locator)
Desktop, 34
saving in Explorer,
432-433
user data, 12, 72
changing, 73
User IDs, mail servers, 421
users, StarSchedule, adding,
473-475
utilities, psetup, 84

V - W

vector images, 110-111
View menu, 61
Beamer, 47
Master view, 393
Status Bar, 36
Toolbars, 39
viewing
Beamer, 41, 47
clip art, 202
images in StarDraw,
113-114
slide contents, 392
task details, 468-471
toolbars, 39

views
Drawing, 390
Slide Sort
copying/pasting slides,
397
deleting slides, 398
moving slides, 396
slides, 390, 393-396

wavy red lines, Auto
Spellcheck, 223
Web browsers, Desktop, 33
Web pages. See Internet
documents
Web servers, email addresses, 426
Window menu, 61
windows
floating, 60
message, 451
Wizards. See AutoPilots
.WMF files, 108
Word file formats, 90-91
backing up copies, 91
exporting to, 96-97
Open dialog box, 134
reviewing, 98-99
styles, 91-92
word processors, import-
ing/exporting formats, 97
WordPerfect files, importing, 93
Work Folder (Explorer), 43,
52
Open dialog location, 133
vs Desktop, 54
Work Folder path, 76
Workplace, 53
moving documents to,
from Desktop, 57
Workplace (Explorer), 43
Wrap submenu, 437

wrapping text, around
images, 211-213

X - Y - Z

X Window System
installing StarOffice, 20
StarOffice installation, 9
starting StarOffice, 25
XPM, 108
xterm windows
setting PATH variable, 26
StarOffice installation, 9
starting StarOffice, 27

Yahoo!, 424

Zoom icon, 113
Zoom selection menu, 37
zooming, StarDraw images,
113